VOICES FROM THE VOLUNTARY SECTOR:
PERSPECTIVES ON LEADERSHIP CHALLENGES
Edited by Frederick Bird and Frances Westley

Voices from the Voluntary Sector contains reflections by practitioners on some of the significant challenges faced by today's not-for-profit organizations in Canada. Broad in scope, these essays present a rich, multidimensional set of vignettes that as a whole express the vitality and humanity of the voluntary sector.

The contributors discuss organizational and managerial challenges, social entrepreneurship, and methods to foster effective global movements. The essays include a discussion of the ways that young people can find the courage to become leaders, a review of the nature and extent of collaborations between voluntary sector organizations and First Nations families, and a consideration of how parental incarceration affects the life prospects of children. *Voices from the Voluntary Sector* is a valuable resource that addresses a wide range of concerns related to the responsiveness, character, and leadership of not-for-profit and non-governmental organizations.

FREDERICK BIRD is a research professor in the Department of Political Science at the University of Waterloo and a distinguished professor emeritus at Concordia University.

FRANCES WESTLEY is a professor and J.W. McConnell Chair in Social Innovation at the University of Waterloo.

EDITED BY
FREDERICK BIRD AND FRANCES WESTLEY

Voices from
the Voluntary Sector

Perspectives on Leadership Challenges

UNIVERSITY OF TORONTO PRESS
Toronto Buffalo London

© University of Toronto Press Incorporated 2011
Toronto Buffalo London
www.utppublishing.com
Printed in Canada

ISBN 978-0-8020-9101-7 (cloth)
ISBN 978-0-8020-9661-6 (paper)

Printed on acid-free, 100% post-consumer recycled paper with vegetable-based inks.

Library and Archives Canada Cataloguing in Publication

Voices from the voluntary sector: perspectives on leadership challenges / edited by Frederick Bird and Frances Westley.

Includes bibliographical references.
ISBN 978-0-8020-9101-7 (bound). – ISBN 978-0-8020-9661-6 (pbk.)

1. Nonprofit organizations – Canada – Management.   2. Charities – Canada – Management.   3. Leadership.   I. Bird, Frederick B. (Frederick Bruce), 1938 –   II. Westley, Frances

HD62.6.V65 2011   658'.0480971   C2010-903967-X

University of Toronto Press acknowledges the financial assistance to its publishing program of the Canada Council for the Arts and the Ontario Arts Council.

 Canada Council   Conseil des Arts
for the Arts   du Canada    ONTARIO ARTS COUNCIL
CONSEIL DES ARTS DE L'ONTARIO

University of Toronto Press acknowledges the financial support of the Government of Canada through the Canada Book Fund for its publishing activities.

Contents

Through the use of excerpts from the personal reflections of youth, this essay explores the emergence of leaders in the Youth in Care Network in Canada. The voices of the young people, who spent difficult years in foster care and found the strength to deal with their inner doubts and external difficulties to become leaders and organizers, highlight the transformative role of such voluntary sector networks.

The author reflects on her own experiences as she moved into a position of local and then regional leadership in her organization. Leaders often become extremely busy with day-to-day activities. This essay reflects on the need to regularly reflect personally on one's own experiences, what can be learned from them, and what has overall priority. Mutoigo also examines the struggles, especially within faith communities, to strike a suitable balance between leading and serving.

BERNARD VOYER

Leaders with considerable charisma have helped to initiate, develop, and renew a number of voluntary sector organizations. However, even as they energize organizations, a leadership vacuum is often created when they leave. This essay explores the ways such organizations can manage the transition that takes place after a charismatic leader departs from an organization. Voyer considers the lessons learned by his own organization after the death of the man who had founded it and served as its inspiration and leader for twenty-eight years.

PART TWO: THE ANALYTIC MINDSET

MARGARET MCGREGOR

Using examples drawn from the experiences of the Canadian Olympic Committee, McGregor reflects on how voluntary sector organizations can better prepare themselves to respond to crises which inevitably will arise. The essay reviews the typical stages of crises and identifies what factors are most important for organizations to manage these challenges successfully.

JERRY V. DEMARCO

This essay examines the criteria used by the Fraser Institute to gauge how voluntary sector organizations deliver services. DeMarco criticizes these criteria and their use for a number of reasons. The measures used disproportionately reflect the norms of the private rather than the voluntary sector, focus excessively on efficiency and cost containment within these organizations, and ignore certain effective and value-creating outcomes.

Langlois employs an ecocycle metaphor to explore the renewal of conventional youth-serving organizations. Youth-infused and community-based management interventions founded on the principles of youth inclusion and empowering leadership are discussed.

PART THREE: THE GLOBAL MINDSET

Informed by her experiences working with First Nations communities in British Columbia, Blackstock reviews the nature and extent of collaborations between voluntary sector organizations and First Nations children and families residing on reserves in British Columbia. First Nations children face more discrimination and higher levels of risk than other Canadian children in family service situations. Unfortunately, these children and families have received very little assistance from voluntary sector organizations in Canada. This essay explores the reasons for this situation and provides recommendations for improvement.

In this essay, Roy examines a number of efforts to coordinate international campaigns orchestrated by civil society organizations around specific objectives. He looks at campaigns that focused on reducing third world debts and eliminating land mines, as well as the efforts to create more favourable trading relations for developing countries. Roy considers various options for how civil society organizations from diverse countries might best work together to promote their common concerns for global peace and justice.

PART FOUR: THE COLLABORATIVE MINDSET

CHARLOTTE CLOUTIER

Cloutier, formerly executive director of the University of Sherbrooke Foundation, argues that charities can and should encourage donors to engage in the kind of dialogue that helps them achieve philanthropic goals that reflect their values. Major gift fundraising is viewed by Cloutier not as a process of marketing or 'selling' a cause, but rather as a unique opportunity to start a discussion that can eventually become, for both donor and charity, a learning experience.

ROBERT RYAN

By weaving together personal stories, experiences, and reflective thought, Ryan's essay highlights some of the joys and challenges fundraisers face as they develop relationships with donors. This is a provocative and stimulating essay by a man who has worked as a fundraiser for both Care Canada and the University of Ottawa.

ELIZABETH MOREAU

The development and dissemination of consumer information is one of the primary functions of voluntary sector health organizations. To help fund health communication initiatives, organizations frequently collaborate with industry, most frequently pharmaceutical companies. Moreau's essay explores ethical questions raised by these collaborations and offers suggestions for resolving key ethical issues that arise in the process.

LILY MAH-SEN

This essay looks at the unique role that an organization like Amnesty International can play as a 'strategic bridging organization' in interactions between the corporate sector and the voluntary human rights sector. Mah-Sen starts by reflecting on her own experiences as an intercultural bridger, and then more broadly considers the correlations between her experiences and Amnesty's experiences as a bridge between voluntary and corporate sectors.

PART FIVE: THE CATALYTIC MINDSET

This essay examines closely the current difficulties and life prospects of the children of offenders, especially single mothers and Aboriginal women. These children are largely ignored by the correctional system. As a result, Bayes argues, expectations for their normal social function is very low, and the probability that they will eventually become offenders themselves is unusually high. Bayes concludes this thought-provoking essay by discussing a number of initiatives to address the needs of these neglected children.

In this essay, Dale explains and evaluates three approaches to fostering public dialogues about pressing contemporary issues. Citizens' Juries (initiated originally in Scandinavia), Participatory Budget Processes (utilized in a number of Brazilian municipalities), and deliberative dialogues (which the author initiated while working for the Canadian Council on International Cooperation) are examined. Dale reviews the strengths and weaknesses of these alternatives, while pointing to the overall benefits that result from any attempt to involve citizens in give-and-take public discussions of important issues.

Social entrepreneurship is an approach that combines the creative delivery of social mission with innovative ways to fund activities, often using earned income streams and other business models borrowed from the private sector. Drawing upon her experiences in Actua, a Canadian charitable organization, as well as comparable experiences of other organizations, Flanagan argues that social entrepreneurship is a mindset that can help organizations marshal the resources required to be more sustainable and to deliver more services.

Foreword

The universe of voluntary sector or 'public benefit' organizations in Canada is vast; indeed, the sector in Canada is second only to that of the Netherlands in size relative to population: over 80,000 registered charities, perhaps double that number of non-profits, 1 million full-time staff and 11.8 million volunteers. Although the sector accounts for some 8 per cent of our GDP, it works largely in obscurity. Feel-good stories in newspapers and, infrequently, reports of malfeasance are the most attention it receives from the media. Governments at all levels rely on the sector to deliver services, build healthy communities, and articulate needs, but seldom consider the impact of legislation or regulations on its vitality. Yet strong voluntary organizations are the essential building blocks of community, both the driving force and the tangible expression of a vibrant democracy.

For decades community organizations have pursued their missions, working within a context that assigned them a role variously defined as complementary to government in the delivery of services to hard-to-reach populations, or addressing 'market failure' in the provision of goods to vulnerable groups, or even as the proverbial 'canary in the mineshaft,' giving early warning of impending social needs and challenges. In the 1990s, however, roles began to blur: business values were increasingly viewed as dominant, with both governments and not-for-profits urged to 'become more businesslike,' which presumably meant more results-oriented and efficient. At the same time, governments began to cut back on social spending, offloading responsibilities to provincial and municipal jurisdictions and, eventually, onto the backs of voluntary organizations. Organizations were exhorted to 'do more with less,' to address root causes and not merely symptoms, and to situate their operations within larger 'systems' of health care, education, and so on.

It was in this changing context that the J.W. McConnell Family Foundation launched a leadership development program specifically for the voluntary sector, in partnership with McGill University. This initiative was new in several respects: it was intended to provide a learning opportunity on a par with what is available to senior private sector executives; it was conceived as a partnership between a funder and a university, requiring a tight marriage of theory and practice in its design and execution; and it was planned as a time-limited program that would reach enough present and future leaders in the sector to constitute a 'critical mass' to influence the sector as a whole.

The essays in this volume, as Fred Bird and Frances Westley explain in their introduction, reflect the themes around which the program was built. Now, several years after the completion of the program, it is evident that it had a profound impact on the participants' careers and their personal lives. Many have gone on to become even more prominent and effective leaders as well as agents of change. The impact on the sector as a whole is more difficult to assess, though one can see new relationships and networks that have been formed, at least in part due to this intense experience of sharing and learning together.

In the past decade the pace of change has accelerated. Terrorism, global health threats, economic shocks, natural disasters, and a changing climate are having a profound impact on the world, and on Canada. At the macro level it is increasingly clear that nation states cannot address these challenges alone; within countries, it is equally apparent that no single sector of society has the capacity to respond successfully. Big Issues call for a societal response, not fragmented efforts, and a commitment to collaborate and to engage citizens in the search for solutions. What has been called the Age of Deference is long over; people no longer expect employers or governments or experts to tell them what to do or how to think. Apparent citizen apathy and disengagement from formal political processes is belied by a willingness to get involved in community-level activity where cooperation can lead to tangible results.

Fifteen years after the first meetings to design a program for voluntary sector leaders, we face a new set of challenges. Some are familiar: a return to government deficits, for example, and the need to make Canada more economically competitive; others are new, like meeting the needs of an aging population. The community sector, in addition to the evergreen problems of managing, staffing, and funding the thousands of organizations that comprise it, is also crafting a different 'narrative' of its role and value to Canadian society, a role that goes beyond caring, causes, and conviction to embrace innovation, entrepreneurship, and creativity. Shifting to a 'green' economy, responsible consumer choices, new models for the delivery of essential services like health care and education, require leadership from the community sector.

The contributors to this volume are evidence that the leadership exists. They explore what is required to focus on the mission while working in complex situations, how Canadian values interact with an increasingly global context, and how organizations must navigate between asserting their separate identities in a competitive marketplace for money and ideas and the need to collaborate for greater impact and effectiveness. The collective portrait is daunting in the scale of its challenges, and inspiring in the commitment and optimism of its actors.

For the Foundation, sponsorship of the McGill-McConnell Program helped to create strong bonds with many important organizations and inspiring leaders with whom we have continued to collaborate. It deepened our understanding of the potential of voluntary or public benefit groups to create positive change, and of the need for targeted support to enhance their ability to do so. It also led directly into our involvement in the field of social innovation and to our commitment to identify, support, and strengthen entrepreneurial individuals and organizations so that they can contribute even more effectively to exploring and implementing solutions to complex social challenges. In the words of Arundhati Roy (2003, n.p.), 'Another world is not only possible, she is on her way. On a quiet day I can hear her breathing.'

Tim Brodhead
President, The J.W. McConnell Family Foundation

Preface

This book is written by a group of leaders in voluntary sector organizations in Canada to voice their concerns about particular contemporary challenges facing the voluntary sector. The topics of their individual chapters range from ideas about better ways to manage unexpected crises (chapter 4) to opportunities afforded by social entrepreneurship (chapter 15); from ways to manage leadership succession in charismatically led groups (chapter 3) to ways to forge effective international links with other NGOs (chapter 8). Some of the essays are quite personal, as leaders reflect on their own leadership experiences (chapter 2) or on their own roles as fundraisers (chapter 10). Several are written to alert readers interested in voluntary sector issues about pressing problems, such as the overlooked situation facing the children of offenders (chapter 13) or First Nations children living on reserves (chapter 7). Several of the authors inquire into the relationship between voluntary sector and private sector organizations when the latter act as sponsors, donors, or partners (chapters 10, 11, and 12). One (chapter 5) is written to raise fundamental questions about appropriate ways of evaluating the effectiveness of voluntary sector organizations. Another (chapter 1) is written to reflect on and celebrate the capacity of some former children in care to transform themselves and become social leaders. One explores the opportunities associated with public dialogues (chapter 14), while another analyses ways of renewing organizations that have become set in their ways (chapter 6).

The essays also vary considerably in style. A few are in the form of research reports. Several others take a more personal approach in order to explore unexamined feelings and assumptions. All are written to speak up and speak out from new angles to address pressing issues in the world, issues facing their organizations and the voluntary sector, and issues facing the authors as leaders.

Readers involved in Canada's voluntary sector – whether as volunteers, professionals, donors, members, participants, students preparing for careers in the sector, or current leaders – will be drawn into the varied worlds of these authors and feel at times sympathetic, outraged, inspired, enlightened, and informed. They will learn about very diverse ways of exercising leadership through administration, listening to others, thought-full analysis or initiating change. In many instances, real leadership development begins, as several of these essays show, by developing one's self.

These essays were all originally written when the authors were participants in a special program co-sponsored by McGill University and the J.W. McConnell Family Foundation. The McGill-McConnell Program – officially known as the McGill-McConnell Masters in Management for National Voluntary Sector Leaders – is described in the introduction. It was not an ordinary academic degree. It was an executive program, which lasted long enough so that three classes of forty leaders could each participate in a series of five two- to three-week modules, along with additional executive exchanges and tutorials, while still continuing their regular professional responsibilities. Working with academic advisors (located at McGill University, as well as York University, Concordia University, McMaster University, Oxford University, the University of Calgary, and the University of Victoria), each participant prepared a major paper related both to what they had learned as part of the McGill-McConnell Program and to challenges in the voluntary sector that especially interested them. Altogether they produced 120 papers, which originally varied in length from 45 to 125 pages. On the basis of recommendations from the academic staff, half of the authors were subsequently invited to present their papers at five specially organized seminars, where the papers were read and critiqued by the participants. Certain authors were then invited to revise their papers substantially for publication. (See also the section 'Additional McGill-McConnell Papers' at the end of this volume.)

Building upon an approach originally developed by the International Masters for Practicing Managers (co-sponsored by five universities in Canada, Great Britain, France, India, and Japan), the McGill-McConnell Program organized its modules around particular themes or mindsets (see Introduction). The sections of the book reflect the modules of the program, with the papers grouped in an approximate relation to the

major themes of these modules. While there are indeed some connections between these broad themes (focusing on leadership and reflection, organizational analysis, global perspectives, collaboration, and
action), most of the essays cover material discussed in several themes
while focusing on a particular challenge.

We have found these essays to be engaging and *provocative* in the root
meaning of this term, namely, as vehicles for *voicing* concerns about
vital matters. It is fitting that these essays are so varied in topic and
style. Diversity is, after all, one of the virtues of the voluntary sector in
Canada.

Frederick Bird and Frances Westley

VOICES FROM THE VOLUNTARY SECTOR:
PERSPECTIVES ON LEADERSHIP CHALLENGES

Introduction:
Leadership and the Voluntary Sector in Canada

FRANCES WESTLEY and FREDERICK BIRD

In 1997, the J.W. McConnell Family Foundation launched a major innovative initiative, in collaboration with the Faculty of Management
at McGill University, to create a new master's degree program, called
the McGill-McConnell Program for National Voluntary Sector Leaders.
Three ideas made this initiative novel in concept: first, that the voluntary sector needed and deserved a leadership program of the same
quality as the best executive business degrees; second, that the sector as
a whole needed to exercise more leadership in Canada, shaping the
public debate so often dominated by corporate leaders and politicians;
and third, that an academic program could contribute to a change of
this kind by bringing voluntary sector leaders together and giving them
a chance to rethink the major challenges facing the sector and build a
community of response.

At the time when the McConnell Foundation envisioned the possibility of such a program, its mission was focused primarily on helping
Canadians deal with change. The foundation saw the voluntary sector
as facing leadership challenges in multiple domains – the most important being collaboration with the private and public sectors. The voluntary sector was in danger of losing its soul, caught between demands
for 'rationalization,' 'accountability,' and cost effectiveness from the
corporate sector, on one hand, and demands from the public sector, on
the other, that the voluntary sector assume delivery of services hitherto
provided by government. A 'colonization' of the voluntary sector remains a real threat.

If the private sector is about commerce and the public sector is about
guardianship (Jacobs 1993), then the voluntary sector remains the chief
arena for debate and dialogue about civil society and those values we

wish to honour apart from considerations of the market or of governance. But how to strengthen this voice? This became the organizing question for the team that designed the program. As most of the team members were from business backgrounds, a secondary challenge was to balance the theory and practice of business management with the value orientations of the voluntary sector, building synergy when possible and identifying difference when helpful.

The program was built around six themes or mindsets, five of which – the *Reflective* Mindset, the *Analytic* Mindset, the *Global* Mindset, the *Collaborative* Mindset, and the *Catalytic* Mindset – are represented in the main parts of this book. These five mindsets represent key leadership functions as identified by Henry Mintzberg: to reflect, analyse, contextualize, collaborate, and catalyse action. The sixth, the *Ethical* Mindset, while increasingly important for the business world in a post-Enron era, was deemed so crucial to the voluntary sector that it was included as a two-day segment of each of the other five modules.

Designing the Program: Leadership Roles and Challenges to the Voluntary Sector

The team of academics who designed the program included Nancy Adler and Michelle Buck (Reflective Mindset); Brenda Zimmerman and Kunal Basu (Analytic Mindset); Nelson Phillips and Tom Lawrence (Collaborative Mindset); Harrie Vredenburg and Rajesh Tandon (Global/ Contextual Mindset); Frances Westley (Catalytic Mindset); and Fred Bird and Travis Kroecker (Ethical Mindset).

From the beginning, team members immersed themselves in the concerns of the voluntary sector, bringing their own management specialties to bear on the challenges of leadership. Workshops were held with voluntary sector leaders around the mindset themes, and from these workshops there emerged a set of sub-themes of particular concern to leadership:

1. *Leadership demands reflection as well as action.* Giving voluntary sector leaders the space and frameworks in which to reflect was key to the program as a whole and became the overriding theme of the first module. Reflection was linked to self-knowledge and discernment, and to the idea that *to be a leader entails a capacity for and a determination to acquire self-knowledge, and to use that knowledge self-confidently in the service of a mission.* This internal focus is quite a departure from the mainstream

business literature on leadership in both the academic and popular press. 'The power of authentic leadership is found not in external arrangements, but in the heart,' says Parker Palmer (1990, 23), who urges us to turn away from a life of ceaseless activity to one of greater contemplation.

To this end, we designed much of the first module and the threads of the rest of the program around the practice of reflection. For some participants in the program this was a challenge on multiple levels. Not only can self-exploration be difficult and disconcerting, but it is frowned upon in the sector as self-indulgent. We found early evidence of this difference through the 360-degree evaluation and feedback instrument we used to assess skill levels before entry into the program – an instrument created by Stephen Schoonover, a Harvard psychiatrist, expressly for the voluntary sector in Canada. On compiling the data for all 120 participants in the McGill-McConnell Program, an interesting pattern emerged. Voluntary sector leaders were stronger than their private sector counterparts in their emphasis on teamwork, their courage and commitment, and their ability to build networks and alliances. They were dedicated, ethical, and determined. But as a group they were less strong than the private sector at delegation, implementation, and what might be considered the command style of leadership. In comparison to his or her counterparts in the private sector, the Canadian voluntary sector leader looks rather like a one-man band, trying to play all the instruments and get the melody right, but then handing off the credit for success to his or her fellow musicians. This is quite a different image from the type of CEO widely praised in the U.S. business press, whose style Mintzberg (1999, 26) terms 'loud management, or Management by Barking Around.'

Instead, voluntary sector leaders in the program were attracted by the idea of the servant leader, the 'leaderful' organization, and shared leadership (Greenleaf 1991). But while these approaches may avoid the excesses of 'loud' leadership, each casts its own different shadow: a tendency to self-effacement, or to self-sacrifice – or both – which *can* get in the way of the organization's mission, despite the leader's best intentions, and which most certainly prevents leaders from the kind of deep self-knowledge we have described above. According to one McGill-McConnell participant,

My most powerful insights came during the course of the first module. I discovered that leadership was not only about what I know and my skills as a professional, but also about 'being.' It requires knowledge of myself and my values, a capacity to reflect on and connect values and action, to listen to various perspectives and weigh various perspectives. Proud of being a professional in the voluntary sector, this subjective dimension to leadership was a total surprise. What had been mostly an intellectual perspective on leadership began to go to my guts, to connect head and soul.

The surprise on our side was the degree of modesty and the self-effacement, which seemed absolutely basic to the sector. For example, a critical leadership skill, which we spent time on in this first module, was that of storytelling. As Howard Gardner and Emma Laskin wrote in their landmark study, *Leading Minds* (1996), 'Leaders achieve their influence through the kinds of narratives or stories they tell; about themselves, their society, and the people with whom they are dealing' (9). The McGill-McConnell Program thus made storytelling a privileged tool for developing leadership, drawing on Gardner and Laskin's ideas, as well as from Joseph Campbell's studies of the role of storytelling in mythology.

But where many leaders had difficulty was in seeing the link between their personal story and that of their organization. Many struggled with feelings that their organizational issues were more important; that to create a story about their own lives as a way to present central issues or dilemmas in their organizations was somehow self-aggrandizement. Most were not even comfortable with the use of the first-person singular ('I did this,' 'I said that'), insisting rather on describing organizational choices in the first-person plural 'we,' even when the individual leader was clearly responsible. Gradually, however, some exciting experiments emerged. One leader was able to see that her experience with the early loss of a much-loved parent was her personal link between her organization and the needy children it served. Moreover, in telling the story she was able to put into words a much more universal experience of loss, of parenting, and of why her organization existed:

When a father dies, a child grieves. I have lost someone I love. When a father leaves, a child feels anxiety and self-blame. What did I do wrong? Why doesn't my father love me? Death is final. He won't come back. Abandonment is indeterminable. What would make him come back?

Yesterday, when a father died, our society affirmed the importance of fatherhood by comforting and supporting his family. Today when a father leaves, our society discounts the importance of fatherhood by accepting his departure with reasoned partiality. Death kills men but sustains fatherhood. Abandonment sustains men but kills fatherhood. Death is more personally final, but departure is more culturally lethal. From a societal perspective, the former is an individual tragedy; the latter is a cultural tragedy.

To reach a place where she could tell this story powerfully required some deep reflection, a search into her own motivations and drives, which for many leaders is disconcerting and difficult. Annie Dillard (1982) describes this as the most difficult journey anyone can take, into 'the substrate, the ocean or matrix or ether which buoys the rest, which gives goodness its power for good, and evil its power for evil' (94); but this journey is necessary in order to arrive at the kinds of truths that it is the leader's responsibility to name and to bring to light.

Part One of this book presents the McGill-McConnell papers inspired by the Reflective Mindset. The essays by Lynda Manser, Ida Mutoigo, and Bernard Voyer illustrate how deep reflection on the part of a leader can be married to organizational mission. These three essays read most like stories, as the authors work to create parallels between their own life narratives and those of their respective organizations.

Through the initial essay, written by Lynda Manser, former executive director of the National Youth in Care Network, readers hear the voices of a number of young people who have experienced rejection and powerlessness but have responded to their circumstances by becoming leaders within the network. They have expressed the 'courage to become.' Manser describes the process by which these young people emerged as leaders as an often difficult journey, by means of which these young men and women were able to identify, affirm, and develop their own particular gifts. In the end she concludes, 'Our capacity to see and change the world coevolves with our capacity to see and change ourselves.' This initial essay explores how people who never would have imagined that they could become leaders find ways to assume both greater charge of their own lives and, in the process, become leaders of others. In the process, Manser's essay moves from interesting and quite engaging accounts and observations about a handful of emerging leaders in one particular organization to a much more general insight about the value for any would-be leaders of identifying and offering as a basis of their leadership their own personal strengths.

While Manser uses her essay to reflect on how some young people, struggling to achieve in spite of difficult conditions, have become leaders, Ida Mutoigo uses her essay to reflect on her own experiences as a leader in an international faith-based organization. She considers her particular calling; reviews various ideas, exercises, and experiences she has found helpful; and spells out a framework for further cultivating her own approach to leadership in a religiously oriented community. What especially stands out in her essay is how important it is for leaders to regularly take time to personally reflect on their own priorities and their sense of what is taking place in their lives, organizations, and worlds. Leaders so often get caught up in continual motion and overwhelmed by the day-to-day agendas. These preoccupations may become even more protracted in faith organizations, Mutoigo muses, where there is such an emphasis on doing things in just the right way. Thus, it is important for leaders to schedule regular times for reflection, so that they can review the larger global situation in which they are working, and the overall purposes of their organization. They can also use these occasions to review, re-assess, and re-affirm their own personal passions and priorities and, in words which Mutoigo uses from Gandhi, 'Be the change you wish to see in the world.'

Bernard Voyer, a director of the Taoist Tai Chi Society of Canada, writes his reflections on leadership quite consciously as a follower rather than as a leader. His essay is especially relevant for any organization, whether religious, political, private, or civil, which has been inspired or directed at any time by a charismatic leader. Voyer states that what was especially interesting about Moy Lin-shin, the charismatic founder of the Taoist Tai Chi Society of Canada, was that Moy expected his followers not to be unthinking and devoted recipients of his direction but rather self-disciplined and well-skilled apprentices in the healthy ways of living that this group promotes. Correspondingly, Moy arranged it so at his death he was succeeded not by a newly designated charismatic leader – in effect, a replacement founder – but by a council of skilled, journeymen-like officials, capable of managing an organization committed to helping people learn and practice certain healthy exercises and lifestyles.

2. *Leadership in the voluntary sector demands the ability to manage highly complex situations and emergence.* For this, the capacity for discernment is required, in order to find useful patterns in the complex world around us. This second capacity is built on the first – because contemplation is required to discern such patterns, and a comfort with self, silence, and ambiguity is necessary to give us the capacity to listen, to wait, and to

contemplate until that pattern becomes clear. According to Gardner (1995), 'Reflecting means spending a lot of time thinking about what it is that you are trying to achieve, seeing how you are doing, continuing if things are going well, correcting course if not; that is, being in a constant dialectic with your work, your project or your set of projects' (294).

In the second module of the McGill-McConnell Program, the 'Analytic Mindset,' we asked participants to look at two pictures: one of a calm beach, the other of a turbulent ocean. We asked, 'When you are managing in your organization, which does it feel like?' Participants invariably suggested the ocean. Leaders in the voluntary sector saw the world not as stable and unchanging, but as highly unstable and connected, 'immersed in and consumed by social connection' with (at times) 'numbing' results (Gergen 1991, 2).

Such social connection has only been intensified by the advent of email. Estimates suggest that the average manager spends at least two hours a day on email correspondence and that it doesn't reduce any of the demands described above. This is what T.S. Eliot called 'distraction from distraction by distraction' (Eliot 1969, 120). Contemporary theorists writing about leadership suggest that this level of distraction, this level of complexity, represents one of the key threats to effective leadership. In such an environment, reflection and its associated skill, discernment, are not luxuries but necessities. It is critical to separate the wheat from the chaff, the key elements from the peripheral, the patterns from the chaos.

This is not easy. The management theorist Peter Senge, who has written extensively about learning organizations, has argued that complexity is defined by a system of non-obvious relationships. What do we mean by that? Well, take the stormy ocean of the photograph. Now imagine you are one ship on that ocean. You have to contend with the waves coming from multiple directions. This feat is complicated, sometimes surprising, but obvious; you literally see them coming. Now imagine that under the waves, you are connected by cables, which you can't see, to numerous other boats that you don't know exist and you can't see, and that they in turn are connected to each other in a complex web. As you attempt to steer your craft in the waves, one of the cables suddenly tautens, pulling you sharply off course; you try to correct by yanking another invisible cable, and so on. These are the non-obvious connections, which Senge says it is the leader's job to anticipate, illuminate or even, under some conditions, design; to this extent leaders must be teachers (Senge 1990).

Leaders as teachers help people restructure their view of reality in order to see beyond superficial conditions and events into the underlying causes of problems – and therefore to see new possibilities for shaping the future (Senge 1990).

These are the underlying system dynamics, which are unseen, but which, like the underwater cables, drive our behaviour. In the McGill-McConnell Program, we began this process of restructuring our view of reality by exploring the notion that in situations of complexity, asking the right questions to reveal the mental models and underlying assumptions within our organizations is as important as giving the right answers. And we introduced the notion of minimum specifications: the notion that in leading under circumstances of complexity, our goal is to strip our requirements to the most basic, and the most essential. According to one graduate of the McGill-McConnell Program,

Conversations have changed in my office, and it has been noticed. We are more honest, straightforward, and supportive of each other. There was not a particular day when it changed. But there is no doubt that 'listening' has become important to the group I work with. If only one lesson remains ingrained with me from the McGill-McConnell program, it would have to be the understanding that 'good conversations take time.' A good example would be my first meeting with a team that had developed a habit of talking all the time, over each other – a style of combative, challenging, intense, no-listening conversation – just go at it! As their new manager, I did not say anything in that staff meeting, just held my own calmly – and when space opened up I still did not say anything, for what seemed like an eternity. There was noticeable discomfort with the non-communicative silence. And I knew that if I was in such a situation two years earlier I would have assumed that such a leader would be seen as lacking in control, and weak. But I was off on a different path, and testing my ability to 'listen' for the real issues as I pulled together threads of their conversation, each one of them, and strung them together into a system. For me it was important that I really heard what they were saying. I didn't have answers for them that day, but I trusted the insight I had learned – that there are times when it is much more powerful to listen than to have an answer ready – because answers without reflection and understandings will not have meaning or be genuine.

The Analytic Mindset is represented by the essays in Part Two. Marg McGregor, Jerry DeMarco, and Mark Langlois all deal with organizational challenges through an analysis which deepens understanding. All three authors assume that organizing and managing complex problems require a systemic, multifaceted, multi-level approach. Again, personal experience is combined with analytical and complexity approaches to illuminate an important aspect of leadership in the voluntary sector.

In the initial essay, Margaret McGregor, who is the CEO of Canadian Interuniversity Sport, especially reflects on the need for timely responses, focusing in this case on guidelines for responding to crises. She draws upon the experience of sport organizations, in order to offer some general guidelines for exerting leadership in times of crises. Observing that crises ordinarily pass through a number of different stages, McGregor indicates when different kinds of responses are called for. In these kinds of settings, she notes in particular that leaders need to have developed the capacity to tolerate both considerable confusion and unanticipated hostility.

In the second essay, Jerry DeMarco, former managing lawyer for the Sierra Legal Defence Fund, criticizes one particular approach that has been developed for assessing how well voluntary sector organizations are performing. He looks at what other organizational analysts have called the 'tyranny of the means,' that is, the rigid focus on efficiency of particular organizational processes, analysed apart from a larger concern for organizational purposes and outcomes. He analyses the Donner Awards for 'Excellence in the Delivery of Social Services.'

While recognizing the need for organizations to evaluate their own performances regularly, he criticizes the way these awards carry out evaluations of voluntary sector organizations. He argues that these awards exhibit a tendency to adopt a business model, which especially looks for and rewards efficient utilization of organizational resources. What is needed, DeMarco argues, is more attention to the varied forms of evaluation geared to the diversity of organizations and their purposes, along with the diversity of objectives they are seeking to realize.

In the third essay in this section, Marc Langlois analyses the experiences of contemporary youth organizations and looks at their prospects for self-renewal. He emphasizes how critical it is for organizations to appreciate where they are in relation to their own life cycle. Renewal may assume different forms, whether organizations are rapidly developing, mature, or declining. Having started a youth organization in Nova Scotia more than twenty years ago, Langlois uses HeartWood, his own organization, as a comparative point of reference for looking at the prospects and problems facing mature youth-serving organizations.

Each of these essays demonstrates a concern for devising lively and fitting forms of accountability. McGregor counsels organizations to analyse the extent to which they are prepared for dealing with unexpected crises. To be accountable entails becoming ready to respond to unanticipated threats and surprises. DeMarco directly criticizes certain approaches to evaluating voluntary sector organizations because they focus attention too narrowly on the efficient use of particular resources. In the process, these forms of evaluation fail to focus enough attention on the wider range of less easily calibrated resources – morale, volunteerism, community feelings – as well as the realization of organizational purposes. To be truly accountable entails devising practices of accountability that foster learning and commitment among organizational members. Langlois counsels mature organizations to fully appreciate possibilities for reviving themselves, while staying grounded in their own histories. To be accountable from this perspective often entails a willingness to relinquish some activities in order to foster others.

3. *To effect real change in the areas which concern voluntary sector leaders, single organizations need to think systemically, across sectors, sub-systems, and scales.* The global context becomes critical for voluntary sector leaders. The kinds of problems that deeply concern them – poverty, youth engagement, homelessness, chronic disease, community development, and the environment – are 'evergreen' issues. They don't go away; they are intractable. Moreover, in an increasingly interconnected world, 'when you try to pick anything up,' as John Muir said, 'you find it connected to everything else' (Muir 1911, n.p.). The drivers of poverty, environmental degradation, or even illness are often global. Understanding the global context is a necessary part of 'thinking like a movement,' working not just to problem solve in the short run but to create change in the long run.

When we move to a global system context, however, we do need to be able to think systemically. Understanding issues such as food markets in China demands an understanding of how industry and environment are interacting at a global scale (Brown 1995). From the point of view of the voluntary sector, to understand how to address issues of poverty, homelessness, social justice, or the environment in a Canadian context, it is important to understand the global drivers of local problems. It also means understanding how the same problems are handled differently in different cultural contexts.

Understanding the global context builds on the capacity of analysis and how to lead change. The McGill-McConnell participants travelled to India, Australia, and Singapore in order to understand firsthand the ways in which economic context and Western values contrast with the more religiously based, local perspectives of the developing world – what Thomas L. Friedman (2000) has famously symbolized as the contrast between 'the Lexus and the olive tree.' In meeting their counterparts in India, in particular, and in confronting the scale and severity of problems there – as well as surprising sources of resilience – participants came to frame some of their own problems differently:

> One of the surprising differences in the Indian voluntary sector was the way in which leaders did not accept service, advocacy, and activism as distinctive organizational missions. Most voluntary sector organizations did all three. In addition, the 'sub-sectors' in the voluntary sector, health, environment, arts et cetera were not seen as entirely distinctive concerns, but rather like separate petals of a daisy, the heart of which was the enhancement of the human spirit. For example, Vendana Shiva noted in a public speech that the environment should be protected, not only because it provided ecosystem services, but also because a beautiful and intact physical environment feeds the human spirit.

Another voluntary sector leader, who headed an organization that worked with street prostitutes, defended the value of an in-house theatre group for the organization's mission. After all, she noted, 'We can tell people how to live, but it is the artists that can tell them why.' This sense of the underlying connection of different sub-sectors further stimulated McGill-McConnell participants to view problems systemically.

The essays in Part Three all take this broader, systemic view of intractable social and environmental issues. Cindy Blackstock looks at the way in which the local experience of Aboriginal populations within Canada is determined by a complex system of drivers that have national and global roots. Alain Roy, in looking at global partnerships, emphasizes the need for collaboration and partnership in order to get traction on global problems – an approach which we call 'thinking like a movement.'

A global mindset entails a full appreciation of cultural diversity, which is an unmistakable characteristic of our increasingly globalized world. Becoming globally aware means more fully acknowledging and seeking to work with the ways others with whom we interact see the world. It is challenging both to recognize these cultural differences and to learn to converse with others in relation to their own valued terms of reference. Correspondingly, to be globally-minded calls for an ecumenical or cosmopolitan attitude: that is, a readiness to seek to understand issues from the perspective of diverse others. In subsequent essays Mah-Sen and Dale respond to this challenge respectively with their analyses of the importance of bridge-building and deliberative dialogue.

In the initial essay in this section, Cindy Blackstock, executive director of the First Nations Child and Family Caring Society, highlights the importance of fostering truly appreciative understanding between the First Nations people living on reserves and voluntary sector organizations in Canada. She begins her essay noting both the risks which these people face and the enigmatic fact that First Nations peoples living on reserves are so poorly served by regular voluntary sector organizations in this country. She then seeks to explore why voluntary sector organizations, otherwise so exemplary in the ways they address social problems, seem to remain so unresponsive to the concerns and needs of First Nations living on reserves. She considers the extent to which this lack of response occurs because of lack of knowledge, differing assumptions about volunteerism, and different cultural expectations. If Canadians are going to respond more effectively to First Nations issues, Blackstock argues, they will need to develop a more attentive and more appreciative understanding of these people.

To the extent that voluntary sector organizations address current issues from a global perspective, they will often, correspondingly, explore ways to collaborate with other organizations in other parts of the world addressing the same kinds of issues. They will explore how to become more effective by finding allies and partners with the same kinds of concerns, whether their interests are related to development, poverty, environmental concerns, youth engagement, animal rights, or health care. In his essay on 'Letting Be or Making Collaborations Happen,' Alain Roy, program director at Amnesty International, reviews varied ways in which voluntary sector organizations from different countries have collaborated globally to share information, engage in dialogues, and work on common projects. He discusses a number of noteworthy examples, such as global, cross-border initiatives to ban landmines, forgive third world debts, address and reduce corruption, raise labour standards, and protest the OECD's proposed Multilateral Agreement on Investment. Roy uses these examples as a basis for inquiring about the diverse ways civil society groups from around the world might work collaboratively to address the issues raised by current forms of economic globalism. What patterns of collaborations, he wonders, are most likely to make the most difference over time? As something like a global civil society begins to emerge, what form is it likely to take?

4. *Because of the reality of the hyper-connectivity, as well as the values of voluntary sector organizations, collaborative frameworks and competencies are a key part of leadership in the voluntary sector.* One of the realities of leadership in the voluntary sector is that it makes increasing demands on a leader's capacity to build sustained collaborations across the sectors. The relative paucity of resources in the sector, as well as the problem-oriented focus of most voluntary sector organizations, makes direct competition, even for resources, counterproductive.

This does not mean that competition in the voluntary sector does not exist; quite the contrary. But it is not valued in the same way as it is in the private sector. As MacMillan points out, the challenge for the voluntary sector is to identify the areas where they should help build up their partners, turn over responsibility to others, and try to win because they indeed are the best organizations to solve the problem. MacMillan recognizes that an emphasis on collaboration sometimes weakens strategic thinking in the sector. This can cause 'mission drift' and a tendency to go after funds reactively as opposed to strategically:

> One approach which combines private and voluntary sector strategic thinking is the use of 'strategic intent' – the creation of a centralized set of ideal goals, a vision of possibility, as it were – in order to stimulate co-ordinated, goal directed activity throughout the organization. The process of arriving at these goals is decentralized, however, allowing for creative means and different approaches. (Macmillan 1983, 70)

Ultimately, however, much more can be gained in the voluntary sector by 'thinking like a movement,' which means combining forces with other voluntary sector organizations, as well as government or private sector actors, to try to induce a 'tipping point' (Gladwell 2000) where initiatives which might be started at a local scale cascade up and cause a whole system transformation. The skills of building partnerships, alliances, and collaborations are therefore key to voluntary sector transformation (Kanter 1989). As one participant said,

Prior to my participation in the McGill-McConnell Program, my approach (to the question of context for educational leadership) would have been straightforward: check opinion polling for attitudes to education; review policy initiatives from across the country, and predict where things might go. Ken Gergen's idea of 'multiple voices all claiming to be the truth and the right' came to mind as I developed a presentation using responses to the 1999 protests against the World Trade Organization in Seattle, challenging us to envisage education as an arena of multiple voices and to explore the implications for educational leaders. An important thing happened: our board's leadership committee decided to reconceptualize its framework for thinking about leadership in education. It determined that it should concern itself with the leadership role that superintendents and others should play in society, and not just in their institutions. As a result, a regular meeting of the board was transformed into a seminar for the board and other national education associations on global trade. It was one of our most successful efforts. A year ago, the board would have said, 'That's not our business.'

Since the end of the program, one of its chief accomplishments has been the number of novel and broadly based collaborations that have sprung up across the sector, as well as collaborations between voluntary organizations and governments or private corporations. Faith communities have collaborated with other NGOs; First Nations organizations have partnered with health- and youth-oriented NGOs. At the sector level, contacts and collaboration have been strengthened and deepened, and some of these have led to continuing, productive relationships. Collaboration within the voluntary sector is not always easy, as many organizations are often in direct competition for funds. Personal contacts established with a colleague during the intensive residency periods of the McGill-McConnell Program paved the way to much more productive dialogue on how collaborative fundraising could be done.

The first two essays in Part Four closely examine the interactions between voluntary sector organizations and the donors who support their activities. In the first essay, Charlotte Cloutier, former executive director of the Newton Foundation, analyses the increased role played by donor-directed contributions to voluntary sector organizations. The astronomical growth of high-involvement giving vehicles, such as donor-advised and venture philanthropy funds, suggests that donors increasingly wish to play a greater role in directing where their gifts go and how they are utilized. Higher levels of donor involvement are not without problems, Cloutier observes, to the extent that donor-directed contributions may lead recipient organizations to shift their orientations and, over time, lose sight of their priorities. Citing several anthropological studies, Cloutier argues that charity 'on the ground' occurs primarily within ongoing and evolving relationships, and is deeply associated with general feelings of identity and community. Correspondingly, voluntary sector organizations should view high-involved giving as an opportunity to build lively and interactive relationships with donors, of the kind that trigger and nurture dialogue, shared learning, and growth.

While Cloutier makes her recommendations as an aspect of professional responsibility, Robert Ryan reaches complementary conclusions in much more personal terms. In his essay 'Can't We Be Friends?' he tells of his experiences soliciting bequests for an international humanitarian organization and a university for which he formerly worked. Imaginatively using Aristotle's discussion of friendship as a point of reference, Ryan explores the fine line between cultivation and manipulation, between respect for the mystery of giving and effectively managing sound financial transactions. After reviewing several ethically ambiguous situations he has encountered as a fundraiser, Ryan wonders whether these kinds of dilemmas can be adequately resolved guided largely by common sense and personal integrity. In the end, he too views fund-raising as an activity that seeks to build relationships, at once utilitarian and personal, between donors and the organizations they support.

In the third essay in this section, Elizabeth Moreau, director of communications and public education of the Canadian Paediatric Society, examines collaborations between pharmaceutical firms and other health care businesses and voluntary sector organizations working in the field of health care. Over time, these organizations have engaged in a number of collaborations, often undertaken to educate various publics regarding beneficial practices, concerning, for example, the immunization of children, sleeping positions for infants, and the value of low fat foods. She predicts that the number and variety of these collaborations will grow over time, as public funding declines. These collaborations have been both necessary and useful. At times, nonetheless, voluntary-private sector collaborations have been abused in ways that seem to advantage particular businesses, evade regulations calling for full disclosure, and infringe upon the priorities of health care organizations. Moreau considers alternatives to respond to these problems. She surveys the diverse policies which groups like the American Medical Society and the World Health Organization have developed to guide health care organizations as they consider and enter into these collaborative relationships. Given the possibility for misunderstanding and misuse, she ends her essay recommending that more efforts be invested in developing useful screening and monitoring procedures for these kinds of collaborations.

In the fourth essay, Lily Mah-Sen, who works as a grass-roots coordinator as part of the Community Activism program of Amnesty International, considers policy alternatives that her organization has been debating. Amnesty has developed its reputation by working to defend human rights, especially the civil and political rights of individuals oppressed and sometimes imprisoned by governments. The organization is now thinking about focusing greater attention on defending as well the social and economic rights of individuals, as they are adversely affected by both governments and businesses. In order to develop this line of action, Amnesty has been exploring the possibilities of collaborating on specific terms with particular businesses. There has been much debate over whether Amnesty, as it engages in corresponding actions along these lines, will have significant impact, will compromise its standards, and/or will divert its energies. To address this question, Mah-Sen, who, as a Chinese-Canadian considers herself to be a hyphenated Canadian, reflects on her own experiences as an alternator and bridge builder in order to consider the degree to which Amnesty has been and can become a bridge builder in the global effort to defend human rights.

5. *The need to act in the face of high uncertainty and high stakes is an ongoing concern for the voluntary sector, particularly those involved with vulnerable clients and populations.* One of the key challenges in voluntary sector organizations is that their work entails not only programmatic but also deeply ethical concerns. When working with fragile and vulnerable populations, the cost of mistakes can be high. If a product line fails, workers may have to be laid off, and profits may decline. But when a youth worker in an international NGO dies far from home, the harm is irreversible. Nonetheless, it remains an ideal to address the needs of the most vulnerable.

When we were in Delhi, we learned something that Gandhi said, that when you're faced with a decision, if you make that decision so that it

benefits the most vulnerable person involved, then you know you are going in the right direction.

Action in a context of high complexity is, as we have noted, based on
low control. An initiative such as a leadership decision may have not
only unexpected, but also devastating consequences. However, without risk there can be no transformation. Palmer (1990) notes the need to
balance contemplation and action, insight and courage. The risks cannot be ignored. But to dwell on them is to risk immobilization. It points
again to reflection and discernment as crucial leadership capacities, but
these need to be combined with the courage to make mistakes, even in
risky situations. As noted by General Roméo Dallaire, the former head
of the UN forces in Rwanda, men went out to fight every day because
they believed in his leadership. Some of them died and, ultimately,
lacking the cooperation of key nations, the peacekeeping effort failed.
But a leader must try; and a leader can't escape responsibility, even for
things that cannot be controlled (Dallaire 2004).

The recognition that mistakes will occur in the voluntary sector is
one thing; the capacity to learn from those mistakes is another, requiring a special kind of courage. It requires the ability to listen deeply to
others, even if that deepens our sense of culpability, to know oneself
deeply, and to be prepared to reveal both strengths and frailties in dialogue with others.

In the first essay in Part Five, Shawn Bayes writes about a particular
problem, namely, the way the correction system puts unanticipated
stress on the children of offenders. As the director of the Elizabeth Fry
Society of Vancouver, Bayes provides compelling evidence of the stress
from which these children suffer and the long-term cost to Canadian
society. In powerful and persuasive ways, her essay is a call to action. It
provides disturbing evidence and then invites readers to explore how
they can find ways to address this situation. As her essay was originally
read by classmates in the McGill-McConnell Program, it has already
aroused others to explore ways in which their organizations might act
to help these children. Effective communication often serves as a means
of rallying people to take action.

Jacquie Dale, who currently is the president and CEO of One World
Inc., also discusses the importance of communicating effectively, but
focuses on a very different form of communicating, namely, interactive public dialogues. Her essay provides accounts of three different
initiatives from Scandinavia, Brazil, and Canada: Citizens' Juries,

participatory budget debates, and deliberative dialogues. All of these tools function as means of opening up public discourse, developing common ground from which plans of action for addressing value-laden, controversial, and potentially divisive issues can arise. They have each had measurable success. In the late 1990s, while still working for the Canadian Council for International Cooperation, Dale initiated a series of public conversations across Canada about international issues, like global trade and world hunger. On the basis of this experience, the council began a consulting firm that Dale manages. It organizes dialogue processes for various public, private, and voluntary organizations.

In the last essay, Jennifer Flanagan, president and CEO of Actua, writes about ways of fostering effective programs of action by integrating commercial activities into voluntary sector organizations. In part, she argues that these money-making activities provide additional sources of funds, without which many program activities might otherwise have to be curtailed. She makes this argument because such commercial activities can provide the most effective way of delivering particular services to targeted groups. Over the years, a number of voluntary sector organizations, such as the YMCA, have developed commercial activities in the form of summer camps, fitness programs, and craft and cooking classes. Flanagan makes another point as well. She wants to call attention to the ways entrepreneurial initiative, so characteristic of many businesses, can be cultivated effectively by voluntary sector organizations.

In spite of their different forms, these essays emphasize the following common points. First, imagination plays an important role in fostering effective action. Imagination can be used by listening to others (Dale), by considering alternative ways of action (Flanagan), and by confronting overlooked information, in this case about the children of offenders (Bayes). Imagination allows us to gain new perspectives, to consider excluded alternatives, and to envision mediating positions between supposed mutually exclusive alternatives.

Second, effective action is often taken by identifying and building on current assets rather than thinking about problems and deficiencies. We can see evidence for this belief in Flanagan's discussion of entrepreneurial activity in the voluntary sector, and in the ways the participants in deliberative dialogues are encouraged to draw upon their own experiences.

Third, effective action calls for people to take risks. Each of these authors points to large risks which typically cause hesitation, anxiety, vacillation, and correspondingly, inaction. The risks in all these cases are real and significant. Bayes reflects both on the risks faced by the children of offenders and the risks that accompany any efforts to address this problem. In the public debates Dale describes, the participants are invited to voice their anxieties about the risk associated with the alternative responses they are discussing. Finally, Flanagan acknowledges the risk associated with the kind of entrepreneurial activities she is championing. These essays are grouped together to compare and appreciate the different ways in which the authors describe methods of addressing risk. Bayes argues that the risks involved in responding compassionately to the children of offenders are smaller than the risks that these children and society will face if we fail to respond. Dale shows how people who otherwise strongly disagree and fear the positions proposed by others can overcome these differences by taking the time to listen to each other. Finally, while acknowledging the risks associated with social entrepreneurship, Flanagan makes a compelling case that the uncertainties are manageable and that the outcomes are well worth the venture.

These five themes, as well as the ethical concerns which run through them all, shaped the conversations in the classroom and shape the essays in this book. The writing of the papers and the process of preparing them for publication made it obvious that the challenges facing today's organizations require not only new understandings but also new forms of knowledge production, best achieved by creating a dialogue between practical academics and thoughtful practitioners. These papers were selected from 120 essays in total; they were nominated by academics who felt that they represented excellent research and practical insights into leadership in the voluntary sector. They were further refined at workshops where practitioners and academics worked together to give voice to areas of key concern for both. What was achieved in this volume is therefore not only an unusual look at the voluntary sector in Canada but also an unusual blend of thought and practice.

As educators, we have discovered in the McGill-McConnell Program a pedagogy of human learning which engages us in the building of knowledge rather than simply the gathering of information, which seeks to foster the development of learning communities in which learners are engaged intellectually, emotionally, and physically.

The essays in this volume are valuable to students and researchers interested in exploring some of the most critical areas of leadership in the voluntary sector. They raise questions for those who want to understand work and practice in this area in greater depth. They also offer new perspectives for the practitioners themselves, providing guidance in their own particular efforts to support social good, social change, and those values upon which civil society depends.

PART ONE

The Reflective Mindset

1 The Courage to Become

LYNDA MANSER

For young people in the care of Canada's already large and rapidly growing child welfare system – dealing with past traumatic experiences, faced with difficult challenges in the future, and lacking effective control over their own lives – life can be intensely frustrating. Many youth in care express feelings of isolation, loneliness, and hopelessness. As a result of this situation, the National Youth in Care Network was started in 1985 by a group of young people from across Canada who were determined to do something about their feelings of powerlessness within the child welfare system and wished to regain control of their lives. Over twenty years later, although the faces have changed, the National Youth in Care Network's purpose remains the same: to empower its youth members and help them, in turn, to empower their peers in care.

The National Youth in Care Network is a national charitable organization made up of young people, ages 14 to 24, who are either in or from state care across Canada. State care includes the child welfare and protection systems, children's mental health systems, and young offender systems. In any year, there are approximately 76,000 young people in the care of child welfare authorities, and 25,000 young people in custody in Canada; countless others in mental health institutions, and still others who fall through the cracks of these systems and live on the streets.

Youth-in-care networks are peer support groups run by and for youth in care, focusing on support and advocacy activities that teach young people skills which will help them to help themselves and their peers. They are the conduits through which youth in care can support one another and effect positive change in the child welfare and custody systems. These networks provide young people with an opportunity to redirect their abused energies in order to help themselves and their peers to heal.

Since I began working with the National Youth in Care Network, I have consistently found inspiration from the youth leaders, even on days that are filled with tears from the horror stories and bureaucratic frustrations that make up a large part of their lives. In gratitude and admiration, I wanted to honour their struggles and their 'courage to become': their ability to find their own humanity within an inhuman system of 'care.'

Storytelling has great power within the Youth in Care Network Movement, and it is the chief mechanism used in this essay to explore the courage to become through reflection and expressive action.

This exploration is an attempt to uncover the common paths taken by young people towards achieving emotional well-being, and to extract the lessons to be learned from their personal experiences of pain and triumph over abusive home situations and the lack of empathy in the child welfare system.

A common theme in these young people's stories is the experience of injustice – of situations leaving youth with a stark choice to act or not to act. When their reaction to this injustice was inaction, they felt despair; but when their reaction was to act, they discovered that they could begin a self-transformation that led to the realization of their own leadership abilities. The creation and narration of their personal stories guided them through a process of expressive action and reflection: an exploration of their motives, their struggles, the others in their lives, their gifts and skills, and the results of their actions. Through this process, they came to know who they were within the context of their personal history and in relation to a community of others like them. They were able to achieve leadership, inspiring other youth in care to begin the process of becoming and increasing the understanding and empathy of others with the situations and needs of youth in care.

Despite the generally positive outcomes in the stories that follow, names have been changed in order to protect the identities and confidentiality of the young narrators.[1]

1. The Injustice: Youth in Care

Physical and sexual assaults are among the most frequent causes of harm and death to children and youth, yet they are also the most difficult to document (Trocmé and Brison 1997). Assaults by family members account for a substantial portion of all assaults against children and youth. These incidents are frequently under-reported because they often take place within the privacy of the home, and involve victims who are dependent on their abusers and who fear the consequences of talking to anyone about their experiences. One victim describes the feelings she had as follows:

> When I think of family violence I think of my father batting me around the house pretty bad. He put me in the hospital. He'd scream and yell at me. You get pretty scared of it. It's like you want to back off. You just want to go, run away and that's what I'd been doing for about thirteen years of my life around there. I'd been running away from home and that really got me even more mad because when I'd get home I'd get the worst of it. When I was first born my mother said she had problems with me even before I was born, that I was the lousiest baby in the whole department. She's always been running me down. And the sexual abuse, well, that put me in a scare because if I didn't do it, what would he do? It's like laying there thinking to yourself, 'When is it going to be over? I want to get it over.' That's all I could think of. My mother could have put a stop to it. She could have gone to the police. She did nothing. She just let it go, and that's why I blame her. I hate my mother. (Raychaba 1993, 17)

There is a general consensus among academics and clinical professionals that family violence has a long-lasting detrimental impact on the lives of child victims (Raychaba 1993). Behaviours commonly exhibited by child victims of violence include non-compliance, hostile and aggressive behaviour, poor peer and social relationships, insecure attachments, low self-esteem, impaired moral development, and an overall sense of anxiety and emotional insecurity. By and large, a history of family violence or abuse is associated with higher rates of delinquency, adult criminal activity, psychiatric illness, and teenage pregnancy (ibid.).

Protection for abused children: The child welfare system

Canada has in place a wide array of legally sanctioned protocols and programs that provide for the protection and substitute care of children and adolescents who either have been abused or, for a wide variety of other reasons, cannot be cared for by their biological families. These were based on the system originally designed for the protection of animals, the Humane Society.

If and when abuse or maltreatment is suspected, a child welfare agency or department of social services initiates an investigation to determine whether or not the allegation is founded, and whether it falls into the jurisdiction's definition of abuse or maltreatment. If the allegation appears to be well founded, child welfare authorities are legally authorized to take the child into custody. The state assumes legal guardianship of young people in need, and thus is considered to be acting *in loco parentis* (in place of the parent). These children or adolescents are then designated as being 'in care.'

Consider the experience of Julie, and her description of how she came into the child welfare system:

> It started when I was about twelve years old and I was always running away from home. At first it consisted of sleeping at friends' houses. Then in stairwells, when my friends' parents would call my mom to tell her that I was there, which defeated the purpose of my running away. Then it turned into longer bouts, became a week at a time. I would be staying up all night in coffeehouses and fast-food restaurants, moving from place to place for as long as I could, as long as they were open.
>
> I lived in the projects in the north of the city with my mom and two brothers. What I remember about my childhood is being surrounded by sadness and poverty. The projects I lived in had mainly single-parent families. There was a lot of drugs and alcohol in our community. It wasn't a safe place to be. So this combined with the mental illness of Mother. She experienced serious depression and found it hard to take care of three kids by herself on top of dealing with her own stuff and everything else in the community. I remember our place on a normal day. The house was always dark, the drapes closed. If you open the fridge, there may be a jar of old pickles and mouldy bread in there. It wasn't a great place: cockroaches and things no one likes to live with. I felt a great deal of responsibility for my brothers, and this caused a lot of conflict with my mother around issues like discipline versus punishment. Her opinion was to punish immediately and physically, and sometimes it got out of hand.
>
> When I was 13, I went to live with Aunt Lucy, who wasn't actually an aunt, just a friend of my mother. She lived in the same neighbourhood as us. Living with her opened my eyes to things. I began to see that things at home weren't normal, that parents didn't have to resort to corporal punishment immediately. Lucy was the same as mother, but she had coping

skills. I lived there for seven months, and during that time my own disposition started to improve. I was happier, safer. I began to realize that there was more to me than 'You're a stupid kid, you're never going to amount to anything.' After seven months, I went back home because I had made decisions in my life with regards to religion and felt that being at home would be better for me.

I asked my grandma if I could live with her. She said no, since my grandpa had just died. But I think it was more because my mom said to her, 'Don't you dare let her live with you.' I think she said that because she was feeling like a bad mom and didn't think it was a good idea. I couldn't live with my father, so my options were to stay put in the institution, or go home. I decided to try to do everything I could to go back home.

People always ask me, 'How can you go back? It never changes.' It's like, no matter what, they are still your parents. No matter what they do to you, they are always your parents. No one else will ever take the place of your parents. You always think that things might be different.

I stayed in that institution for almost a month. The day before I was to go home, a psychiatrist came to my room and asked me, 'What would you do if your mom didn't want you back?' I said, 'I guess I would be on the streets.' My mom had told them she didn't want me back, but she hadn't told me. They had already contacted the ministry, and had planned for a social worker to come the next day and take me to a receiving home. I found out that Mom had known about this for a week and had already packed up my stuff, without saying a word to me. I freaked out and spent the afternoon crying. The only thing that helped me that day was one of [the] co-op students came into my room and closed the door behind her. She didn't say anything for a while. Then, in a quiet voice she said, 'I don't normally tell anyone this, but I'm telling you this to help you.' She told me that she had been in care and it was the best thing for her because of her own home life. She told me that going into care saved her life, and that it may be a good thing for me too. She told me that it was only temporary, and that it didn't make me a bad person, it didn't make me abnormal. She was supportive, and that gave me a source of strength to help me get through it.

But I still had a lot of things that hadn't been dealt with. I was still in depression and using drugs, and basically living a double life. Going to school was really hard, as I was constantly getting the 'What did you do?' or 'You must be a bad ass' or 'You must be easy because girls in care are easy.' After going to three different schools in less than two years, you learn to keep your mouth shut and you don't say anything. You just hope you'll meet a nice person who will become your friend. But, without fail, I always met up with people who smoked pot or had no respect for life and I would just end up sitting under a bridge doing drugs. I was supposed to be getting counselling and tutoring, but I think that no amount of counselling would have helped me, because I didn't feel ready to do it. I didn't realize at that time that I was not the bad person.

The experience of being in the care of the child welfare system

The experience of being in the care system is unlike anything one would want a child to experience. Children and adolescents frequently have difficulty adjusting to the disintegration of their families and subsequent removal from their home. Being placed in a stranger's home with little more than a garbage bag of belongings compounds the barriers for adjustment. While some social workers, judges, or foster parents may attempt to explain to them that they have been removed from their families 'for their own good,' the children, removed from everything that is secure and known, typically feel that they, not their parents, are being punished for the abuse they have suffered.

Once placed in the care of the state, youth are frequently moved to new foster or group homes, causing further ruptures in what stable relationships they have. This transiency may be the result of inadequate placement selection, insufficient contact with caseworkers, inadequate supervision, or a caseworker's misdiagnosis of the child's needs. Emotional and behavioural problems resulting from past histories of family violence often manifest themselves in anti-social, hostile, and aggressive behaviours, also leading to the breakdown of a placement (Raychaba 1993).

Unfortunately, although this 'acting out' is a natural response to their earlier separation and loss, displaying this response leads into a self-perpetuating and unhealthy cycle of non-attachment and disruptive behaviour. Successful experiences with attachment provide children and youth with the psychological security and confidence necessary for them to cope with stress, fear, frustration and worry later on in life, while providing the foundations upon which future relationships are built.

Unfortunately, the experience of the child in care is often associated with considerable instability. This situation is undesirable for any child, especially one who has an unhappy background that has been characterized by an unstable relationship with parents (Cruikshank 1991). Youth in care living transient lifestyles over a sustained period of time tend to develop a conditioned inability and an understandable unwillingness to interact, integrate, and become emotionally connected to or attached with either peers or adult caregivers (Raychaba 1993).

They Soon Forget

You came,
You became a number
You ate
You slept
They kept your mind under lock and key.
They chained you to rules,
To their way of life.
You went,
They waved,
They soon forgot,
But, did you?

Anonymous, *Youth Exchange* (1987, 2)

2. The Reaction to the Injustice: Courage in the Lives of Youth in Care

In the midst of these unhealthy conditions, and despite the interference of a system originally designed to ensure the protection of animals, some youth survive. They become strong enough to overcome the impact of a vicious childhood and stop the cycle of violence. And some excel, leading organizations that support young people who suffer under the same unhealthy conditions and oppressive bureaucracies. They have the courage to work with the perceived enemy, to prevent their experiences from happening to other, younger children. At some point in their lives, they have sensed their own possibilities beyond their immediate existence and have chosen to represent those possibilities to others. But what is it that drives some to live with courage, while others are forever trapped in a cycle already determined for them?

The courage to become

Courage refers to the attitude of facing and dealing with anything recognized as dangerous, difficult or painful, instead of withdrawing from it. *Webster's Ninth New Collegiate Dictionary* defines courage as 'mental or moral strength to venture, persevere, and withstand danger, fear, or difficulty.' Mark Twain's saying, 'Courage is resistance to fear, mastery of fear – not absence of fear,' adds an important nuance. The word comes from the Old French word for heart (*cuer*, from the Latin *cor*). We develop courage for those things that speak to our heart, to the centre of our will and seat of our intellect. Our courage grows for things that affect us deeply, things that open our hearts. Once our heart is engaged, it is easy to be brave (Wheatley 2002).

In *The Courage to Be* (1952), Paul Tillich describes 'the courage to be' as the self-affirmation of being in spite of non-being, the courage to accept oneself in spite of being unacceptable. For youth in care, this means accepting themselves as worthy of a life of meaning, despite having little positive affirmation or support throughout their childhood and adolescence. The experience of being abused for no apparent reason, of being pulled out of their reality without their consent or even consultation, and of being referred to as a case file number lead many youth in care to believe that they are not valuable human beings. In Tillich's terms, these experiences communicate and reinforce the anxiety of non-being – a source of profound psychological and spiritual anguish.

Tillich identifies three forms this existential anxiety takes. The first of these is *ontic* anxiety, the anxiety of fate and death. We live with the awareness that one day we will be extinguished by death, and we are constantly reminded of our vulnerability through encountering factors affecting our lives over which we have no control. The second form is *spiritual* anxiety, the realization that humanity lives with the threat of meaninglessness. To live meaningfully is to have a source of ultimate concern that gives purpose and value to existence. Ultimate concern is the source of our spiritual centre – that is, our capacity for self-affirmation – and without it we incur the risk of self-disintegration. The third form is *moral* anxiety, the anxiety of guilt. To live is to live with the responsibility to affirm or to realize oneself: to fail to do so creates a sense of guilt that our essential nature has been neglected (Tillich 1952). These forms of anxiety are termed 'existential' and are so called because they are integral and inescapable dimensions of human existence.

According to Jean-Paul Sartre, existentialism's first effect is to make man aware of what he is and to make the full responsibility of his existence rest on him. Courage is the principle that enables people to recognize the threat of non-being and to affirm one's own being in the face of it. It is the principle that enables people to define their identity not only as social beings but also as isolated individuals. This process is similar to Carl Jung's process of individuation, whereby we come to know who we are inside. The first step in the process – the first act of courage, as Jung describes it – is to acknowledge and come to terms with one's own 'shadow.' From there one will be able to integrate one's soul:

> ... it is therefore necessary to integrate the unconscious into consciousness. This is a synthetic process which I have termed the 'individuation process.' As a matter of fact, this process follows the natural course of life – a life in which the individual becomes what he always was. (Jung 1981)

According to Margaret Wheatley, life is born from an unquenchable need to be. One of the most interesting definitions of life in modern biology is that something is considered alive if it has the capacity to create itself (Wheatley 2000). The term for this is *autopoiesis* – self-creation – derived from the same root as 'poetry.' At the very heart of our ideas about life is this definition that life begins from the desire to create something original, to bring a new being into form.

The courage to become can be seen through the stories of reflection and action, the stories and poetry of those youth who have come from the cycle of abuse and the system into their own, bringing other oppressed youth with them. It is through these stories that the process behind the courage to become can be understood. It is also through the creation of their own stories that these youth have discovered their own courage and begun to be.

The power of storytelling in discovering the courage to become

There is a great power in storytelling. The voicing of one's own story and experiences is powerful, both for one's own healing but also for increasing the understanding of another. Carl Jung maintains that every person has a story, and when derangement occurs, it is because this personal story has been denied or rejected. Healing and integration is possible when the person discovers or rediscovers his or her own personal story. Marc, a former youth-in-care leader, describes how the mastery of one's story is the basis for one's journey to become:

> The capacity to see and change both the world and ourselves co-evolves on an ongoing basis. It has to begin with the challenge and the assurance that, at its most fundamental, youth in care have mastery over themselves. Nobody can tell me that my experience is wrong, because it's my experience. The first thing I master is my own experience, then I come up with

my own voice, I master my own story. Then, when I've decided for myself, I begin to clarify and further develop what that experience was, a fine-tuning mastery of my story. Eventually, I begin envisioning a positive alternative to what happened to me. It's not just knowing where I've been and where I am, but envisioning where I could be that is the ultimate mastery of experience.

Stories enliven the capacity to change and help to establish relations with others who have experienced similar situations. For many youth in care, telling their stories to each other is their first attempt to begin the process of developing healthy relationships. And it is successful because the similarity of their experiences works to break down the barriers and lessen the distance between them. Good conversations help us to connect with others on multiple levels. They help us to remember that we are part of a large whole. From this we gain a sense of shared wisdom, as Wheatley (2002) writes:

> Good conversation connects us at a deeper level. As we share our different human experiences, we rediscover a sense of unity. We remember we are part of a greater whole. And as an added joy, we also discover our collective wisdom. We suddenly see how wise we can be together.

Anthony, a former youth in care leader, describes the power of sharing stories with others like himself:

> When I opened myself up to the others, then they responded. When you share with kids like you, they'll understand that they can relate to you. They'll understand that, as hard as it is now, they can do it; that when you're fifteen years old and things are hard and you can't see anything good, in ten years you'll be able to pick out the good things in life. It's hard to pitch to someone that their real life shittyness will be a solid foundation for them some day. But it means everything to hear it.

Through stories, youth in care can discover their courage, begin the process of becoming and inspire other youth in care to do the same.

The conditions of injustice

Common to all youth in care are the feelings of powerlessness, fear, instability, emotional disconnection, and a lack of support. These are not the prime conditions for displaying courage or for having an understanding of one's self beyond one's immediate existential reality. Raychaba (1993) makes this clear:

> Family violence … It brings to my mind pictures of being in my bed, covering my head and just being afraid. Being afraid of everything. Being afraid to cry in case anybody hears me. Being afraid to move, to draw attention to myself. Walking on eggshells. Being terrified. Being angry. Blood. Pain … Lots of pain. (ix)

For some, these feelings are enough to threaten one's being. In Tillich's terms, they threaten one's ontic self-affirmation, relatively in terms of fate, and absolutely in terms of death; one's spiritual self-affirmation, relatively in terms of emptiness and absolutely in terms of meaninglessness; and one's moral self-affirmation, relatively in terms of guilt and absolutely in terms of condemnation. These existential threats are severe enough to drive some young people to seek distraction through drugs, to shut down emotionally, to take to the streets in search of human connection, or to seek death through suicide. Yet, for others, these threatening feelings turn into a drive for survival. And, for a few, the fear for their own survival turns into courage and translates into passion for one's actions and life direction.

Motives followed by inaction lead to despair and distraction

According to Parker Palmer (1990), an initial exposure to an injustice, followed by an inability to ignore or accept that injustice, results in a motive or calling. This motive will either lead to inaction or to action. When injustice leaves us with inaction, we feel despair. Consider the story of Marc, as he describes the despair he felt upon his entrance into the child welfare system:

> I grew up in single-parent household, but I had regular contact with my father. My only sister is eleven years older than I am. She left home early, as she and my mother didn't get along. The situation with my mom grew worse as I grew older, but I was an introvert and I just internalized the abuse and oppression. My mom called the Children's Aid Society.
> When the social worker came into my home, I was the focus and got the blame for everything. I heard that they thought I was a fire-starter, but the workers never confronted nor challenged this. At one point, the worker

said I had to go to Sick Kids Hospital for a quick assessment. I didn't want to go, so I talked to my sister about it. She said to play along, so I went to what they called a quick 'meeting' with other people watching behind a one-way mirror. At the end of the meeting a lady came out to speak with me. She told me that I would remain at the hospital for a one-week assessment. This quick 'meeting' occurred in June, and at the end of the meeting, my clothes were taken away, a nightgown was handed to me and I was seriously sedated. I shut down. I didn't speak to anyone. I zoned out like a zombie for two months, the whole summer.

During my 'zombie' summer in the hospital, I stayed with some other, more seriously mentally ill youth. At the end of the summer, I was finally sent to a foster home. I was sent to some stranger's home.

This despair can also translate into distractions of other sorts. Consider the story of Anthony:

I was born into the child welfare system. I was destined to be transient … I was moved from home … to foster care … to home … you get the picture. My mom was on her own, no support, no job, no future other than a lifetime cycling of abuse and neglect that is so common on First Nations reserves. She drank, and soon I was taken away from her and placed into a foster home. Then another, then another. Eventually, I was adopted by a set of white parents: my mom, who stayed at home while I was young, and my dad, who was a police officer. My parents, though, were not in great shape … my father was a chronic alcoholic. In fact, the only difference between my dad and one of those guys on a street was his badge.

I spent as much time as I could away from the house and from him. As soon as I was old enough, I started hanging out in the arcades. One day I didn't want to go home, but I ran out of coins, so I was just sitting around in the arcade. An old guy, probably in his thirties, came up to me and asked me if I wanted to go to his house to play a new video game he had. I didn't want to go home, so I said sure. At his house after a few hours of playing the game, he asked me if I wanted to try some cocaine. I did, and before I knew it I had turned my first trick. I was eleven years old. I got hooked right away, on the drugs and on how easy it was to get stuff just by turning a few tricks. And it kept me away from home and from my father. But soon my parents got fed up with me and I was back into the system. First into a foster home, then another, then a group home, then onto the streets, then in jail, you name it.

Motives followed by action lead to courage

When injustice leads to action, we discover courage. According to Margaret Wheatley (2002), we are often moved to courage by the recognition that if we fail to act, nothing will happen: 'the greatest source of courage is to realize that if we don't act, nothing will change for the better ... reality doesn't change itself ... it needs us to act.' This discovery of one's courage through action is echoed in the story of Joe, as he describes what brought him into the care of the child welfare system:

> I grew up with my dad and brother and sister. Our dad was physically abusive. He drank lots and as a result, beat us up a lot. Our mother ran away from him early in our lives, when all three of us were five or under. Our dad used to tell us in countless lectures that our mom was a wicked bitch who abandoned us to foster care when we were just infants. No soft mother. No nurturing or tucking in at bedtime. Things were really hard. And I wanted to kill myself from a really young age, nine or ten. I often thought that God had abandoned us and left us for dead; torture would be more like it.
>
> Anyway, things were bad for many years. I experienced racism in schools from white kids, white male kids especially, because I was the Aboriginal kid. I experienced hopelessness after a while because Social Services had been called many times but my dad got away with 'it' every time. I experienced fear of the cops, because I was a bad thief. I stole bikes, toys, everything. I had a really long young offender record, all before I was twelve years old. I had no concept of school, or hard work.
>
> When I was twelve years old, a social worker had the balls to give me the phone number of the Crisis Intervention Mobile when my dad was in the washroom during a home visit. Later that week, the next time my dad flew off the handle, I used that number.
>
> Anyway, the next time my dad tried hitting me, I ran out the door and down the driveway. I had pre-planned the run away because I had a place to go ... And I went to foster care. Those fucking losers actually believed me and took me in. Not only that, but they went and got my bro and sister. I was really scared, about retaliation from my father. About getting stalked down and beaten.
>
> I like to think that I ran away when my brother only left for a while. I like to think a lot about how I left and did it for myself, but it was good for them too. Not too many people have heard my run away night story.

Maybe five or ten in the last thirteen years. Today I'm in AA and doing shit with my life. If the world stopped turning today and we all had to meet our makers, my bro and sister would have to scrounge for positive things. Like, they seem to still be there, in that house in some ways. Like, they haven't said, 'Fuck you, asshole, I'm leaving,' to his face, and left. I think there's a lot to be said about a moment of courage lasting a lifetime.

But at what point does the fear for one's own survival turn into courage and translate into passion for one's actions and life direction? Consider Joe's story:

I learned to feel helpless and hopeless. I was afraid and terrified. All my life I have felt a lack of love and void of courage. I felt the unforgiving eyes of my peers calling me a coward. And to be a coward was the worst thing I could be, all my life. But real courage was something that came from trial and error. You try it and see what happens. As leaders, we can only hope to lead.

I always hope that my life will inspire other youth to leave abusive homes. I always hope that I will stay healthy and raise a good set of kids, and not beat them, and not have them quiver at my arm movements. I have hopes that my stories will tell people that they can live, in spite of the odds, that God has not left them for dead and that we are responsible to one another once we have survived.

I think if we can survive, our life will be sufficient enough to lead people out of abuse. Like Marc Rachayba did for me, I want to show a person that even though you don't know the details of my story, it was bad, but now I wear nice clothes and have a haircut and go to university.

For us the concepts of leadership and courage are deeply rooted in self-esteem and spirituality. We suffer from deep spiritual wounds and our self-esteems are abnormally affected. The youth that come from abuse are special. Not many of them will survive. But as you know, those who do make enormous impact in their area of passion. I like to think I have affected the National Youth in Care Network in a good way and the child welfare system as well. I don't think of myself as a drain on the system.

Perhaps for some, it is as deceptively simple as what Margaret Wheatley (1992) says when she argues that we tend to be shaped by what we pay attention to: 'We become what we choose to notice. We create ourselves by what we choose to notice. Once this work of self-authorship has begun, we inhabit the world we've created' (n.p.). Or perhaps, for some, it comes when we look into ourselves, beyond our immediate existence. We have the greatest capacity to make a difference when we dare to open ourselves up, to expose our most honest nightmares and our most heartfelt dreams (Kahane 2001). The Tibetan teacher Chögyam Trungpa Rinpoche describes the 'dark time' as one in which people forget who they are, lose confidence, and so lack the courage to speak. He feels that courageous acts are born when we can acknowledge our goodness. One youth in care describes the risks and courage needed to speak, to acknowledge one's goodness:

> Us youth in care were betrayed by those of you who were in a position to love and protect us. Over and over again our trust and our spirits have been broken, and yet most of us survived. Speaking about some of these unbelievable experiences often gives life to things we may have minimized or pushed away into one of the many corners of our minds. We usually do not bring up the past, because speaking about it has a tendency to make it real again. Knowing all of this, we still took that risk. We are survivors and we are breaking the cycle of abuse. (National Youth in Care Network 1996, 1)

The role of action and reflection in the courage to become

An action in response to an injustice on its own can create frenzy – an effort to impose one's will on the world or survive against the odds. Contemplation on its own creates escapism – a flight from the world into a realm of falsity. Some youth in care who never contemplate enter into the world of networking and leave a few months later completely burnt out. Other youth in care who never take action experience such overwhelming feelings of isolation that they end up in mental institutions or on the streets. Those who move on to become leaders of the National Youth in Care Network have found ways to act and to contemplate in harmony long enough to complete some of their work. Both action and contemplation are needed. To reflect and contemplate is to unveil the illusions that masquerade as reality, to reveal the reality behind the mask, which leads to discernment. Instrumental action is a means to an end, using the logic of success. Expressive action, on the other hand, refers to an action that expresses one's own inner truth – one's motives, struggles, gifts and skills, and relationships to others – so intimately that to refuse such action would be, in effect, to deny one's own nature. According to Paul Tillich (1952), 'the courage to be is the ethical act in which man affirms his own being in spite of those elements of his existence which conflict with his essential self-affirmation' (3). Expressive action and the self-understanding it requires are thus essential to spiritual self-affirmation through the courage to become.

3. The Courage to Become: Reflection and Expressive Action Motives

While the first contact of youth in care with networks may be coerced, what makes them stay is something that is felt deep inside themselves. It signals a possibility and triggers the courage to become that possibility. Consider Julie's story of her initial involvement with a network and how it transformed into her calling.

My stay with the Joneses kind of failed in the end. And from there I had another four foster placements, then was moved into a semi-independent home. Part of that time I was in open custody, and I continued to run away no matter where I was living. It was like I was not feeling, like not caring if there were people worried about me or if I would be punished; I would deal with it when it happens, and that is that. Throughout that time, my social worker kept pushing me to get a job, and finally sent me to PARC, a youth-in-care network and support organization. I went, but was really sick at the time. I was always sick, which was a recurring theme, a result of a lifetime of bad nutrition and a parent who didn't know how to take care of a sick child. Irwin took me into his office and he said, 'You look sick. You should go home' … I told him to get me a job first. So he hooked me up with a summer job working in nursing home.

I think Irwin took an interest in me because I never talked and scowled a lot … He took me aside once and said, 'I think there's more going on. I think you should come in and talk to people.' I said I had had enough social workers talking at me, and he said, 'No, not a worker, I want you to talk to others your age, a youth-in-care network.' So I went and saw all these kids, a very diverse group of kids. At the time I didn't know they were all in care, but there was something about them that made them seem like a big family. Something was said in the group that struck a chord with me and made me want to open up. I got more involved. I kept doing more speak outs.

When I was eighteen years old, I was living two blocks away from PARC. I wasn't in care anymore, and I was trying to make a living and trying to get education. Things got bad for me. I was getting into some heavy chemical drugs. No one even noticed. I was acting stupid and was keeping things to myself.

But it wasn't until I started seeing things happening to the others I was with that I felt a sense of urgency to change. When my friends started dying, getting murdered, going to jail, disappearing, getting AIDS, doing heavy drugs, that's when I realized I was surrounded by a huge bubble of shit that I didn't want to be around. But what other options did I have? I knew that this was not the life I wanted for myself. People say that when you don't like your life, you have to stop complaining and change it. I realized that I needed to stop blaming my childhood and my parents for what I was or else I'd be just like them. It took me until I was twenty years old to remove myself from that community. I stopped going with those people and replaced them with PARC. It became my life every day. I stopped doing the things that were destroying me, and things started to happen for me right away because of it. I started volunteering my time, and telling people that I wanted to be more involved. They gave me more and more responsibility, and I learned how to fundraise, speak in public, help peers, and stuff like that. By the time I was twenty-two years old I was employed at PARC full time. And when the position at the NYICN came up, I went for it.

The struggle

LEADING WHILE BECOMING

Due to their early life experiences, many youth in care have an inability and unwillingness to develop a healthy emotional intimacy with others. These issues are ones that they continue to deal with throughout their lives. Their initial exposure to youth-in-care networks is quite often their first attempt at establishing healthy relationships. Unfortunately, the time that youth are involved with networks is relatively short. On average, youth in care become involved in the National Youth in Care Network around the time of their emancipation from care, and continue their involvement for approximately four years, until they are no longer considered to be 'youth,' which, according to the National Youth in Care Network by-laws, is age 25.

Quite often the initial contact is instigated by a concerned social worker or foster parent who sees the youth 'heading in the wrong direction' and in need of additional support. While the short time of their involvement is adequate for establishing a consistent form of supportive relations, it is extremely short for the journey from 'on the margins' or 'at risk' to 'leader,' in terms of personal and skills growth. One of the clearest advantages of the National Youth in Care organization is that it is clearly peer-run. Therefore the difficulties must be dealt with, for both the organization and the individual. This difficulty is described by Sam's experience of trying to lead, while still dealing with the same issues as the ones she was trying to lead.

> It seemed like everybody, particularly those of us who worked as staff, went through horrible burnout. So many of us had a hard time – constantly articulating our experiences. There was a four-year overlap where I was on the board and still involved in drugs and the sex trade. We were working for change, but it hadn't happened yet. Our involvement with the National Youth in Care Network was in a leadership role, and yet we were looking for support too ... It kept me very raw for a long time ... To try and make a distinction between the personal and professional is pretty hard.

It is also extremely difficult to try to support other youth through their issues while still dealing with issues of one's own. While time might not be devoted directly to one's own healing during their journey to leadership, the very work that they do, their own actions, allow for the progression of their courage and journey to become.

Action can be the outward manifestation of an inward power; but as we act, we not only express what is in us and help give shape to the world, we also receive what is outside us and reshape our inner selves. When we act, the world acts back. This dynamic action works to co-create both the world and ourselves. Our action is a mixture of ego and innocence. Our most constructive impulse is often accompanied by a destructive impulse, made all the more destructive by the fact that we usually remain oblivious to this sinister energy within us. But this duality is dynamic, and its tension helps us grow. Every action involves self-transformation. The tense dynamic of the duality within us, even when subconscious, presents us with risks. We may choose to avoid those risks and continue to live inactive lives of disillusionment, or we may choose to take risks through actions, risks that may reveal the tension between our duality.

RISKING AND LEARNING
Through our actions we both express and learn something of who we are and of the kind of world we want. By risking, we may learn more

about ourselves and our world; the bigger the risk, the greater the learning. Our capacity to see and change the world co-evolves with our capacity to see and change ourselves (Kahane 2001).

At some point, we realize what we can and cannot control in this world. To attempt to exercise control where we have none is illusory. To exercise control where we have the capacity to do so is a form of wisdom. For the former, only action is required. For the latter, both action and reflection are required. The challenge is to know the difference, and that requires action and reflection, chaos and contemplation. To understand one's self is to get in touch with what one believes and values, and to assess how one translates these beliefs into action. Often our values and beliefs create personal energy.

Contemplation and solitude

Contemplation is difficult for many, because so much is invested in our illusions. These illusions serve a variety of societal functions, including maintaining our status quo, preventing insanity, inhibiting rage, and numbing our pain. The function of contemplation is to penetrate our illusions and touch reality. It is difficult to experience the moment in which our illusions and false hopes are stripped away, because it is a kind of dying. When our contemplative journey is prompted by disillusionment, our familiar comforts are replaced with an inner emptiness in which new truths emerge that are often alien and unsettling.

Yet solitude means to be in possession of one's heart, its identity and integrity, and a refusal to let one's life be dictated by others or imposed on by an impersonal culture. Solitude is someone who is able to give her heart away because it is hers to give, her possession. The only things we have to bring to others are ourselves, so the contemplative process of recovering our true selves in solitude is never selfish; ultimately, it's the best gift we can give to others (Palmer 1990).

Julie also talks about the role of solitude in her life:

> Solitude was sometimes wanted and sometimes just the way it was. I had tons of solitude living at home with my mom, and it wasn't necessarily good. There were many days in a row when I would be locked in my room. But I learned a lot about myself at a young age. I learned to be okay by myself. I was so used to being myself; it was like hanging out with a friend. When I would get through it, I realized that I was strong and able

to rely on myself. I know that I can pick up my stuff in a moment and leave all by myself and everything will be okay now.

The journey downward to knowledge and true compassion

The journey to knowledge is a spiral downward within oneself to where there is both the capacity for good and evil.

According to Parker Palmer, there are three elements that turn one's action from detached 'do-gooding' towards the beginnings of true compassion:

1. Hearing rather than seeing, which makes you more engaged.
2. Being frightened, which reveals real emotion and involvement.
3. Failing and allowing yourself to suffer, which is the key to growth, as it shows a willingness to confront, acknowledge, and explore failure.

According to Frederick Bird, people are morally deaf to the degree that they do not hear and do not respond to moral issues that have been raised by others (Bird 1996, 55). They fail to hear, recognize, and pay attention to the moral concerns expressed by others. The capacity to respond to the needs of others makes us responsible. And the degree to which we are responsible, or responsive, determines the degree of morality we possess. This responsiveness or morality is necessary because the consequences of inattention are harmful to others; likewise, the consequences of attention are beneficial.

The following passages from Margaret Wheatley's *Listening as Healing* (2001, n.p.) describe the power of hearing in its role in healing:

Great healing is available when we listen to each other.

Listening is such a simple act. It requires us to be present, and that takes practice, but we don't have to do anything else. We don't have to advise, or coach, or sound wise. We just have to be willing to sit there and listen. If we can do that, we create moments in which real healing is available.

A young black South African woman taught some of my friends a profound lesson about listening. She was sitting in a circle of women from many nations, and each woman had the chance to tell a story from her life.

When her turn came, she began quietly to tell a story of true horror – of how she had found her grandparents slaughtered in their village. Many of the women were Westerners, and in the presence of such pain, they instinctively wanted to do something. They wanted to fix, to make it better, anything to remove the pain of this tragedy from such a young life. The young woman felt their compassion, but also felt them closing in. She put her hands up, as if to push back their desire to help. She said: 'I don't need you to fix me. I just need you to listen to me.'

She taught many women that day that being listened to is enough. If we can speak our story, and know that others hear it, we are somehow healed by that. During the Truth and Reconciliation Commission hearings in South Africa, many of those who testified to the atrocities they had endured under apartheid would speak of being healed by their own testimony. They knew that many people were listening to their story. One young man who had been blinded when a policeman shot him in the face at close range said: 'I feel what has brought my eyesight back is to come here and tell the story. I feel what has been making me sick all the time is the fact that I couldn't tell my story. But now it feels like I've got my sight back by coming here and telling you the story.'

Our natural state is to be together. Though we keep moving away from each other, we haven't lost the need to be in relationship. Everybody has a story, and everybody wants to tell their story in order to connect. If no one listens, we tell it to ourselves and then we go mad. In the English language, the word for 'health' comes from the same root as the word for 'whole.' We can't be healthy if we're not in relationship. And 'whole' is from the same root word as 'holy.'

Listening moves us closer; it helps us become more whole, healthier, and more holy. Not listening creates fragmentation, and fragmentation is the root of all suffering. Archbishop Desmond Tutu describes this era as a time of 'radical brokenness' in all our relationships. Anywhere we look in the global family, we see disconnection and fear of one another. As one example, how many teenagers today, in many lands, state that no one listens to them? They feel ignored and discounted, and in pain they turn to each other to create their own subcultures. I've heard two great teachers, Malidoma Somé from Burkino Faso in West Africa, and Parker Palmer from the United States, have both made this comment: 'You can tell a culture is in trouble when its elders walk across the street to avoid meeting its youth.' It is impossible to create a healthy culture if we refuse to meet, and if we refuse to listen. But if we meet, and when we listen, we reweave the world into wholeness, and holiness.

4. The Other

For every action there is another, with whom the actor is in partnership and on whom the action in part depends. It is a joint action, the result of the dynamic meeting between an actor and another. The result is co-creation.

Life needs relationships in order to exist. Gaia is not lonely. It is impossible to look into the natural world and find a separated individual. As an African proverb states: 'Alone, I have seen many marvellous things, none of which were true.' Biologist Lynn Margulis expresses a similar idea when she comments that independence is a political concept, not a biological concept. Everywhere life displays itself as complex, tangled, messy webs of relationships. From these relationships, life creates systems that offer greater stability and support than life lived alone. Organisms shape themselves in response to their neighbours and their environments.

Knowledge of potentials and limits

We must know and revere the nature of the other if action is to be fruitful. This includes knowledge of the potentials and limits both of the other and of ourselves.

Julie describes her struggles of knowing the potentials and limits of others, as well as herself:

> One thing I did struggle with was allowing other people to come into my life in such a way that they could help me. I have friends, but asking them for help is difficult, because I think, in some way, it will weaken me. I won't go through the experience on my own, and somehow not having that experience is going to weaken me. But at the same time, other people's stories have been a source of courage for me. We're all still going through things, and probably will be for the rest of our lives. But seeing how far they've come, and not wanting to fake that everything is okay myself has given me courage. I want it to be good and be able to say it is good because I worked for it.

If we violate the nature of the other, we violate ourselves as well. Joe describes his experience with this type of violation:

> I was involved in a personal conflict with another youth that has persisted for a long time, still does a bit. It was about resentment, insecurity, selfishness, competition, all that. We didn't want to share the spotlight with one another in the same group in the same city. I had several heated discussions with him, and it came out that he didn't like the way I was hogging the spotlight. He called it the 'Joe Network,' and was really critical about the way I was running the network. I wasn't going to him with a warm invitation either … As leaders, we need to support youth, but we also need to have competence within the group … Resentment can kill a person. It's the worst thing for any occupation to resent someone you work with, going into work every day thinking about that person, going home thinking about that person, just wanting to jump on him for being so incompetent. Maybe I didn't handle it well as a leader, because there were times when I tried to turn people against him through gossip. I had lots of struggles. Gossip and accusation shit can come back to bite you.

These destructive actions tend to perpetuate themselves through vicious cycles. The key to an action that knows and cares for another is to know and care for yourself.

The interaction of self and other for 'right' action

A live encounter in the spirit of 'right' action is an encounter between the inward truth of the actor and the inward truth of the other that penetrates all external appearances and expectations (Palmer 1990). An action that distances us from the other can never be right. We cannot do 'good' by standing back and pulling levers that drop bounty on people who need it. 'Right' action can only be an immersion of ourselves in the reality of relationships with others, through which we find our place in the organic nature of things (ibid.). Even though we may mean well, or have deep feelings of sympathy for those who suffer, it does not follow that we know the appropriate action to take in order to help. To suffer with another person means to be there in whatever way possible. It is a source of inspiration and courage to face suffering along with others, to share the circumstances of the other's life as much as one can – not to add to the world's pool of suffering, but rather to gain intimate understanding of his or her wants and needs. In fact, however, our actions may be far removed from the needs of the other; misjudging our distance, we may have no clue as to what their reality requires.

Leaders who influence history do so because they live a paradox. They have enough courage to commit their lives to affecting the changes that they want to see. At the same time, they have the courage to engage with others, even their enemies, and to give up the illusion of being in control, to venture beyond detachment and to surrender to the process (Kahane 2001).

The healing power of the other

There is comfort and healing in the presence of people who know how to be with others, how to be fully there. Our inner energy grows exponentially when the common values of others interact with our own (Born 2003). A synergy of values and vision create energy that has purpose.

David LaChapelle (2001) says the following about the power of the group:

> In our coming together we are bearing witness to a remarkable gift of the cosmos: the capacity of human beings to transcend their condition by generating a presence amongst them which inspires, activates and nourishes.
>
> The emergence of this presence is the release of the guiding capacity which is biologically and spiritually encoded in each individual. Our bodies are an evolutionary experiment that is still in flux. As we listen to the deepest longings within our souls we feel the call towards something more whole, integrated and full. Our inner lives are in motion, dynamic in their intentionality to become more complete.
>
> Sorrow, greed, inhumanity, lack of hope – the innumerable afflictions that confront us arise from an insensitivity that is not innate; no human being is born without compassion. The biological imperative of their body and the emergent creative potential of their inner capacities are all seeking to find expression, an expression which is manifest and reflected in the moon upon the water and the curl of a leaf in the morning sun.
>
> Whenever a group of human beings gather there is, in the moment of the gathering, the possibility of engendering a quality of presence, which opens outward into the dreams, hopes and aspirations which live in the heart of us all. It is the collective debris of the conditioned self, which narrows the focus of the mind and afflicts the heart.

Consider Marc's description as he talks about the healing presence of others:

There was healing through being with others, in that others told me that my work was good, which was diametrically opposed to what my mother told me all my life. Healing is a gradual process, and there are limits to what networking can do. Some youth in care are so damaged that they are beyond repair. That is a sad reality. But when there is something to work with, it has the potential to be powerful, impactful. The healing of networking is literally a matter of finding one's voice, and discovering one's gifts.

Consider Anthony's experience of the power of the group:

Being in the presence of others, like Nicole, Joe, Yve, and Delia, was better than ten years of therapy. Having those people around was what let me accept my faults. When we were together, everyone knew everything about each other. We were able to be honest about our strengths and weaknesses. It was really critical, having those tight relationships. That's what makes the National Youth in Care Network so strong.

Having adults around in the same way was brilliant, because it made me know what I wanted to be: strong, supportive, and helpful like they were. They were able to be supportive, but at same time hold me accountable. It was the good balance that showed me what I wanted to be like.

Joe talks in this way of the healing of others:

If I had to sit down and plan out my life with God, I couldn't have expected some of the things I experienced. The group consciousness helped me to cope and deal with my raw abuse issues. There was major healing with the National Youth in Care Network. Some of the best friends of my life have been youth in care. There's no room to be a child in abusive environments, but this lets us recapture some of our childhood ... like our day in the sun ... It has built me into a man ...

Also, consider Sam's words on the power of being with others:

It has shaped me. It's who I am, what I do, what I'm about. For me, it was support, people who really understood me whether I was doing well or wasn't doing well. It's funny, because state care didn't help me with the transition, but the National Youth in Care Network did ... making the transition from dependent child to independent adult. The National Youth in Care Network helped me to go through that. I didn't have an adolescence in care, and I certainly didn't have one in the sex trade, so the National Youth in Care Network gave me that time to go through it. It let me be angry, and it let me be sad, and it let me heal. It stayed with me as I began to understand change in my life, within myself. And that doesn't even capture it.

5. Gifts and Skills

The courage to become is a process of self-transformation, which at its roots involves the ability to take inventory of and utilize one's gifts and skills. To become fully alive is to discover our ability to acquire and develop real competence in the areas for which we possess a natural aptitude. Listen to Anthony' describe how his competence developed:

I needed to trust my judgment. I learned about that, and I learned to let myself trust my judgment through my journey to leadership. I had it to some degree when I worked in the sex trade – there were cars I didn't get into, and homes I didn't go to. But then it was a survival skill. When I was a kid it was just a survival skill to have good judgment and make good choices. It was only through my involvement in the network that it became a life skill. There is a difference between surviving and living. At the National Youth in Care Network, that's where I learned skills to live, not just survive.

Yet it is hard to discern those gifts. Our culture says that gifts are not real; we must earn or make everything we get. Many of our gifts are so central to us that we take them for granted and are never aware of them. We assume that because we already have them, they are not gifts. We assume that because we did not work or struggle to develop those gifts, they are not skills.

Julie expresses her perspective on her gifts and skills this way:

I learned that I am intelligent and can do a lot. I haven't even realized my own abilities yet. There are things that I did that I never would have thought I could have done, like travelling to present to the bar association in Japan, or starting an international movement, or being a part of my brother's life. Then I think, if I've done all that in just this amount of time, I get really excited to think what I might be doing over the next part of my life. There is more to life than being in care, and thank goodness there is.

For some youth in care, the gift they have is simply to remember, to understand their family history and personal development, and to tell others of these experiences. To remember is literally to re-member, to reunite the hidden wholeness in us that is so easily torn apart by the powers within and around us, to transcend the motives and contexts that mitigate and distort our actions, and to enter into our own versions of fasting, forgetting, and dying. By accepting this process, they are healing. By telling it to others, they are helping.

Their commitment to becoming, to understanding one's self, translates into a passion and dedication for healing, of themselves and of others. Leaders who make a difference are extraordinarily committed, body and soul, to the change they want to see in the world, to a goal much larger than themselves (Kahane 2001).

6. Results

Expressive action is the expression of one's own inner truth, and therefore, the results of those actions will be in accordance with who one is, with one's self and one's values. The results emerge from the intricate interplay of the actor, the other, and the context of the action. They are based on motives, struggles, others, and gifts, and occur through a balance of action and reflection. If we can give up our expectations for specific results and surrender to the organic realities of one's self, the other, and the adventure of the action itself, then we will see results that are in line with who we are (Palmer 1990). This yielding of our expectations requires us to confront our fears.

We have a need to control results because of our obsession with projecting expected results and gearing our actions towards those projections. This obsession is based on fear; the fear of what will happen if we lose control, which is due to a lack of confidence that life is trustworthy, that a life of live encounters will take us towards wholeness. This results in us forever feeling the need to manipulate, through the strategy of goal-setting and results projection.

Marc talks of the results of expressive action:

> I believe that the mandate of the National Youth in Care Network to be a support for all youth in care is unrealistic. The beauty and magic of certain moments were not because they were scheduled or programmed; they just happened. I feel my actions were based on an expression of who I was or wanted to be.

The process of becoming is an expressive action insofar as it expresses one's own inner truth. When youth in care are in a position of leadership, their emerging reality is constantly affecting and being affected by the others, young and old, whom they are leading. Their innermost dreams and nightmares are being revealed; and these self-revelations in the process of becoming likewise affect those whom these young people lead, and in many cases inspire them to discover their own courage to become. Just as these young leaders discover their course of action through a feeling of connection, so too they create this new and powerful feeling in others.

We lead when we touch one another in such a way that our intimacy with life deepens, as we realize our courage to live through the obstacles we encounter, and discover the wellspring of creative capacity that lies within the heart of every human being.

We lead, in such moments, because we ourselves have been led by our opening outward into the fullness of life; by our risking becoming sensitive to one another; and by authentically experiencing and embracing the individual with whom we have become attuned. This moment of recognition does not become blind to the pain, struggles, and difficulties, but it also does not lie down in front of them. To lead is to move through the contractions that limit the elegant unfolding of the human flower, and touch the sensitive, emerging desire of every human being to be part of life itself: to contribute, to nourish, to support, to embrace, to inspire, to act, and to hold dear this precious existence we share. As LaChapelle (2001) writes, 'This is not a leading by imposition of one will upon another. This is a mutual exploration of the inherent beauty of life, the tender moments of pain and difficulties, which beset us, and the sensed emergent capacities of the soul present in each one of us.' Through their involvement with youth-in-care networks, they came to realize that their experiences were much the same as those of others who had survived family abuse and mistreatment by the child welfare system – they were all 'others' together. This sense of 'unity in otherness' encouraged them in their own discovery of their courage to become, and in return, to find this potential for healing in others that ultimately leads to solidarity and intimacy.

7. Conclusion

The experience of violence alone is enough to force some people to withdraw from the outside world. Youth in care must also deal with ruptured family bonds and unstable environments. Developing a clear sense of and trust in one's identity, much less the outside world, is a difficult task. To validate their essential beings in the face of threat of violation by abusive parents or the structurally insensitive state protection systems requires them to discover their courage to be: to become who they are called to be, to define their identity not just as isolated beings, but also as social beings.

This courage to become is seen in the stories and poetry of former leaders of the Youth in Care Network Movement, as well as by other poets and philosophers. Common to these stories is the experience of reflection leading to expressive action. These Youth in Care leaders came from situations of extreme injustice, and as a result, they were motivated to either inaction or to action. When experience of injustice reduced them to inaction, or provoked them to react without self-awareness or a clear purpose, they were driven to despair. When injustice spurred them to action, they discovered their own courage to become and began a self-transformation that eventually led to the realization of their own capacity for leadership.

Throughout this self-transformation, they were forced to struggle with issues such as leading others while still in the process of becoming themselves – risking and learning through contemplation and solitude, on the journey towards self-knowledge and compassion. They discovered that by opening themselves up to others, they were able to understand themselves better. They began to understand that their action and self-expression did not occur in isolation; that every action involved other persons who shared their reality and came to share their courage to become. This realization reshaped both themselves and the outer world in an act of reciprocal creation. As they progressed through self-transformation, they began to identify and develop these skills, and consequently, their results began to merge with their actions, coalescing with their identity rather than with structured goals.

This self-transformation through expressive action would not have been possible without reflection and contemplation. Reflection was necessary for them to become aware of their own motives, face their struggle with greater awareness, learn respectfully from the others in their world, identify and develop their skills, and be able to renounce expectations of specific results in favour of enjoying the exploration of their actions, themselves, and the world. They came to know who they were within the context of their personal history and in relation to a community with common bonds. They were able to journey to leadership, inspiring other youth in care to begin the process of becoming, and increasing the understanding and empathy of others to the situations and needs of youth in care.

NOTE

1 Excerpts from interviews conducted with former National Youth in Care Network leaders, staff, and volunteer board members are printed with permission. Some excerpts contain pseudonyms and altered details to ensure anonymity and to highlight the concepts being explored.

2 How Then Shall I Lead? The Journey of Leadership in a Faith Community

IDA MUTOIGO

1. Crossroads

At certain points in my life, important opportunities have arisen which have allowed me to make formative choices in developing my character, vocation, and leadership abilities. One of the most important of these 'crossroads' experiences was the call that I felt, at the age of thirteen, to serve in a developing country. Although it took over twelve years before that call became a reality, my faith in God and His direction for my life served a critical role in facing and developing as a result of life's crossroads.

Another major crossroads I faced was the death of my mother. I was fifteen, and had to assume a role of responsibility without authority as the oldest of nine children. Yet another crossroads experience led me to a fourteen-year career with the Christian Reformed World Relief Committee (CRWRC) in Uganda, where my roles as a development consultant and leader brought new challenges of working and living in cross-cultural contexts. These experiences tested my flexibility and relational skills. Living in north-eastern Uganda for four years, an area of great political insecurity at the time, tested my courage and commitment.

In 1994, I faced another crossroads in my life when I returned to Canada to serve as a national coordinator of volunteers for ServiceLink, a program with the Christian Reformed Church (CRC). For the first time in my leadership journey, I was required to put an idea for a new volunteer coordination program into practice, and to translate a vision into reality. This experience increased my strategic planning and public relations skills.

At every crossroads on this leadership journey, I have discovered that the most significant challenge – but also the greatest joy – has been serving in the Christian Reformed Church that I belong to. I wrote this essay in order to share and learn from the experiences I have faced, and continue to face, as a leader in my faith community and within an increasingly complex world.

The framework of this essay is inspired by Anthony D'Souza's suggestion that one's leadership style depends upon four major factors: the nature of the environment, the personality of the leader, the personality of the group or organization members that he or she leads, and the nature of the task or goal (D'Souza 1989).

2. The Leadership Wheel

I believe the image of a wheel is symbolic of leadership. In a motionless state, a wheel is loaded with latent energy. When it moves, it has kinetic energy, or energy in motion. Similarly, when leadership is only focused on maintaining positional power, it is largely motionless and has not been used to its full potential, although it still may have plenty of latent power. When leadership is focused on movement, it is leadership as I believe it should be, moving people towards achieving a vision. Just as a wheel requires good balance to keep it moving steadily, the leadership wheel that is well balanced is easy to maintain (Born 1999).

A well-balanced leadership wheel requires healthy, strong spokes to keep it moving. There are at least five spokes that I have learned are essential to keep the leadership wheel moving well. All the spokes are important and need to have an integrated relationship with each other:

1. Understanding my reality: 'The inside'
2. Determining direction: My vision or call
3. Communicating the vision
4. Considering the environmental context: 'The outside'
5. Taking appropriate action

If any one of these spokes is missing or has not had enough attention, a leader's journey can be very difficult, even impossible. For example, my vision may be very clear and I may be able to communicate it well to people in my team; but if it is not meeting a felt need in the communities that we serve, people will eventually lose their enthusiasm for the vision. If I insist on still going in the same direction, people would

FIGURE 2.1
The leadership wheel

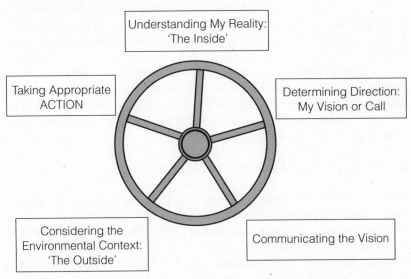

eventually resist, rebel, and try to find another leader who has a vision more relevant to their interests and needs.

Understanding my reality: 'The inside'

Who am I as a leader? Who do I want to be as leader? These are important questions to answer in order to understand how I best fit with the context, organization, and group of people I need to work with in order to achieve a vision. The team I lead is largely energized by relationships that are built on trust and commitment to a common cause. Thus, when I build good relationships with country and regional consultants, supervisors, and other agency staff and volunteers, my leadership is sustained and can energize others for many years.

Robert Greenleaf (1991) aptly describes the kind of leadership style and the values I try to practice: 'People will freely respond only to individuals who are chosen as leaders because they are proven and trusted as servants' (10). The motivation for my servant leadership comes from my faith. The role model for my relationships is Jesus Christ, who 'did not consider equality with God something to be grasped, but made himself nothing, taking the very nature of a servant' (Philippians 2:6 NIV).[1]

Yet this strength of servanthood is my ultimate challenge. My drive to meet the needs of others sometimes reaches levels that negate my ability to lead with foresight and vision. When I become consumed with responding to staff relationship concerns and dealing with requests from partner organizations, there is no time for reflection, creativity, or visioning. My Christian faith sometimes contributes to this dilemma because of its emphasis on servanthood. I feel pushed to do too much and not allow myself enough time to reflect and relax.

A 360-degree assessment confirmed that I needed to develop skills in visioning, alignment, and communication of vision.[2] Although I have the ability to integrate an ethical perspective into strategic business decisions, I need to improve my capacity to juggle multiple tasks and work demands (Schoonover 1999). The leadership that our CRWRC faith community organization needs is one with an ability to manage time effectively. Constant motion does not necessarily mean effective leadership, especially if it is not going in the right direction. I now realize that there is no validity to the excuse that I don't have the time to plan creatively for the future of CRWRC. The problem is not a lack of time, but how I choose to use my time. I need to prioritize more of my time for reflecting, reassessment, and imagining.

Another cultural value of our faith community that affects my leadership is the drive towards perfection. In response to the greatest commandment that Jesus gave, to 'love the Lord your God with all your heart and with all your soul and with all your mind' (Matthew 22:37 NIV), as well as his challenge to 'be perfect, therefore, as your heavenly Father is perfect' (Matthew 5:48 NIV), I tend to focus more on perfecting the details of tasks than on overall vision or mission. Micromanagement then consumes my energy, at the cost of completing the important macro-level tasks of leadership. I have discovered that 'routine work drives out non-routine work and smothers to death all creative planning, all fundamental change in any institution' (Bennis 1989, 15).

Overall, I have learned that the same values of perfection, good relationships, and servant leadership that are important to facilitate my leadership are also detrimental when they negate my ability to determine and communicate vision effectively. There is a serious cost to our organization and the faith community's ministry when this happens. Already there are indications that volunteer placement ratios are declining because I have not been proactively and creatively planning for more volunteer opportunities. CRWRC and the CRC faith community are also experiencing a decline in donations. Our leadership has not focused enough on communicating the vision in a way that engages constituents. In the increasingly globalized world we live in, this focus on micromanaging produces a naïveté about global forces and an inability to proactively address them.

Determining direction: My vision or call

Before I can address the issue of organizational vision, I need to consider my own personal call and vision for life. In August 1999, I realized God had a more specific call for me in a leadership role in my faith community. During a lunch conversation, a man told me the story of how his wife died. While I listened to him, my eyes and heart were opened to the enormity of his pain. I believe God used this man and his story to challenge me to think of how I must be transformed as a leader and open my eyes to see with my heart before I can encourage transformation in other people or the communities we serve. His story inspired my specific vision to develop more leaders who can serve with impact in our faith community, as well as communities around the world. Thus, the essence of my vision for my role in my faith community was to cultivate *transformed leaders that fostered community.*

Accordingly, the critical questions for me as a leader in CRWRC were: What stories can we tell to motivate people to become committed as donors and partners? How can the vision be communicated so as to inspire others?

Vision can be inspiring when it focuses on real needs and opportunities to meet a need. It cannot be defined through an academic exercise that produces a dispassionate statement.

The question I ask myself as I search for a clearer vision is this: How can I become a good listener? Listening to the story of one man opened my understanding of my specific call. Listening to the voice of God opened my heart and mind to find meaning and purpose in that call. I now realize that the type of leader CRWRC needs is one who generates energy and passion. This requires setting aside time and events where staff, partners, and community participants can share their stories. It also means selecting stories that illustrate the vision and use appropriate media to communicate its meaning. After all, if our faith community values a way of life that is *in* the world but not *of* the world, there needs to be an effective communication of vision that will engage all of us *in* the world and impact it.

There are also some important tools that I have discovered which will be useful to move my leadership from a micromanaging and perfectionist approach to a focus on vision-setting and setting priorities for the future. During a strategic planning meeting that I organized in 2000, Appreciative Inquiry (AI) and scenario-planning tools were used with stakeholders to determine future priorities, especially in relation to engaging Canadian constituents in the work of the CRC faith community agencies.

Appreciative Inquiry (AI) is a tool or process used in organizational development that involves engaging stakeholders in what works and brings life to the organization, instead of trying to fix what doesn't work. This is done through a four-stage process: discover, dream, design, and deliver (or create). AI was developed by David L. Cooperrider of Case Western Reserve University.[3]

The AI process encouraged participants to answer the questions: What gives life to our organization? What is the strength and success of this program? At first, it was a challenge for the team to articulate the dream of 'what might be the future of our organization,' because participants were more comfortable with judging each other's contributions and sticking to traditional views than discovering new ideas and ways of thinking about the future. However, through successful facilitation and an emphasis on values that foster learning, they were encouraged not only to focus on vision but to become visionaries themselves.

I discovered that our organization could not become visionary merely by creating a vision statement. Instead, through AI we became visionary by following a core ideology, while at the same time having a powerful drive for progress that enabled change, adaptation, and creativity (Flower 1995). We became more visionary when we clearly understood how our vision could meet significant and relevant needs in our community, and how it could change the reality of our current context in the direction of a much better future. There was much life, positive energy, and growth generated by using this tool. The AI effectively helped us to frame the issue regarding our organization's future, and helped to determine strategic priorities where we should focus our energies. In terms of the leadership wheel, then, it helped me to generate and direct the energy of our team more effectively.

Scenario planning was a new analytical tool that we used during the same meeting to build on our AI experience. Scenario planning is an eight-step process for performing an in-depth analysis of several equally plausible future alternatives in order to develop effective strategic plans, thus allowing management or leadership to be prepared for, and able to influence, all potential futures for the organization. Steps in the scenario planning process include 'uncovering the decision' (i.e., where the organization is going); information hunting and gathering; identifying driving forces, predetermined elements, and critical uncertainties; composing scenarios and analyzing possible decisions in response; and selecting leading indicators (Schwartz 1996).

Both tools confirmed that youth and retirees were the major constituent groups that needed to be engaged in the future. Both tools emphasized first what we wanted to 'be' and then what we wanted to 'do.' Both clarified the vision and values of our organization. This experience provided a catalyst for change because the vision was shared and values were quickly and powerfully tied to action steps. One example of this was our staff committing themselves to writing and sharing more success stories because they realized it was these stories that communicated vision.

Communicating the vision

It is not the story that in itself can communicate vision. *How* the vision is communicated is as important as *what* is communicated (Westley and Mintzberg 1989). If leadership is an art, then communicating vision is part of that art. How can I best communicate the vision of the Christian Reformed World Relief Committee? To communicate well, the audience has to be considered, including their issues, attitudes, concerns, and background (MacGwire 1999). Who is the CRWRC audience? In my analysis, I noted that they are staff, volunteers, donors, and partner organizations. Each requires a different communication medium. For example, youth volunteers are most attracted and committed to CRWRC's vision when other post-service youth volunteers, especially their peers, narrate their experiences personally. Websites, post-service celebration parties, youth meetings, and youth magazines are also very effective.

In my experience, vision is communicated best not only when it is accurate in content but also when it is dramatic, when it captures the senses and emotions of the audience. Through feedback I have received about my presentations to church groups, I have discovered that the most powerful impact of communication occurs when emotional appeals are connected to values. If my vision communicates values, especially biblical values, an audience from a faith community readily embraces it. Here again I am able to leverage my strengths of understanding my faith community and integrating an ethical perspective into vision building and communication.

If leadership is energy and leaders are effective when they are moving people towards achieving the vision, I need to determine what energizes each audience to be engaged and active in our vision. In a faith community like ours, values like love and compassion give energy. Thus by appealing to these values as expounded in biblical passages such as 1 Corinthians 13 and James 1:27 (NIV) our faith community members can be energized to serve and give to the cause.

Considering the environmental context: 'The outside'

My experience of growing up in a faith community within a Christian family and education system influenced my view and perspective of the world. As a child, I learned to see the world outside of my family and church community as an 'enemy,' largely due to the many messages I heard about keeping oneself from being 'yoked to unbelievers' or 'polluted by the world.' As my faith matured and was tested by various life experiences, I learned that this dichotomization of the physical world as 'unholy or evil' and the spiritual world as 'holy or good' was not correct or even biblical. After all, Colossians 1:20 (NIV) speaks of Jesus as having reconciled *all* things on heaven and on earth to himself. This implies that God cared about saving the whole world from destruction, not just parts of it.

Although attitudes may change, the dichotomization of life continues to be a challenge in practice with our faith community's organizational culture. My experience as a leader in the Christian Reformed Church denomination is one where we still operate largely in a 'bubble,' trying to protect ourselves from the world, or trying to keep ourselves from interacting too intimately with the world outside our church community. The challenge I face as a leader in my faith community is to be more engaged in transforming the world, without compromising a biblical worldview and understanding of truth.

The hesitancy that our faith community has in engaging with the world has often led to an ignorance of the context that we as leaders operate in. As a result of this, we have ignored the impacts of one of the most significant aspects of our world today: globalization. It is this ignorance that has prompted me to reflect, in this section, on globalization and its implications for leadership in our faith community. If I intend to lead with clear vision and strategy, I need to learn how to understand and respond to the forces of a globalized world and context.

I assume that by examining the forces of globalization, I will increase my knowledge and the skills necessary to juggle those forces more innovatively and effectively. 'Globalization refers to increasing the global interconnectedness, so that events and developments in one part of the world are affected by, have to take account of, and also influence, in turn, other parts of the world' (Tiplady 2003, 2). Globalization impacts every aspect of life, including the spiritual and cultural aspects. Since I believe that the whole of life needs to be directed to the service and glory of God, who is the source and creator of life, it is important for me to understand the forces that affect my ability to do this. If globalization promotes a culture and value system that affects my cultural values and that of my faith community, I need to understand what that culture is in order to respond to it appropriately. This raises a key reflective question: *What are some of the threats and opportunities of globalization in this context of leadership that I find myself in today?*

One opportunity that the globalized business culture presents to the voluntary sector, of which our faith community is a part, is an emphasis on professionalism and higher-quality service. One threat of adopting business principles is that it creates a highly competitive environment. During a visit to Australia in 2000, I learned that the public sector implemented a 'winner take all' business-oriented strategy, which rewarded the voluntary sector organizations that were the most *efficient* – but not necessarily the most *effective*. This competitive approach made economic viability the primary goal, at the expense of the voluntary sector's ability to consider important social consequences.

One of the most positive opportunities that the technological advances of globalization provide is the increase in networking and collaboration between voluntary sector organizations, as well as between the voluntary sector, the corporate sector, and the public sector. Those who have access to communications technology can also have a greater understanding of a common future, along with greater access to resources for addressing virtually any organizational or technical issue. The challenge that this technology presents for voluntary sector leaders is how to manage the volume of information (read: email!) that is available, taking care to focus on what has the greatest impact for their work. Virtually every leader I meet in Canada, Australia, and India faces this challenge.[4]

Globalization has also encouraged more opportunities for cultural exchange, language courses, and festival celebration, taking into consideration global media coverage and a global market (Patel 2000, 3). Increased media exposure to global events has increased the interest of volunteers and donors in our faith community, who want to be more engaged in the work that CRWRC does with communities. The challenge is to accommodate their interests without compromising the needs of those we serve and the partners with whom our agency works.

Although CRWRC is influenced by these broader global forces, it is important to determine which ones have the highest influence, especially in terms of our two major constituents: the donors from North America and the members of developing communities. During a workshop that focused on strategic directions related to constituent involvement, stakeholders noted these forces as the most important ones affecting North American donors (financial and volunteer):

- People of all ages are interested in being more personally involved in a cause, and not just giving money.
- There are increasing requests from youth groups searching for service opportunities during their spring break or the summer holidays.
- There are increasing requests for service opportunities overseas, yet openings are limited.
- More youth and young adults are viewing volunteering as a way of building their résumés.
- An ever-increasing diversity in volunteers demands greater flexibility in recruitment strategies, support and training strategies, recognition systems, and communication strategies.
- More volunteers with high levels of professional expertise are looking for service opportunities.

Taking appropriate action

As I consider this globalized context and ponder the question, *How, then, shall I lead?* I see six major ways in which I, as a leader in our faith community organization, CRWRC, can respond to globalization: *reflect, resist, redirect, relieve, reinforce, and recreate.*

REFLECT

Just as a farmer listens faithfully to the weather report because he knows the forces of weather greatly affect his crops, so the voluntary sector leader needs to regularly reflect on the weather of globalization, its forces, and impacts. There are several ways in which I can encourage this reflection and analysis in CRWRC:

- Organize staff and volunteer exchange visits and work assignments from one country or region to another.
- Attune myself through the reading of relevant books, websites, and other articles on a regular basis, and share this knowledge and discuss impressions with staff and other leaders in our CRC faith community.
- Encourage dialogue regarding globalization impacts during long-range planning meetings, orientation sessions, regular coaching visits, and global forums with other stakeholders.
- Design special assignments and use new research tools such as power analysis tools to determine the impacts of globalization at community levels where we focus our energies and staff resources.

RESIST

At times, forces of globalization are known to have high negative impact. A clear example can be seen in India, where many corporations have no regard for the pollution they are creating in poor neighbourhoods, or where dams are built with no regard for the displacement of the low-caste 'Dalits.' With my work in CRWRC, we face similar challenges. In the slum areas of Nairobi, Kenya, where our partners were working, powerful landlords and business owners bulldozed property without notice. CRWRC and its partners could implement a 'resist' response in a number of ways:

- Advocate for the poor and powerless. Challenge the corporate conscience and negotiate with business leaders and landlords: encourage them to act as caring companies or leaders, and to be seen as such.
- Use the national newspapers and other news media to pressure political leaders towards more just and sustainable development.
- Resist the manipulative measures (whether they are bribes or false charges) used by corporate or public sector leaders to silence advocates in the communities that are affected.

- Educate the poor and powerless on their rights to mobilize for action in ways that impact those in power. Sometimes it is not until the privileged are inconvenienced that the disadvantaged get anything at all.

REDIRECT

At times, the most effective approach to dealing with the forces of globalization is to redirect them. One of the best examples of this is the use of the news media. In Uganda, where CRWRC works, the government refused to renew our registration; it based its refusal on a newspaper article that contained false information. By using this same newspaper to present a true report about the positive contributions that CRWRC made towards the development of people and their communities, the government's NGO certification board grew in their understanding and appreciation, and eventually approved CRWRC's registration.

There are additional things that I can do in my organization to redirect the forces of globalization:

- Use the same global media sources that portray negative examples of the voluntary sector to promote our work in a positive light. Tell stories that report and celebrate the good done by CRWRC.
- Use international linkages for dissemination. For example, use the Internet to promote alternative messages.
- Make appropriate technology a quality product, not merely a source of cheap entertainment, by using it in ways that foster development. For example, teach communities to access the Internet for information about better agricultural methods, rather than using it merely for entertainment.
- Join civil society networks to influence the discourse about what development and social transformation really should be.

RELIEVE

Of all the responses that CRWRC and our CRC faith community gives to globalization, the 'relieve' response is the one we do best. It is our core competency. We play a strong role in providing a social safety net for those who are victims of globalization, especially those affected by global economic forces. As a leader, I feel there is no need to change our activities that are focused on disaster relief interventions and on the capacity-building of community leaders, partners, and their community groups. But there is a need to create a new wave of thinking, or to reframe our thinking to develop more powerful strategies (see 'Recreate' below).

REINFORCE
There are several ways to use globalization forces so as to enhance the achievement of our organization's vision and transform the lives of the disadvantaged and poor:

- Help the increasing numbers of youth and retiree volunteers who are tired of an uncaring corporatist society to get involved in serving communities that may be economically poor but socially rich.
- Use information technology to tell stories reflecting and celebrating the true spirit of volunteerism.
- Engage the increasing number of corporate sector leaders who want to have a more 'caring' image by strengthening our collaboration with partners worldwide.

RECREATE
It is interesting that the corporate sector often asks how it can strategically globalize, while the voluntary sector only asks how it can respond or work with global trends or forces instead of *creating* them. It is high time our Christian Reformed Church faith community, including CRWRC, started to become more proactive towards, rather than reactive against, the forces of globalization. Although this deserves more attention, I see one possibility we could start with. Given global capitalism's promotion of competition, to be 'the winner,' to be 'number one,' we need to create a new meaning for what a winner is – not only in economic terms, but also in social or spiritual terms that reflect our core values. We need to create a new philosophy, theology, and strategy for development. At our Leaders' Conference in 2000, Kathy Vandergrift shared some thoughts on how to do this:

> As foreign aid declines and trade advances, the focus is more on rules and standards rather than a simple transfer of resources from rich to poor. We have moved from development as the delivery of goods through development as providing service; now we are moving to development by leverage on other actors through new types of relationships with governments, corporations, and local communities. The goal is to make the powerful

systems that impact on people's lives meet the needs of the poor – or at least stop hurting them. I know this organization can be very strategic to maximize dollars and impact for direct assistance and building capacity of community groups. If the same strategic thinking and priority were applied to justice work, I think this organization could have an impact far beyond its size. (Vandergrift 2000, 7)

3. Conclusion and Recommendations

In this reflective essay on my leadership journey, I have learned several key things about the 'spokes' that keep the leadership wheel moving well. Probably the greatest lesson for me has been that change needs to start with myself first. Mahatma Gandhi once said, 'Be the change you wish to see in the world.' Indeed, how can I expect the Christian Reformed World Relief Committee or my faith community to change and move in a more visionary direction, if I don't change myself to become more visionary? Some ideas for building visionary leadership – the second spoke of the leadership wheel – include:

- Allocating a full day each month to focus on clarifying and communicating vision as well as creative long-range planning. This would be informed by meditation and prayer, seeking to gain insight and understanding of God's plan for the future.
- Evaluating my use of time. At the end of each week, review my schedule and start to drop activities that are not important, delegate some that are routine, and set priorities for the next week.
- Allocating a half day each week, preferably Friday, to listen to and write stories of impact and achievement of vision.

I have also learned that I need to leverage my strengths more deliberately to provide the leadership that CRWRC needs. For example, when sharing stories of impact, I can design my presentations more carefully to use my strengths of courage, commitment, and positive attitude to influence my audience, sharing more openly and passionately what my commitment is. A great leader's courage to fulfill his vision comes from passion, not position.

My reflective analysis has also highlighted the importance of using new tools to understand and address old issues. In my faith community, there is often a mindset that there is one and only one 'right' or 'best' way of doing things. Unfortunately, this causes a prejudgment or dismissal of many options, instead of a more thorough exploration of the possibilities or options available. Appreciative Inquiry and scenario planning exercises have shown me that my attitude to leadership must be one that accepts and fosters a diversity of responses to complex issues. There may be more than one good way to respond to them. As a leader in a faith community organization that operates within a context of increasing change, I should have an attitude that appreciates the unknown more than fears it and that values learning more than quick solutions.

To build a stronger understanding of the environment and context – the fourth spoke in the leadership wheel – I have discovered a need to move outside the protective 'bubble' of my faith community. After my privileged exposure to global issues in India and Australia, I realized my attitudes as a leader in this faith community must change from these exclusivist tendencies. Instead of thinking and acting locally, I must think globally and act locally.

To think globally and act locally requires making significant decisions on how to respond to the external forces and the forces of globalization that impact them. Although our faith community organization espouses biblical values and has articulated its major organizational values, I still need to take action that articulates and communicates these values appropriately in a given context. For example, the principle 'Love your neighbour as yourself' is fairly broad in scope. There may be numerous ways to express this love in terms of practical action. I have learned that an appreciative approach helps me to discern those specific actions (and there may be more than one) that may be effective, depending on the person, time, and context.

I have learned that this discernment includes responding appropriately to the global forces that impact our organization, and discerning whether that action should: use global forces to our advantage; prevent and mitigate the negative impacts of these forces; help persons harmed by these negative impacts; or create new forces so that our vision and purpose can be better achieved.

My actions as a leader in our faith community organization should extend beyond the core competency 'Relieve,' and begin to:

- be more involved in justice and advocacy
- be more involved in civil society networks
- educate stakeholders about the impact of global forces
- use media and information technology appropriately to communicate and create a new reality of a holistically developed society that develops the full potential of people in communities.

As I move towards a greater understanding of globalization and responding to it, I have also learned that I need to be wise in my response to pluralism as one of the hallmarks of globalization. Pluralism calls for openness to diversity however, as it insists that relativism or 'the belief that no truth is final truth' is necessary for authentic openness (Lundy 2003), it can actually promote the dogmatism it is seeking to avoid. The overall attitude for me to adopt is to accept the diversity of expressions of truth (practice) that different ideologies and cultures may have, while remaining committed to the foundations of truth (principle) in my own faith that are consistent over time and place. For me, it takes prayer and reflection to discern what is the difference between the principle and the practice.

Finally, I have learned that change is essential for growth to take place in a leader within our faith community organization. By promoting a learning environment that encourages risk taking, while remaining focused on vision and values, I can foster greater energy and excitement for change within myself and in others with whom I work. But change merely for the sake of change is wasteful.

My world view is one in which I believe God is not interested in preserving the status quo, but in bringing an entirely new order of creation in us, in our organizations, and in the world outside our organizations. We are God's agents of change. That requires us to step outside of our 'bubbles,' to move from our sheltered church communities and into our neighbourhoods as His messengers in actions of love, hope, justice, mercy, peace, reconciliation, and healing. And these actions may be expressed in a diversity of ways, depending on the context and persons involved. In that sense, expression is emergent. As we change and create change in this increasingly complex and diverse global community, the values and vision that God has given us remain constant. After all, this is what gives us life, energy, and courage to lead and serve. It is in this spirit, a spirit both of change and constants and of deliberative and emergent approaches working together as God intended, that I shall then lead. The fascinating journey continues.

NOTES

1   All quotations from the Bible are taken from The NIV study Bible: New international version, ed. Kenneth Barker (Grand Rapids, MI: Zondervan Bible Publishers, 1985).

2 The 360-degree assessment is a tool used to assess a staff member's or leader's capacity and performance through the involvement of peers (horizontal relationship internal to the organization), supervisors (vertical relationship upward), subordinates (vertical relationship downward), and service recipients or customers (horizontal relationship external to organization). In this case, the persons involved in the author's 360-degree assessment included Mr Jacob Kramer (peer), Mr Ray Elgersma (supervisor), Ms Amanda Kleinhuis (subordinate), and two volunteer customers.

3 For resources online, see the Appreciative Inquiry Commons: http://appreciativeinquiry.case.edu.

4 Information technology today allows disadvantaged people to market a finished product, instead of selling only raw materials. My friend Alam from Crane Bank in Uganda gives an example from his home country of Bangladesh that is quite remarkable. When the Grameen Bank placed computers in communities, one peasant women's group that was producing rugs started to advertise their products on the Internet. Within a short time, the rugs were being sold to an overseas market, ultimately increasing the income of these women by thousands of dollars.

3 Life after a Charismatic Leader

BERNARD VOYER

The Taoist monk Moy Lin-shin was born in 1931 in Toisan (Taishan), a township near Guangzhou (Canton), China, and passed away in Toronto on 6 June 1998. The establishment and organization of the International Taoist Tai Chi Society, a multi-corporation non-profit organization[1] which he founded in 1970 and which today consists of some 40,000 members in 28 countries, may be considered the crowning achievement of his life. For over twenty-five years, I have been a follower of this charismatic leader, apprenticing under him first in Taoist arts and later, together with several of my peers, in Confucian administration.

At the age of 27 in 1982, when I first met Mr Moy, I was a young member of his fledgling organization. Five years later, upon being selected for employment by the Society, I agreed – without quite knowing what I was letting myself in for – to undergo a classical Confucian administrative training, akin to that which prevailed in China for centuries before the communist revolution.

Under the Confucian education of public administrators, the notions of 'taming of the heart' and 'cultivating virtue,' for instance, take precedence over academic achievement or technical skill sets. It was my immense good fortune to have had Mr Moy himself as my teacher, along with other instructors who had undergone similar training. Today, as one of the elders of this Canadian-based international organization, I share the benefits of my training with members who are committed to Mr Moy's vision of promoting health in the community through the practice of the Taoist Tai Chi™ internal arts of health.

Mr Moy's humble passing in 1998, leaving behind few personal possessions, was very much in keeping with his unassuming lifestyle; yet he bequeathed an inestimable treasure to the world: the powerful internal arts and methods now registered under the trademark 'Taoist Tai Chi,' a harmonious human community that shares a common vision worldwide, without regard for cultural, political, and demographic barriers; and an economic and infrastructural foundation of successful past achievements and challenging future projects.

Based on my firsthand experience and on some academic research, this essay discusses a fundamental aspect of charismatic leadership: the question of succession. How can an organization that grew out of this type of leadership carry on with its mission after the death – or retirement, or resignation – of its founding charismatic leader?

This essay is addressing the voluntary sector as its primary readership. The narration of my experience in a personal voice, with some further articulation in managerial language, should encourage organizations where the leader and followers are (or have been) connected in a relationship of a charismatic nature to engage in conversations about succession.

1. A Foot in Two Worlds

Every organization is, in a sense, unique with respect to its origin, history, and culture. To better make sense of the singularities and issues with which the International Taoist Tai Chi Society had to grapple in the course of its development, it will be helpful to begin with a brief overview of its organizational configuration.

It has been long accepted within the Society that ours is a 'top-down' *and* 'bottom-up' social organism that evolves through a generative relationship between its Eastern and Western components. Figure 3.1 illustrates the Society's organizational design.

Our Western side

Our Western side is rooted in the written tradition, and very much exists as a *society of rights*. Its constitution embodies all the familiar components and processes of a typical occidental corporate entity. It includes the traditional tools of governance (such as letters patent and by-laws), management (structures and procedures), analysis and decision-making (data gathering, formation of task forces and committees). Being intimately intertwined with the concept of a democratic society, our Western side expresses itself via its commonly accepted doctrines

FIGURE 3.1
Organizational configuration of the Taoist Tai Chi Society, an organization that is both top-down and bottom-up.

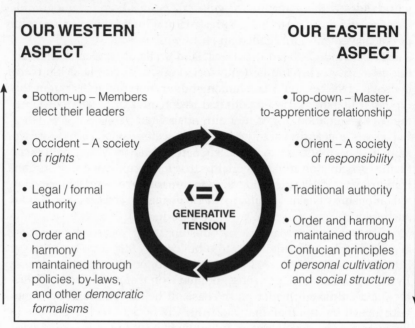

('*Vox populi, vox Dei*'; 'One person, one vote') and its familiar secular
rituals (committee meetings, AGMs) mediated by elite professional authorities (lawyers, accountants, and managers); often it appeals to some
higher human power such as the Law, Government, or Standard
Procedure, the name of which, inevitably, is sometimes taken in vain.

Viewed from our Eastern side, our Western side is often perceived as
a necessary evil, required to broker our relationships with the imperatives of the world around us. It operates at four hierarchical levels: from
the international board down to the branch committees, through the
national boards and regional management committees. It is represented
by a bottom-up arrow in figure 3.1, in reference to the electoral process,
where power and authority are assigned upwards from grass-roots
constituencies.

In terms of advantages, obligations, and limitations inherent in its
constitutional makeup and everyday operations, ours is a fairly typical

occidental voluntary sector organization, except for the fact that it is entirely financed by its membership and that, with an employee to member ratio of about 1:1,500, it is run almost entirely by volunteers.

Our Eastern side

Our Eastern side, on the other hand, is radically atypical. It is founded on a system of beliefs, values, and social constructs that had flourished in the Pearl River delta of Guangdong province during the late imperial Chinese dynasty, and then migrated to a coastal English protectorate during the mid-twentieth century. In other words, it is rooted in Hong Kong culture. It is also largely influenced by the unified teachings of the three religions of China: Buddhism, Confucianism, and Taoism. Central to our Eastern-side belief system are the practices related to 'the Dual Cultivation of Body and Mind, so as to return to one's original nature.'[2]

This belief system originates in a *society of responsibility* and expresses itself through oral tradition. We were introduced to it by our venerable founder and teacher, Master Moy Lin-shin, and by his contemporaries, many of whom participated in the building of the temples in Hong Kong after the Maoist revolution and in the founding of the Hong Kong Taoist Association. He patiently initiated us into the Confucian principles of personal cultivation as the basis of world order and of family structure as the regulator of relationships.

Organizations in this system follow the 'master-to-apprentice' tradition, in which the necessary bond of trust between a virtuous teacher and a worthy student is implicit – the top-down arrow represented in our organizational model (fig. 3.1).

Members who are heavily immersed in their Western customs often experience frustration with the cavalier manner in which decisions and actions appear to emerge from our Eastern side. They take exception to the absence of clear Western-style processes; they begrudge the apparent disdain for 'win-win' type consensus and they dread the unilateral pronouncements occasionally made by more senior members. Our Eastern side is the province of education, tradition, and culture; it tolerates, and sometimes encourages, the equivocal, the subjective, and the seemingly arbitrary. This may be irritating to newcomers or to managers trained exclusively on Western principles, especially when someone who takes issue with a decision is served the typical Confucian dictum, 'It is more important to act harmoniously than to be right.' It would be a mistake to interpret this as an exemption from resolving disagreements, or as a dictum enjoining silence. Rather, Confucian propriety encourages one to ask for explanations in lieu of the Western-style expression of outright disagreement. This makes for an uncommonly 'chatty' organization.

This approach has singular results. As an international, multi-corporate, and membership-based organization, the Society has never compiled a policy manual, as would be typical of even much smaller NGOs. Yet no decision – from the design of T-shirts to the purchase of a property – will be made without quoting from 'The Way We Do Things,' an unwritten, evolving compendium of collective experiences, referenced with varying interpretative influence and experiential 'weight' by those who shared in its compilation. Consequently, while the Taoist Tai Chi Society of Canada leadership may well have more than its share of loquacious, strong-minded personalities, no national resolution has ever been passed in Canada that was not unanimous – the capacity of *just letting go* being an equally strong organizational value as that of *firmly holding your ground*, thanks to our Eastern perspective.

Generative tension within the paradox

The 'equal' sign in the middle of figure 3.1 represents the accepted notion that harmony prevails through some sort of balance between the Western and Eastern organizational hemispheres. Balance is achieved by one side deferring to or, at least, considering the other. This may sometimes result in decisions appearing to go around in circles. But most often, the process generates a healthy tension, which sometimes brings the Society near the edge of chaos. This state of affairs closely resembles what Zimmerman, Lindberg, and Plsek (1998) describe as the attributes of a complex adaptive system: 'a densely connected web of interacting agents, each operating from their own schema or local knowledge' (8). In our worldwide Society's case, the local schemata are rooted not only in our members' various ethnic, geographical, cultural, and religious origins but also in their disparate personal experiences, beliefs, and values. And the webbing is provided by a single common mission and by the acceptance of a shared organizational *supraculture*, as outlined above.

Yet, admittedly, this 'being pulled from two sides,' as members sometimes say, may be uncomfortable. Those who cannot bear the pressure of that tension, or who lack insight or appreciation of our singular organizational heritage, may sometimes fall back on platitudes. For instance, a common tendency is to diminish the uncomfortable generative relationship between the two arrows by equating the Society's administrative functions only with the Western side, while equating its instructional functions only with the Eastern side. This *reductio* deprives its proponents of a heightened managerial experience rooted in *paradox*, another favoured theme of complexity science, which holds that 'creativity and innovation have the best chances to emerge precisely at the point of greatest tension and apparent irreconcilable differences' (Zimmerman, Lindberg, and Plsek 1998, 33).

In reality, the dynamic double-arrow is present as a *fractal*, a 'unit of structure that is replicated at various levels [as] a harmonious, self-organizing feature of nature' (ibid., 149), in every subset of the organizational structure and every process that carries the growth of our organization to new frontiers. It is nonetheless accepted that those branches and members who were closest to Mr Moy – whether geographically or culturally – developed a hypertrophied Eastern side and an atrophied Western one. While 'dust collected on the by-laws in Canada' (a catch-phrase within the Society), where Mr Moy resided and where a benevolent hegemony prevailed, more distant branches developed efficient regulations and decision-making processes to maintain order among the membership. In consequence, tremendous efforts were deployed after Mr Moy's passing to fill the gap between the two societal orders.

2. Charisma as the Basis of Authority

While the Society is in many regards unique, the bond that united Mr Moy and his students in their effort to edify the organization is not completely unfamiliar. The vast literature on leadership that has accumulated in recent decades abounds in theories that seek to explain how relationships evolve between leaders and followers, and practically every publication that discusses 'what makes organizations tick' has come up with an elegant epithet to qualify the ideal organizational leader. One adjective that has been repeatedly slipped under the academic microscope during the past thirty years is the label 'charismatic.'

Until the mid-1970s, when organizational studies became more tangibly interested in charismatic leadership, discussions regarding this basis of authority were limited to the fields of sociology and political science. A noteworthy exception is religious studies, where charisma is a subject of interest, if not scrutiny, especially with regard to what are known as 'new religious movements' (Chryssides 2001, 10). During the past three decades, by way of a plethora of studies, the notion of charisma has mutated into a number of spin-off concepts that are more palatable to the pragmatic minds of today.

Most literature reviewed for the present purposes refers back to the essential notion of 'charismatic authority,' first introduced between 1910 and 1914 by Max Weber, the renowned 'father of modern sociology.' All subsequent studies of the field unmistakably flag Weber's definition of charisma:

> The term charisma will be applied to a certain quality of an individual personality by virtue of which he is set apart from ordinary men and treated as endowed with supernatural, superhuman or at least specifically exceptional powers or qualities. These are such as are not accessible to the ordinary person, but are regarded as of divine origin or as exemplary, and on the basis of them the individual concerned is treated as a leader. (Weber 1968, 48)

Weber defined these charismatic grounds of authority in a broader discussion of 'three pure types of legitimate authority': (a) *legal* authority or 'rational grounds – resting on a belief in the legality of patterns of normative rules and the right of those elevated to authority under such rules to issue commands'; (b) *traditional* authority or 'traditional grounds – resting on an established belief in the sanctity of immemorial traditions and the legitimacy of the status of those exercising authority under them'; and (c) *charismatic* authority, or 'charismatic grounds – resting on devotion to the specific and exceptional sanctity, heroism, or exemplary character of an individual person, and of the normative patterns or order revealed or ordained by him' (ibid., 46).[3]

It should be noted that a given leader or authority may, to varying degrees, exhibit traits similar to one or all of these 'analytic types.' They should therefore be understood as heuristic terms of reference rather than a formal classificatory scheme.

Weber attaches to his definition of *charisma* (literally, the gift of grace) another fundamental notion, which he presents as non-dissociable from the personal qualities of the leader who is deemed charismatic: 'What is alone important is how the individual is actually regarded by those subject to charismatic authority, by his "followers" or "disciples"' (ibid., 48).

This would necessarily open the door to an exploration of how charismatic leadership impacts on the lives of those who are committed to the vision of such a leader. It is not the purpose of the present paper to discuss the nature of followers as such. Suffice it to specify, for purposes of clarification, that in Master Moy's case, the title 'master' (in Cantonese, *sifu*, meaning 'teacher,' with the connotation of the Latin *magister*) was juxtaposed to his name at the request of the students, not of the leader.

From traditional to charismatic authority

Examining Master Moy Lin-shin's leadership is interesting mainly because it stirs up a more elaborate reflection about the three types of legitimate authority postulated by Weber.

Except perhaps in indigenous societies, it can be said of very few leaders of large constituencies that their leadership rests on no legal basis whatsoever. One of the remarkable aspects of Mr Moy's leadership is that he never had a leg to stand on in terms of legal authority. For one thing, he had settled in Canada illegally, and remained without Landed Immigrant status until 1975, when the federal government declared an amnesty for illegal immigrants. Even afterwards, he never aspired to hold office in the organization that he had created. In fact, as the Taoist Tai Chi Society continually expanded its membership and created several legal entities to gain status and stature in the growing number of provinces and countries where it branched out, Mr Moy repeatedly made a point of saying, 'I've never signed any papers,' as a way of insisting that it was up to the various boards of directors to oversee the Society's Western administrative obligations and to deal with the civil authorities, as he held no official office.

If Mr Moy's authority never rested on legal grounds, it probably may not have appeared very charismatic at first glance, either. Members who were active during the first decade of the Society's history often recount stories of how Mr Moy used his skills at the martial aspect of Tai Chi to get attention. This may be looked at from two equally important perspectives.

First, it seems clear that Mr Moy needed to establish 'a high level of domain competency'[4] – to at least measure up to, if not surpass, the other Chinese martial arts teachers who were already active in Canada's Chinatowns at defining 'Tai Chi' in Western minds. In 1970, Mr Moy was, after all, the new neighbour on the block; he had to demonstrate his credibility immediately and unequivocally and there was no better way to do so than literally to use a 'hands-on' approach. It is hardly surprising, then, that the initial members of the Society were young people, males for the most part, including many Chinese immigrants. They didn't mind being pushed around if the lessons demanded this, as many had dabbled in Kung Fu and in other forms of Tai Chi. Their youthful resilience constituted a solid and energetic foundation on which to build the future organization, if only they could be given a direction in life.

The other reason for initially resorting to a martial arts approach is apparent only in retrospect: it embodied an accessible, comprehensible code of conduct on which Mr Moy could build what Weber termed 'traditional-grounds authority.' Human rapports in the Chinese martial arts milieu are regulated by a complex grammar and vocabulary of do's and don'ts that Mr Moy was able to communicate with great fluency, thus enabling him to gain the respect of all in his culture of origin.

He most likely gained an experiential appreciation of the traditional code and of its privileges and sanctions during the tribulations that marked his flight from communist China and his subsequent establishment as a *sifu* (master or teacher) in the parks of Hong Kong. The behaviour of Chinese martial artists is, for the most part, regulated by oral tradition derived from precepts of the Confucian social order, particularly those expounded in a sacred text known as 'The Eight Virtues.' Most Chinese expatriates are familiar with its main tenets, at least on a superficial level. During the 1970s, when Chinese culture was being defined for the benefit of young occidental minds by the resounding box-office success of Bruce Lee's cloak-and-nanchuka blockbusters, Westerners were also becoming aware that belts and diplomas don't make a martial arts master, and that true learning comes with a certain amount of associated discomfort and aggravation.

For instance, anyone who aspires to walk in the Tao should expect to eventually engage in an arduous process sometimes referred to as Taming of the Heart. It is integral to the alchemical transformation of body and mind via the practise of Taoist arts and within the rigorous dynamics of a master-to-apprentice relationship. It involved a strong degree of what at the Society has become known as 'ego-trimming,' in which the teacher relentlessly points out deficiencies to the student, and of periods of subsequent reflective silence, where master and apprentice reciprocally re-evaluate the meaningfulness of their relationship. The apparent nit-picking, correcting or even scolding may take place publicly or privately, on the practise floor, at dim sum, or in club hallways alike. It is characterized by a constant gauging of the rapport between action and intention, and by intervening in such a way as to foster the emergence of a 'centred heart.' Mr Moy's 'traditionally grounded authority' remained solid until the very end, and the oral code on which it was based still lives on in the social rapports among the 'first-generation' members of the Society, most of whom were not even born in the culture where it originated. Yet several key members who had responded well to this traditional authority in the early years abandoned the path during the following decade, when another facet of Mr Moy's spirit began to shine. In the 1980s he asserted a new demand. No longer did he merely require of his students that they 'pay forward' the acquisition of Tai Chi skills by sharing the benefits with others as volunteer instructors in Taoist Tai Chi™ internal arts of health. We were now expected to make the necessary inner accommodations in our lives that would enable us to transform the skills acquired from a *martial* art into those of a *healing* art. Not everyone was prepared to become a healer. Many students came and went; yet many others stayed to learn, and their numbers continue to grow.

To foster the transformation of so many people, Mr Moy had to recount his own path of change and demonstrate first-hand his healing skills – so much so that, by the early 1990s, when the Society's instructors numbered nearly a thousand in various countries, Mr Moy was coming across as something of a 'magus,' in the words of George Chryssides (2001), or 'someone who possesses skills in oriental "magic" ... and who displays extraordinary wisdom' (7), not just metaphorically.

By then, his authority had clearly become charismatic; yet he made no personal claim to be the source of the teachings and skills that he shared with us. He and his contemporaries belonged to a diaspora of believers in a spiritual system. They had seen its infrastructures destroyed by the Maoists and had been cast away to such places as Hong Kong, Taiwan, and Singapore. Mr Moy introduced us to some peers, and even to his own teachers. For that reason, he might also be appropriately characterized as a 'disciplic successor,' again following Chryssides' nomenclature (ibid., 8).

3. Succeeding Our Teacher

By the mid-1990s, members had become increasingly comfortable with the charismatic nature of Mr Moy's authority. The corpus of his knowledge seemed unlimited, his judgment was impeccable, and he had, moreover, consistently maintained a Spartan lifestyle, apparently unmotivated by personal gain. Hence, twenty years after the foundation of the Society, someone again asked Mr Moy if we could call him *sifu*, and he finally accepted. Interestingly, while one came to easily recognize the vintage of fellow Society members by whether they addressed our teacher as 'Mister Moy' or 'Master Moy,' the more recent members using the latter designation, why he delayed so long the acceptance of that title remains unclear.

In developmental psychology, there is a well-known phenomenon called 'generativity,' whereby individuals arriving at mid-life feel compelled to pass along their accumulated knowledge and experience (whether relevant or not) to the younger generation. This, according to Erikson (1980), is motivated as much by a concern for future generations as it is by a will to leave behind some sort of social contribution after one's passing.[5] It would explain, for instance, why some grandparents tend to take advantage of family reunions to revisit the past with long narratives and musings that don't always sit right with the younger members around the dinner table. Generativity also may explain the arm-around-the-shoulders walks along the corporate hallways that sometimes punctuate a mentoring relationship. Although some of these elders may merely be seeking attention, others are literally attempting to 'invest the mission in one's children,' to use an expression applied figuratively by Biggart (1989, 144). The psychological predisposition described above may not alone explain the lengths to which some leaders will go to pass on the baton to the next generation.

What is remarkable about the fact that Mr Moy 'never signed any papers' isn't so much that he was a CEO without a briefcase, but that he could manage organization affairs skilfully while leaving all the paperwork to others. Many aspects of his succession were thus built directly into the administrative apparatus as the organization was growing. Was this intended or not? If 'the first duty of a leader is to find his [or her] own replacement' (another common saying in this Society), it probably was.

This concern for succession is probably not a forefront issue in every organization that owes its inception to a charismatic bond. In the best cases, an event will trigger in the leader a need to start preparing for the afterlife – or life after leadership, at least. But many organizations never survive the retirement, death, resignation, or dismissal of their founding leader. Such is the haunting perspective that comes to inhabit followers whose lives revolve around a mission greater than themselves.

Researchers as early as Weber recognized that organizations based on a charismatic style of leadership may become dependent on charisma and, as Bryman (1992) pointed out, the dilemma is that it is very unlikely that a succeeding charismatic leader will be found to replace the founder. Organizations that wish to live on after the departure of their charismatic founder must base their future on a more stable foundation. Weber calls the first step in this process 'routinization,' which, when successful, leads to institutionalization of the organization that was once founded on one person's charisma. This process doubtless is more likely to succeed if the charismatic founder gives it a head start.

'Préparer les lendemains'[6]

A striking instance of successful routinization of an organization founded on charismatic leadership is the case of Alcoholics Anonymous. In the early stages of AA, its co-founders, Bill Wilson and Dr Bob Smith, with their initial group of followers, established '(1) an effective administrative apparatus independent of the founder[s], (2) rites that diffused charisma among the members, and (3) written and oral traditions that sustained the [leaders'] message over time' (Conger and Kanungo 1998, 28).

This reminds me of the circumstances in which it suddenly dawned on the leaders of the Society that Mr Moy had no intention of appointing a given successor – not even one who would look after the crucial preservation of the quality of instruction, let alone the administrative matters (then considered secondary by many members). Instead, he insisted that his successorship be assumed in a collegial fashion: 'You are all, together, the successor.'[7]

Conger and Kanungo (1998, 30) point out that such 'fostering of a charismatic presence among the founder's children' is not uncommon in family businesses. The Society can be understood in similar terms, given its Confucian social structure, which is closely related to a family structure.

It is not unlikely for the founders of organizations to rehearse their retirement: for instance, by assuming a semi-active, backseat presence for a time after their official retirement, occasionally reasserting their influence while the succeeding authorities build up experience and confidence with the membership and stakeholders. Lee Kuan Yew, the founder of modern Singapore, who moved his country from a third-world state to a world-class nation, resigned as prime minister in 1991 after thirty-five years in power. During the last decade of his leadership, he put his cabinet of old-guard loyalists through what he called 'self-renewal' (Lee 2002). Yet, at the time of writing this essay, Lee still maintains an active presence, having been appointed senior minister by Goh Chok Tong, the successor that he had personally groomed for the position. His eldest son, Lee Hsien Loong, has been prime minister of Singapore since 2004.

Similarly, Mr Moy maintained a high level of activity after he declared himself 'retired' on his sixty-fifth birthday – so much so that the board was uncertain about what issues to bring to his attention. On some issues, directors would approach him before coming to a decision, only to be told, 'Why do you ask me? I am retired.' Consequently, on other issues, decisions were made without consulting him. Hearing about these after the fact, he would complain, 'It's not because I am retired that you should stop consulting me.' These uncomfortable dynamics went on for several months.

One day, I asked, in an oblique way, what the defining line was between what he wanted and did not want to hear. 'Mr Moy,' I said, 'it has been several months since you declared yourself retired, yet you have not slowed down. You travel as much as before, you continue raising funds, and you still are involved in administrative affairs. What do you mean by *retired*?'

'The difference now is that I no longer feel personally responsible for the financial stability of the Society,' he replied without hesitation.[8]

This self-divestment of the responsibility of accumulating patrimony is typical of retirees, for whom the wheel of fortune turns counter-clockwise as they liquidate assets to provide sustenance for the final years of their life. It is also deeply rooted in the Chinese family tradition, where three generations live under the same roof – both parents working outside the home to support the family, while the grandparents educate the grandchildren. This later-life period, when the ageing parents' health declines and as they become financially dependent on their maturing children, is a time when their educational efforts should come to fruition. From early on, Mr Moy had provided an additional incentive to pursuing the organization's mission after his passing, by embedding the Confucian values (for the lay members) or the virtues (for the more spiritually inclined) of filial piety directly into the Society's foundation, setting it up as a three-generational community.

The 'mourning after': New claims on charisma

Given that the mission and methods of an organization founded by a charismatic leader are so intimately and subjectively related to his commanding presence, the sudden and irreversible loss that takes place when the leader dies can leave a gaping hole in the organizational structure of authority. On the economic side, the void never stays open too long in an organization that has accumulated conventional assets in material goods, liquidity, and goodwill, since some committed individuals will move in quickly to protect the organization's shared equity against the sudden assaults of opportunists. Things are not so clear when it comes to preserving the organization's human assets.

Time and again, during the first few years that followed Mr Moy's death, I witnessed the resilience of the Society's leadership against certain self-interested individuals who sought to usurp a share of his charismatic authority. Of the four people who eulogized Mr Moy at his funeral, three are no longer connected with the Society. They left of their own volition, some slamming the door on the way out when their claims to a distinct personal status (allegedly deriving from their exceptional relationship with our teacher) were denied. This, according to Weber (1968), is the rule rather than the exception: 'The process of routinization is not free of conflict. In the early stages, personal claims on the charisma of the chief are not easily forgotten and the conflict between the charisma of office or of hereditary status with personal charisma is a typical process in many historical situations' (61).

In retrospect, these sporadic assaults on the heritage left by Mr Moy were quashed thanks to his own foresight. Indeed, for many years, he had made it a practice to use his personal influence over the voting delegates in order to constitute boards consisting of directors who would eventually prove steadfastly dedicated to furthering the bequeathed slate of projects in its entirety, including his principle of collegial successorship. To assemble such a team, he had to resist the trappings of political correctness and its short-term benefits. Indeed, more than once he had been second-guessed on his choices of candidates, which were often heavy on male presence and light on geographical representation. Yet it must be said in fairness that the harmony among 'siblings' was largely preserved by the Society's Confucian culture, particularly by the assertion of the principle that 'the children should change nothing in the home for three years after the passing of the father.' This gave every member the opportunity to re-evaluate his or her commitment to the Society's mission in the new environment, while gauging the ability and appropriateness of the new leaders. Not surprisingly, few of the directors who had figured prominently on Mr Moy's slate stepped down from office after his death. But more importantly, many of the processes dear to the founder have been repeated so often since 1998 as to have become routinized, if not institutionalized, within a very short period.

Voluntary routinization

The legacy that Mr Moy left behind at the time of his passing can be summarized as follows:

1. Extraordinary health arts, deeply rooted in, and still actively connected to, the Taoist spiritual tradition from which they originated.
2. A harmonious multinational, plurilingual, heterocultural, and socio-economically diversified human environment framed within a common organizational culture, tradition, and four decades of shared experience.
3. A network of infrastructures (the Society owned properties – urban clubhouses, rural training centres, temples, etc.) that give the organization a permanent physical presence in areas where it has reached maturity.
4. An elaborate slate of ongoing and future projects to focus individual energies.
5. An articulate set of aims and objectives.
6. A reserve of resources and a practical method to generate additional resources, as needed.

All this may sound pretty solid. Yet the initial solidarity displayed by the majority of members during the time of mourning remains cemented only with the delicate fibres of connection to the mission and with individual goodwill.

At present, however, there is every reason to feel confident that history will look back at the first generation leaders of the Society as having safeguarded the heritage entrusted to us by our founder and made it available to a more recent generation of members. This is already quite an achievement, considering how many organizations soon fail after the passing of their founders. It is attributable to a common frame of mind shared by the vast majority of the Society's leaders, which emerged during the hours following Mr Moy's passing and was very much intuitive, even if it is closely related to Weber's principle of post-charismatic routinization:

> To take on the character of a permanent relationship forming a stable community of disciples or a band of followers or a party or any sort of political or hierocratic organization, it is necessary for the character of charismatic authority to become radically changed. Indeed, in its pure form charismatic authority may be said to exist only in the process of originating. It cannot remain stable, but becomes either traditionalized or rationalized, or a combination of both. (Weber 1968, 54)

Patrimonial authority versus hegemonic succession

The commencement of this routinization of the Society was marked by a number of consensual decisions among the leadership – directors, advisors, and elders. Somehow energized and inspired by our grief, we made a defining decision during an informal meeting that took place on the same day as Mr Moy's funeral, in the large living room of the temple he had co-founded. At that meeting, we rapidly came to the decision not to look for another *sifu* and to stand in the way of anyone who would dare to pose as the next master.

We made this choice intuitively, unaware that the consequences of a choice between *patrimonial* authority and *patriarchal* authority had long before been articulated by organizational researchers and social scientists. We were aware of what we were getting into, if not the sheer amount of energy that would be required to manage the Society's affairs through consensual decision-making, collegial instruction, and collective action.

4. Legitimacy and Recognition

According to Weber (1968), a number of decisions specifically linked to the followers' need to confer legitimate authority upon the new ruler(s) or regime will punctuate the formerly charismatically driven movement's progression through routinization to a choice between patrimonial authority and hegemonic succession (54–8).

Recognition of legitimacy

As stated earlier, organizations based on a charismatic style of leadership often become dependent on charisma, and therefore resort to a variety of strategies to secure a continued hegemonic leadership to which they have become accustomed. Weber (1968, 57) identifies four such strategies:

1. *To search for a replacement leader, in which legitimacy is established by the similarity of distinguishing characteristics.* This is the option that the leaders of the Society promptly decided against in their meeting after the funeral. Nonetheless, in the early years after 1998, several pretenders to leadership attempted to avail themselves of apparent opportunities. One of these was a former peer of Mr Moy who was vaguely known to have studied together with our founder under an older master. Although Mr Moy is said to have shown some respect for this man's Tai Chi skills, he had never introduced him as being a *susu* (literally, 'uncle') as this man claimed to be; and so our drifting self-appointed *susu* was accorded no greater acknowledgment than a polite greeting and a send-off. Surprisingly, this was the only attempt by an outsider to hijack the Society. A few other attempts came from the inside, as explained earlier, but were quickly warded off. Usually in the Society, ambition manifests itself in the form of aspiration to fiefdoms – a tendency that is also discussed by Weber (1968, 59) – most often, by attempting to steer a branch or group of members away from the Society and towards oneself. As for members who are unable to make the leap from patriarchal to collegial organization, they usually leave the Society to hook up with one of the many self-styled *sifus* on the martial arts market.

2. *To seek a successor through supernatural revelation.* In some forms of Buddhism, for instance, the faithful rely on oracles, dreams, and omens to find the next supernaturally destined leader. When the Lama passes away, the elders set off in all directions around the world, looking for the young male infant or child in which he has been reincarnated. Here, the legitimacy of the authority is established through recognition of the legitimacy of the technique itself. While there are many divination techniques in Taoism and Confucianism, the Society has never considered relying on such to find a successor to Mr Moy – though if everyone were to have the same dream at the same time, it would certainly get our attention.

3. *To recognize a hereditary successor.* The principle of primogeniture has been established as governing the inheritance of authority in several national cultures, including those of Japan and a few of the remaining monarchies of medieval Europe (in the United Kingdom, it was abolished in England and Wales by an Act of Parliament in 1926 and in

Scotland in 1964); it is also prevalent in certain family businesses.[9] Here recognition is not paid to the charismatic qualities of the inheritor per se, but to the legitimacy of acquiring his position by inherited succession. Mr Moy had no children, so this never was a consideration.

4. *To validate the original charismatic leader's choice of a successor.* In this case, it is the stature of the decider that confers legitimacy. This is the route that Singapore's Lee Kuan-Yew took when he stepped down from the prime minister's office and indicated that Goh Chok Tong was his candidate of choice for that position. In Chinese martial arts schools, *sifus* usually transmit their skills and knowledge to a designated successor, often known as the 'Favourite Son.' As recounted earlier, Mr Moy clearly indicated that he did not want to avail himself of the privilege of designating a single individual as successor. However, to a certain extent, it can be said that by using his influence when submitting a slate of candidates for election to various boards, he did leave an imprint that sealed the legitimacy of the directors, who are still in place today. The grooming methods and selection processes undergone by prospective successors before accessing their particular position would make for interesting academic research. In the case of many leaders of the Society, the Taming of the Heart training, briefly described earlier, may have some equivalency, at least metaphorically, to yet another source of recognition of legitimate successorial authority, in which 'charisma may be transmitted by ritual means from one bearer to another or may be created in a new person. In this case, the belief in legitimacy is no longer directed to the individual, but to the acquired qualities and to the effectiveness of the ritual acts' (Weber 1968, 57).

Such transmission may have referred originally to some sort of initiation, anointment, or coronation where the charisma was passed along by a priest or an elder in a ceremony or ritual. Strictly speaking, no such ritualistic transmission has ever taken place in the Society. Yet, as most of the current leaders of the Society have been subjected to some direct confrontation with Mr Moy during which their ego was publicly quashed through the 'heart taming' process, such encounters may be viewed a posteriori as a rite of initiation, which determined members' suitability for higher office.[10]

It is difficult to say which of – if even either of – the nomination for office by our founder or the quasi-ritualistic ego-trimming would have initially weighed heavier on the scales of successorial legitimacy for the leaders of the Society during the grieving years. The directors were nonetheless granted a considerable degree of respect by their first-generation contemporaries, and this has now rubbed off onto the next generation. To this day, all remain committed to a collegial approach.

The legitimizing of recognition

Foreseeing quite early on that they themselves must eventually pass the baton to another generation, leaders of the Society became acutely aware of their singular condition of having come of age in hegemonic times and of having ridden on the coat-tails of Mr Moy's charisma after his passing. Times would soon change, so the future urgently needed attention.

This awareness arose in the midst of three short, consecutive periods, each marked by a prevailing characteristic, and which may be considered as subroutines of the routinization process:

TAKING STOCK OF THE PATRIMONY

The first period was a time of taking public inventory of Mr Moy's legacy during the first three years after Mr Moy's passing, when 'the children must change nothing in the house after the passing of the father.' One of the outcomes of this process was the realization that, as an organic organization, the Society was indeed greater than the sum of its members' experiences, and that its particular cultural significance would depend on how we could make our way through each episode of generative tension between our Eastern master-to-apprentice traditions and the imperatives of a Western democratic environment, as described earlier.

As the Society gradually emerged from its three-year mourning period, the leaders became increasingly self-conscious about their role as collective custodians of Mr Moy's heritage. To protect it over the long term, some constitutional adjustments would need to be made and the ensuing new policies would not be very popular with the grass-roots membership. In fairness, we couldn't just leave it to 'the next guys' to stick their necks out, so when our terms were up, we had to renew our mandates on our own steam, which was not an exciting prospect. Although none of us had personal ambitions around further longevity in office, we were aware that a premature changing of the guard could cause damage to the organization. And yet it was clear that in order to move forward on possibly controversial decisions, our legitimacy must receive unequivocal confirmation from all members.

MAKING A FEW SIGNIFICANT TRAJECTORY CORRECTIONS
The following is an example of a typical conversation between two
Society directors during the period known as 'the first three years':

> *Director A:* 'We can no longer do that.'
> *Director B:* 'But Mr Moy used to do it.'
> *Director A:* 'Sure, but none of us is Mr Moy.'

Two significant corrective governance amendments were passed just as
the Society emerged from its three-year inventory period. While purely
the outcome of an intuitive reflection, they were founded on a concern
that, in retrospect, is not unrelated to Weber's (1968) argument that 'the
routinization of charisma also takes the form of the appropriation of the
powers of control and of economic advantages by the followers or disciples, and of the regulation of the recruitment of these groups' (58).

Our first amendment, in which the Society's leaders chose to divest
themselves of an economic privilege that had been conferred directly
onto them by Mr Moy,[11] would seem to run contrary to Weber's argument. The rationale was that in renouncing this privilege, the leaders
were levelling the economic playing field on which first-generation and
'next-generation' members were to meet. Thus, here the routinization
was in the very act itself of redefining the distribution of economic
advantages.

The second amendment, which constitutionally established electoral
nomination committees at all hierarchical levels, was more clearly in
line with Weber's argument regarding 'the appropriation of the powers
of control.' The role of these committees was to take all acceptable steps
to ensure that, in Weber's terms, 'only the proven novice is allowed to
exercise authority' (ibid.).

ENTERING INTO A PERIOD OF REFLECTIVE GESTATION
From the period early after Mr Moy's passing, when Society leaders
consciously clung to the past when making decisions, they gradually
moved to a different state of mind, characterized by the need to make
imaginative and intuitive leaps between the past and the future when
deciding for the present.

I have named this period our 'reflective gestation.' As figure 3.2 shows,
it has evolved from the days of mourning, marked by interplay between
nostalgia and uncertainty, through the dynamics between retrospection
and prospection that still influence many Society leaders in the present

FIGURE 3.2
Reflective gestation matrix. Maturing individually in order to move on collectively.

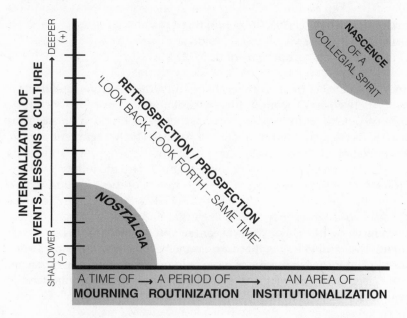

times. The 'gestation' is integral to the slow march towards institutional-ization, as routinization is a form of active gestation – like the chrysalis phase when the pupa becomes a butterfly, or the 'dark phase' in the Western alchemical process. The outcome of this quiet transformation should be, for many, an internalization of the past that will include not only our years with Mr Moy, but also the defining years after his passing – those for which the present generation of leaders will be remembered, and the time of our own 'attainment of eldership.'

* * *

Postscript: Twelve Years Later

Currently, the Society is at a defining moment of its history. Leadership at the local and, increasingly, at the regional levels is now in the care of those whom my peers call 'next-generation members' – those who did not know Mr Moy or had little contact with him. It is only because so many first-generation leaders have now crossed the threshold of legitimacy and have struck a delicate balance between the legal and traditional bases of authority that the next generation has connected to our founder's vision, has internalized our organizational culture, and is advancing our mission.

First-generation members are still actively calling the shots at the national and international levels; but the younger leaders are moving up, and will soon be in charge. Currently, present leaders are more than ever involved in preparing our own collective succession. As the circumstances are different, so are some challenges. But the images of Mr Moy's care in leaving behind a house in order are still very vivid.

NOTES

Special thanks are due to my thesis director, Professor Jan Jorgenson, for pointing me in the right direction in the course of the literature review for this essay, as well as for his interest and support throughout my studies in the McGill-McConnell Program. Thank you to my elders, peers, and students, and to my parents, siblings, and children for your patience and forbearance.

1 Four corporations are registered national charitable organizations: two with 'health' objects (the Taoist Tai Chi Societies of Canada and of Great Britain) and two with 'religious' objects (the Taoist Tai Chi Society of the USA and the Fung Loy Kok Institute of Taoism). All other corporations in the twenty-five other countries where the International Taoist Tai Chi Society is active are non-profit organizations; some are awaiting charitable status.

2 The reader may want to consult www.taoist.org for more information about the Taoist Tai Chi Society and the Fung Loy Kok Institute of Taoism's history, mission, and activities, and also to consult Lai (2003) for a brief backgrounder about Taoism in Hong Kong.

3 I should caution the reader that, in 1951, Max Weber also wrote a book about Confucianism and Taoism that was later criticized as 'theoretically biased.' His take on these spiritual traditions, as reported by Lai (2003, 459), in no way corresponds to my own experience of them.

4 This expression is borrowed from Howard Gardner's 'Six Constants' from his *Leading minds: An anatomy of leadership* (1996).

5   In a recent review of Erikson's studies, Houde (2002) places the age range of this stage of life at 30 to 50 years. From my own observations, the urgency to leave something behind increases exponentially each time one confronts the milestones of ageing: disease, loss of loved ones, and so on.

6   'Prepare for tomorrow.'

7   The episodic constitutional saga that would eventually culminate in the unification of the fourteen founding corporations that now form the Society in Canada lasted seventeen years, from 1985 to 2002.

At a meeting in the late 1980s, about 30 members spent the weekend around a table in our Orangeville Centre, discussing yet another draft of the proposed unification by-laws. On Sunday morning, we asked Mr Moy if he would provide us guidance, as we pondered chapter 9, entitled 'Succession,' outlining provisions to be enacted in the event of our founder's untimely death so as to designate a member to the position of 'successor' in instructional affairs. We had even been so bold as to 'name a name' of the likely successor: an 'alpha-type male,' who was widely respected by his peers, and had been repeatedly pointed out publicly by Mr Moy as possessing excellent skills and experience.

Mr Moy's response to chapter 9 came sharply, even before the translator had finished relaying our request to him in Cantonese. 'You have understood nothing,' he told us. 'In the old days in China, the teacher would appoint a successor among his "favourite sons." The problem is that the successor is always weaker than the master, and thus his teachings get lost over time. That is why, for almost twenty years now, I have endeavoured not only to give you the blueprint and foundation of the arts we practice but also to build an organization that will sustain it, and to which you all belong. The teachings are entrusted to all of you together. You are all the successors, together, as a fellowship, as an organization.'

Chapter 9 was promptly deleted to make way for what I now understand as a more 'patrimonial' approach to post-charismatic governance.

8   Even if he expected the Society's board to take over the financial responsibility of the organization, Mr Moy managed nonetheless to single-handedly raise $3 million during the last three years of his life following his retirement, to help cover the costs of the crowning infrastructure project that he had instigated: the Fung Loy Kok Institute of Taoism's Quiet Cultivation Centre, now located on the grounds of the International Taoist Tai Chi Centre in Orangeville, Ontario.

9   In my province of residence alone, three industrial family empires that were passed down from father to children come to mind: Pierre Péladeau's Quebecor media empire, drug store mogul Jean Coutu's eponymous empire, and Joseph-Armand Bombardier's transportation empire.

10 Up to 1991, individuals who wished to join the (then known as) Fung Loy Kok Temple had to undergo a traditional initiation ceremony, usually led by the co-founder of the temple, Mr Mui Ming-to. That year, Mr Moy insisted that individuals who wished to share in the advancement of the charitable mission of Fung Loy Kok (essentially, the relief of suffering) should not be put in a position of renouncing their faith of origin. He therefore laicised access to the temple by abolishing the initiation rite and changed the corporate name to the 'Fung Loy Kok Institute of Taoism.'

11 The constitutional privilege abolished was known as the 'Ten-year Plus Exemption,' which entitled any member who had paid membership dues for ten consecutive years to be exempted from further payments of dues.

PART TWO

The Analytic Mindset

4 Leadership in the Eye of the Storm: Lessons in Crisis Management for National Sports Organizations

MARGARET MCGREGOR

SARS, West Nile Virus, terrorism, British Columbia forest fires, fifty million people left without electrical power, mad cow disease, Canada's national airline in bankruptcy protection, fears of an avian flu pandemic, Hurricane Katrina – it all sounds like a bad dream or a plotline from a far-fetched late-night movie. Unfortunately, far from being a fantasy, all these events have taken place in recent memory and have had a significant effect on individuals and organizations in the voluntary sector.

Organizations are often confronted with scandals, emergencies, and high-visibility controversies. Crises are inevitable and recurring (Andriole 1985, 4) and recent world events would certainly support that point. 'The need for preparing for crises has never been greater. The need to prepare for the unthinkable has never been greater either' (Mitroff 2004, 15). The enormous complexity of today's sports organizations and the global environment in which they operate is one of the biggest contributing causes to crises (Mitroff and Pearson 1993), yet despite people's best efforts and intentions, there is no way to avoid crises altogether.

Crisis management is a discipline that needs to be practised and mastered.[1] Unfortunately, all too few leaders prepare for a crisis while the skies are clear and before disaster strikes. Most organizations do not view crisis management as an important element of their core business, and few see the need until they are in the eye of the storm. In the face of pressing daily responsibilities, leaders do not invest sufficient time in proactive risk-management strategies to reduce the likelihood of crisis situations.[2] The 'unconscious conspiracy to get immersed in the routine' rather than deal with larger issues (Bennis 1989, 17) keeps leaders from deepening their understanding of crisis prevention and management. Hesselbein (2002) contends that 'there are too few outstanding examples of leaders who prepared the organization for an emergency, who instilled values that would support a powerful, ethical response and who – when the crisis hit – led from the front and communicated in an open and powerful way' (4). Crisis management is as much an expression of leadership as it is of organizational responsiveness.

This essay explains the stages of a crisis, discusses the skills of effective crisis leadership, and offers suggestions on how to steer a national organization through the eye of the storm. It is intended to help national voluntary sector leaders better understand what can be done to reduce the likelihood of a crisis and lessen the impact when (not if) a crisis finally occurs.

1. Why Crisis Management Is Important for Sports Organizations

The world of sports has entered a new era. Under the spotlight of global media attention, national and international sports have transformed into entertainment properties with brand identity, huge followings, and associated revenues.

As recently as twenty years ago, sports were played primarily for the pride of the school, community, or country. The joy of participation was sufficient reward for an athlete. Money was not the major motivating force. Today, a sports organization's image and 'branding' are among its most precious assets. Many sporting events have become global entertainment events (Wingate 1995). Athletes and sports organizations are being held accountable to the public and the press. Infringements of principles and compromised ethical standards in sports attract international attention and impact heavily upon a wide range of stakeholders. In 1999, for instance, the International Olympic Committee (IOC) acknowledged that the series of scandals it had encountered had severely undermined the 105-year-old organization's credibility. Sports organizations are beginning to declare their deficiencies in the context of crisis management, and are seeking strategies to manage crises more effectively.

The repercussions of unethical conduct and crises affect a wide range of stakeholders in the sports enterprise.

1. *Parents may hesitate to encourage their children* to pursue high-performance sport (McGregor 1998). Highly visible sexual abuse scandals, frequent doping infractions, and incidents of corruption do little to engender faith in parents that sports organizations will take good care of their children.

2. *Politicians and bureaucrats may become nervous about the investment of public dollars* in a sector that seems plagued with embarrassing scandals

and controversies. In his report on the Ben Johnson doping crisis, the Honourable Charles Dubin (1990) declared: 'If public funds are being used by our athletes for drugs and other banned practices, financial support should not be continued because such practices defeat the justification for the expenditure of public funding' (501).

3. *Corporate sponsors may withdraw or reduce support* in the context of recurring crises in sports. In the aftermath of the 1999 IOC corruption crisis, insurance giant John Hancock cancelled negotiations for $20 million worth of Olympic-related advertising with NBC, and removed the Olympic symbol from its annual report (*Toronto Star* 1999). Many sports organizations that have relied heavily on government support over the years are facing growing financial difficulties and are looking to alternate sources of funds. Fundraising, donations, and corporate sponsorship are becoming the major alternate sources of revenue, and these new revenue streams are very easily blocked by any change that might affect the organization's image or reputation.

4. *Public cynicism towards sports may escalate,* fuelled by doping and corruption scandals, along with other crisis situations. This cynicism does a disservice to the majority of athletes, who pursue their sport simply for the love of the game. Participants in a 1991 Decima Research focus group spoke of athletes' disillusionment with the Olympics and other high-profile international competitions due to cheating, commercialism, and banned substance usage.[3]

5. *Fans may lose their commitment and withdraw support* for athletes in the face of growing numbers of scandals and televised violence in professional sports. Junior hockey, for example, is in danger of eroding its fan base because parents are refusing to take their children to a spectacle that features fighting rather than skill (*Toronto Star* 1991).

To avert mismanagement of crises and its consequences – permanent injury to athletes' reputations, damage to an organization's image, and the loss of important sources of funding – national sports organizations must enhance their capacity to predict, prevent, understand, and respond to crisis situations.

2. What Is a Crisis?

A crisis is:

- Any damaging event or incident that threatens the viability of the organization. This includes physical damage to a facility or to an image (Wingate 1995, 3).

- A major, unpredictable event that has potentially negative results. The event and its aftermath may significantly damage an organization (Barton 1993, 2).
- A serious incident which has either received or been threatened with adverse publicity (Bland 1998, 5).

Common features of a crisis are (based on Barton 1993; Bland 1998):

- Someone is to blame.
- Something is at stake (profit, reputation, survival).
- Someone finds out.
- Leaders must act in a hurry, initially without full knowledge.
- There is usually someone ready to second-guess those in charge.

To distinguish what does and what does not constitute a crisis, Bland (1998) gives the example of lightning striking a building. The building burns down and employees are injured. This is an accident and people sympathize. But if the injuries were caused because the lightning rod was not in working order, or the company's evacuation procedures were inadequate, then it is a crisis.

Leaders should not get too bogged down in definitions, because there are no clear boundaries and there is rarely a single moment when an incident or issue transforms into a crisis (Bland 1998, 5). It is best to adopt a low threshold when defining a crisis, and err on the side of caution. Sometimes even a seemingly minor episode can escalate into a crisis at an astonishing speed.

A crisis is a fluid, unstable, dynamic situation where things are in a constant state of flux (Fink 2000, 20). Crises can come in pairs, clusters, or series. They are never cut and dried, and never black and white. By definition, the context and intensity of any crisis are highly unpredictable.

3. Stages of Crisis Management

There are at least four distinct stages of crisis management:

1. Avoiding the crisis: the early warning stage.
2. Preparing to manage the crisis.
3. Containing, managing, and resolving the crisis.
4. Learning from the crisis: the post-mortem.

These stages may occur within a short time span, or be extended over a long period of time (Fink 2000, 20). Having an appreciation of what stage of the crisis an organization is in may help with the successful management of the crisis.

Avoiding the crisis: The early warning stage

In the early warning stage, clues or hints of impending trouble begin to surface. These signals are often, though not always, clearly present before a major crisis occurs (Barton 1993). Leaders must know how to read the signals of impending disaster. If the warnings go unperceived, then the subsequent stages can strike swiftly and mercilessly. The leader's challenge is to sharpen his or her awareness so as to spot and act upon the warning signals before events escalate. Even if the leader cannot prevent the crisis, just being aware of its impending arrival can make it much easier to manage.

Warning signals that might have alerted leaders to an upcoming crisis often go unrecorded, unrecognized, or unattended. In the 1999 Columbine High School shooting in Littleton, Colorado, the police already knew that on several occasions the two teenaged snipers had threatened their classmates, and had even submitted written assignments in school warning of violence. In Canada, during the Dubin Inquiry hearings on banned practices in sports following the 1988 Olympics, it was learned that track and field officials were aware of the rumoured drug use among some members of the national team before Canadian sprinter Ben Johnson tested positive for steroids (Dubin 1990, 177).

In the fall of 2005 in the aftermath of Hurricane Katrina, the U.S. government was heavily criticized for ignoring repeated warnings it had received months, even years, in advance that New Orleans and surrounding areas would sustain catastrophic damage from Category Four hurricanes. The Bush administration came under severe fire for failing to organize relief in advance of the disaster.

Once a signal is sounded, it must be heard by the right person, one who knows what to do about it (Mitroff and Pearson 1993). In the aftermath of the *Challenger* space shuttle explosion on 28 January 1986, the Rogers Commission appointed by President Reagan to investigate the accident learned that the engineers responsible for flight safety checks at the Kennedy Space Center had warned of a flaw in the O-rings on the shuttle's solid-fuel booster rockets. Yet senior management in the NASA organization had systematically ignored this crucial technical information, as well as other risks (Feynman 1988).

One of the commission's members, the theoretical physicist and Nobel laureate Richard Feynman, was highly critical of the flaws in NASA's 'safety culture.' In a personal appendix to the final report, he famously concluded, 'For a successful technology, reality must take precedence over public relations, for nature cannot be fooled' (Feynman 1988, 237). Feynman's words apply in a broader sense to the culture and techniques of crisis management in general.

Although most leaders are well-intentioned, many attempt to manage their organizations in a state of denial, rather than being open and attentive to clues that should trigger a proactive response to an impending crisis (Barton 1993, 3). Open lines of communication should be developed, supported, and encouraged between the bottom, top, edges, and centre of the organization. These lines of communication or 'voicing systems' should enable employees or members to speak up when something is troubling, questionable, or amiss.

Canadian Interuniversity Sport has integrated such a voicing system as a key part of its operations. Meetings of the board of directors include an agenda item dedicated to 'crisis management early warning signal detection.' This provides an opportunity for board members to voice concerns while problems are still in their infancy. Board members are asked, 'Where are we vulnerable? What small problems might become large issues? And what crises have other sports organizations faced recently?' This discussion serves as an early warning to determine whether or not some sort of action or intervention should be initiated to meet the issue head-on, and if possible, resolve it before it escalates into a paralysing crisis.

Signals must also be assessed in order to calibrate their risk potential. Not every signal merits a response, and the leader's challenge is to differentiate important signals from background noise.

Preparing to manage the crisis

This stage involves developing action plans, communication plans, staging mock crises or fire drills, and establishing essential relationships that may be called upon in the midst of the crisis. R. Norman Augustine suggests that while prevention is 'perfectly unattainable,' preparation can make a big difference: Noah started building the ark before it began to rain (Augustine 2000, 12). The maxim 'practise makes perfect' likewise applies to crisis preparation.

Leaders should be prepared and positioned to manage crisis situations. Ever since the bombing at the 1996 Atlanta Olympics and the September 11, 2001 terrorist attacks, key decision-makers within the sports sector have become acutely aware of the multitude of risks and issues surrounding major international sports events. Elaborate measures and plans are put into place in order to anticipate security crises.

In January 2006, an outbreak of H5N1 avian flu was confirmed in Turkey, not far from the site of the 2006 Olympic and Paralympic Winter Games in Torino, Italy, scheduled to open in February. Leaders from the Canadian Olympic Committee anticipated that the athletes' village, populated with people from around the world, was an ideal breeding ground for infection, and that the Canadian Team could be touched by bird flu. Consequently, they secured antiviral drugs and designed a plan to evacuate Canadians should the need have arisen (Morris 2006).

Generally, the safest place for Canadians during major games is within the confines of the secured games venues and villages. Without going so far as to recommend that athletes restrict themselves exclusively to secure zones, the Canadian Team leadership typically supports the suggestion that whenever possible, athletes minimize their movements outside of secured areas. Risk reduction suggestions are given to athletes to travel in pairs, wear clothing that identifies them as Canadian, and inform team leaders of their whereabouts whenever they leave the secure zones.

During the preparation stage, organizations should form a crisis management team (CMT) empowered to make and implement decisions rapidly in the midst of a crisis. If the crisis occurs in multiple jurisdictions, one of the first tasks of the CMT is to contact the other stakeholders involved. The CMT will ensure consistency and coordinate the responses of the key players so it is clear who acts when and so the responses are synchronized. Team members should be provided with cell phones, BlackBerry devices, or other mobile technologies for easy access. Team leaders should also have satellite phones to serve as a backup in case landlines and cellular networks go down. The crisis management team should take media relations and crisis communications training.

The CMT should draft plans to confront examples of crises to which their organization could be susceptible. These 'what-if' plans serve as templates during an actual crisis. The plans should include: (a) principles or philosophy, (b) action plans, (c) communication plans, and (d) essential relationships. This process will ensure that instructions and assignments are clear, current, and well rehearsed. The 'what-if' plans should outline initial responses to situations, identify key audiences to communicate with, identify channels through which to speak to the public, and indicate key messages to be delivered. Augustine (2000) contends that the heat of a disaster is the poorest possible time to establish new relationships with needed organizations.

Containing, managing, and resolving the crisis

This stage is characterized by avalanche-like speed and intensity. Fink (200) describes this stage as 'the point of no return' (22). The warnings have slipped by unnoticed or have been ignored. The hot spot has erupted. Normal operation of the organization is often compromised at this stage. The situation typically falls under intense public or media scrutiny. Some damage has already occurred; how much additional damage will occur depends upon the organization's leader.

This phase is commonly referred to as 'damage control.' Efforts must be made to contain the crisis so that it does not contaminate other parts of the organization. Augustine (2000) contends that it pays to search for subtleties – the second-order effects. Surviving the immediate threat may not be as difficult as having the long-term capability to cope under sustained pressure. Often, the leadership of an organization diverts its full attention to containing the crisis and other parts of the organization can suffer.

Augustine (2000) offers hard-hitting advice to institutions facing an organizational crisis: 'Get it right, get it quick, get it out and get it over' (22). Some kind of reasonable, decisive action is almost always better than no action at all. The American humorist Will Rogers once said, 'Even if you're on the right track, you'll get run over if you just sit there.' This subtly echoes Augustine's point that a crisis will not wait: 'It's like wrestling a gorilla. You rest when the gorilla wants to rest' (ibid., 20).

Learning from the crisis: The post-mortem stage

Once the crisis is past, it is time to calculate the damage, recover emotionally, conduct inquiries and audits, and congratulate those who performed well. It is also time for management shake-ups (Fink 2000, 24). In most poorly managed crisis situations, a high-profile person usually pays with his job (Welch 2005). In extreme cases, the organization may cease to exist altogether.

In the post-mortem stage, it is important to distil the critical lessons from the crisis and put these lessons into practise for the future. This involves reflection about why the crisis occurred and what might have been done to prevent it or lessen its impact.

It is essential that these lessons not be ignored, as the public's tolerance for repeat offenders is limited. For example, Firestone was involved in five of the ten largest tire recalls in U.S. history. Many dealers and consumers said subsequently that they would not use Firestone tires of any kind (Mitroff 2004, 30). Within the Canadian sports sector, in 1988, the Canadian Olympic Committee and Commonwealth Games Canada both underwent intense scrutiny for not providing sufficient bilingual services during the Canadian team receptions, first at the Winter Olympic Games in February and again at the Commonwealth Games in July. These communications crises took place within five months of each other and the media and politicians were very critical of both organizations for making the same mistake twice.

Welch (2005) suggests that immunity to crises comes from the postmortem stage. Crises can teach us what is broken. Taking action to fix what went wrong makes the organization stronger. 'It is very unlikely, for instance, that Johnson & Johnson will ever have another product-tampering disaster like Tylenol' (4).

4. Leadership in a Crisis: Skills, Behaviours, Actions

The Internet and twenty-four-hour news channels allow a worldwide audience to watch, dissect, and evaluate on an hourly basis how a leader responds to a crisis. Commentators offer their analysis, criticism, and second-guessing of a leader's effectiveness during a crisis.

Crises provide leaders with opportunities – if they are able to capitalize on them. They challenge management's ability to lead, yet there exists the potential for leaders to fail if they are unable to take decisive and appropriate action that is linked to the organization's mission and values. However, if leaders are able to manage the crisis with aplomb, they can transform their organizations.

Effective crisis managers have the ability to (a) frame events, (b) keep them in perspective, (c) tolerate confusion and hostility, and (d) be decisive, despite incomplete information. Effective crisis leaders must be willing to get their hands dirty and be present as a visible leader.

In May 2000, seven people died in Walkerton, Ontario, and more than 2,000 fell ill as a result of drinking from the town's water supply, which was infected with E. coli. The Walkerton Judicial Inquiry commissioned Roger Martin, the dean of the Rotman School of Management at the University of Toronto, to conduct a management analysis of what went wrong. In his report, Martin found that the failure to admit to mistakes was at the root of the Walkerton crisis: 'When pushed beyond our comfort levels, we will engage in defensive behaviour aimed at avoiding failure and the resulting embarrassment. We will avoid telling the truth or asking questions. The result is that we will cover up mistakes, even if it makes a bad situation worse' (*Ottawa Citizen* 2001, A5).

Crisis management literature suggests that the most effective crisis managers are unconventional thinkers who have the ability to stay calm and be rational under extreme pressure and stress (Wingate 1995). The term applied to those qualities most valued in crisis is 'cosmopolitan leadership.' Today's organizations must respond to environments that are multidimensional, discontinuous, conflicting, and highly interdependent (Andriole 1985, 4).

Mental agility is needed to imagine crisis management solutions that cross traditional boundaries. Kanter (1985, 89–98) describes cosmopolitan leaders as those who can forge links between organizations and who are comfortable operating across boundaries. Cosmopolitan leaders are diplomats who can influence people and organizations to work together to find a common cause. The success of managing a crisis often involves bringing people together to think through common problems and discover common solutions.

Framing skills

Leaders who are most effective during crises are able to frame events and issues while under intense pressure and in the absence of full information. They are able to lead an organization through the rough-and-tumble of a crisis by keeping the big picture and the opportunities for learning before them. Leaders who succeed stay connected with their organization's values, mission, and vision.

Failures, setbacks, and missteps occur often under the pressure of a crisis. However, with each failure comes a learning opportunity, which can be capitalized upon. Controversies and crises offer opportunities for learning, provided the experiences are dissected and the lessons are absorbed (Gardner 1996).

The challenge for leaders at this stage is that 'you don't know what you don't know.' Augustine (2000, 21) states that there may be too little information – or too much – with no easy way to sift out what is important. In the first minutes of the 28 March 1979 accident at the Three

Mile Island nuclear power plant near Harrisburg, Pennsylvania, the partial core meltdown triggered over one hundred alarms; but there was no system for suppressing the unimportant signals so that operators could concentrate on the significant alarms. Information was not available in a clear, prioritized, and understandable form.

In the heat of crises, CEOs must operate swiftly in murky situations, often in the face of conflicting advice. 'The legal department will warn "Tell 'em nothin' and tell 'em slow," the public relations department will appeal for an immediate press conference, the shareholder relations department will be terrified of doing anything and the engineers will want to disappear into their labs to conduct confirming experiments' (Augustine 2000, 21).

Augustine's experience is that it is preferable to err on the side of over-disclosure, even at the risk of harming one's legal position, in order to say *something*. If the CEO is not prepared to talk, reporters will find someone who is. In the age of immediate, global Internet information exchange, 'No comment' is an unacceptable response. The media will locate sources anywhere on the globe. Leading businessperson Warren Buffett sets out clear priorities: 'First, state clearly that you do not know all the facts. Then promptly state the facts you do know' (Augustine 2000, 22).

Leaders' visibility in the eye of the storm

Immediately dispatching the senior responsible individual to the scene of the problem sends two important messages: 'I care,' and 'I am accountable.' As stated above, effective leadership under extreme pressure and timelines can be more easily provided when the organization has thought out its position and principles well in advance of a crisis. 'Organizations that cope well with crises have their houses in order; they know what their values are and have a well articulated mission that permeates the organization. They know what they stand for' (Hesselbein 2002, 4).

In March 1989, Exxon CEO Lawrence Rawl made a serious mistake in leadership during the *Exxon Valdez* environmental crisis off the Alaska coast, by sending a succession of lower-ranking executives to deal with the eleven-million-gallon oil spill flowing from the grounded tanker, instead of flying to the disaster site himself and personally taking control of the situation in a forceful and highly visible way. (Rawl did not visit Alaska until three weeks after the spill.) Top officials at Exxon refused to comment on the vast environmental damage for almost a week. This apparent lack of a forthright official response made Exxon appear uncaring (Barton 1993, 5).

Similarly, in the fall of 2000, Russian President Vladimir Putin was intensely criticized when he chose not to cut short his holiday on the Black Sea in order to return to Moscow to deal with the crisis associated with the sinking of the *Kursk* submarine.

On the other hand, New York City Mayor Rudolph Giuliani was widely praised for his response to the September 11, 2001 terrorist attacks on the World Trade Center, especially his commanding and compassionate presence at Ground Zero during and immediately after the attacks. In contrast, Ontario Premier Ernie Eves was criticized for his delay in speaking to the citizens of Ontario during the first few hours of the August 2003 power blackout.

People want to see and hear leaders in a crisis. They want to be reassured that someone is in charge. They want candour. At the same time, people often look for a scapegoat or someone to blame. If the leader is not accessible, he or she is more likely to become that scapegoat (Barton 1993, 8). No response or a poor response from the leader is viewed as a sign of weakness and can keep the crisis alive longer than if the leader had acted promptly and with compassion.

Tolerating confusion and hostility

Michael O'Connor, the author of 'Crisis Decision Making,' explains some of the common features of decision-making in the heat of a crisis: there is uncertainty about critical events, the stakes are high, time is short, there are conflicting values and multiple constituencies (cited in Andriole 1985, 240).

Leaders will be better able to tolerate confusion if their organization has a clear sense of purpose and a mission that articulates what the organization stands for. Connecting to the organization's mission, values, and beliefs can serve as ballast during times of confusion. When leaders get into highly stressful situations, they will know how to react if they have a strong core and sense of organizational values.

Effective leaders during a crisis must be able to tolerate confusion and hostility, separate what is important from what is background noise, and make well-organized decisions. O'Connor advocates a 'decision analysis' process for determining the course of action during a crisis. This involves convening a group of decision-makers in a room at a site removed from the workplace. 'The session involves assessment of subjective inputs with supporting rationale, computer analysis, display of results, sensitivity analysis and modification until the outputs make sense, decision recommendations and associated discussions and if relevant, an implementation plan' (cited in Andriole 1985, 245).

5. Lessons Learned from Crisis Management in Sports Organizations

The following is a summary of the lessons learned in the course of my research on crisis management in sports organizations. These observations have been distilled from discussions during an extensive interview with one of the leading figures in sports management in Canada. Sue Hylland has managed crises with high-profile athletes at high-visibility events, under the microscope of worldwide media attention at the Olympic Games from 1984 to 2000. Her assessment of the elements of each crisis, the characteristics of the environment, and the aspects of crisis management approaches that succeeded (or failed) provides a rich insight into the reality of front-line crisis management in sports.

The lessons also incorporate the reflections and experiences I had when I served as the *chef de mission* for the Canadian team to the 2002 Commonwealth Games in Manchester, England, and the 2006 Paralympic Games in Torino, Italy. Although these lessons originate from crises that have occurred in sports organizations, they are relevant for all voluntary sector organizations.

In times of crisis, take action

Paralysis and indecision immediately after the outbreak of a crisis are worse than taking some moderate form of action. When the crisis occurs, lead from the front and communicate in an open way that is connected to, and consistent with, the vision and values of the organization. State clearly what you know – and what you do not know. Do not make up facts or overstate the situation. Keeping your sense of humour will help you keep cool in the heat of the crisis. Don't forget that during a crisis you still have the rest of the organization to take care of. You are the 'go-to' person who will be asked, 'Now what do we do?' Others are looking to you for reassurance.

An extensive risk analysis must be conducted around all major sporting events, such as the Olympic Games, involving a large number of Canadians travelling offshore. Prepare crisis management plans in advance.

In major Games situations, the voluntary organization and its leaders do not have a great deal of control. It is simply impossible to control 500 or more Canadian athletes in a confined area, under high-pressure conditions, for extended periods of time. Still less is it possible to control everything the athletes and coaches do in the years and months leading up to the Games. Voluntary organizations cannot control acts of terrorism, either. The most a national sports organization can do is to set guidelines that explain what factors are controllable and suggest appropriate responses to events that are uncontrollable, in a manner consistent with the values and principles of the organization.

Crises come at unexpected times ... and they rarely come alone

It is not improbable – sometimes it is even predictable – that a crisis may occur during the Games; but crises can also arise before the team leaves Canadian soil. Several issues arose prior to the Sydney Olympics in 2000, including equestrian athlete Eric Lamaze's cocaine infraction and a steroid infraction with a track athlete. During the Games in Sydney, however, things were surprisingly quiet and calm. The Canadian Olympic Committee kept waiting for something big to explode, but the minor crisis in these Games had already happened back home prior to the departure of the athletes.

At the 2002 Commonwealth Games, the first crisis, a positive doping infraction, occurred just two hours before the opening ceremonies, an event where all the Canadian media were in attendance and looking for a news story. This crisis had not been resolved before the next one occurred, which involved Canadian team leaders arguing before the International Rugby Union to reinstate a Canadian athlete. A third major issue, the detention by Manchester police of a Canadian for allegedly falsifying Games accreditation, arose while leaders were still trying to cope with the first two crises. Crises often do not come one at a time, nor do they happen at a convenient moment when one is well rested, well fed, and well prepared.

Institutionalize the lessons learned

After every Olympic Games, it is important to talk about what went wrong from a crisis management perspective. After the 1996 Olympics in Atlanta, the Canadian Olympic Committee (COC) held an extensive post-mortem. We acknowledged we were unprepared with an appropriate response when the bomb exploded in a downtown Atlanta plaza. We identified what we needed to do the next time a crisis arose involving a terrorist act at the Olympics. Last but not least, we made a point of institutionalizing the crisis management lessons from Games to Games. Each set of Games offers a new and unexpected crisis to deal with, and the issues are rarely the same. However, debriefing each situation helps to build a repertoire of crisis leadership skills.

On the evening of the Atlanta explosion, key people on the Canadian team were awakened and briefed on the details of the bomb. Team leaders from each sport were asked to confirm the whereabouts of their athletes. A head count was done, giving the COC reasonable assurance that all Canadian athletes were safe. The COC was most concerned about the swim team, because they had finished their events and had planned to go downtown and celebrate. For the Canadian teams, the initial phase of chaos resolved itself very quickly.

The COC also learned about the importance of communications during a crisis. Parents in Canada were concerned about their children's safety and needed to be reassured. The COC set up a mechanism for parents to connect with their children.

Develop relationships with other stakeholders

During preparations for the 2002 Salt Lake City Olympics, the threat of terrorism was a very real concern of the Canadian team. The Canadian Olympic Committee joined forces with the other Games organizations such as Commonwealth Games Canada, Canadian Interuniversity Sport, and government agencies that specialize in risk assessment to develop crisis plans. Most voluntary organizations do not have the resources for an in-house risk manager or crisis leader, so it is important to rely on external expertise as needed.

At the 2002 Commonwealth Games in Manchester, Canadian officials were notified at 2:00 p.m. that they were to appear before the International Court of Arbitration for Sport at 10:00 p.m. that night to argue a case related to a doping infraction. Having established relationships in advance of the Games helped the Canadian Team to secure British legal counsel and prepare arguments in time for the adjudication. The arbitrator decided in favour of the Canadian team, and ruled that Canadian triathlon athlete Kelly Guest was not eligible to compete for Canada at the 2002 Commonwealth Games as a result of a doping infraction.

Follow a crisis to its end stage

Surviving the chaotic initial phase of a crisis, when the storm breaks, is only the first step. Do not let your guard down prematurely. After surviving the eye of the storm, staff and volunteers may be exhausted and not operating at full speed or efficiency. This can make other areas of the organization vulnerable to contamination.

An incident occurred at the 2002 Commonwealth Games when silver medallist swimmer Jennifer Carroll brought a fleur-de-lis flag onto the medal podium, in a breach of unwritten protocol. The issue was dealt with later that night by Canadian Team mission staff. While we thought the flag issue had been resolved on the Games site, it surfaced again back in Canada several months later, creating a media furor, with calls for the resignation of the head swim coach and threats to cut off government funding to Swim Canada. A formal inquiry took place five months after the incident occurred. Crises are not necessarily over when you think they are, or when you want them to be.

Incorporate crisis management activities into strategic plans, into the CEO's job description, and into the budget. In advance of a crisis occurring, get information on how to set up a toll-free telephone number that can be promptly activated. Insurance coverage should be reviewed to determine risk protection. It is also important to store all essential supplies – spare cheques, letterhead, envelopes, media contact lists, backups of the database system, and emails – in an accessible, off-site location.

Enhanced safety and security reviews

Since the terrorist attacks of September 11, 2001, our notions of security have changed in terms of both actual and perceived comfort levels of Canadian athletes. Because Canada has a large number of athletes travelling internationally, evacuation plans must be put in place. Being unprepared is not an option. In order for athletes to perform well, they must be able to focus intensively on their performance, without having to worry about other issues. Athletes and their families need to be reassured that their safety and security have been looked after.

Nor is terrorism the only international threat. Headlines suggesting an impending pandemic of avian flu were commonplace in the months leading up to the 2006 Olympics and Paralympics. It was important to address this threat to team safety and to put contingency plans in place. These plans involved the medical staff and logistics staff, and included stockpiling a twenty-four-hour supply of antiviral drugs and developing an evacuation plan.

Listen to the early warning signals

Snowboarding was first admitted as an Olympic sport in 1998. Snowboarders are, by and large, free-spirited, counterculture athletes. By contrast, the IOC, a very traditional blue-blazer crowd, governs the Olympics. Sue Hylland admits that had the members of the Canadian Olympic Committee been tuned in to the early warning signals, they could have anticipated a confrontation between the traditional International Olympic Committee and the snowboarders.

The snowboarding event took place on the opening day of the Winter Olympics in Nagano in 1998. The victory of Canadian Ross Rebagliati was a pleasant surprise. The next day, the Canadian team's atmosphere of celebration turned to apprehension, after Rebagliati's urine sample revealed traces of marijuana in his system.

The COC management team decided to appeal the positive doping infraction ruling, based upon the technicalities of the doping rules. The COC crisis team turned over the management of the crisis to the lawyer in charge of the appeal. The International Federation (IF) regulations on marijuana were shown to be unclear and ambiguous. The case against Rebagliati was dropped, and he retained his medal. However, the Japanese police were planning to incarcerate him, because drug use in Japan is prohibited by harsh laws. The Canadian Embassy was contacted and arrangements were made to fly Rebagliati back to Canada immediately. This brought the acute stage of the crisis to a conclusion.

Leadership matters

At least three leadership lessons can be gleaned from the Rebagliati crisis. First, a crisis can occur on many levels. It was not enough to resolve the gold medal issue; the local police issue was also at hand and had to be incorporated into strategies to manage the crisis, while still maintaining focus on the Olympic athletes who remained behind.

Secondly, there are moments when the leadership on the crisis file may have to change hands, from technical, to legal, to communication, and finally to diplomatic experts. Keeping key stakeholders alerted to the developments and remaining agile in handing off leadership can be critical to successful crisis management.

Thirdly, the athletes who are not directly involved must also be helped to maintain their focus on their performance in the midst of a crisis. The moment for which athletes have prepared for a lifetime should not be unnecessarily or unfairly placed at risk or contaminated by surrounding events and crises. To some degree, competing athletes must be numb to a crisis, even if it affects a teammate.

.Leaders who are involved in crisis management are called upon twenty-four hours a day to address and resolve issues. This unremitting schedule will take its toll, emotionally and physically. It is important for leaders to eat well and get some sleep whenever possible. The leader, however, must learn to recognize his or her own limitations and, if necessary, stand down in order to recover enough to be an effective decision-maker. When a leader is stressed and tired, it helps to have a clear sense of the organizational values and principles.

6. Conclusion

Crisis management is as much an expression of leadership as it is of organizational responsiveness. History tells us that crises are inevitable. Crises can cause organizational collapse, but they also can present remarkable opportunities for organizational transformation. The saying that unless we learn from past mistakes, we are destined to repeat them certainly applies to crisis management.

Sports organizations are under the intense spotlight of public scrutiny. Leaders must take steps to prevent crises. When an 'impossible to imagine' crisis occurs, leaders must be prepared to navigate the eye of the storm. When asked 'Now what should we do?' they can apply the crisis management suggestions contained in this essay. They can lead from the front. They can communicate in an open and powerful way. They can express their leadership by responding to the crisis in an ethical manner that is linked to the values of their organization.

NOTES

1 I was inspired to explore the topic of crisis management in order to better prepare myself as a leader. I have served as the *chef de mission*, the top position of leadership, for the Canadian teams competing at the 2002

Commonwealth Games and the 2006 Paralympic Games. I am the 'go-to' person that the team turns to in those 'Now what do we do?' moments.

Today's major international sporting events, with their worldwide media visibility and scores of dignitaries in attendance, are prime targets for terrorists. An atmosphere in which 'anything and everything is possible' has replaced the sense of security that athletes once felt while competing internationally. If an 'impossible to imagine' scenario occurred during my watch, I wanted to be prepared for the heat of battle. I wanted to know that I had taken steps to prevent an incident, and that I was prepared to respond effectively to a crisis after it occurred. I wanted to be wiser, and to learn from the experience of other sport leaders who had managed crises in sport. Out of concern for Canadian athletes, and a desire to value and protect them so that they could concentrate on achieving their high performance goals, I set out on a journey to learn how to lead in the eye of the storm.

2 Wilf Wedmann, interview with author, Burnaby, British Columbia, 17 November 1999. In 1988 Wedmann was president of the Canadian Track and Field Association at the time of the Ben Johnson doping scandal.

3 Quoted in *Sport: The way ahead*, report of the Minister's Task Force on Federal Sport Policy (1992), 170.

5 Evaluating the Performance of Non-Profit Organizations: An Examination of the Performance Index for the Donner Awards*

JERRY V. DEMARCO

> 'What gets measured gets done.'
> David Osborne and Ted Gaebler, *Reinventing Government*

> 'In every move, in every decision, in every policy, the non-profit institution needs to start out by asking, Will this advance our capacity to carry out our mission?'
> Peter F. Drucker, *Managing the Non-profit Organization*

> 'Change is not necessarily progress. Change is adaptation.'
> Michael Quinn Patton, *Utilization-focused Evaluation*

Non-profit performance evaluation and Darwinism are two quite unrelated topics, it is clear, but I will attempt to weave them together to help convey my concerns about a relatively new Canadian quantitative non-profit evaluation tool. To begin, I wish to set out the general parameters of the discussion to follow. First, I recognize that non-profits are without the benefit of simple quantitative evaluation tools that could be used to assess their overall performance. Second, I believe that, despite the many complexities within business models, the common evaluative denominator remains focused on quantifiable profit, which makes those models not wholly transferrable to the non-profit arena. Third, I believe that the lack of a simple, quantitative, evaluative

---

* This chapter is used with permission of the Canadian Evaluation Society. A longer version was originally published in the *Canadian Journal of Program Evaluation* 19, no. 1 (Spring 2004): 61–96.

tool for non-profits inspired the creation of the Fraser Institute's Performance Index for the Donner Canadian Foundation Awards for Excellence in the Delivery of Social Services (the 'Donner Awards'), and that as a new entrant to the field of quantitative evaluation tools for non-profits, the Index holds a 'first on the scene' advantage. Fourth, I believe that there are inherent difficulties in attempting to create a one-size-fits-all evaluation tool for non-profits and that these difficulties militate in favour of considering a range of utilization-focused evaluation tools (Patton 1997), in a context-specific and mission-driven manner.

1. The Importance of Performance Evaluation

Critical to any organization is the question of how well it is performing. As noted by Patton (1997), '[c]orporations, philanthropic foundations, and non-profit agencies are increasingly turning to evaluators for help in enhancing their organizational effectiveness' (15). Evaluation is normally intended to serve one or more of the following purposes: 'rendering judgments, facilitating improvements, and/or generating knowledge' (65). While the choice of which measures and factors to use in such evaluation exercises is open to debate, it is evident that a non-profit organization should strive to perform to the best of its abilities. Critical to such performance is knowing how well an organization is doing vis-à-vis its mission and how it can improve itself. How one goes about this process of evaluation in the non-profit arena is not the subject of any consensus, and many different approaches to evaluation are available (see Hall, Phillips, Meillat, and Pickering 2003, 38; Patton 1997, 387–413; Wood and Clemens 2002, 80–4).

In the for-profit world, there are at least some common denominators revolving around measures of profit that can be used to compare performance across organizations, though it is recognized that the for-profit arena is not simple to evaluate. In the non-profit world, no obvious common denominator provides even the basic measuring stick that profitability measures offer to for-profit enterprises. But this should not be used to excuse an organization from evaluating performance.

2. The Performance Index and the Donner Awards

The Donner Awards are a collaborative initiative of the Donner Canadian Foundation and the Fraser Institute. The Awards are based on a two-stage process. First, non-profit organizations in nine different areas of social services (alternative education, childcare, counselling, crisis intervention, prevention and treatment of substance abuse, provision of basic necessities, services for people with disabilities, services to seniors, and traditional education) complete a quantitative-based questionnaire regarding ten areas of performance management (financial management, income independence, strategic management, board governance, volunteers, staff, innovation, program cost, outcome monitoring, and accessibility) (Wood and Clemens 2002, 5–6), which are then analysed by the Institute according to a Performance Index (see appendix 5.1).

Second, based on the results of this quantitative exercise, three or four finalists in each category of social service are selected to respond in essay-style format to five questions dealing with strategic management, outcome monitoring, program delivery, innovation, and affirmation (Wood and Clemens 2002, 7). Based on these answers, as well as independent letters of support, $5,000 awards for excellence are issued in each of the nine categories of social services, and a single $20,000 award is issued to the overall winner. Accompanying the awards is an annual performance report (Wood and Clemens 2002) that provides aggregate results from all applicants and graphs of how each class of organization scored in each area of performance measurement.

Though the awards are the key public outcome to the process, the performance evaluation also results in organization-specific 'Confidential Performance Reports,' which each applicant receives 'to identify particular areas of weakness' and 'to discover ways to improve performance' (Wood and Clemens 2002, 14). Thus, this evaluative process appears to focus on two of the typical general purposes of evaluation set out by Patton (1997, 65), namely, rendering judgment and facilitating improvement.

The Performance Index is relatively uncommon in its attempt to provide a quantitative performance evaluation system to measure the excellence of social service programs in many very different areas of endeavour. Wood and Clemens (2002) consider their approach to be a 'comprehensive' system that is a 'major step forward in the ability of non-profit organization managers to assess performance on an objective and quantifiable basis' (9). Considering that it seeks to provide a comprehensive approach to assessing the excellence with which social services are delivered in nine completely different areas, the Performance Index system is quite simple. The application form is a self-assessment questionnaire that is four pages in length and contains just over fifty questions (appendix 5.2). A four-page guide for applicants is also provided to assist in completing the questionnaire (Fraser Institute 2003d). The literature associated with the Donner Awards refers to the general concepts of performance, effectiveness, excellence, and efficiency as the matters being evaluated by the Performance Index.

Given that a key aspect of the Performance Index is to provide non-profit organizations with information that they can use to improve their performance, it makes sense to first examine whether the guidance provided by the Index is well suited to the organization and the non-profit sector. This is a key aspect of 'utilization-focused evaluation' (Patton 1997) and 'practical program evaluation' (Newcomer, Hatry, and Wholey 1994, 2). Consistent with the notion of 'evaluability assessment' (Wholey 1994, 17), one must be cognizant of how an evaluation will be used and whether it will be useful and practical for the organization or other stakeholders. This involves examining whether the tool is well suited to the particular milieu and, if it is not, whether acting on the results may provide little added value or even detract from the organization's mission (Hall et al. 2003, 2).

To help examine the potential impact of an evaluation tool on an organization's evolution, I will use a Darwinian metaphor. Will the Performance Index cause non-profits to *adapt* to the wrong *environment*? Will participating organizations *select* characteristics that help them better accomplish their mission or better emulate business, or both? Does the process assist the organizations in becoming more *fit* for their mission-driven *environment*, or more *fit* for another type of *environment* (e.g., a business-like world)?

It is worth noting that the Fraser Institute's program director, who oversees the Donner Awards, invokes a Darwinian metaphor in his call for the non-profit sector to become more 'business-like.' With reference to the current debate surrounding this alleged need, he remarks (Clemens 2000):

> Not all non-profit organizations embrace change. Some continue to believe that good words speak for themselves. They believe the language and practice of business have no place in the world of volunteers and compassion. Others go further, blaming business for creating a Darwinian world of winners and losers — and then turning its back on the losers. (B11)

Because the use of the Performance Index is in many ways a specific example of the larger debate about becoming more 'business-like,' it is particularly relevant (see Drucker 1977, 19). The Index exemplifies the collection of traits generally reflective of business approaches, which some advocate should be used in the non-profit arena. Whether one views the increased emphasis on business-like approaches as unwanted colonization or useful cross-pollination, the phenomenon itself is very present in the current non-profit environment. Legitimate calls for more accountability, better disclosure of outcomes, increased efficiency, and so on, can all lead a non-profit organization to look to the business world as a source of guidance.

3. Competition and Progress

The competition metaphor, which Darwin emphasized in some of his writings, is endemic to business models, and its influence on the Performance Index is quite evident. The Donner Awards brochure (Fraser Institute 2003e) states that the results of the Performance Index provide 'a useful tool for corporations, foundations and individuals to evaluate the organizations *competing* for their charitable dollars' (emphasis added). The byline from a Donner Awards media release noted that it is the 'only program in Canada to measure performance *against* peer groups' (Fraser Institute 2000; emphasis added). As well, the annual performance report (Wood and Clemens 2002) notes: 'Data from the application is then used to objectively assess the agency's performance on a comparative basis in ten performance areas ... Agencies are, therefore, *rated against each other* rather than assessed on the basis of an imposed standard' (6; emphasis added). The veracity of the claims to objectivity and to not measuring against an imposed standard will be discussed further below, but the above passages do help underline the important role of competition in the Performance Index. Non-profits are competing against each other to perform best, win awards, and attract funders.

The idea of evolving to a higher or more progressed state of being and how those terms were defined was an issue that Darwin struggled with. For Darwin, progress simply meant achieving a better state of adaptation to the current environment (Gould 1977, 37). This provided no guarantee of long-term prosperity or survival, of course. A rapid change in the environment could easily leave behind those forms that were more highly adapted to the previous conditions. Without expressly invoking a Darwinian metaphor, Patton (1997) speaks about the fact that changes within organizations are not necessarily improvements, either: 'changes are dictated by your current perceptions, but the commitment to change doesn't carry a judgment that what was done before was inadequate or less effective. Change is not necessarily progress. Change is adaptation' (106).

Evaluating performance and improving an organization are, however, geared towards progress. If the point of an organization is to accomplish a given mission and it is not yet completely doing so, then there is room for progress – to reach a higher level. But how one defines progress is key. Applying this to the Performance Index, one can see that organizations are being judged against an ideal 'higher' state. Despite the model's contention that the organizations are only being judged against each other, it is quite obvious that they are being judged against each other according to a particular set of standards. Admittedly, using statistical methods, the relative distribution can be expressed in any manner thought desirable – a scale of 0 to 10 (which is what the Index does use), as a percentage of the highest scoring organization, and so on – but who scores high and who scores low is very much correlated with what exactly the standard is. An organization that buys into the standards set by the model will do better on the Index, whether it be by, for example, reducing staff turnover, building up an accumulated surplus, or avoiding unstable government funding. 'Higher' performance means progressing towards the Performance Index's view of what is desirable. If the Index's definition of progress were compatible with a definition based on progress relative to mission accomplishment, then no difficulties would likely arise. However, these two types of progress are not synonymous. High performance under the Performance Index could help an organization perform better, but many other important variables are also at stake. Questions that might arise in process and impact evaluations (Scheirer 1994, 40) – such as What impact did the services have on the beneficiaries? Were resources put towards the areas of greatest effectiveness? Was the cause of the problem giving rise to the need addressed? and Was the organization's mission fulfilled in whole or in part? – are not the focus of the Index.

To say that doing well on one indicator of success (the Performance Index) translates into overall excellence in non-profit service delivery is a large leap of faith. The fact is that only the top 10 per cent of scores in the Index are eligible to carry on to the second stage of the Donner Awards process (the qualitative essay questions and references process), and thus, the 90 per cent of the organizations that may be excelling on a wider definition of performance are weeded out – they are 'lower' and less fit for the environment defined by the model.

4. The Influence of Business Perspectives

As noted above, the Performance Index approach is rooted in a business view of the world. Consistent with the general approach of the Fraser Institute (Fraser Institute 2002), the Index borrows much from the lessons learned in the competitive world of the market, and the awards program does not hide the fact that it helps non-profits become more 'business-like' (Clemens 2000). Being more business-like and efficient is assumed to be naturally better. Several authors challenge this assumption, however, as it applies in other fields (Ehrenfeld 1978, 246–7; Evernden 1992, 5–6; Livingston 1994, 72, 91, 176–97; Worster 1985, 315).

There is a difference between a very utilitarian business-like view of the world and one that places value on the experience of a particular beneficiary of social services instead of just the numbers served. There are legitimate differences in what is deemed to be good and desirable, according to different perspectives (Zimmerman and Dart 1998, 15). The Performance Index tries to respond to these differences by creating an external authority to which we can look for direction. That authority is rooted not in the values of the non-profit sector but in the perspective of market solutions to social problems. Given that the driving forces behind the two sectors are very different, it is naïve to believe that a business model is appropriate across the board in the non-profit arena, or vice versa. I share the concern of Zimmerman and Dart (1998) that business models are presently permeating society, including the non-profit sector:

> If we accept the assumptions underlying the commercial model without examining the context or limitations of their application, we could blindly or unconsciously apply inappropriate decision models to societal choices … The market ideology is powerful because it has 1) the support from groups that control the resources; 2) a consistent, coherent language; and 3) measurement tools. The market rules and logic will 'decide' which charitable activities are valuable in society. (16–17)

The Performance Index is clearly a 'measurement tool' steeped in the business model mindset, and this general warning seems particularly apt to any discussion of the Index's potential influence on non-profits. The ability to measure is alluring. Stein (2001) discusses the attraction of simple, efficient measurement within two main public services (health and education):

What is measured matters, because what is measured is what people do ...
It matters profoundly which measures of effectiveness are chosen. It matters because these measures – once they are socially accepted – feed back
to, and drive, the performance of those who provide public goods. (151–2)

In the non-profit context, Kanter and Summers (1987) (see also T.
Hayes 1996, 86–91; Kerr 1995, 7–14; and Patton 1997, 159– 61, 316) warn
that a tendency can arise to manage for the indicators of effectiveness,
instead of performance itself, which is particularly likely for organizations that serve very broad, and thus difficult to define, missions:

> When goals are vague or ill defined, effectiveness criteria may themselves
> become substitutes for goals, particularly when they are more precise and
> suggest concrete actions ... When immediate effectiveness measures set
> the standards for the organization, a tendency can arise to favor the short
> term over the long term – to maximize the score on indicators of today's
> performance. (156)

Knowing how effective an organization is depends very much on what
definition of effectiveness or performance is being used. As noted by
Kanter and Summers (1987, 156), attention needs to be paid to the 'larger mission' and to the temporal aspects as well (short-term and long-
term effectiveness measures may be very different). Generating this
type of knowledge is necessarily subjective in part, because it will depend on the nature of the organizational mission. No 'true' overarching
measure like profit will be found for all non-profits to gauge their overall performance.

Simple and attractive measurements (such as the Performance Index)
pose a risk: organizations may manage for them because there is no
easy alternative. Rather than recognizing that an organization's mission can be translated into some specific measurable (indeed, quantifiable) goals against which performance can be judged, the simplistic
one-size-fits-all approach may become the convenient choice – especially where it leads to a direct monetary reward. To borrow a term
from Gould (1981), simple measurements may in some cases simply be
mismeasurements. In his discussion of biological determinism, Gould
(1981, 24–5) examines how simplistic measurements and the fallacies of
reification (i.e., converting 'abstract concepts into entities') and ranking
('ordering complex variation as a gradual ascending scale') have helped
perpetuate historical discrimination within the human species.

The Performance Index suffers from both types of fallacies. Because it converts an abstract notion (or at least a diverse one), that is, the accomplishment of many different types of missions in the non-profit sector into one simple entity, a performance excellence score, it suffers from reification. More obviously, by ordering many types of organizations (with different missions, even though they are in similar fields) into one ascending scale, it is clearly based on ranking. But reification and ranking are not conducive to an examination of diverse, complex matters such as judging performance across entities that have different missions. The Performance Index may be an efficient attempt to judge performance with the resources its proponents have assigned to the project, but it is not likely accurate in gauging overall performance. As such, its utility in actually accomplishing what it sets out to do (i.e., recognizing and rewarding excellence in non-profit program provision and providing useful, pertinent performance information to assist non-profits to improve service delivery) is questionable (Fraser Institute 2003e).

Alongside the notion of competition, efficiency occupies a prominent place in the business world, and the Performance Index is heavily influenced by the concept of efficiency. The Donner Awards place significant emphasis on efficiency of service delivery. But filling a non-profit role may have little to do with the numbers that provide the handy metric in the business world, as noted by Zimmerman and Dart (1998, 17–18) in their study on charities undertaking commercial ventures. They emphasize, in particular, the temporal differences in approach between the non-profit and business sectors (e.g., long-term vs. short-term). Another simple example would be the many important services for the needy for which there is no prospect of profit. Clients with no capacity to pay may create an important need for non-profit services but create no profit-oriented niche in the market economy. These long-term and wider-view needs, typically serviced by the non-profit sector, may be given less attention if that sector adopts more of a business-like mentality. Zimmerman and Dart (1998) warn:

> If a commercial mentality is essentially based on self-interest, charities undertaking commerce run the inherent risk of losing their focus on the public interest. Also, and at a more macro level, the public risks losing its understanding of the distinct moral metrics of the public and charitable sectors. (18)

Many of the general conclusions reached by Zimmerman and Dart (1998) shed light on business-like approaches to performance evaluation.

Just as undertaking commercial ventures can cause a fundamental shift in the culture of an organization (Zimmerman and Dart 1998, 42), undue attention paid to the Index's individualized 'Confidential Performance Reports' may unnecessarily or unwisely lead to decisions to change the nature of an organization. Before the recommendations implicit in these reports are acted upon, I believe that an organization must first return to its mission, goals, and objectives as a starting point for deciding whether to evolve in the direction pointed to by the Performance Index (Drucker 1990, 87–8; Scheirer 1994, 40; Wholey 1994, 15; Zimmerman and Dart 1998, 42).

5. The Performance Index as an Answer to the 'Measurement Challenge'

The 'Measurement Challenge,' a section of the Wood and Clemens (2002) report, sets out part of the rationale for the development of the Performance Index:

> Unlike the for-profit business sector, the non-profit sector is hampered in its ability to assess performance due to the lack of an objective, quantifiable performance measure. The for-profit sector relies on a number of objective measures to assess performance, including profitability, market share, and return on assets. The existence of standard, objective performance measures in the for-profit sector allows for comprehensive and comparative performance analysis. Unfortunately, there is no such parallel for the non-profit sector ... The performance measurement system developed for the Awards Program represents a major step forward in the ability of non-profit organization managers to assess performance on an objective and quantifiable basis. (9)

The suitability of more quantifiable measures to the non-profit sector, however, is open to question. As Kanter and Summers (1987, 155) contend, non-profits define themselves around their mission or services, not around their financial returns, and it is this 'centrality of social values over financial values' that makes measurement complicated. Similarly, Drucker (1990) notes that 'the results of a non-profit institution are always outside the organization, *not* inside' (81, 107–8; see also Patton 1997, 13). Rather than inward-looking empire-building institutions, non-profits are outward looking in their approach – seeking to effect change pursuant to their particular mission. In other words, the question of whether a non-profit organization is excelling at carrying out its mission will not be conclusively answered by posing questions about the internal workings of the organization. This leads us to the question of whether the Performance Index and the Donner Awards are intended to measure the excellence with which an organization carries out its mission or whether they are intended to measure only the efficiency aspects of performance.

The literature published in conjunction with these awards is somewhat confusing on this point. Different words such as excellence, efficiency, performance, and effectiveness are used to describe the thrust of the initiative (Fraser Institute 2003b, 2003c; Wood and Clemens 2002, 6). There are important differences between, for example, efficiency and effectiveness, as noted by Osborne and Gaebler (1992, 351). The Performance Index's ten areas of measurement (each of which gets equal weight in the final overall performance score) emphasize efficiency measures (cost containment, program spending versus overall spending, size of accumulated surplus relative to expenses, use of volunteers relative to staff, turnover, cost per hour of programming provided, etc.). The areas of measurement include some components that could, in theory, help measure the important outcomes pointed out by Drucker (1990), which relate to mission. In particular, the 'Strategic Management' and 'Outcome Monitoring' areas appear to be good candidates. However, both areas of measurement constitute very rudimentary inquiries into these critical subject matters. Under 'Strategic Management,' five simple questions are asked of the organization (see appendix 5.2), which could honestly be answered in a way that yields high scores even if the type of strategic management that is undertaken is failing to achieve good results. More specifically, it is possible to have a concise mission statement, annual goals, and objectives for programs, staff, and volunteers, a structured mission updating process, and staff involvement in strategic management and goal-setting, but such would not necessarily equate with either effective strategic planning or achievement of desired outcomes. What is being measured is whether strategic management tasks are being carried out, not whether they are being carried out well. Most competent organizations would meet these criteria and, in fact, the annual performance report concludes that a substantial proportion of organizations demonstrate 'superior performance' in this area:

> There were strong performances in all service categories in the area of Strategic Management, with the average and median scores ranging

between 7.8 and 9.9 [out of 10]. Almost one-third of agencies received a score of 10 for Strategic Management, which indicates superior perform-ance. (Wood and Clemens 2002, 21)

While such high scores might indicate 'superior performance' in some circumstances, it is more likely that what is actually being measured is the ease with which an organization can get a high score when such basic indicators of good 'Strategic Management' are used as the evalua-tion tool. This demonstrates the importance of choosing valid indica-tors of performance.

Similar concerns arise in the 'Outcome Monitoring' area of measure-ment, also comprising five simple questions (see appendix 5.2). What the questions measure are not actual outcomes but rather whether out-comes are monitored within an organization. The problem, of course, is that one could diligently monitor outcomes, but fail miserably year after year in reaching them, yet still receive a high score in all five cat-egories. Seemingly oblivious to the effects of having chosen such basic measures of performance, the annual performance report notes:

The scores for Outcome Monitoring are relatively high with the average and median scores for all categories falling in the range of 7.1 to 9.5. This indicates a relatively high level of average performance in terms of man-aging and pursuing outcomes. One-third of all agencies received a score of 9 or 10, which indicated high performance. (Wood and Clemens 2002, 33)

The graphs set out in the annual performance report (Wood and Clemens 2002, 20, 32) confirm that the vast majority of organizations are clustered in the top performance classes for both 'Strategic Management' and 'Outcome Monitoring.' Given the lack of statistical differentiation among organizations in these two areas, they end up having little effect on the overall outcome of which organizations will be considered high performers under the index. The remaining eight areas reveal much greater ranges in performance, and their relative im-pact on the overall comparative results is consequently higher (that is, though each of the ten areas gets equal weight, if some categories yield nearly identical results for all organizations because they are so simple to pass, the relative weight of the other scores thereby increases as they provide better means to differentiate amongst organizations). The re-sult is that these two critical areas of performance ('Strategic Management' and 'Outcome Monitoring') have, mathematically, only a

20 per cent effect (2 out of 10 equally weighted areas in the overall score). Further, their actual impact on which organizations emerge as finalists is likely much lower, because the shallow measures being used are not uncovering critical differences among organizations.

Does the Performance Index simply suffer from asking too easy questions in these critical areas? Should the search begin for better questions that will better reflect good or excellent performance? Better questions will inevitably be context-specific. If other factors were measured, similar to those suggested by Drucker (1990) (e.g., did performance improve, did we put resources in the areas of high results, what percentage of beneficiaries achieved the outcome sought, to what degree was the mission accomplished?), a more informative picture of excellence in these two areas might be painted. Unfortunately, meaningful results could be elusive. Indeed, the reason that such basic measures were chosen for the Performance Index may be that this is all that is common across non-profits in these critical areas of measurement. Delving further might require actually undertaking organization-specific inquiries, but the Performance Index notes that 'the scope for comparison is limited and costly' (Wood and Clemens 2002, 9) in this kind of subjective inquiry. By searching for the common denominator on critical performance issues, the developers of the Index may have inadvertently proved a very key point – that is, that meaningful performance evaluation does not lend itself to a simple one-size-fits-all recipe based on a few basic measures, which, on their own, may have little correlation with those organizations that perform their missions well.

It is the vast area of context and mission-specific questions that will likely reveal more about performance. To ask these types of questions, one would have to abandon the 'common denominator' approach. This is not to say that quantitative approaches are to be avoided. Both quantitative and qualitative approaches have an important place in evaluation (Patton 1997, 273–7). Rather, rigorous performance evaluation, whether quantitative or not, will require approaches tailored to the organization's mission and its many constituencies. Indeed, mission-driven, context-specific performance evaluation questions can still be quantitative, as Drucker (1990, 107–8) notes. Yet it is difficult to conceive of any overarching generic questions that will accurately gauge performance and be applicable across a wide range of non-profit organizations. The common denominators that might emerge, such as 'for the public or common good' or 'for the public trust' yield no measurable metric that can be used across the entire sector.

In essence, with the Performance Index, non-profits embark on a journey (towards finding the common, objective measure of non-profit excellence) whose destination might not exist. Its proponents can assert that 'until now' the non-profit sector has been 'hampered in its ability to assess performance due to the lack of an objective, quantifiable performance measure' and that the index 'represents a major step forward in the ability of non-profit organization managers to assess performance on an objective and quantifiable basis' (Wood and Clemens 2002, 9). But alas, it is only an assertion – strongly stated but without much evidence.

The question then remains: What does the Performance Index measure? Is it possible that aspects of the model are worth retaining? The Performance Index may assist in measuring efficiencies and financial performance, two areas that are critical to high performance in the business world. Many of the criteria would help an organization gauge its financial stability, its growth, its efficient use of staff, volunteers, resources, and so on, and lend themselves to easily quantifiable measures. If one accepts the assumptions behind the standards set, one can judge performance in some of these areas. For example, if one agrees with the proposition that the 'optimal size of the accumulated surplus is equal to one year's annual expenses' (Wood and Clemens 2002, 19), the index will assist in evaluating performance towards that goal. Of course, it is far from certain that each non-profit organization should accept that this is the optimal situation for itself. Circumstances vary, and in some cases non-profits may rightly choose to adopt a high discount rate and to spend an accumulated surplus (for instance, when an unusual opportunity to help fulfil its mission arises). Nevertheless, as long as non-profits are aware of the assumptions underlying some of the simple measures in the Performance Index and check their validity against their current circumstances, some of these measures may be helpful in improving efficiency, financial management, and so on in the organization. They may be useful in a targeted way.

Even so, this generalized approach and the assumptions that underlie it are open to question. For example, the Index examines sources and concentration of revenue, in particular with respect to government sources, and in so doing assumes both that long-term funding stability is necessary and that reliance on government funding runs contrary to this goal. These assumptions may be questionable, however, for many non-profits.

First, with regard to government funding, while at the macro level in recent times in Canada, government funding of many non-profits has not been stable, it has been stable or increasing for others. Why should the latter organizations be penalized in the Performance Index simply because their individual circumstances are not reflective of the general trend? Indeed, for them, it is possible that long-term stability is better achieved through government funding than through other sources. The Index's approach to government funding is very much in line with the Fraser Institute's desired state of affairs of less government spending. It is an open question as to whether the Index was intentionally designed to cause organizations to evolve and adapt to such an environment. But insofar as the model singles out unstable government funding, and not unstable funding generally, it leaves itself open to criticism that its assumptions may be ideologically driven (i.e., towards lower government spending) instead of logically driven to penalize all types of unstable sources.

Second, the assumption that unstable sources (including government sources and others) are not worth pursuing is questionable as well. If an organization is cognizant of the instability of certain sources, it can pursue them but be on the ready to live without them as well. Planning and living with many uncertain sources may in the aggregate allow the organization to better fulfil its mission than relying on smaller stable sources. Yet those organizations that pursue unstable sources of revenue (such as some government sources) and plan accordingly will be penalized under the Performance Index. Further, since this measure looks at the total amount of revenue from all levels of government, an organization that is funded by many different types of government agencies would be penalized, even though it would be very unlikely that its entire portfolio of government funders would dry up simultaneously. While such an organization would be rewarded for having a diversified income portfolio, it would be penalized under the government funding criterion.

6. The Evaluation Purposes of the Index and Awards: Judgment and Improvement

The importance of the evaluation design to the intended users is underscored when an evaluation also includes an improvement facilitation purpose (Wholey 1994, 17), as the Performance Index explicitly intends. These 'formative'-type goals (as opposed to 'summative' goals that render judgment) focus 'on ways of improving and enhancing programs' (Patton 1997, 67). The Fraser Institute was ambitious in trying to satisfy equally these two very different types of purposes, given the different characteristics of each type of evaluation. As Patton (1997) explains: 'Using evaluation results to improve a program turns out, in practice, to be fundamentally different from rendering judgment about overall effectiveness, merit, or worth' (68).

While attempting to satisfy both types of purposes, this particular evaluation tool is notably weighted more towards the judgment-oriented approach. And yet it is far from evident that the judgment-oriented aspects of the evaluation protocol have employed defensible and supported criteria. Indeed, the criteria are notably lacking in the critical results-based measurements that would be needed to render judgment about whether services were in fact delivered with excellence. The critical questions of how the life circumstances of beneficiaries changed as a result of the service that was delivered, and how well the organization's mission was carried out vis-à-vis those beneficiaries go unanswered in the evaluation.

The Performance Index and Donner Awards suffer from two key design weaknesses vis-à-vis their stated purposes of recognizing and rewarding excellence and providing information to improve operations. First, the program shows little evidence of having chosen criteria that are direct indicators of excellence in service delivery or of having employed criteria that are broadly supported by users other than the program's proponents and those organizations that succeed in obtaining an award. Second, the program fails to include nearly all the approaches typical of evaluations intended to improve operations as discussed by Patton (1997, 68–70). It is rigid and judgment-oriented and focuses on providing direction on how an organization can improve in the next year's judgment-rendering exercise. This tends to create an incentive for non-profit users to manage for the indicators of success rather than managing for actual results. This is especially true in the design of this particular evaluation protocol since the two components that may provide some guidance on managing for actual results ('Strategic Management' and 'Outcome Monitoring') are too simplistic to provide meaningful organization-specific guidance. Table 5.1 summarizes what I see as the main deficiencies in the Performance Index.

We now turn to a consideration of the practical implications for non-profit organizations.

Table 5.1
Key Deficiencies of the Performance Index

- Its one-size-fits-all approach, which compares and ranks performance across organizations, is not adapted to the diversity of missions in the non-profit sector.
- It focuses on efficiency and process, with little emphasis on actual service delivery effectiveness or outcomes.
- It may cause users to manage for performance indicators in order to improve their score for the awards rather than to manage directly for excellence in accomplishing the organizational mission.
- It makes unsubstantiated claims to objectivity and claims not to rank non-profits against an imposed standard.
- Its emphasis on simple, quantifiable measures leads to superficial assessment in key areas like strategic management and outcome monitoring.
- Through its desire to encourage non-profits to be more business-like, the Index appeals to values that are often at odds with the charitable activities and the public interest outlook of many non-profits.

---

7. Implications for Non-Profit Organizations

The Donner Awards typically receive hundreds of applications and have enjoyed the credibility associated with having the awards given out by the Lieutenant Governor of Ontario each year. Award recipients have also received, for example, positive coverage in the media and recognition in the Hansard of legislatures. As well, according to the testimonials from non-profits provided by the Fraser Institute, the Performance Index is having a direct impact on these organizations and the funding community (Fraser Institute 2003a).

As well, the Donner Canadian Foundation has made it clear that it hopes the Awards will attain greater currency. The proponents hope to have an effect on other funders by providing 'a useful tool for corporations, foundations and individuals to evaluate the organizations competing for their charitable dollars' (Fraser Institute 2003e, 1). Indeed, the performance report profiles many non-profits that have performed well in the Awards Program and includes detailed information on each organization, presumably to affect, in part, the decisions of other funders (Wood and Clemens 2002, 39–78).

Given the intended influence of the Index and Donner Awards on the decisions of non-profits and funders, it is critical that the approach benefit these intended users. The evaluation must be designed so that it exerts a positive influence on the evolution of the non-profit organizations being evaluated. The difficulty, however, is that what is to be considered positive will very much depend on the individual characteristics of each non-profit organization. The nature of one non-profit organization may lend itself to adding more volunteers, reducing government funding, having a substantial accumulated surplus, and so on, but for many others, this may not be the case. By generalizing what it means to be doing well, the model misses the mark on what is most important to every non-profit organization: whether the decision will improve its ability to carry out its specific mission.

If organizations do not keep these questions in mind and too easily adopt the blunt and simple evaluation instrument offered by the Performance Index, they may embark on a series of changes to improve their performance according to the index's methods. Evolution can happen very quickly in an organization, if it explicitly embarks on a new path. If the index gets widespread support (in this case perhaps because of the lack of any other allegedly comprehensive, quantitative non-profit evaluation tool as a competitive force), rapid changes to participating non-profits may occur. But will they be more adapted to their overall environment, or just more fit to the micro-environment of an artificial breeder?

I believe that a diversity of approaches is preferable – that non-profits explore a range of evaluation tools and employ those that are best suited to their circumstances and able to provide guidance on better accomplishing missions. There is no single sequential path like the Performance Index that is suitable for all organizations to follow. As Gould (1977) notes in describing humankind's place in the process of evolution: '*Homo sapiens* is not the foreordained product of a ladder that was reaching toward our exalted estate from the start. We are merely the surviving branch of a once luxuriant bush' (62). The danger of having only one artificial breeder acting as the evaluation environment is that we would lose the diversity of the non-profit 'bush' and evolve towards a monocultural approach, under the mistaken notion that the 'ladder' will lead us to the promised land. But if we have a range of evaluative tools, each acting as a different selective force on different organizations, diversity might be retained or fostered.

I agree with Zimmerman and Dart (1998, 11–13) that, at a minimum, diversity is needed across the societal sectors and within the non-profit sector. The question is how that diversity within the non-profit sector might be affected by the use of one dominant tool for quantitative evaluation.

The quantifiable aspects inherent in business models make them attractive to many audiences. Zimmerman and Dart (1998) put it this way:

> Part of the appeal of commerce is the tidiness of the models. There are excellent measurement tools, evaluation tools and decision models within the market framework. We have not put the same effort into developing alternative measurement concepts, language or evaluation concepts for community or public good actions. (45)

Will these alternatives ever be developed? If an equivalent approach could be found that succeeded in effectively evaluating non-profit performance, it would be inappropriate to reject it simply because it shared some similarities with business models. However, I doubt whether simple common denominators like profit or return on investment have analogues waiting to be found in the non-profit sector. The non-profit sector is so diverse that the evaluative tools that could be seen to be transferable sector-wide could only be very general in nature. The search for very specific quantifiable tools is probably one that should be undertaken only at the organizational or subsectoral level (i.e., within a group of similarly situated organizations) for the tools to be meaningful and appropriate for their contexts.

Part of the answer may lie in the words we use to describe the sectors themselves. One sector is the profit sector, the other non-profit. The former is incredibly diverse, of course, but shares the common thread of making a profit, which is quantifiable (though I admit that performance evaluation is not, therefore, 'easy' in the for-profit sector). The latter is the non-profit sector, which by definition can encompass almost anything else. Can this residual 'anything else' be characterized by any common thread or common denominator? I would argue that the sector does share a common thread (e.g., seeking the betterment of society) but that this very general common thread is neither amenable to a common metric nor even amenable to a common definition. Indeed, the missions of two non-profits could have polar opposite goals because the members being represented or the constituency being served hold opposite views of what constitutes the betterment of society. One of the consequences of a heterogeneous society and social relativism is that different groups may have completely different concepts of 'what constitutes the good life' (Evernden 1992, 5–6). Just as there is a diversity of views about what standards of excellence should be striven for at the individual level, so too is there a diversity across non-profits. So long as that diversity persists, the one-size-fits-all non-profit excellence evaluation tool will never be found, because it will not exist.

8. Adapting Evaluation to an Organization's Environment

On the subject of performance evaluation for non-profits, I would like to suggest a path that is more similar to Gould's branching bush than to a ladder. Different evaluation questions should be posed for different branches (sub-sectors) within the non-profit field. By knowing what adaptations are potentially useful to their specific missions, organizations can try to evolve and better adapt to the circumstances within which they are embedded. Patton's (1997) repeated focus on making evaluation useful for the intended users is especially apt in this context: 'Utilization-focused evaluation is a problem-solving approach that calls for creative adaptation to changed and changing conditions, as opposed to a technical approach, which attempts to mold and define conditions to fit preconceived models of how things should be done' (131–3).

Patton's (1997, 135) general call for more 'situational responsiveness' fits well with a more context-specific and mission-driven approach to non-profit performance evaluation. Patton goes on to state that part of being situationally responsive includes being respectful of the stakeholders by not intimidating or manipulating intended users (137–8). The Performance Index points the way along the 'business-like' ladder, without ever acknowledging that businesses are just as susceptible to failure or underperformance, even with their objective measures of profit. What makes a particular business prosper has little to do with the availability of a common denominator like profit, but everything to do with its specific strengths and weaknesses in relation to the particular market environment in which it is acting (which makes performance evaluation in the for-profit sector much more involved than simply looking at profit margins). These important, context-specific matters are left out entirely from the Performance Index and enter into the equation only for the handful of organizations that score high and are eligible for the final stage of the Donner Awards process, during which essay questions are posed and letters of support provided (Wood and Clemens 2002, 7).

In his call for useful evaluations, Patton (1997) discusses the standards developed by the Joint Committee on Standards for Education

Evaluation: utility, feasibility, propriety, and accuracy. He concludes: 'Implementation of a utility-focused, feasibility-conscious, propriety-oriented, and accuracy-based evaluation requires situational responsiveness, methodological flexibility, multiple evaluator roles, political sophistication, and substantial doses of creativity, all elements of utilization-focused evaluation' (16–17). The Performance Index lacks many of these characteristics.

While I can offer no simple alternative to the Performance Index for non-profits, I agree that testing performance remains a key task to be undertaken, for performance 'is the ultimate test of any institution [and] every non-profit institution exists for the sake of performance in changing people and society' (Drucker 1990, 107). Finding or creating evaluation tools that help to measure just that – how an organization's actions have effected real change – is what is needed. For each organization, fashioning such a tool should not be exceedingly difficult, though for the long-term goals included in some missions, very long time horizons may be involved, making evaluation challenging.

Returning to Drucker's (1990) notion of focusing on the outside rather than the inside, it makes sense to look at what change is occurring as a result of the non-profit organization's performance:

> The non-profits are human-change agents. And their results are therefore always a change in people – in their behavior, in their circumstances, in their vision, in their health, in their hopes, above all in their competence and capacity. The non-profit institution therefore needs to set specific goals in terms of its *service* to people. (85)

This outward-looking perspective nests well within mission-driven approaches. As Drucker notes (1990, 87–8, 108–9), the mission of non-profits is not simply to build a well-run non-profit organization, but to build a better society. In addition, performance measurement needs to be cognizant of the many constituencies at play (funders, donors, clients, the public, etc.) (Hall et al. 2003, 1; Kanter and Summers 1987, 164). Because, for example, most non-profits have very different stakeholders when it comes to funders and beneficiaries (except in commercial fee-for-service areas), it is important to demonstrate performance to funders and the broader public. Non-profits, especially charities, are given certain privileges (such as those relating to taxation and charitable tax receipts), and that means that members of the public (through government but not exclusively) need to be able to gauge performance if interested in doing so. The diversity within the sector makes such communication difficult, and as a result there will always be those that state that the sector is therefore unaccountable. In truth, the sector is not defined by an obvious quantifiable common measure, but a non-profit organization can still be accountable by establishing a mission that provides a public benefit, carrying it out well, and providing evidence that it is doing so through performance measures that are appropriate to it.

Organizational change is clearly a matter of choice. In many ways, it is about deciding how to evolve, or more passively, how to be bred and moulded by others. While acknowledging the risks of pushing the Darwinian metaphor perhaps too far, I submit that adopting diverse mission-driven evaluation processes is a more *natural* fit to the non-profit setting than the one-size-fits-all business-like approach advocated by the Performance Index.

ACKNOWLEDGMENTS

I wish to thank the late Bruce Miller and my other colleagues in the McGill-McConnell Team Integrative Project (Shawn Bayes, Karen Flannery, Marc Johnson, and Valerie Wilder), whose collective idea it was to critically analyse the Performance Index as a group project. In the course of preparing our team report and presentation, they developed many of the insights that I present herein. I also wish to thank Anne Bell, Fred Bird, Michael Quinn Patton, Janice Gross Stein, Frances Westley, Brenda Zimmerman, and the *Canadian Journal of Program Evaluation*'s anonymous reviewers.

Appendix 5.1
Components of Performance Measurement in the Performance Index

SOURCE: Wood and Clemens 2002, 10–11, used with permission of the Fraser Institute. See www.fraserinstitute.ca for more information on the awards program.

Area of Measurement and Components

1. Financial Management
- annual surplus – composite measure of the 4 year average and most recent year
- revenue increase – composite measure of the 3 year average and most recent year
- cost containment – composite measure of the 3 year average and most recent year
- program spending versus overall spending – composite measure of the 4 year average and most recent year
- financial reporting

2. Income Independence
- number of sources of income adjusted for the average size of the donation
- percentage of revenue provided by largest revenue source
- percentage of revenue provided by government
- size of accumulated surplus relative to expenses – composite measure of the 4 year average and most recent year

3. Strategic Management
- use and prevalence of a mission statement
- level of objective and goal setting
- depth of involvement

4. Board Governance
- independence
- financial contributions
- level of involvement as measured by frequency of meetings
- level of participation as measured by attendance at meetings
- policy guidelines to avoid conflicts of interest

5. Volunteers
- use of volunteers relative to staff – composite measure of agency total and program total
- recruiting activities
- management and development of volunteers
- donations other than time by volunteers
- turnover

6. Staff
- level of programming provided by employees
- percentage of employees working in programs
- turnover
- management and development of staff

7. Innovation
- uniqueness of agency's program
- level of restructuring/ change
- use of alternative delivery systems/ technology in the delivery of services

8. Program Cost
- cost per hour of programming provided
- cost per client – *information only*
- hours per client – *information only*

9. Outcome Monitoring
- defining desired outcomes/ goals for program
- measured actual outcomes
- desired versus actual outcome comparisons
- plans to deal with divergences

10. Accessibility
- process of assessing need and targeting assistance
- measurement of the level of usage by clients
- determination of the cause of a client's difficulties

OVERALL SCORE Composite of ten areas of measurement

Appendix 5.2
2003 Application Form for the Donner Canadian Foundation Awards for Excellence in the Delivery of Social Services

---

SOURCE: Fraser Institute 2003d, used with permission of the Fraser Institute. See www.fraserinstitute.ca for more information on the awards program.

SECTION ONE: AGENCY INFORMATION (Source of information: Whole agency)

1 a)   Name of Organization _____

1 b)   Street Address, Postal Box _____

1 c)   City, Province, Postal Code _____

1 d)   Phone Number (_____)_____ Fax Number (_____)_____

1 e)   E-Mail / Web Site _____

1 f)   Contact Person _____ Title _____

1 g)   Year Organization (Local) was Founded _____

1 h)   Indicate the program area **(one only)** to which your organization is applying for recognition

(see category definitions in the Guide).

- Child Care Services
- Alternative Education
- Provision of Basic Necessities
- Crisis Intervention
- Traditional Education
- Services for People with Disabilities
- Counselling Services
- Prevention and Treatment of Substance Abuse
- Services for Seniors

SECTION TWO: FINANCIAL MANAGEMENT (Source of information: Whole agency)

2 a)   **INCOME STATEMENT**. Please complete the following tables using the **four** most recent years available. (Revenue and expenditure information should be available in your agency's income statement.)

Most Recent Year	Previous Year	2 Years Previous	3 Years Previous

     (i)   Total Revenue ($)
     (ii) Total Expenses ($)
     (iii) Total Program Spending ($)
     (iv) Total Non-Program Spending ($)
     NOTE: (iii) plus (iv) should approximately equal (ii)

2 b) **BALANCE SHEET INFORMATION**. Please complete the following table using the **four** most recent years available. (All information should be available in your agency's balance sheet.)

Most Recent Year	Previous Year	2 Years Previous	3 Years Previous

     (i)   Total Assets ($)
     (ii) Total Liabilities ($)
     (iii) Accumulated Surplus/Deficit or Fund Balance ($)
     NOTE: (ii) plus (iii) should approximately equal (i)

2 c) To what extent does your agency regularly report its financial performance to its members and donors? *(Please use a scale of 1 to 10, where 1 = No Reporting and 10 = Detailed Periodic Reporting Beyond the Annual Report)* _____ (#)

2 d) Are your agency's financial statements either 'audited' or 'prepared under review engagement'?
(circle one) Yes / No

SECTION THREE: INCOME INDEPENDENCE (Source of information: Whole agency)

3 a) How many separate sources of revenue does your agency maintain?
_____ (#)

3 b) What percentage of your operating revenue is provided by your single largest revenue source? _____ (%)

3 c) What percentage of your agency's operating revenue is provided by government sources? Include all levels of government. _____ (%)

SECTION FOUR: STRATEGIC MANAGEMENT (Source of information: Whole agency)

4 a) To what extent does your organization have a clear, concise statement of purpose that is on display and known by staff, volunteers, and clients – commonly referred to as a mission statement? *(Please use a scale of 1 to 10, where 1 = No Statement and 10 = Concise, Written Statement)* _____ (#)

4 b) Does your agency establish, on the basis of the mission statement, annual goals and objectives for: (circle one)
     (i)   programs? Yes / No
     (ii) staff? Yes / No
     (iii) volunteers? Yes / No

4 c) To what extent is there an annual process for updating the mission statement and consideration of its appropriateness in the face of changes in the environment, the clients, and/or community needs? *(Please use a scale of 1 to 10, where 1 = No Process and 10 = Frequent Structured Process)* _____ (#)

4 d)   What percentage of the program staff, managers and senior support staff are involved in the strategic management process? _____ (%)

4 e)   To what extent are the staff mentioned in question 4 d) involved in the setting of goals and objectives? *(Please use a scale of 1 to 10, where 1 = No Participation and 10 = High Participation)* _____ (#)

SECTION FIVE: BOARD GOVERNANCE (Source of information: Whole agency)

5 a)   What percentage of voting board members are also employed staff members? _____ (%)

5 b)   What percentage of board members are also financial contributors? _____ (%)

5 c)   How many times did the Board of Directors (or the executive committee) meet last year? _____ (#)

5 d)   As a percentage, what was the average attendance of Board members at Board of Director meetings (or the executive committee) throughout the last year? _____ (%)

5 e)   To what extent does your organization have policy guidelines in place to avoid conflicts of interest involving Board or staff members? *(Please use a scale of 1 to 10, where 1 = No Policy Guidelines and 10 = Formal, Documented Policy Guidelines)* _____ (#)

SECTION SIX: VOLUNTEERS (Source of information: Whole agency)

6 a)   How many full-time-equivalent (F.T.E.) volunteers does your agency have in total? _____ (#)

6 b)   To what extent are volunteers screened for eligibility? *(Please use a scale of 1 to 10, where 1 = No Screening and 10 = Detailed Screening Process Including Reference Checks)* _____ (#)

6 c)   To what extent are volunteers assessed for job allocation? *(Please use a scale of 1 to 10, where 1 = No Assessment and 10 = Detailed Initial Assessment and Ongoing Reassessment)* _____ (#)

6 d)   To what extent does your agency have a volunteer training program in place? *(Please use a scale of 1 to 10, where 1 = No Training Program and 10 = Ongoing Training Program)* _____ (#)

6 e)   To what extent does your agency have a regular evaluation process in place for volunteers? *(Please use a scale of 1 to 10, where 1 = No Evaluation Process and 10 = Detailed Periodic Evaluation Process, Beyond an Annual Evaluation Process)* _____ (#)

6 f)   To what extent does your agency attempt to recruit **eligible** past adult clientele for volunteering? *(Please use a scale of 1 to 10, where 1 = No Attempt Made and 10 = Actively Promotes Volunteering to Eligible Past Clientele)* _____ (#)

6 g)   What percentage of your agency's **eligible** adult clientele is asked to volunteer? _____ (%)

6 h)   What percentage of your agency's volunteers donated money or goods and services in-kind, in addition to the donation of their time? _____ (%)

6 i)   What was the percentage turnover of your agency's volunteers in the previous year? _____ (%)

SECTION SEVEN: STAFF (Source of information: Whole agency)

7 a)   How many full-time-equivalent (F.T.E.) staff does your agency have in total? _____ (#)

7 b)   What percentage of the total full-time equivalent agency staff work primarily in the delivery of all programs? _____ (%)

7 c)   What was the percentage turnover of your agency's **total staff** in the previous year? _____ (%)

7 d)   What was the percentage turnover of your agency's **total program staff** in the previous year? _____ (%)

7 e)   To what extent are staff regularly evaluated? *(Please use a scale of 1 to 10, where 1 = No Evaluation Process and 10 = Detailed Periodic Evaluation Process, Beyond an Annual Evaluation Process)* _____ (#)

7 f)   To what extent does your agency maintain a formal hiring process? *(Please use a scale of 1 to 10, where 1 = No Formal Hiring Process and 10 = Extensive, Formalized Hiring Process)* _____ (#)

7 g)   To what extent does your agency have a staff training program in place? *(Please use a scale of 1 to 10, where 1 = No Training Program and 10 = Ongoing Training Program)* _____ (#)

SECTION EIGHT: PROGRAM COST & PROFILE (Source of information: Program)

8 a)   Name of the program being submitted for recognition: _____

8 b)   Started in: _____ (Year)

8 c)   Total cost of the program in the most recent year of operations: $ _____

8 d)   Number of full-time equivalent (F.T.E.) volunteers involved in the program: _____ (#)

8 e)   Number of full-time equivalent (F.T.E.) staff involved in the program: _____ (#)

8 f)   Number of clients served in the most recent year: _____ (#)

8 g)   Number of program hours (or units for the Provision of Basic Necessities category) provided in the most recent year by the program applying for recognition: _____ (#)

SECTION NINE: INNOVATION (Source of information: Program; Questions 9e and 9f: Whole agency)

9 a)   To what extent does the government provide or finance programs in your community similar to the one your agency offers? *(Please use a scale of 1 to 10, where 1 = No Level of Provision or Financing and 10 = High Level of Parallel Provision or Financing)* _____ (#)

9 b)   To what extent does your agency's program resemble similar programs in your community? *(Please use a scale of 1 to 10, where 1 = High Level of Similarity and 10 = Completely Unique)* _____ (#)

9 c)   What percentage of your current program was considered for restructuring or changing in the last year in order to improve the program? _____ (%)

9 d)   What percentage of your current program was actually restructured or changed in the last year in order to improve the program? _____ (%)

9 e)   To what extent (percentage) are computers and similar technology incorporated in your agency's operations? Include both non-program and program functions. _____ (%)

9 f)   If an innovation in your program has been implemented in the last year, what approximate percentage of the whole agency's operations was affected by the innovation? _____ (%)

ONLY EDUCATIONAL SERVICES AND CHILD CARE PROVIDERS SHOULD ANSWER QUESTION 9 G). ALL OTHER AGENCIES PLEASE SKIP QUESTION 9 G).

9 g)   To what extent (percentage) are computers and similar technology incorporated in the delivery of your agency's program? _____ (%)

SECTION TEN: OUTCOME MONITORING (Source of information: Program)

10a)   To what extent has your organization defined the desired outcomes for the program? That is, what it is that the program is attempting to achieve? *(Please use a scale of 1 to 10, where 1 = No Desired Outcomes Defined and 10 = Detailed Statement of Desired Outcomes)* _____ (#)

10b)   Given the program's desired outcomes, what type of assessment is made of the actual outcomes? *(Please use a scale of 1 to 10, where 1 = No Measurement of Actual Outcomes and 10 = Formal, Documented Assessment)* _____ (#)

10c)   How often does your agency compare the actual outcomes [question 10 b)] against the desired outcomes [question 10 a)] of its programs? *(Please use a scale of 1 to 10, where 1 = No Comparison Made and 10 = Regular, Documented Comparisons)* _____ (#)

10d)   To what extent is there a process for dealing with differences between the actual and the desired outcomes? *(Please use a scale of 1 to 10, where 1 = No Process Defined and 10 = Documented Periodic Process, Including Action Plans, Monitoring, and Follow-Up)* _____ (#)

10e)   To what extent does your agency attempt to track past clientele for progress? *(Please use a scale of 1 to 10, where 1 = No Attempt to Track Past Clientele and 10 = Regular, Documented Tracking)* _____ (#)

SECTION ELEVEN: ACCESSIBILITY (Source of information: Program)

11a)   To what extent does your agency restrict the receipt of services based on an assessment of need? *(Please use a scale of 1 to 10, where 1 = No Restrictions and 10 = Restrictions Applied According to a Standardized Process of Needs Assessment)* _____ (#)

EDUCATIONAL SERVICES AND CHILD CARE SERVICES SKIP QUESTIONS 11 B) TO 11 D).

11b) To what extent does your organization attempt to ascertain the cause of a client's present circumstance? *(Please use a scale of 1 to 10, where 1 = No Inquiry and 10 = Detailed Inquiry)* _____ (#)

11c) To what extent does your agency measure the frequency of usage by clients? *(Please use a scale of 1 to 10, where 1 = None and 10 = High)* _____ (#)

SERVICES FOR SENIORS AND SERVICES FOR PEOPLE WITH DISABILITIES SKIP QUESTION 11 D).

11d) To what extent does your agency restrict access to services based on the frequency of usage? *(Please use a scale of 1 to 10, where 1 = No Restrictions and 10 = High)* _____ (#)

11e) To what extent does your agency charge a fee for use of its services? *(Please use a scale of 1 to 10, where 1 = No Fee Charged, 5= Flat Fee Charged and 10 = Fee Charged that is Geared to Client Income (Adjusted Based on Income Levels))* _____ (#)

END OF APPLICATION

6 Renewal of a Youth-Serving Organization: Lessons and Stories Shared through an Ecocycle Metaphor

MARC LANGLOIS

Organizations are open and living systems that naturally cycle and change. With that in mind, the entrepreneurial dream of one continuous upward climb to organizational health and prosperity is unrealistic. Setbacks, crises, and conflicts are bound to occur. Parts die off and new parts emerge. Attempts to suppress crisis only create more setbacks and hold the system back from reaching new heights. After a time, organizations reach a stage of maturity, when the chief preoccupation is to manage the existing systems rather than attempt new beginnings. Energy stagnates and routines predominate. Such organizations are in need of renewal. But is renewal possible – and if so, how?

This essay reviews my experience as the co-founder and executive director of a youth-serving organization (YSO) called HeartWood, as it went through its own challenges of maturity and processes of renewal. Examples and comparisons are also drawn from the field, in particular with Scouts Canada, one of the longest-established leaders in the youth sector.

Two core organizational principles and two program strategies are presented as central to guiding an organization through its next level of development. The ideas in this essay are presented with the help of a theoretical framework communicated metaphorically in terms of the ecocycle in naturally occurring systems.

1. Why a Comparison between HeartWood and Scouts Canada?

Established in Halifax, Nova Scotia, in 1989, the HeartWood Centre for Community Youth Development promotes and supports young people as community builders. To generate lasting personal and community changes, the organization acts as an intermediary on multiple levels with youth, adults, community organizations, institutions, and government. Locally and nationally, its activities include leadership development, organizational development, community development, professional development, forums, and research. Over more than seventeen years, HeartWood has grown to be recognized as one of the most innovative organizations in Canada working to engage youth in building stronger communities. HeartWood has now developed a Community Youth Development Model that draws together practices of youth development with those of community development.

Robert Baden-Powell (1857–1914) founded the Scouts organization one hundred years ago with a desire to improve society (World Scouts Bureau 1998). This was a goal he believed could only be achieved by improving the individuals in society. This proud organization has made a significant imprint on the youth development sector and has had a positive impact on the lives of thousands of young people in Canada. Internationally, the organization has reached 28 million young people and adults, boys and girls, in 216 countries and territories, 212,000 of these in Canada.

Today, Scouts Canada is struggling through its maturity. Unless dramatic changes are made, the current membership downturn points to Scouts Canada disappearing from significance in the youth sector in the foreseeable future. It would by a great loss for the youth of this country and the youth sector, a loss that I maintain could be avoided. It is not any one thing that has gone wrong at the Scouts, nor are the factors involved unique to this organization.

HeartWood's vision and culture have been described by a senior Scouter as being similar to the vision and culture of the Scouting movement in its earliest days. Both the Scouts and HeartWood were founded on principles of self-development and incorporate practices of outdoor adventure and service to others.

In this essay, I draw comparisons between management practices at HeartWood and the Scouts organization, in the hope of shedding light on the circumstances in which problems of organizational maturity surface and how they might be managed. I offer the comparison with respect for the greatness the Scouts organization has achieved and with recognition of what a younger organization with some shared values might offer by way of lessons at a time when renewal is called for.

Though HeartWood has faced its share of challenges in efforts at renewal, it was able to adapt, learn, and move forward at a pace that the

Scouts, and other larger organizations with long histories, find more difficult to achieve.

2. The Adaptive Cycle

A friend of mine practices ecoforestry,[1] in a beautiful and diverse 200-acre area along the LaHave River on Nova Scotia's South Shore. Ecoforestry follows a set of practices sensitive to the natural rhythms of the forest, with an eye to the sustainability of the forest and forestry business. A walk with my friend through the forest can teach me a great deal about how to 'manage' a system naturally. He follows a strict practice of 'letting things be,' not suppressing, not directing. While keeping his eye on individual trees ready for harvest, his selection is inextricably tied to his knowledge and appreciation of the forest as a whole system. His practices can teach us a great deal about managing the complexity that surrounds the YSO, and serves as an apt introduction to the ideas highlighted by the Adaptive Cycle.

C.S. Holling led an international group of ecologists, economists, social scientists, and mathematicians through a five-year collaboration that led to the development of the theoretical framework referred to as the Adaptive Cycle (Holling 2001). I apply their work as an aid in analysing and communicating how a youth-serving organization might aptly respond to a call for renewal.

Like the forest, an organization experiences many natural life cycles: change is constant; balance is not a static state. Recognizing this cycling suggests a framework in which to consider what types of intervention to undertake, and at what point in the organization's development it might be most receptive or vulnerable to such interventions – including what the organization might be willing to destroy deliberately in order to begin a renewal process.

The work of the Adaptive Cycle is communicated through a natural systems metaphor. Organizational change dynamics are categorized in the four phases of an ecocycle: Birth (exploitation), Maturity (conservation), Creative Destruction, and Renewal (mobilization). The Creative Destruction and Renewal phases of the cycle are referred to as the 'back-loop' (indicated by a perforated line in figure 6.1).

The Adaptive Cycle does not suggest that an organization ought to be in one phase or another at any given time. On the contrary, Holling advocates that a healthy organization, like a healthy forest ecosystem, must operate in all phases simultaneously – a concept known as 'patch

FIGURE 6.1
The adaptive cycle

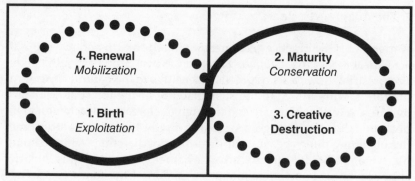

4. Renewal
Mobilization

2. Maturity
Conservation

1. Birth
Exploitation

3. Creative
Destruction

Source: Holling (2001)

dynamics' (Zimmerman, Lindberg, and Plsek 1998, 175). As in a forest, it is the characteristics of the patch dynamics that reflect a resilient organization. It is to the detriment of the organization and the forest alike to rely too heavily on any one management practice or service, thereby limiting unnecessarily one's response to the diversity and the resilience of the whole system.

The back-loop cycle represents the greatest potential and the most intriguing dynamics for change. This is the cycle managers know the least about and fear the most. It is characterized by chaos, uncertainty, and anticipation. It stirs emotions that range from fun and excitement to fear and frustration. The back-loop progresses much more quickly than the slow and more deliberate growth of the front-loop (Birth to Maturity). Since these two phases of the Adaptive Cycle hold the greatest opportunity for progressive change, the focus of this essay is on back-loop strategies and ideas relevant to YSOs.

3. Packing for the Back-loop Journey

Two principles were central to HeartWood's own successful renewal: youth inclusion and empowering leadership. Both principles were alive in a set of organizational and community practices. Being aware of these principles enabled HeartWood to maximize its human resources and remain 'nimble' during its transition. These two principles lay the foundation for my discussion of how a YSO can successfully navigate through the back-loop journey to a place of renewal.

Youth inclusion

Ironically, in public and private youth-serving agencies, there is seldom any real input from young people into the programs and services designed to serve them. In YSOs, as in the larger society, decision-making primarily rests with adults. Traditionally, these organizations have done things for young people, rather than actually working with them. Though this is the accepted modus operandi, when you consider that the mandate of most YSOs ultimately is their clients' empowerment, the standard begs questioning. Not to involve young people in decision-making within the organization is, at best, a missed opportunity and, one could argue, hypocritical.

The impact of youth inclusion for a YSO can be profound. Not only does the inclusion of youth in decision-making roles improve operational effectiveness but also client services inevitably become more relevant. The majority of YSOs have a mandate related to the empowerment of young people – to help them feel needed, worthy, and able to contribute to society. Child welfare, youth justice, homelessness, education, employment opportunities – whatever the YSO's primary focus, the opportunities to provide empowering experiences within the organization are plentiful. Robert Greenleaf's ideas on 'servant leadership'[2] are instructive here. In describing the ideal exchange between agency and client, Greenleaf (1991) says that 'the first order of business is to build a group of people who, under the influence of the institution, grow taller and become healthier, stronger, more autonomous'(30).

The challenge Greenleaf puts forth is a worthy one for the youth sector. Unfortunately, it is far too common that youth-serving institutions, agencies, and organizations that unintentionally leave young people with whom they interact feeling less rather than more empowered from those interactions.

One young HeartWood staff member, who after years in the 'care' of a child welfare system moved out on his own, describes it this way:

It's like I was in a box with boundaries all around me. I stopped thinking for myself, and I lost touch with what is important to me. It became about what other people needed or wanted from me. I started to feel powerless, like I could do nothing right anymore. When I did speak up to express my needs and wants, nobody heard me. I find it so ironic that this service existed to support me, yet I was the one that had to accommodate their needs, constraints, and polices.[3]

Young people involved as staff and volunteers at various levels of an institution, agency, or organization can help other youth address this deficit.

Youth are an important component of HeartWood's back-loop journey. Personally, I find their fresh perspectives, passion, and energy life-giving. I find young people generally more at ease than adults with the chaos and uncertainty common to back-loop activity. This may be due to young people's tendency to want more 'doing' and less 'planning.' With the complex decision-making circumstance of the back-loop, it was in the 'doing' that HeartWood's real learning surfaced. Other organizations, including Amnesty International, are experiencing the same kind of results.

Amnesty International Canada has enjoyed commendable success with its youth inclusion effort, but not without plenty of doubt and uncertainty in the early stages. The episodic activism of youth, with a lack of continuity was considered by many in Amnesty as a barrier to youth involvement in the organization. Commenting on the structure of a meeting that was attempting to be more 'youth-friendly,' an Amnesty staff organizer said, 'For an organization that is characterized by its ability to produce tons of paper and analytical planning frameworks, which is used to following the Robert's Rules of Order at meetings, the idea of holding a meeting with just a one-line statement of objectives, no pre-set agenda or assigned meeting facilitator, was seen as downright crazy' (Mah-Sen 2003). It is not structured procedures per se that are being suggested as a problem, but when those procedures get in the way of inclusive and generative exchange, they can become one. Attempts at structuring what are popularly referred to as 'youth-friendly' meetings generally translate as attempts to increase the personal touch and interaction of a meeting. It is important to note that structuring a meeting in a manner that encourages youth participation has been found to maximize adult participation.

Young people provide new perspectives and encourage creative problem solving, characteristics Holling associates with the Renewal phase – a time to question assumptions and make room for innovation and new insights. HeartWood's young staff demonstrated a strong inclination towards spending time getting to know one another, to talk things through in a transparent manner, and for the importance of hearing the voice of the youth we served. These findings are consistent with Sheperd Zeldin's study (2000) on the adult and organizational impacts from youth inclusion.

· A participatory evaluation report completed at HeartWood on a program of the Nova Scotia Department of Employment Support Services supports the notion of youth ability to stimulate a system: 'The best way to gain curiosity in the Department's services and programs is to have youth involvement at every level possible. Their first-hand experience and knowledge are what will help the Department gain the greatest insight on how to address youth needs and wants' (Lavers 2004, 14).

Leadership that empowers

The stimulants capable of advancing a mature organization into the Creative Destruction phase generally lie hidden within the organization. In natural systems, accumulated resources lie sequestered for the growing, maturing ecosystems. The tightly interconnected system also represents a gradual increase in the potential for many other kinds of ecosystems to emerge in the future. For many YSOs, the greatest and most readily accessible resources for positive change lie within the hearts and minds of its volunteers and youth constituents. It remains only for a gifted leader to create the environment and circumstances for these volunteers to step forward.

When an organization finds itself on the verge of a Creative Destruction phase, the most common reaction is fear, and the most frequent tendency in response is to hire a technocrat leader to hold things together and to rein in, control, and put a stop to the chaos. A case in point is the Scouts organization's policy of recruiting new CEOs from within its own ranks. Not only does this limit the pool from which the organization can draw candidates, but also it runs the risk of getting a top manager who lacks new vision or the capacity to embrace change. Such hiring practices may hasten the organization's disintegration.

Rather than fight disturbances during the rapid changes and multiple uncertainties of the back-loop phase, a wise leader is able to unleash energy and direct it towards contributions that build new possibilities. The same lesson is learned from observing natural systems. Several studies have demonstrated that the suppression of disturbance will diminish the ability of the ecosystem to renew itself

(Holling 2001, 133). The Renewal phase is a time of reorganization. It requires that the organization excel in reflective learning, pausing to look around, listen, and act on immediate information and respond to every crisis as an opportunity. The effective leader at this time will excel in listening, watching, connecting, and directing all of the various pieces towards a common end. Henry Mintzberg describes the leader's role during this phase as not to preconceive deliberate strategies but rather to manage a learning process from which novel strategies can emerge (1999, 208). Essentially the leader is creating a 'container' in which ideas can bounce around, without losing sight of the organization's core competencies. If the leader listens carefully, he or she will unearth a wealth of opportunities to which staff will respond with passion and determination. This is leadership that empowers.

A former executive director of Santropol Roulant (SR), a youth-run Meals on Wheels program in Montreal, was one of the best leaders I've met for maintaining a 'container' for ideas and allowing projects to emerge and grow. During an evaluation I conducted for the agency during my PhD studies, one staff member said, 'We and the volunteers have the space and time to explore.' Another said, 'I had the time to be unproductive and explore.' These comments provide insight into the wisdom at SR. As is often the case, it came down to having a leader who recognized that her job was to create the 'elbow room' that would allow staff and volunteers to connect and grow. According to an organizational document, she put it this way: 'The Roulant is always consciously involved in a thousand conversations' (Nilsson 2003, 31). The combination of an empowering culture and a young staff results in Santropol Roulant spilling over with energy and enthusiasm.

4. Maturity

The mature forest is sheltered and quiet. Dappled light filters through the canopy of trees to the sparse understory, where the intricate relationships between plant species occur, in which nutrients are consumed and wastes are generated. Likewise, in the Maturity phase of human organizations, the more established policies, processes, or programs take up the majority of the available resources. In the forest, the result is a high level of stored energy known as biomass, which cannot be released. The equivalent in human systems is 'human capital' – all the ideas and human potential held back from surfacing.

In human organizations, travel along the 'S-curve' – moving up from the lower left quadrant (Birth) of the Adaptive Cycle framework – has long been the mainstay of business wisdom. Strategic planning, budgeting, and most control systems are designed for this process of consolidation and improving efficiency. 'Streamlining operations and allocating resources with more predictable returns is considered good management during the maturity phase' (Zimmerman, Lindberg, and Plsek 1998, 173). The mature organization reflects a high level of sameness and the component parts show a high degree of connectivity.

Like a single-species tree plantation, the programs and services of most mature organizations are not sufficiently diverse. With a tight, well-established system, the organization's ability to bounce back from the impact of a large crisis, or reverse a slow and steady decline, is hampered. In the case of extreme and growing rigidity, these systems become accidents waiting to happen. Basically, they are sitting targets. 'The trigger might be entirely random and external – a transient drying spell for the forest, a difficult board member ...' (Holling 2001, 45).

The mature youth-serving organization

Much of Canada's conventional youth-serving sector – public agencies and voluntary sector organizations – remain mired in old paradigms and practices. Not from lack of effort to renew – structures imposed on often skilled and passionate staff and volunteers limit their routines, relationships, and expectations to familiar territory. Staff energy is consumed by established processes that hamper the development of new organizational skills and competencies. With little light filtering through to support new thinking, many agencies struggle in the dark of the Maturity phase, never experiencing the excitement and energy that can result in a new way of doing business.

The challenges of the Maturity phase in an organization are perhaps most apparent in youth sector stalwarts such as the Scouts, as they search for new ways to attract young people. Fundamentally, little has changed in the way they run their programs. Organizational systems that have been growing for one hundred years are now rigid and tightly interconnected. Management looks to past practices, with a focus on repairing the old organizational fabric, rather than leveraging potential and future opportunities. This can lead to a situation like the unresolved debate, which began in the Scouts Canada organization in the early

1980s, on whether to keep their traditional British-style military beret as part of the Scouts uniform. With risk aversion prevalent, there seems to be little willingness to make difficult decisions that impact many interconnected parts of the organization. However, courageous action is needed, or these older organizations risk disappearing from significance. Holling likens this situation to the natural ecocycle conditions in which accumulating nutrient and biomass resources become more and more tightly bound within existing vegetation, preventing other competitors from utilizing them (Holling 2001, 35). According to Holling (2001), 'Several studies have demonstrated that suppression of disturbance will diminish the ability of the eco-system to renew itself' (133). In the context of human systems, clear cases of suppression are demonstrated in two examples in the Scouts' organization.

In a recent visit to a provincial Scouts headquarters, I was struck by the cavernous and mostly empty building that the organization had held on to for years, despite its own declining demand for the space. Though the building tied up much-needed capital and stressed operational funds, fond memories for senior members charged the debate on selling it with emotion. Only with persistence on the part of the executive director was a decision nudged ever so slowly forward.

The second example concerns a widely distributed memo sent by a senior staff person in a branch office, a lifetime Scouter, to the national CEO of Scouts Canada. The memo was an attempt at constructive criticism of the practices and plans of the national office that had implications on branch offices. The author of the memo backed up his concerns with examples and suggestions for alternative strategies. Three and one-half weeks later, the author was dismissed from his position, much to the surprise of the local volunteer board to which he reported.

Circumstances such as these are not unique to the Scouts organization. An organization can only suppresses 'hot-spot' fires for so long. Eventually, the flames will consume all that is dry and ready to burn. Scouts Canada appears in the above examples to have choked out the beginning of new life forms, even when handed to them by a respected senior staff member. In his research of great companies, Jim Collins has written: 'Leadership is about creating a climate where the truth is heard and the brutal facts confronted' (2001, 74). Let's hope for the sake of the many committed volunteers, staff, and youth associated with the Scouts that their upcoming centennial celebrations usher in a new way of operating that, while respecting the rich history of the organization, recognizes the need to creatively let go of those giants that hold back renewal.

HeartWood at maturity

Though HeartWood was a relatively young organization, after fifteen years it too began to sink into the established patterns and routines of the Maturity phase. Using summer camp facilities and wilderness settings, we had spent ten years running programs for youth. With our focus on encouraging youth to lead in their home communities, it seems ironic now that these programs were in wilderness and rural settings, usually quite far away from the young people's communities. There are programmatic reasons for the tradition of youth leadership programs being based in the wilderness; HeartWood shares the practice with more than 650 summer camps in Canada. By the standards of this summer camp sector, HeartWood had been quite successful, with an enviable service reputation, and over 24,000 alumni (children and youth) who had benefited directly from the organization's leadership training and environmental education.

Our work seemed honourable enough: we had taught these young people about leadership. We had taught them to believe in their dreams. We had encouraged them to contribute to their communities. Yet, like most summer camp youth programs, HeartWood took no responsibility for helping its young participants keep the flame alive in their own communities. HeartWood's responsibilities commenced and ended at the gates, doors, and trailheads of their program sites. Unfortunately, graduates of HeartWood's leadership programs faced communities and institutions that were neither prepared for nor interested in young people showing leadership. No matter how empowered young people might feel while at a leadership program, once they leave the safe confines of peer support and adult guidance, their motivation and sense of direction back home often dissipates.

Although HeartWood was encouraging young people to act as change agents in their communities, we provided them with no direct training to take action, nor did we provide ongoing support; this reality represented both the deficit and the opportunity of our work at the time. It is in their own communities, whatever these might be, that young people have the best opportunities to learn about leadership. I began to become critical of the practices behind our claim to be champions of youth leadership. HeartWood was at a crossroads: we had to either suppress the call for deeper work or start a journey that would take the organization in unknown directions. To suppress seemed unnatural, risking a circular spin between Maturity and Creative Destruction – what Holling describes as a 'poverty trap' (2001, 96). My sense at the time was that ignoring the call to deeper work meant accepting a 'flatter' future: less innovation, less passion, less organizational learning. I sensed that HeartWood would eventually lose some of the passionate and skilled staff who kept the workplace exciting. Passionate people want to learn and be challenged; they also want to give something of significance back. If an organization doesn't grow with them, they will leave in search of a more empowering work culture.

There is, as well, my own personal side to the story of HeartWood's journey into Creative Destruction. I knew the leadership challenge ahead would be significant. Admittedly, I was tired after a ten-year stint building the organization up from its modest beginning. I was feeling ready for a change of roles and venue. My agitation with having to make a decision at all was palpable. The passionate founder in me, though, found the prospect of HeartWood moving into a condition of complacency even more unsettling. The strongest pull I felt was the need for a deeper connection to the youth and communities HeartWood served. I came to see that the vibrancy of the new community work we had begun was capable of carrying us into a new and better way of thinking, being, and serving. It was my responsibility to open the door, get out of the way, and look after myself along the way.

5. The Creative Destruction Phase

Natural ecosystems have taught us that, despite human attempts to suppress disturbances, destruction will eventually occur. Creative destruction occurs when previously tightly bound biomass accumulates and nutrients become increasingly fragile – in systems terms, overconnected – until suddenly released by agents such as forest fires, drought, insect pests, or intense pulses of grazing (Holling 2001, 394). The destruction must occur before a process of renewal can begin. However, the system is seldom fully destroyed; previously stored resources from the conservation phase are released and become available to energize new beginnings, whether they are nutrients in the forest or material and social capital in the human organization. The feeling at the organization is one of identity crisis, anxiety, and relationship change. The people who do well with crises and new beginnings tend to do well at times of Creative Destruction.

The role of the leader at this time is, in essence, to stand still: to observe, be available, and assess results. It is a fascinating challenge of leadership to consider the concept of creative destruction in an organization. The phrase 'Creative Destruction' is well chosen; it is in the manifestation of *creative* force that the real challenge lies. In the ecologically managed forest, the choice to harvest a tree is based on the tree's health and maturity, and what new life its removal will bring to the grove. The same can be applied to the organization; it is a time to look at what the organization might stop doing or 'harvest,' in order to embrace new life. The important thing at HeartWood was not to throw away all we had been doing and destroy rampantly, like a short-sighted clear-cut. With the assets necessary for organizational renewal already in the system, it becomes important to preserve the integrity of the system.

HeartWood in creative destruction

We were at the end of a day-long visioning session, which we had shared with community stakeholders. We talked about what we liked, about what HeartWood was doing, and where we hoped it would go. Overall, the organization received ample feedback on what it was doing right. The predominant pull that day, however, was towards facing uncharted waters. We moved forward with a sense of excitement and overwhelming anticipation, even though we already felt 'maxed out' at our jobs as they were. We laughingly labelled the journey ahead as our 'abyss.'

It was not all smooth sailing, and I don't expect it often is in periods of Creative Destruction. We endured endless meetings about the minute details of a program framework that has since only minimally been implemented. We invested money and time in programs that failed, and had meetings that seemed to go nowhere. Yet other meetings and successful program efforts produced the basis for a model that has been central to our ongoing work. Through it all, we learned.

At the time of writing, HeartWood's activity is very different than what it was five years earlier. In my last years as executive director, the organization completed the transition from offering primarily youth leadership programs to those that support the involvement of youth within community organizations and agencies. The period of transition was difficult and exhilarating simultaneously. I liken it to the feeling of being on shore after jumping into the cold Atlantic on our beloved South Shore of Nova Scotia: difficult to get yourself in, sometimes numbingly cold while you are there, refreshing when you are out.

A strategy for creative destruction: Let some giants fall

Creative Destruction is not a 'quick-fix' process, a matter simply of getting rid of the 'right' program so that all else will immediately flourish.
There is work involved that requires tenacity and patience. At HeartWood,
it was only through an ongoing process of reflection about the organization as a *whole system* that it became possible to imagine and make adjustments to its structure, finances, and program. Strategies for the
back-loop will be unique to every organization. Each will learn and see
different lessons through the lens of the Adaptive Cycle. At HeartWood,
however, we did discover a strategy for navigating the back-loop that we
found particularly helpful in our own change process.

The large sunspots of rainforests fascinate me. These areas are created when a giant tree falls and opens a spot to the sunlight, where a
new diversity of life can breed and flourish. Sunspots are oases of vibrant green and light that sharply contrast with their dense and dark
surroundings. The YSO wanting to creatively destruct needs first to
take a hard look at what 'giants' of their programs or practices may be
blocking fresh ideas – and whether or not deliberately toppling some of
these 'giants' will let the sunshine in.

By way of example, with close to one hundred years of programming
traditions at Scouts Canada, certain taboos have developed. One such
taboo concerns the selling off of summer camp lands. In one provincial
Scouts riding, keeping a particular underutilized camp on the books
cost the organization in the range of $250,000 annually. Senior staff
members have complained that the organization is so risk-adverse it
has avoided what could be the unpopular decision of closing at least
some of these properties. Avoiding such issues denies the possibility of
alternative options emerging, as well as often badly needed financial
resources.

Another example comes from Amnesty International Canada's 'fell-
ing' of established member meeting and engagement practices. In the
early stages of Amnesty's youth inclusion initiative, young people were
saying, 'The message [we] get is that Amnesty is for adults only. All the
materials, opportunities for involvement are all directed at adults ...
Only adult community groups can take on long-term human rights work
... You say that you want us to get involved, but really, what you want us
to do is to put up posters and do all sort of "Joe jobs"' (Mah-Sen 2003, 2).

To Amnesty International's credit, the organization embraced the opportunity for new forms of participation by youth. 'There was such a

loss of potential; AI adults were not able to benefit from the enthusiasm and fresh ideas from youth, and the youth were not able to benefit from the insights and experience of the adults' (ibid., 2). With the push to experiment and shed old ways of doing things, it becomes increasingly limiting for YSOs to hold tight to traditional practices of adult-controlled and directed programming. In characterizing the results of its new youth engagement practices, Amnesty says there has been 'a fundamental change in Amnesty culture that is being felt throughout the organization internationally' (ibid.).

Before attempting to decide what an organization might strategically 'let fall,' a prudent first step is to assess its core competencies and core business. Core competencies are not those things an organization 'has'; they are things it 'does.' Inevitably they are 'bundles' of the organization's strengths – not merely what the organization is competent at doing, but rather which of these things the organization wants to be central to its purpose or mission. What does the organization do that is distinctive and valuable? How inimitable and durable are its competencies? These questions call for both analysis and decision-making.

At HeartWood, we identified our competencies as program design, customer service, experimentation, government relations, maintaining a healthy organizational culture, and inspiring young people.

With core competencies identified, an organization can move forward to determine its core business. Again, this is not simply a list of products and services; rather, it is those aspects of what it does that the organization wants at its core. HeartWood identified its core business as project management and training.

We then turned to a third and final set of questions. Which programs least addressed the core of our business and enlisted our competencies? Who in the organization had passion and skill to unleash? Was anything blocking a compelling idea from moving forward? What funding expectations or costs blocked renewal? Answering these questions was the key to stripping away the inessentials and focusing on how the organization would move forward.

At HeartWood we ceased to offer our popular annual public canoe trips, which we had been offering for over thirteen years. We could no longer justify either the time or resources that they consumed relative to the number of children and youth they served. Though I was ready to see us end the programs two years earlier than we did, the emotional attachment for the staff was significant. It was through the process of reviewing our core competencies and business that we were reminded that it was wilderness programming we felt a deeper connection to, not those specific canoe trips. With a recommitment to an outdoors experiential component for our newly emerging programs, we were able to release the energy held by the canoe trips. This opened prime time in the summer calendar, which is now filled with program activities that generate more significant community and youth development outcomes.

'For Scouts Canada ...'

For national organizations with branch offices, ecological systems offer a unique lesson in Creative Destruction. Conditions in a forest allow a local ignition to create a small ground fire at times, which spreads first up to the crown of a tree, then to another, and eventually to the crowns of a whole stand of trees. Each step of that cascade moves the transformation to a larger and slower level (Holling 2001, 398). Important to note in the cascade is that though the foliage at the crowns burns, the trees remain intact to grow another day.

Branch-based youth service organizations can often identify at least one branch whose work moves beyond the status quo in the organization. Imagine for a moment releasing this one branch from its ties to the established national policy structure, thus (figuratively speaking) igniting a small 'ground fire.' Although inevitably some chaos may ensue, the parent organization will have established a 'laboratory' for experimentation. The burn at the branch level will find fuel in the extra baggage: policies, procedures, and programs that may hold back innovative new work. Like the tree in the forest, the crown burn will not have immediately effected the national organization, and will move slower as it cascades in search of more fuel into other parts of the organization. During this phase, the wise leader can watch, listen, and learn to monitor the slower moving cascade. Creative Destruction will have commenced in the organization without immediately challenging the integrity of the larger system.

---

6. The Mobilization Phase

Moving through the back-loop from Creative Destruction to the Renewal phase in a human organization is a time of high chaos and uncertainty. The excitement of changes afoot is sometimes tempered and sometimes fed by an accompanying sense of fear. 'This shift represents a time of explosive increase in uncertainty ... conditions might arise for formal chaotic behavior' (Holling 2001, 45). Latent ideas, human resources, opportunities, and capital likewise present pieces of a puzzle – without the benefit of the cover photo of the completed puzzle. The reorganization phase of the Adaptive Cycle is essentially equivalent to one of innovation and restructuring in an industry or a society (ibid., 35). In a natural system, the Renewal phase is found in those parts of the forest overgrown with many competing species, all vying for the same nutrients. Though organizational potential in this phase seems high, the leader must exercise maximum awareness in order to identify it and direct it. In natural ecosystems, the equivalent of the leader's job is performed by the soil, as it works to manage the loss of nutrients and prepare them for the emerging phase of exploitation.

Ironically, most managers expend much time and worry on carefully articulated strategic planning documents, though most action taken by organizations is in response to learning that is emergent (Mintzberg, Ahlstrand, and Lampel 1998, 208). If the leader is in tune with the living nature of its external and internal systems, he or she will continuously adjust the 'plan,' redirecting resources so as to sustain action towards desired outcomes.

A certain mindset is required of a YSO if it wants to thrive in this fast-changing environment. Humility, adaptability, and willingness to connect with the community will help the organization to embrace the uncertainty and foster change. In these circumstances, both the organization and the individual will learn better if there is control over the level of risk, with supportive peers nearby. In my work over the years as an adventure-based experiential educator, this learning edge is referred to as 'stepping out of the comfort zone.' It is well known in that field and most other personal and group development modalities that challenging oneself within a supportive context leads to growth and development. Ralph Stacey, in his work with systems learning, describes this learning edge as a 'zone of complexity,' a time, he adds, that contains high uncertainty and little agreement in an organization (Zimmerman, Lindberg, and Plesk 1998, 140). Stacey argues that traditional approaches to solving problems will not be very effective here, but it is a time of high creativity, innovation, and breaking from the old ways of doing things. Frances Westley adds, 'The interaction between established routines and novel situations is an important source of learning' (Mintzberg, Ahlstrand, and Lampel 1998, 185).

The Renewal phase is a time to 'learn by doing,' with many false starts, new ideas, and actions surfacing. For the leader, it is a time to intensify the exchange of information and encourage connections between various parts of the organization internally and externally.

HeartWood's transition in the Renewal phase to a new way of programming involved establishing what we called 'Youth Action Teams': community-based groups of young people and adults concerned with personal, group, and community development. We already had our own experience with emergent learning and adaptation during the period of experimenting with this new work. In one community, we discovered too late that the young people we had engaged with disagreed with our endorsement of a certain sponsor and volunteer mentors. In another, we regretted initiating activity without first having adult mentors in place. In yet another community, a sponsoring agency expected the young people to provide service only for their agency, much to the chagrin of the young people. After two years of watching, responding, and learning from these teams, it was clear we were on our 'learning edge.' There was a reciprocal relationship of learning between HeartWood and the Youth Action Teams. The most valuable lessons came from our responses to the teams' needs and questions as they arose. Our responses were not based on any preconceived policy or plans; adaptability was the order of the day. The circumstances were new and the situation was complex. The lessons the organization learned were of the kind that is uniquely available the first time a new project or initiative is attempted. Our work during those days still informs HeartWood's method and principles of engagement with organizations and communities today.

Strategy for the mobilization phase: Community youth development

The back-loop phase at HeartWood was the organization's most challenging and rewarding transition since its beginnings in 1989. Emerging from the three years we had labelled our 'abyss,' HeartWood adopted a new, overarching program framework. After years of providing primarily leadership programs for youth, the organization expanded its core services and philosophy to embrace a vision of meaningful participation by youth in building healthy communities. We found resonance in the language and principles of Community Youth Development (CYD).[4]

For YSOs, CYD offers both a framework for renewed community engagement and a stimulant for organizational renewal. Across Canada, there is a growing wave of activity focused on including youth in community processes. The movement needs guidance and ambassadors. Citizens are turning to the youth-serving sector for guidance.[5] This is a call for YSOs to get to the place where they can stand up and loudly advocate for youth inclusion in community decision-making processes.

The opportunity for YSOs to make an impact on the lives of young people and communities is unprecedented. A YSO may variably take on roles as trainers, facilitators, conveners, or intermediaries between young people and their communities. HeartWood found its own increased engagement in the community very fulfilling work. It brought the organization to a deeper place with its work, calling on our competencies to service real community needs. Community collaborations, programs, and forums immediately increased. The principles of CYD gave the organization a framework for making choices between the many options, needs, and ideas that surfaced in HeartWood's mobilization phase.

I have found that, when given the opportunity to engage in a meaningful way, most young people are quite willing to step up to the plate. In the words of one young person in a local public meeting, 'Youth really want to be involved. That's the whole point that we are trying to get to. Let us get involved. Let us be a part of our town.' Young people have what Alec Dickson, the visionary founder of Britain's Voluntary Service Overseas, described as a basic human desire to be needed (Dickson 1976). What I find particularly exciting is that when a community does call on a young person for leadership, a ripple of energy stirs from deep in the soul of the young person and extends outward into the community. Young people bring forward a rich diversity as well as a difference from adults in approaches and priorities to community development.

A compelling reason to engage youth in community building is that communities are searching for fresh support and creativity in addressing mounting economic and social demands. The heart of a community's social capital is the diversity of interactions taking place within the community. It is in the nurturing and building of these interactions that young people can make their most significant civic contribution. Leading youth researcher Julia Burgess (2000) points out, 'Young people are able to bridge many of the perceived differences within communities, especially racial and ethnic, that keep adults from working together' (4). If youth-serving and community organizations leverage this natural strength of young people, there is a real possibility of positive community outcomes not previously considered in the realm of youth development efforts.

The following three CYD practices warrant special attention for the potential they represent to assist a YSO moving through reorganization. These practices may help frame and ground some of the many ideas that arise during the chaotic rebuilding that follows Creative Destruction.

YOUTH SPENDING THE YOUTH DOLLAR

If plagued with indecision on the fate of a marginal program, the agency leader could turn to a group of young people for guidance. I find it ironic that entrusting youth with decisions on how to expend resources for youth programs is considered a 'radical' practice. However, a growing number of 'youth philanthropy' programs in North America are taking this approach. Groups of young people across North America are disbursing grants for youth-related services in their communities. Supported with training and adult guidance, these programs are generating impressive results for the agencies, community, and the youth. The rigour and values that youth apply to grant making decisions such as these has been noteworthy. A YSO could apply a similar practice to funding for a particular issue, or to expend a percentage of an annual program budget. An agency responsible for youth services in the community could also consider establishing a small grants program for its constituents, with granting decisions made by a trained and supported youth team.

COLLABORATION

Good collaboration has the potential to move a YSO into Creative Destruction and to assist the organization in navigating the back-loop. Though not all collaborations turn out well, with shared learning and action and effective communication between partners, the potential is great. Ideally, a collaborating partner has something special to offer (e.g., expertise, networking, experience) for a particular action or initiative. In periods of high complexity and chaos, collaboration can shed much-needed light down otherwise dark alleys.

Collaboration can also be a means of offloading a program or service that, while holding your organization back, may be attractive to some other organization or agency. Passing a program over to another organization can breathe new life into the program, while freeing up financial resources or emotional energy at your own organization.

For example, there was talk at a senior level of plans for a potential collaboration between Scouts Canada and Kids Help Phone.[6] From a distance, I thought the idea showed great promise. The initiative was discussed with great enthusiasm in both organizations, and the reciprocal benefits were obvious. When I later asked about the collaboration, a senior Scouts staff member replied that there were 'some pretty big issues on the table ... and the collaboration was not seen as a big priority.'[7] Considering the stresses on their organization, it was understandably difficult for the Scouts to see the benefits of the Kids Help Phone collaboration clearly at the time. Yet the collaboration may have held some of the properties needed to lubricate the Scouts' tightly wound organizational machinery.

YOUTH ACTIVISM

Marginalized youth populations are most willing to take action for a cause that they see as being close to home. There is a contagious energy connected to social action for causes youth find meaningful, particularly those that influence their friends, families, and neighbourhoods directly. In the San Francisco Bay Area, youth activists supported by adult-based organizations convinced officials to commit $1.4 million for health clinics and mental health centres in high schools (Cervone 2002).

For a YSO, facilitating action or service for a cause has the potential to stimulate renewal and connect it more directly to the community. For a conservative organization like Scouts Canada, adopting a national issue such as the environment, poverty, or child abuse could leverage the 'do-good' image of a Scouter and stimulate the moral imagination of society.

Imagine if the Scouts, with their attempt to rekindle their organizational spirit and update their image, organized a large group of Scouts to stage a peaceful sit-in on Parliament Hill, as a call for increased action against child pornography, child labour, or in support of the people of Tibet – all justice-based issues with broad public support. Those in the Scouts organization who might dismiss the idea as too radical or risky might want to reconsider the current membership decline and the greater risk of do nothing radical at all. In his popular book, *Bowling Alone* (2000), Robert Putnam weighs in on the need for a new kind of activity and image for the Scouts. 'What we need is not civic broccoli, good for you but not appealing – but an updated version of Scouting's ingenious combination of values and fun' (406).

Carefully framed and managed, a social justice action by a conventional YSO could deliver a clear message that the organization will stand up and get involved in support of a cause for just society. Focusing on what 'could be' versus 'what is' or 'is not' begins the process of projecting a new organizational future.

7. Conclusion

Youth Service Organizations have long been considered an important element of community life. Their role in helping to prepare young people for healthy futures has been relied on to complement the work of schools and family life. In their maturity, however, many YSOs experience significant financial and program challenges. Old ways of working internally and in the community are no longer sufficient. At the same time, there are increasing appeals to get young people more involved in community processes and in the organizations and agencies that provide youth services. To maintain its relevance, the mature YSO needs to adapt and find ways to renew its organization and practices.

Youth inclusion and leadership that empowers are suggested as two key principles on which YSOs might base a process of renewal, bearing in mind the Adaptive Cycle framework (Holling 2001) and applying its ecocycle metaphor as a tool for exploring and navigating through major change.

Any mature organization that recognizes the need to change must also be prepared to enter the back-loop phases of organizational development: Creative Destruction and Mobilization. Drawing from my experience at the helm of a YSO, one key strategy is discussed to navigate each phase: in Creative Destruction, to let go of outmoded practices that sequester resources and redirect these resources to implement new emerging ideas. In the Mobilization phase, the concept of Community Youth Development is a strategic way to frame and ground organizational renewal. Youth philanthropy, collaboration, and activism are presented as examples of CYD that can move a YSO forward into a new phase of effective operation and valuable community service.

NOTES

1   Ecoforestry is the science of preserving fully intact forest ecosystems while providing for appropriate levels of commercial timber extraction. It is

adaptable to the inclusion of ecological, cultural, heritage, scenic, recreational, wildlife, and fisheries objectives within the value set identified for mitigation or maintenance. For further information, see the Ecoforestry Institute website, http://ecoforestry.ca/default.htm.

2 The servant leader is a servant first. It begins with the natural feeling that one wants to serve, to serve first. Then conscious choice brings one to aspire to lead (Greenleaf 1991).

3 Author's personal conversation with a colleague who had experienced the child welfare system first hand, Halifax, NS, 2004.

4 Community Youth Development is an approach that espouses the principle that the enlistment of young people as active agents in community-building contributes positively both to youth development and the community. (See Hughes and Curnan 2000.)

5 I am indebted to B. Braganza of the HeartWood Centre, M. McKnight of Big Brothers Big Sisters Canada, and E. Burton of the Boys and Girls Club of Canada for comments and correspondence on Community Youth Development.

6 Kids Help Phone (http://www.kidshelpphone.ca) is a non-profit organization that provides toll-free, twenty-four-hour, bilingual, and anonymous telephone counselling to young people in Canada.

7 Anonymous, confidential conversation with author, 15 March 2002.

PART THREE

The Global Mindset

7 First Nations Children and Families: In Search of the Voluntary Sector

CINDY BLACKSTOCK

There is convincing evidence that First Nations children and young people are among the most disadvantaged in Canadian society, and yet they receive far fewer resources than other Canadians (RCAP 1996; CCRC 1999; McDonald and Ladd 2000; Nadjiwan and Blackstock 2003; Blackstock et al. 2004; Blackstock et al. 2005). This evidence runs counter to the prevailing Canadian stereotype that First Nations are the preferred beneficiaries of Canadian society. It also challenges the claim that Canada's voluntary sector reaches out to the country's most vulnerable citizens.

This essay describes the findings of a study I conducted in 2002 in cooperation with First Nations Child and Family Service (FNCFS) agencies and with child, youth and family serving voluntary sector organizations (Blackstock 2005). This study was intended to determine the degree to which First Nations children living on-reserve in British Columbia benefited from voluntary sector services. The results confirmed First Nations reports that despite significant need and a desire by First Nations to form respectful partnerships with the voluntary sector, only a handful of Aboriginal children were receiving any benefit from the relevant voluntary sector organizations (VSOs) or philanthropic funders. This lack of service, which has not materially improved since the 2002 study, is compounded by inequities in government funding and low levels of family income. In the pages that follow, possible reasons for the lack of voluntary sector services on-reserve are discussed and policy solutions are proposed.

1. Background

As the United Nations Committee on the Rights of the Child (2003) has observed, Aboriginal children in Canada face pervasive and disproportionate risks to a degree not experienced by other Canadian children. First Nations children are more likely than other Canadian children to be born into poverty, live in unsafe housing, be placed in child welfare care or the justice system, and not succeed in school (Blackstock et al. 2004). Increasingly, studies show that the key drivers of these risks are poverty, poor housing, and substance misuse born out of the experience of colonization (Blackstock et al. 2005; Trocmé, Knoke, and Blackstock 2004). Redressing these inequities would, over the long term, provide sustainable benefits for First Nations children and young people. However, getting there will require increased investment in community-driven development plans by the corporate, public, and voluntary sectors (Cornell and Kalt 2002).

Ramping up to ensure that adequate resources are available to address these structural risks begins with understanding what is currently available. Contrary to prevailing stereotypes in which First Nations figure as preferred beneficiaries of Canada's resources, children on-reserve currently have significantly *fewer* resources available to them than children off-reserves (see table 7.1).

Given this inequality in resource access, it is not difficult to understand why First Nations families are finding redressing the impacts of colonization so challenging. After all, it is likely that Canadian families, too, would experience significant decreases in quality of life if they had to make do with the very limited social supports that are available to First Nations families on-reserve.

Off-reserves, the voluntary sector (VS) has a significant impact on the socio-economic well-being of Canadians. Along with providing the services, advocacy, and information critical to maintaining the standard of living that Canadians enjoy, the voluntary sector is a leading employer; its expenditures have a direct impact on local economies. It also has a direct influence on government policy and on the development of public policy as a whole (Milne 2002). In British Columbia, Imagine Canada (2005) reports that there are over 22,000 voluntary sector organizations: collectively, these represent over 1 million hours of volunteer service that are valued at over $2.7 billion. This significant pool of resources is distributed throughout British Columbia to benefit a myriad of causes, including social welfare and justice, recreation and sport, the arts and the environment. Although there are no data indicating how many of these organizations have the well-being of children, youth, and families as their specific mandate, anecdotal evidence indicates the numbers are significant. First Call, a cross-section coalition of child, youth, and

Table 7.1
Contrasting social supports for children on- and off-reserve in Canada

Sector	Off-Reserve Supports	On-Reserve Supports
Public Sector	Federal programs Provincial programs Municipal services	Federal programs based on population count
Corporate Sector	G8 economy provides family incomes of $37,757 for non-Aboriginal workers in Canada (Campaign 2000)	Limited corporate sector annual family income of $7,165.00 per annum (Beavon and Cooke 2001)
Voluntary Sector	Canadian non-profits employ 1,000,000 people. Together these organizations collect over $115 billion per year in annual revenue (Canadian Council on Social Development 2003)	Extremely negligible anecdotal evidence of VS service delivery or funding of FN-based forms of volunteerism

family organizations, lists over 50 provincial child-, youth-, and family-serving voluntary sector organizations (CYFSVSOs) among its members, and the United Way of British Columbia lists hundreds of community child, youth, and family organizations on its website (First Call 2002; United Way 2002).

The voluntary sector's collective efforts have undoubtedly contributed to the well-being of children and families. However, as the sector's influence on Canadian public policy increases, so too does its responsibility to ensure it is inclusive of all Canadians – particularly populations that experience significant social exclusion or social risk, as Aboriginal peoples in Canada do. My research findings suggest that, as of 2002, the voluntary sector was providing services to First Nations children on-reserve in only the most exceptional of circumstances, despite an overwhelming need for increased social supports (Blackstock 2005).

2. Research Method

In order to measure the degree to which child-, youth-, and family-serving voluntary sector organizations (CYFSVSOs) were providing services to First Nations children on-reserve in British Columbia, a study was conducted in 2002, using survey methodology. Respondents included First Nations Child and Family Services agencies serving 47 of the 196 First Nations in British Columbia. The survey for voluntary sector organizations was distributed to over 60 CYFSVSOs through provincial networks; however, only five responses were received (Blackstock 2005). This low response rate is problematic in terms of better understanding why the voluntary sector is not meaningfully engaged with First Nations. Nonetheless, the BC survey represents a significant step forward in research. It was the first study of its kind in North America, and it provides foundational knowledge upon which future research can be developed.

3. Findings

Results of the BC survey indicate that voluntary sector organizations have only marginal awareness of the needs of First Nations children and families. None of the VSOs reported providing a service to a child, youth, or family on-reserve in the year prior to the survey. First Nations Child and Family Services (FNCFS) agencies mentioned only four instances where a voluntary sector organization had provided services to a child on-reserve in 2001. However, the FNCFS agencies rated the four VSOs' quality of service, for the most part, as fair to excellent. One FNCFS agency commented: 'Some families are more comfortable working out family issues with people they don't see on a social basis. [The VSO] skills are good.' Another noted that the First Nation in question had a desire to develop the capacity to deliver the services on-reserve to reflect more closely the cultural context of the clients they serve.

Overall, only seven of the 47 First Nations serviced by agencies participating in this survey reported having any engagement with the voluntary sector during the past year. This limited engagement would seem to indicate that the citizens of the 40 remaining First Nations did not receive services from the voluntary sector in 2001, since FNCFS agencies act as the primary service referral agents for children, youth, and families on-reserve. In fact, FNCFS agencies in urban areas were the *least likely* to report collaboration with the CYFSVS. This fact is important, because it debunks the notion that geographical distance is a significant barrier to relationship building between First Nations and the voluntary sector.

Interestingly, this service vacuum occurred despite the fact that all of the voluntary sector respondents saw a role for the sector in providing services to children, youth, and families on-reserve. Several voluntary sector respondents indicated that the reason why they did not provide services on-reserve was because First Nations did not want them there. Interestingly, when asked how they came to form that opinion, none of the respondents had actually asked the First Nations Child and Family Services providers; they simply went on the basis of assumptions that were informed by television shows or social norms. Whatever their opinion of the voluntary sector, the FNCFS agencies were unanimous that VSOs had a role to play in meeting the needs of First Nations children, youth, and families on-reserve. Here are just a few of the agencies' responses:

'Yes, I see a need for other non-profit organizations in a community. Our agency can't do it all because of time constraints and funding issues. Too many jurisdictional issues to deal with when working on- and off-reserve.'

'Yes, meal programs for on-reserve schools, transportation is a HUGE need (no public transit), hitchhiking is the only transit in remote communities. VS could fund community buses, after school programming, sports equipment, field trips, and exchange options to provide hope to youth.'

'Yes, when population size does not support the creation of an entire program, on-reserve partnerships may contribute to their development and success.'

Among the main barriers FNCFS agencies identified in forming relationships with the voluntary sector was the need for voluntary sector organizations to enhance their understanding of the cultures, histories, and organizations when working on-reserve with children, youth, and families. Among other issues were the agencies' lack of information about the voluntary sector, lack of time to form collaborative relationships, and the remoteness of voluntary sector organizations' offices and resources from reserve communities.

In contrast, when the voluntary sector respondents identified the main barriers to building relationships with FNCFS agencies, a slightly different set of factors emerged:

- Four out of five respondents listed lack of time as the most serious barrier to forming collaborative relationships with FNCFS.
- Four out of five respondents indicated the lack of knowledge of First Nations Child and Family Service agencies as a key factor.

Other barriers frequently cited were ignorance of Aboriginal cultures, lack of awareness about the needs of First Nations children, youth, and families, remoteness of First Nations reserve communities, and hesitancy to assume that VSOs would necessarily be welcome on-reserve.

As a cornerstone of successful collaboration, FNCFS agencies identified a shared vision of community development that builds on the assets of the community. Building community capacity, not dependency, was strongly emphasized. In order to achieve this, FNCFS respondents stated that the voluntary sector 'must have knowledge of cultural and traditional ways of that community. Voluntary sector workers must be non-judgmental and be vigilant about not forcing their own values/morals on our community. There must also be a willingness by voluntary sector organizations to support First Nations directed resources and voluntary activity.'

In reflecting on what would assist relationship building between VSOs and FNCFS agencies, two voluntary sector respondents indicated that there needed to be a forum to facilitate relationship building: 'If FNCFS wanted to work with the sector, then a respectful space to meet and create relationship [is needed], which has as its main goal relationship building, but as well includes some form of concrete, easy-to-deliver project.' Another respondent said it was important that all the collaborators 'have a firm understanding of the history of each of the groups involved, so that you don't get blinded by a romantic idea of what is happening. A realistic, clear-eyed grasp of the situation at hand is always a good place to start.'

Other suggestions included:

- A team approach that would find resource opportunities that would allow VSOs to hire First Nations staff.
- Integration of First Nations culture and context into training programs for voluntary sector staff.

4. Discussion

While there were differences in some responses, findings indicate that there is very little evidence of engagement between CYFSVSOs and FNCFS agencies in BC. This is distressing and puzzling, given the significant needs of First Nations children, youth, and families and the voluntary sector's desire to be inclusive and responsive to the needs of all Canadians. One hopeful finding, however, is that all respondents, both from First Nations and the voluntary sector, agreed that there was a role for the voluntary sector in building on the assets of communities to respond to the needs of children, youth, and families. The FNCFS agencies and CYFSVOs that took part in the BC study have identified a myriad of ways to foster collaboration.

Because of the small sample size of voluntary sector organizations in the BC study, there is no definitive way, based on the data, of explaining the social exclusion of First Nations children, youth, and families. In order to promote further dialogue on the etiological drivers of this exclusion, I will explore four possible rationales:

1. lack of information
2. the liberal tradition of the voluntary sector
3. differing values and beliefs on volunteerism
4. colonization, racism, and reconciliation

Although I have organized these into four separate discussions, it is my belief that it is in the blending of these and other possible dimensions that the experience of both the voluntary sector and First Nations Child and Family Services agencies is best reflected.

Lack of information

Information has been identified by collaboration theorist Rosabeth Moss Kanter (1989) as a critical component in the effective development and maintenance of organizational collaborative relationships. Although there is no specific information that lets us assess the nature and extent of historical knowledge, particularly regarding First Nations peoples, among voluntary sector leaders and organizations, we can draw some information from national studies. In 1998, the Dominion Institute and the Canada Council for Unity commissioned Ipsos-Reid to conduct a poll on Canadians' knowledge of their history. Only half of respondents passed the test. (Interestingly, this test of Canadian history contained no questions about Aboriginal peoples.) An Ipsos-Reid poll in September 2001 indicated that 76 per cent of Canadians are embarrassed by their lack of knowledge about Canadian history (Ipsos-Reid 2001). So why do we know so little about our history? What are our institutions of knowledge such as schools and the media doing about it, and what implications does this have for the shaping of Canadian society?

Canadian historian Jack Granatstein (2000) sums up the teaching of history in Canada's elementary and secondary schools as follows:

... astonishingly, four provinces have no compulsory Canadian history courses in their high schools. Others bury it in a mishmash of civic, pop sociology and English as a Second Language, eliminating anything that might offend students, parents and school trustees, in an attempt to produce an airbrushed past free of warts (except for the officially approved historical sins that can be used for present-day social engineering). (4)

If elementary and high schools leave Canadians with an inadequate understanding of Canadian history, then what about the colleges and universities that graduate many of the voluntary sector leaders? Michael Ignatieff (2000) has written of the exclusionary account of Canadian history that still prevailed at the University of British Columbia when he taught there, and the obvious role it played in perpetuating Canadians' historical ignorance:

[The] reason the history I was teaching wasn't national history was that it left out almost all of the people. It was a history of the politics, diplomacy and warfare that led to the creation of British North America and the Canadian political system. While this has to be core of any national history, it leaves out a lot ... and as for the aboriginal peoples, whose civilization had marked the history of the Pacific Northwest, if my students wanted to study them, they had to head over to the anthropology department. Their achievements – and their tragedy – had no place in the Canadian story. (8)

Historical ignorance allows Canadian governments and the voluntary sector to claim a higher level of morality and justice on the international stage and to hold tight to the values of democracy, freedom, compassion, and peace upon which we found our national identity. We call on countries such as South Africa to end apartheid and China to recognize the distinctness of Tibet, and on members of the G8 to end child poverty; yet Canada is home to the *Indian Act* (Government of Canada 1985). First Nations children live in conditions that lag far behind that of other Canadian children, and little progress has been made to recognize Aboriginal rights and titles in this country. According to Aziz Choudry, 'Many social justice campaigns, NGOs and activists in these countries operate from a state of colonial denial and refuse to make links between human rights abuses overseas, economic injustice, and the colonization of the lands and peoples where they live' (Choudry n.d., n.p.). Choudry emphasizes that it is not possible to understand the contemporary context or experience of Aboriginal people in Canada without knowledge of the history. Considering the significant socio-economic needs in Aboriginal communities and the ready access to meaningful information in reports such as that of the Royal Commission on Aboriginal Peoples (1996), it is unconscionable that the voluntary sector should continue to bask comfortably in its own ignorance, especially if it sincerely wishes to serve all Canadians.

If voluntary sector leaders are seriously willing to engage in renewed relationships between Canada's non-Aboriginal and Aboriginal peoples, then they must actively seek out multiple sources of historical truth and perspective on which to base their future actions. If the enthusiastic support for increased collaboration and learning from both FNCFS agencies and VSOs participating in this project are any indication, there is reason for hope. But now that hope must be mobilized into deliberate and thoughtful action.

The liberal tradition: The mask of inequality and diversity

The voluntary sector is largely premised on the Western liberal tradition that seeks to affirm individual rights through organizational governance and service delivery structures that do not discriminate on the basis of issues such as race, religion, gender, or political affiliation (Taylor 1994). This is admirable, but it also assumes a lot. For one thing, the liberal approach presupposes that the recipients of state benefits and social services all share, or in any case will be receptive to, a cultural framework founded in the liberal tradition. It also assumes that the misapplication of liberal ideology will be obvious and preventable.

The problem is that these liberal assumptions are only half-truths, even when applied to non-Aboriginal Canadians, let alone to First Nations, who experience political, economic, and social oppression to a degree that is not shared by other Canadians. Thus the difficulty arises, in that the liberal tradition in unanticipated ways propagates and supports inequality through the *equal treatment of unequals*. This type of ethical blindness is easily sustained when it is couched in the language of universality and non-discrimination.

The perpetuation of inequality, although often not deliberate, can be as destructive in its consequences as intentional discrimination. In the case of the Canadian voluntary sector, with its service delivery modelled in the liberal tradition, this apparently has resulted either in the exclusion of First Nations children, youth, and families as service recipients or in a cultural mismatch between services provided and the cultural context of the service recipient. A conversation with a non-Aboriginal director of a child and youth VSO provides some insight into how the liberal tradition manifests itself in practice. When told of the disproportionately low numbers of First Nations children in care that were being serviced by her organization, she remarked, 'We don't focus on First Nations children; we look out for the interests of *all* children' (her emphasis). While looking out for 'the interests of all children' sounds admirable, it can, in practice, lead to the development of universal programs that fail to consider the inequalities and contexts experienced by Aboriginal children, who in this case accounted for over 40 per cent of the organization's clients.

An over-reliance on universal descriptors such as 'aboriginal,' 'indigenous,' or 'native' to guide voluntary service governance or service delivery can also mask the significant differences between Aboriginal peoples in Canada, resulting in numerous services and programs that do not adequately respond to various constituencies. Take, for example, the issue of the nature and extent of engagement between the voluntary sector and FNCPS agencies that is reviewed in this essay. If the question were reframed to measure whether or not VSOs provide services to Aboriginal peoples, I would hypothesize that the engagement rates would have been somewhat higher in light of the higher profile of urban Aboriginal voluntary sector organizations such as Friendship Centres and Aboriginal Head Start Programs. By asking specifically about voluntary engagement with on-reserve FNCPS agencies, a significant gap was identified. Another example is Michael Chandler's research on youth suicide in First Nations communities in British Columbia. His study found that although Aboriginal youth in Canada are at higher per capita risk of suicide than any other culturally identifiable group in the world, there were First Nations in BC that had a zero youth suicide rate over the past thirteen years. In comparing First Nations where suicide rates are high with those where youth suicide was not a concern, Chandler found that decreased suicide rates were highly correlated with increased community self-government and self-determination (Chandler 2002). This finding supports other research suggesting that community self-government precedes improvements in economic and social well-being in First Nations communities (Cornell and Kalt 2002). If Chandler had not unpacked the term 'Aboriginal' to examine differences in suicide rates among diverse First Nations communities, this critical preventative factor for youth suicide would have not been identified.

Another example of the misuse of social taxonomy is the tendency to include First Nations as part of the 'multicultural' community in Canada. While at first glance it may seem appropriate to lump First Nations in with other peoples of colour, the First Nations experience and impacts of colonization, assimilation, and expropriation of lands supported by Canadian legal, political, and social instruments is so significant that cross-comparisons with immigrant groups cannot be substantiated (Bennett and Blackstock 2002). Although the multicultural service delivery approach offers the value of simplicity for the service provider, it essentially denies the diverse realities of the service user and in this way perpetuates the paradox of homogeneity in diversity, which the multicultural approach seeks to inculcate and, ultimately, exploit.

The liberal tradition, while seeking to satisfy an ideal of non-discrimination, in the end fails to recognize that the services that liberal democracies provide are not culturally neutral and that the needs and contexts of populations targeted for social benefits are neither consistent nor universal. Respecting difference and responding to difference takes time and attention, and it is definitely a more complicated goal than can be attained on the basis of liberal presumptions of neutrality regarding cultural differences. Nonetheless, it is incumbent on the voluntary sector to try. The lack of engagement of the BC voluntary sector with First Nations Child and Family Services agencies is a strong signal that current approaches need to be reconsidered and redesigned if the voluntary sector wishes to contribute to the well-being of all Canadian children, youth, and families.

Differing values and concepts of volunteerism

As noted in *Strategic Planning for Aboriginal Input*, a document produced in July 2001 by Aboriginal participants for the Voluntary Sector Initiative (2002), concepts of volunteerism can be influenced by differing values and beliefs. For example, civic engagement in First Nations communities is based on a strong tradition of interdependent communal life that is reflective of cultural values, beliefs, and practices. Volunteerism, in the Euro-Western sense, implies individual choice. In First Nations communities, civic engagement is not, strictly speaking, elective; it is an expectation necessary to ensure the sustainability of community. Both of these traditions are valid. However, if the voluntary sector organizes itself strictly around the Euro-Western framework, it will fail to recognize and support other forms of civic engagement.

There has been much debate on what constitutes a voluntary sector organization in Canada but this has mostly been confined to whether the VSO is run by volunteers or relies on paid staff (Nadjiwan and Blackstock 2003). The debate on how to support First Nations cultural constructs of volunteerism within a multicultural Canada requires further thoughtful deliberation by the voluntary sector, government funders, and the philanthropic community.

5. Colonization, Racism, and Reconciliation

On 7 January 1998, the minister of Indian Affairs and Northern Development, Jane Stewart, read a Statement of Reconciliation (Government of Canada 1998) on the floor of the House of Commons in Ottawa. This statement was intended to signal the beginning of a new relationship between Aboriginal and non-Aboriginal Canadians, informed by history and founded on respect and honour. The Statement contained the following passage:

> Reconciliation is an ongoing process. In renewing our partnership, we must ensure that the mistakes that marked our past relationship are not repeated. The Government of Canada recognizes that policies that sought to assimilate Aboriginal people, women and men, were not the way to build a strong country. We must instead continue to find ways in which Aboriginal people can participate fully in the economic, political, cultural and social life of Canada in a manner that preserves and enhances the collective identities of Aboriginal communities, and allows them to evolve and flourish in the future. Working together to achieve our shared goals will benefit all Canadians, Aboriginal and non-Aboriginal alike. (Government of Canada 1998)

Although there is significant debate as to whether the Statement went far enough in apologizing for Canada's colonial policies and whether the government has met its commitments in the Statement, it is important that the Statement was made: it indicates a need for the redistribution of power so as to restore First Nations self-determination, and calls for a significant renovation of the relationship between Aboriginal peoples, the state, and other Canadians. Many stakeholders, both inside and outside of government, agree that empowerment, often termed 'capacity building,' should be supported in First Nations communities. The difficulty is that empowering First Nations peoples necessarily results in the *disempowerment* of the colonial interests of government and mainstream Canadian society. It is here that the road forward is often blocked.

A revitalization of reconciliation begins with an authentic understanding of the harm done to First Nations – without attempting to rationalize or explain it away. It requires the acceptance of responsibility for the past and the involvement in the solutions that pave the way forward. For the voluntary sector, this means accepting responsibility for its knowledge and lack of knowledge, for past actions and inactions, and for its collective and individual relationships with First Nations peoples.

It also calls for a greater understanding of the insidious normality that clothes racism, and how it envelops itself in the language of public security, community, and justice, making it so damaging and pervasive in public affairs. Zygmunt Bauman's (1989) definition of racism emphasizes how it can become so normalized in our daily experience that we hardly notice it at all:

> Racism stands apart by a practice of which it is a part and which it rationalizes: a practice that combines strategies of architecture and gardening with that of medicine – in the service of the construction of an artificial social order, through cutting out the elements of the present reality that neither fit the visualized perfect reality, nor can be changed so that they do so. (65)

As a part of a constructed reality, racism can permeate and influence our construction of just and safe communities (Bauman 2001). This threat may come from the most unexpected directions. 'Community' is a word we all feel good about – a blanket that wraps around us, making us feel safe and secure. The need to maintain that 'feel-good' sense of community at a local, regional, or national level can result in a progressive tendency to protect the concept of community by rejecting and oppressing peoples or ideas that are inconsistent with it (ibid.). In this way we become morally blind to the realities experienced by the others, and either we fail to see the connections between our actions and their situation or we rationalize those actions as being necessary to ensure community safety. The massacre at Wounded Knee in 1890 is a historic example of how mass murder of Indian peoples was rationalized as being necessary to ensure the safety of the non-Aboriginal settlers. In more recent times, the unarmed protest by First Nations peoples to protect an ancient burial site at Ipperwash Provincial Park in Ontario in

1995 brought out the Ontario Provincial Police Tactics and Rescue Squad, which resulted in the shooting of an unarmed Ojibwe protestor, Dudley George, and the beating of two others (Edwards 2001). Media reports and exposés surrounding the killing of Dudley George and the subsequent criminal prosecution of a police officer have put in focus again how race influences perceptions of threat, leading to an excessive use of force by the police that is supported by mainstream society. Canadian human rights mechanisms continue to focus on individual rights violations, making it very difficult to address collective rights violations that result from structural discrimination and oppression.

As this study highlights, the voluntary sector community has somehow constructed structural barriers between itself and First Nations peoples in Canada. This social exclusion has persisted over time regardless of the degree of devastation experienced by Aboriginal peoples, including the pervasive abuse and deaths of children in the notorious residential schools. Even today, statistics outlining the landscape of harm facing First Nations children – racism, poverty, social exclusion, institutionalization, and lack of social support – are normalized. We have pushed our collective tolerance for rights violations of Aboriginal children and youth to such a point that it is hard to imagine how bad things need to get before we demand the focused action and attention that is required to redress their conditions. Exclusion and moral blindness are so antithetical to the role and values of the voluntary sector that we are compelled to try to understand why they occurred, why they are occurring now, and what we can do to make sure they do not occur again.

I have had many informal conversations with leaders, staff, and volunteers of non-Aboriginal and Aboriginal VSOs which provide some insight into the silent supports that exclude Aboriginal peoples. Although all the non-Aboriginal VSO staff and volunteers I spoke with were well-intentioned people who personally supported social inclusion, many acknowledged a distinct discomfort when thinking of how to involve Aboriginal people in their organizations.

It is important to acknowledge that this discomfort is real in the voluntary sector, as it can lead to decisions to not involve the Aboriginal community or, after one or two failed attempts at engagement, to simply stop trying. One voluntary sector leader described how each year, during the board's strategic planning session, the issue of involving more Aboriginal people in the organization would surface. The board would agree that this was important. Someone would then ask if anyone on the board knew someone Aboriginal whom they could contact. No one did, and so the question was put off until the next year.

An Aboriginal man told me how the exclusion occurs in even high-level meetings of those involved in children's services. He said that he was the only Aboriginal participant in a group that was setting national priorities for action. He shared with this group the data and stories mapping out the significant (and disproportionate) risks faced by Aboriginal children and the solutions that had been developed to redress those risks. After he finished, there was silence – no one said anything – and then the group moved on with the rest of the discussion. At the end of the day, the experiences of the Aboriginal children were not included among the top ten priorities for action.

Another Aboriginal man said that still in Canadian society, one of his key roles is to be a contradiction – to be what the stereotypes say he *cannot* be: educated, articulate, generous, caring about people across cultures, and not wearing regalia all the time. Like many of my Aboriginal friends, he is told, 'You're different from the rest [i.e., other Indians],' or 'You're good at walking in both worlds.' Although well-meaning, these compliments reflect a failure to appreciate the implied power imbalance, when 'walking in both worlds' is only an honourable duty for Aboriginal peoples and visible minorities, but not for mainstream Canadians, who fail to understand that the 'success story' they see before them is not an exception among Aboriginal peoples but rather a glimpse of what was lost in Canadian society when Aboriginal peoples and their gifts of knowledge and caring were relegated to the status of the 'other.'

I have experienced what I call the 'set-aside,' where Euro-Canadians, not understanding the harm or wanting to avoid discomfort, set aside the concerns of Aboriginal peoples. Over the years I have participated in many non-Aboriginal working groups in the voluntary sector, and I find that the conversation of rights violations is too often centred on those violations that affect non-Aboriginal Canadians whose basic rights have already been recognized. Legitimate middle-class concerns, such as ensuring family-friendly workplaces and improving recreation parks, overshadow the need to eliminate the race-based *Indian Act* or the significant risk factors facing Aboriginal children. Too often the violations of our rights as Aboriginal peoples are only an uncomfortable interruption in the conversations of the privileged. And so it is in many rights-based publications that our story is often relegated to the back chapter of a book under the headings 'vulnerable,' 'at risk,' and 'marginalized.'

These stories underscore the reality that, even among enlightened social organizations where there is a desire to engage with the Aboriginal
community, there is often too little shared commitment, information,
and action. There are positive exceptions, of course, and these need to be
highly recognized and supported in order to inspire more general action
within the voluntary sector and not lull us back into complacency.

It is natural, when working in cross-cultural contexts, for there to be
some apprehension over cultural etiquette, understanding, and language, as well as the crucial need to understand local history and context. Canada's voluntary sector, through its work in international
development, has routinely demonstrated success in collaborating with
distinct cultures worldwide, including Aboriginal peoples in countries
like Brazil and Peru whose conditions parallel the ranking of First
Nations living on-reserve in Canada. Yet it seems more difficult for
people working in the voluntary sector to collaborate with First Nations
in Canada.

Perhaps Bauman is right. Perhaps for too many Canadians, acknowledging the history of First Nations not only brings a great appreciation
for the Aboriginal peoples and cultures of this land but also calls to account the values of justice, peace, honesty, democracy, equality, and in-
dividualism upon which Canadians found their identity – whether as a
country, a voluntary sector, or citizens. It explains why, as a country, we
celebrate aspects of Aboriginal and First Nations culture that are consistent with our perceived values (as exemplified by the presence of
Aboriginal art in Canada's airports, museums, and government buildings) while we turn away from the conversations of reconciliation, resti-
tution, inclusion, and accountability. That is what assimilation looks
like today: the celebration and inclusion of First Nations arts without
the celebration and inclusion of First Nations peoples. It is a masquerade of acceptance and humanitarianism towards First Nations which
Canada sends out to the world, blinding itself to its continued efforts to
make First Nations fit into Euro-Western constructs of humanity.

Breaking the silence requires promoting the voices of First Nations to
quicken our national moral deliberation and action. Frederick Douglass,
the former slave and Abolitionist leader, in his great Independence Day
address of 1852 used words that must inform the courageous conversation ahead:

> It is not light that is needed, but fire; it is not the gentle shower, but thun-
> der. We need the storm, the whirlwind and the earthquake. The feeling of
> the nation must be quickened; the conscience of the nation must be roused;

the propriety of the nation must be startled; the hypocrisy of the nation must be exposed; and its crimes against God and man must be proclaimed and denounced. (Douglass 1852, n.p.)

Some may say that such bold actions are unnecessary to address violations of civil, cultural, and human rights in a modern civilized country such as Canada; but we also know that the major civil change called for by the Royal Commission on Aboriginal Peoples has not happened in its absence. We also know from the fine examples of Ghandi and Martin Luther King Jr that often civil change and development have been preceded by courageous, loud, and often controversial conversation framed within non-violent resistance.

In all dimensions, the voluntary sector's role in reconciliation must be shaped by an understanding that First Nations peoples are knowledgeable, resilient, and valuable peoples in their own right. Despite the ravages of colonization and assimilation, we are not a broken people waiting to be fixed by Euro-Western 'community development' approaches. We have our own answers, which need to be heard, respected, and acted upon. These answers must guide the involvement of the voluntary sector. This includes setting the pace for change. It is true that for many First Nations communities, the road back to the restoration of peace and harmony for children, youth, and families is a long one; voluntary sector organizations working in collaboration with First Nations should not be deterred if their acts of giving do not show any immediate change. The goal is to affirm and strengthen what works for the community and to be patient and respectful as the community and its members increasingly embrace confident action towards a future that they themselves define.

6. Conclusion

If you have come here to help me,
You are wasting your time ... But if you have come because
Your liberation is bound up with mine,
Then let us work together.
                    Lilla Watson, Australian Aboriginal educator and activist
                                                        (Cooney 2000, 3)

What is it that is so powerful that it separates us from one another? What makes us believe, as long as we ourselves are not hurting, and cannot hear the cries of another, that all is well? What makes us believe these are matters best dealt with by chosen leaders and not by the rest of us? What is the story, the fact, or the picture that needs to flash upon our collective consciousness to understand that loving and caring about ourselves means loving and caring for the 'others'?

Canada's voluntary sector needs actively to resist the temptation to rationalize not only its past but also its present. The consequences of Canada's voluntary sector standing still in the face of pervasive rights violations has had devastating consequences for Aboriginal children and youth. As frightening as it might feel to take steps to do something, we cannot feel morally absolved in standing silent. We must, with our entire humanity, embrace what hurts so that we can ensure a world fit for children – all of our children.

NOTE

This chapter is adapted from the article 'Same country: Same lands; 78 countries away: An exploration of nature and extent of collaboration between voluntary sector and First Nations Child and Family Services agencies in British Columbia,' published in the *First Peoples Child and Family Review* (2005). Copyright 2005 by Cindy Blackstock.

8 Letting or Making Global Collaboration Happen? An Exploration of Collaborative Efforts among International NGOs

ALAIN ROY

I first wrote this essay in the days that followed my participation in the People's Summit, held just prior to the Summit of the Americas in Quebec City in April 2001. This experience had left me excited, but also worried, about the prospects of NGO collaboration in the future.

I had been moved by the tens of thousands of people that had come together to share their frustrations about globalization, understood here as the worldwide drive towards a global economic system based on rapid growth in international trade, investment, and capital flows, and without much accountability to democratic processes or national governments. During the People's Summit, I had the opportunity to meet and exchange views with small farmers from France and southern Ontario, labour union representatives from Brazil and Eastern Canada, indigenous group representatives from South America, and concerned citizens of Quebec City. These encounters were invigorating. Lively debates occurred in forums on human rights, agriculture, labour, and the environment. It felt a lot like democracy – people from different backgrounds and experiences exchanging views and debating them openly and respectfully.

The People's Summit was not without its flaws and limitations. The deliberations were often chaotic, sometimes a cacophony of discordant voices and emphasis: engagement versus non-engagement, no trade versus different trade, sustainable development versus protection of the environment. While most participants offered thoughtful interventions, some presented apocalyptic visions, blaming globalization and international trade for everything that was going wrong in the world at present. I also worried that the Quebec People's Summit, though successful on many counts, was not building on the participants' previous experiences. It was hard to see how this gathering could become a stepping-stone towards building a broader people's movement. In some ways, it seemed an isolated event, without strong connections to similar events that had been held in Seattle, Washington, and Prague in previous years. The visible part of the People's Summit – the street demonstrations, and the now inevitable confrontations between a small group of radical protesters and the police – seemed merely a re-enactment of events we had seen elsewhere, instead of being a step forward in the evolution of the anti-globalization movement.

What also worried me was the increased radicalization of the movement, and this trend's potential consequences for the prospects of further broadening its base of support. I had taken my children to the World March of Women held in Ottawa in 2000, and to other such events. I had also seen families and individuals from all walks of life take part in the People's March in Quebec City in April 2001. Even some of my conservative acquaintances were beginning to acknowledge that this popular movement was raising important concerns and asking valid questions. The public was increasingly sympathetic to the movement. All this, however, began to change as soon as the media images of the protests became more violent. The rock-throwing, the physical confrontations with the police, and the destruction of private property were alienating not only outsiders but also many of the movement's supporters, leaving the field to radicalized, highly committed individuals willing to risk harm and arrest – demonstrations were certainly not the place to bring your children anymore.

These feelings and concerns have led me to reflect further on transnational NGO collaboration, and to explore whether such collaboration, in the light of organizational theory and NGO experience, might yield useful ideas and lessons that would let the movement grow without becoming institutionalized and bureaucratic.

Relatively little coordinated activity and no transnational structures seem to be needed in order to stage protest marches or schedule panel discussions during 'alternative' summits. However, if the anti-globalization movement is to succeed in bringing about important, systemic changes in the world order, it will require some type of organization as well as networks of actors, along with some conventions and processes in order to unite and coordinate actors and actions in pursuit of these common goals.

Rereading this essay in the fall of 2005, it seems as relevant as it did four years ago to try to find answers to my initial research questions: How do organizational structures used by the anti-globalization movement impact upon the effectiveness of its advocacy? And what organizational structures are most likely to improve the effectiveness of this movement?

1. Collaboration Experience and Theory

The precursors of transnational NGO collaboration

The idea of cooperating across borders is not a new one. Over the past century, declining costs of transportation and communication have led to increased linkages of peoples across borders, and the formation of international agencies and transnational non-governmental organizations (NGOs). One of the first such transnational NGOs was the International Red Cross, which, since its inception over a century ago has been providing protection and assistance to individuals, communities, and even whole regions in distress. Its beginnings were quite modest: in 1863, a committee of five eminent Swiss citizens organized an international conference, calling for the humane treatment of wounded soldiers and the founding of national relief societies whose members would be distinguished on the battlefield by a white armlet bearing a red cross. These proposals led, the next year, to the signing by twelve states and kingdoms of the 'Geneva Convention for the Amelioration of the Condition of the Wounded in Armies in the Field' – the first of the four great Geneva Conventions. One hundred and forty years later, the Red Cross has grown into a universal movement comprising, besides the International Committee of the Red Cross, 137 national societies with about 250 million members, and the societies' world federation, the League of Red Cross and Red Crescent Societies. Over time, the International Red Cross has contributed significantly to the development of international humanitarian law. With millions of dollars in material assistance channelled yearly to countless persons the world over, easing their suffering in times of war and peace alike, the Red Cross is perhaps the most visible transnational NGO.

Another example is the International Labour Organization (ILO), founded in 1919. The impetus provided by worker organizations contributed in part to making the ILO the world's only tripartite international agency, bringing together governments, workers, and employers in its executive bodies. The labour movement, though perceived as declining in North America, is still the most structured and best financially resourced of all social movements. It can count on union locals, provincial and national federations of labour, and an International Trade Unions Confederation that is very active in international forums.

Transnational NGO collaborations are now numerous and quite visible. The increased movement of information and news has contributed both to the visibility and the growth of NGO collaboration. Increased public awareness and dramatization of grievances have turned parts of the 'audience' into adherents and participants in transnational social movements. Media coverage of Greenpeace activists' confrontations with whalers, the events of Tiananmen Square in 1989, or the protests at the 1999 World Trade Organization's (WTO) Third Ministerial Meeting in Seattle brought these battles into the living rooms of millions of people around the world.

Changes in the international context have also contributed to increased transnational collaboration on peace, environment, and health issues among NGOs. In my experience, however, such NGO collaboration very rarely goes beyond basic information sharing. Seldom are the issues worked through, shared goals identified, and action planned deliberately. This emerging, rather than deliberate, nature of NGO collaborations is not necessarily a negative; in fact, some authors have argued that the emerging nature of NGO collaborations is an asset. The fact that NGO campaigns are driven not by budgets and organizational structures but by ideas and a vision of a better world is a quality to be preserved (Korten 1991). Others have said this emergence makes NGO campaigns agile and hard to oppose because of the absence of a precise shape and leadership structure. It also allows organizations and individuals to participate in the collaborative effort on their own terms.

Still, I wonder if NGOs would not benefit from a further structuring of the mechanisms they use to collaborate across borders. The idea is not necessarily to aim to create new global structures or bureaucracies, but to develop work methods and ongoing commitment to collaborative action, allowing key actors to effectively come together to strategize and act when needed.

The pursuit of various objectives through collaboration

Scholars have argued that collaboration can bring people and organizations together to solve problems in ways that competition cannot, because 'parties who see different aspects of a problem can constructively explore their differences and search for solutions that go beyond their own limited vision of what is possible' (Gray 1989, 5).

NGOs may collaborate for various reasons. Some, such as the aware-ness-raising work of environmental groups over the past few decades, seek to call attention to a problem area; others may seek to protest or resist particular actions (as in cases of NGOs opposing the building of dams and other infrastructure deemed to have detrimental effects for people and the environment). Still other collaborations involve sus-tained action over time towards precise objectives. The Jubilee Debt Campaign (calling for the cancellation of 100 per cent of unpayable and unfair poor-country debts), and the international campaign to ban landmines are good illustrations of this type of collaborative action. It is thus helpful to classify collaborations along a continuum, according to their objectives. I have distinguished among four broad types of col-laboration objectives: *information sharing, dialogue, agenda building,* and *action* (see table 8.1). These categories, though not definitive, are useful in identifying the different processes for reaching the stated objectives, the particular type of leadership required, and the most effective mech-anisms or tools to make the collaborations work.

With regard to the typology described in table 8.1, I do not wish to suggest that collaborations focused on action are necessarily more de-sirable or worthy than others. However, it seems obvious that the inten-sity of the collaboration, the depth of exchanges, and the frequency of interaction increase as the collaboration moves from information shar-ing to action. It also seems (though information sharing is not without its obstacles) that there are increased challenges as collaborators at-tempt to identify common assumptions, process information, and iden-tify courses of action that call either for collective efforts or a division of labour among collaborators.

I would argue as well that the more collaborators focus on basic in-formation sharing, the easier it is for people and organizations to par-ticipate and to feel that they are part of the collaboration on their own terms. Collaborators may share information without having to agree on a particular analysis or strategy. At the other end of the spectrum, ac-tion-focused collaboration calls for at least some level of agreement or commitment to a particular analysis or strategy.

Finally, I would note that these categories are not mutually exclusive, and that people are often collaborating at various levels simultaneously. This seems to have been the case in the protests of November 1999, dur-ing the World Trade Organization Third Ministerial Meeting in Seattle. As I will show in section two of this essay, the people who went to Seattle clearly collaborated at all levels. The collaboration was most

Table 8.1
Collaboration typology

Type of Collaboration	Objective	Type of Leadership	Process	Mechanisms	Examples
Information Sharing	Share information	Information provider Processor	Making connections Identification of potential collaborators	Print communication Email Internet Face-to-face meetings	CIVICUS International Council of Voluntary Agencies
Dialogue	Draw on the knowledge of various organizations to create a holistic view of issues	Convener Moderator	Bringing people together in a way that makes them consider themselves potential collaborators	Conversations Teach-ins Seminars Learning circles LISTSERVS Chat groups	Anti-globalization movement Peace movement World March of Women
Agenda Building	Work through issues Consensus building	Facilitator Negotiator	Data analysis Choice work Consensus building	Face-to-face meetings Public deliberation methodologies Electronic forums	Anti-globalization movement Jubilee Debt Coalition
Action	Organizing Sharing resources Joint action	Organizer Motivator Empowerment	Resource mobilization Organization	Conversations Networking Awareness raising Mobilizing	Transparency International Oxfam International Coalition to Ban Landmines Jubilee Debt Coalition

obvious at the level of information sharing, but there was also evidence of dialogue among a core group of organizations and individuals, as well as several efforts to work through a common set of principles and to build a common agenda that would continue to oppose a certain type of trade liberalization. There were also some concrete, coordinated actions at the tactical level. Groups tried to coordinate some of their protest efforts to ensure maximum impact. Public events and media relations were carefully planned.

Collaboration and collective behaviour

In the 1970s and 1980s, protests against the Apartheid regime in South Africa were held on the African continent and in Europe, the United States, and Canada. During the Vietnam War, protests broke out not only in the United States but also in Canada, Western Europe, and elsewhere around the world. In recent years, a variety of voluntary groups, philanthropic organizations, and international agencies came together to create movements in favour of human rights, the preservation of the environment, and the promotion of rights and opportunities for women, to name just a few major issues. How can we explain these diverse manifestations of international collective action? How do these international collective efforts take shape? How do people from around the world sometimes come to act in concert?

It is useful here to look at Mayer N. Zald's typology of collective behaviour (Cooperrider and Dutton 1999), which distinguishes three broad types: (1) the *'demonstration effect'*; (2) networked *social and environmental campaigns*; and (3) *transnational NGOs* (international organizations).

Because collaboration behaviours are dynamic, there are many grey areas that make it difficult to pigeonhole some organizations into behaviour types. Over time, collaboration can move from the 'demonstration effect' type to the networking type, or vice versa. On the other hand, it is probably extremely rare (though not impossible) that a transnational NGO will move back to a looser form of collaboration, once a certain number of its collaboration processes have become institutionalized.

The 'demonstration effect'

In the simplest cases, people and groups take collective action without much intentional planning and coordination. Simple demonstration and diffusion processes are at play (Cooperrider and Dutton 1999). The 'demonstration effect' occurs when individuals or groups come to model their own behaviour on the behaviour of other groups or individuals with whom they are not formally or directly interacting. Such mimicking usually happens between groups that share values and other important characteristics. This demonstration effect seems to have occurred among the groups questioning 'globalization' and the 'Washington consensus on trade liberalization.' Many groups and individuals from around the globe, without any direct contact with each other, came to adopt similar behaviours and take similar actions against the type of economic order that was being proposed. There is little indication that strong links originally existed between the various groups in Latin America, Africa, South Asia, Europe, and North America, other than a sense of similar realities across vast distances, and a perception that similar behaviour, strategies, and tactics were appropriate. They staged the early protests, marches, and rallies against 'free trade' agreements and boycotts of multinational companies around the world.

Information flows are key for the demonstration effect to occur. Media coverage of the anti-globalization movement was particularly important in generating the demonstration effect, since national boundaries play no role in preventing such copying behaviour unless government authorities are able to suppress the flow of information. NGO actions in one part of the world have made people realize that their grievances were not unique, and spurred individuals and groups in other regions to identify others in their communities who shared their grievances and to stage similar actions.

There are limits to the ability of the demonstration effect to sustain parallel movements around the world. As long as acute problems or grievances persist and large public mobilization is displayed, the effect can occur. When public mobilization energies diminish, the participants' attention wanes and the momentum and enthusiasm required to attract people is reduced. Copying behaviour then declines, as the issue loses perceived importance and immediate relevance. However, the demonstration effect can sometimes be reproduced over time. The cycles of mobilization of the peace movement exemplify this phenomenon.

Social and environmental campaigns

The International Union for the Conservancy of Nature (IUCN), formed just after the Second World War, was one of the early focal points for networking on environmental issues. This hybrid organization, comprising states, NGOs, and government agencies, still plays this role today, although it now fits the description of a full-fledged transnational organization more than a network.

Although many 'global' environmental organizations exist, such as Greenpeace, Friends of the Earth, and the World Wildlife Fund, much of the global power of the environmental movement derives from the global network they have built rather than from specific individual organizations. While one NGO can lead efforts on a specific issue, it is usually the combination of efforts from the broader environmental network that puts the issue firmly on the public and political agenda. In addition to the large transnational environmental NGOs, there are thousands of small, active environmental groups, often working locally but which are also active internationally. It is these groups with connections to international development NGOs in Canada and other northern countries, as well as in the South, that were core initiators of campaigns to make multilateral development banks more accountable for the environmental impacts of the projects they supported.

There are now thousands of loosely connected environmental networks, each comprising dozens, even hundreds, of organizations, sometimes working separately on specific issues but also coming together at times on common campaigns. Most of the umbrella organizations for these networks are organized along traditional lines, with a board of directors, which, in principle, sets policy and oversees the organization's activities; they also have staff responsible for various programs, who report to an executive director. In practice, however, these are relatively flat organizations with blurred, hierarchical lines. These organizations also count on a membership base that has grown significantly over the last thirty years. The total number of members of Canadian environmental groups is estimated at several million.

The international organization

Although there are many forms of international organizations, I shall focus on two forms often seen in the NGO world: the *networked organization* and the *confederation*. While the idea of a network can conjure up the image of voluntary, reciprocal, and horizontal patterns of communication and exchange rather than a single organization, in the NGO world there are many hybrids. These hybrids often call themselves networks, but the way they function and the image they project is that of a single organization with shared goals, close alignment of strategies, a certain chain of command, and a chain of reporting or communication.

The Third World Network, the Canadian Environmental Network, and Transparency International are examples of this type.

The confederation, on the other hand, is an easily identifiable form of transnational collaboration, exemplified by organizations such as Amnesty International, Oxfam International, and Friends of the Earth. Groups associated with these transnational organizations often come together under common international headquarters and increasingly develop common functions, such as research, advocacy, and public relations, in addition to agreeing on a division of roles among the parts of the confederation. For example, at CARE, certain national member organizations play a leadership or coordinating role in certain countries (e.g., CARE Canada was the 'lead' CARE agency in Cameroon and Haiti in the late 1990s).

Fredrik Galtung has described in detail the workings of Transparency International (Florini 2000). In many ways, this is a simple type of transnational network: what started as a network of individuals (mainly academics) seeking to curb international corruption turned into a single, international, non-governmental organization, which gained recognition and became effective quite rapidly in the 1990s. Transparency International (TI) now has national chapters actively designing their own national anti-corruption strategies in more than seventy countries. Over time, TI has set up a secretariat in Berlin, with a growing team of paid management and staff whose main work is to support national chapters and conduct the core research for TI's 'Corruption Perception Index.' Although these national chapters retain some autonomy, there is a trend towards more integration and alignment of strategies. Through international meetings and communication, TI now has its members work in a coordinated fashion around key objectives, which the national chapters then focus much of their energies and resources towards achieving. Others have noted that TI's emphasis on institutional change rather than exposés and high-profile media coverage of corruption scandals may well have promoted top-down leadership rather than grass-roots mobilization, and thus contributed to this increased centralization of its objectives and operations.

In a study of thirty transnational social movements, Chadwick Alger found that at some point all, without exception, created a transnational organization with headquarters, periodic meetings of representatives from a number of countries for policy-making on one or more global issues, and permanent secretariats to help implement these policies (Smith, Chatfield, and Pagnucco 1997). These transnational social movement organizations tended to emerge from more informal networks composed of local organizations and individuals linked through common concerns, but they all created a 'new' organization – a structure – at some point. There are certainly exceptions. In the Conservation Breeding Specialist Group, an NGO based in Minnesota, the individual members (many of them scientists) work both independently and cooperatively to fight the increasing speed at which the extinction of various species is threatening biodiversity. *Observatoire de la mondialisation*, a group of European intellectuals, is researching the impact of globalization and trying to develop alternatives to the dominant models. Nonetheless, most movements or networks have found that the benefits of institutionalization outweigh its costs (Cooperrider and Dutton 1999).

2. The Emerging Organizational Shape of the Movement Opposing Economic Globalization

The anti-globalization movement is somewhat different from the transnational movements mentioned in the previous section. Instead of having a single goal or a clearly defined set of objectives, the movement is characterized by the parallel pursuit of compatible, though not necessarily identical, goals. Although better global governance and increased social justice are goals probably shared by the majority of members in the movement, most individuals and organizations are pursuing particular agendas: better working conditions, protection of the environment, elimination of certain tariff barriers, increased foreign aid – or, more ambitiously for some groups, the end of capitalism. While there is regular communication among the NGOs, the flow of information is lopsided, with a few organizations at the core of the movement dominating the conversation, and with loose information loops. Despite occasional efforts to discuss or review strategies, there is much less sense of a deliberately coordinated strategy than in the other collaboration efforts reviewed earlier.

The other interesting characteristic of this emerging movement is that it is turning its focus away from national governments as key advocacy targets. Although some of the UN conferences of the 1990s and some campaigns aimed at the World Bank had global entities or processes as targets, much of the advocacy was directed at national governments. The emerging movement contesting the dominant model of economic globalization puts, quite clearly, less emphasis on lobbying national governments. The main target is different, and it seems at once clearer and more elusive. The international trade agreements produced by the World Trade Organization, with its vast bureaucracy in Geneva and its ministerial conferences, such as the November 1999 meeting in Seattle, have been the clear target of the protests to date. However, a review of the materials and analyses of the organizations at the core of the movement underscores the fact that the target is more diffuse. The real target is the globalized economic system, seen as being dominated by corporate trade and financial institutions that are not accountable to democratic processes or to national governments. It is also sometimes referred to as the 'Washington Consensus,' after a set of policies agreed upon by the United States Government, the International Monetary Fund, and the World Bank, policies that are recommended to, and, at times, allegedly imposed upon national governments throughout the world.

It is thus important to distinguish between two levels of campaigning. At one level, the movement is about whether particular policies, rules, and trade agreements are unjust or oppressive. This campaign includes specific challenges to trade and intellectual property agreements, such as those that deprive people of access to life-saving medicines. The movement also denounces sections of the WTO Agreement on Agriculture, which reduces food security by forcing people out of subsistence agriculture and into export cash-crop production, exposing them to the instability of global food markets. The trade rules that frequently prevent governments from making and upholding agreed-upon international rules to protect the environment, and trade clauses that threaten the provision of public services such as health care and education, are also condemned.

The broader campaign – the second level – is about democracy, accountability, and a just adjudication of disputes between countries. WTO trade rules and other agreements, such as the North American Free Trade Agreement (NAFTA), have come to cover a broad range of areas and issues, from investment, to border controls, to intellectual property, with major implications for domestic economies and policy choices, regulation, and enforcement.

For the movement opposing economic globalization, current trends in trade liberalization indicate a lack of attention to developmental needs and poverty eradication, and a focus on market access as the end goal. This is due in part to unequal power relations among countries, and in part to the need for national development strategies to be locally relevant. Harvard University Professor Dani Rodrick (2001) has shown how the WTO is devoted largely to market access despite its stated purpose to 'raise living standards around the world' (1). Rodrick convincingly shows that free trade is not the typical outcome of the trade process. Consumers and their welfare do not seem to be high on the trade agenda, which has been shaped in response to a tug-of-war between exporters and multinational corporations in developed countries, on the one hand, and import-competing interests (mainly labour) on the other. Consumers, the supposed beneficiaries of the trade process, are nowhere to be found in the WTO. Thus, the trade agreements are largely the product of intense lobbying by specific export groups in the United States and Europe, or else of compromises among multinational companies and domestic interests. Observers in the anti-globalization movement argue that there is nothing in the multilateral trade negotiations process that ensures that their outcomes are consistent with development goals.

Trade rounds are bargaining sessions to which the wealthy countries send vast armies of lawyers, industry representatives, bureaucrats, and trade specialists to prepare and conduct negotiations. Not surprisingly, countries that lack the vast resources of the world's economic and political giants cannot successfully defend their own interests. The dispute settlement mechanisms that have been established to mediate trade arguments between countries also require major resources and expertise.

While in theory WTO decisions are reached by consensus, the real decision-making authority lies with the countries with the greatest economic power and political clout. This reality has been formalized to some extent with the creation of the 'Quad' group – the U.S., EU, Japan, and Canada. While some large developing countries, like Brazil and India, do play active roles at times, the Quad basically drives the agenda. According to Walden Bello, 'The problem with transparency and democracy [in the WTO] is that even within the official process they do not exist ... The Quad countries basically determine which issues are important and come to the floor, and which issues do not come to the floor' (Senevirtane 1996, n.p.).

The battle in Seattle

'Seattle' has been described in many ways. The columnist Charles Krauthammer, writing in *Time* magazine (13 December 1999) declared that the protests signified the 'return of the Luddites.' The television networks, which focused on the clash between protesters and police forces, dubbed it 'the battle in Seattle.' NGO leaders, on the other hand, described Seattle as a 'watershed,' with the dramatic collapse of the talks, and a 'beachhead' for 'the mobilization of mass resistance to the WTO by civil society groups ... [which] set the stage for a potential rollback of the agenda for economic globalization' (Barlow and Clarke 2000, 1).

Many accounts in the media attempted to characterize the events in Seattle as a spontaneous outburst of frustration felt by a variety of disparate special interest groups (Krauthammer 1999). It is true that the 50,000 or so protesters present in Seattle were loosely connected; just how much coordination and collaboration existed among the various groups is not entirely clear. Even people who were closely involved in the pre-Seattle planning are not entirely sure how it all came together in the way it did. A panel discussion that brought together representatives from organizations at the forefront of the Canadian protests revealed that although key actors knew each other, they had had very limited contacts.[1] But some of the principal architects of the international protests have described 'Seattle' as the focal point of a year or more of real collaboration among NGOs, which started to take a clearer shape as soon as the European Union and Japan announced their agreement in early 1999 to launch a new round of negotiations. NGOs from around the world – some having worked on the protests against the GATT Uruguay Round Agreements, and others that had been involved in the fight against the Multilateral Agreement on Investment (MAI) – came together at that time to sketch out a campaign plan. Thus it seems fairly clear that the Seattle events were not spontaneous; rather, for several months at least, NGOs had come to some agreement on an overall analysis, and had been planning actions around the WTO meeting.

The international campaigning involved each of some thirty country-based campaigns. In Canada, for example, the Council of Canadians, the Polaris Institute, and the Canadian Labour Congress played leadership roles. Similar campaigns were established in the UK, France, Germany, and Australia. Active campaigns were also mounted in India, Indonesia, and other southern countries.

A series of meetings in late 1998 and in early 1999 brought together the leaders of several of these country-based campaigns, as well as intellectual leaders from civil society. U.S.-based Global Trade Watch acted as the main convener of most of these meetings. Global Trade Watch, a division of Public Citizen, the national consumer group founded in 1972 by Ralph Nader, had built substantial capacity and diverse contacts with NGOs in the U.S. and around the world, making it a legitimate convener.

These meetings, however, were few and far apart. This limited the extent to which the groups were able to work through issues and strategies together. Even though we often talk of a shrinking world, distances still matter. New technologies, including email, certainly make information exchanges faster and more convenient. However, they don't necessarily improve the quality of the communication or exchanges between people. As activist Lori Wallach has pointed out, 'Even though the Internet is used to share information, the real deep planning and organizing is still done person to person' (Naim 2000, 47). Video conferencing and live chat services are available, but costs and different levels of access to technology have prevented the group of collaborators from using them to work through issues. This has left them with the very rough tool of one-to-one emails and LISTSERVs to come up with joint statements or strategies. Such processes are still rudimentary, with a handful of people providing the intellectual leadership to civil society and drafting such statements.

Nonetheless, in this way the 'WTO: Shrink or Sink' petition circulated worldwide in the wake of the collapse of the Seattle talks, and was signed by more than 1,500 organizations. This particular statement was reviewed and agreed upon by some thirty people; it was then posted on the websites of different members of the loose set of collaborators involved at the time, including Public Citizen (U.S.), and the Third World Network (Malaysia), where organizations were invited to sign on. People had the option to sign it or not. But there was almost no opportunity for discussion or modification.

This type of process did not foster a deep level of collaboration. The imperative of getting as broad a coalition as possible to support the statement, and the limited time available to draft it, meant that the statement stayed at the level of very broad principles. Very few people, even opponents of the collaborators, would oppose the principles of protecting the environment and ensuring social development.[2]

Even so, the statement proved to be quite effective as a blueprint for strategies to counter specific items of the world trade agenda. The more pointed criticism about the lack of transparency and accountability, and the request to stop the expansion of the WTO agenda, still allowed a wide range of people to participate in the campaign on their own terms.

I believe the lack of forums for the collaborators to work through issues together also had the effect of inadvertently concentrating power and leadership in the hands of a few individuals, to whom others loosely involved in the collaboration looked for guidance and direction. Almost all of the NGO documents I reviewed point to the same sources of leadership and analysis. Most of these are based in the United States: the AFL-CIO, Public Citizen, the International Forum on Global Exchange, and the Institute for Agriculture and Trade Policy. Other leading organizations were ATTAC (France), the Third World Network (Malaysia), Focus on the Global South (Thailand), and the Centre for Science and the Environment (India).

These groups played a key role as information processors. They had the resources to stay on top of the rapidly evolving trade agenda and provide early warning and interpretation of proposed negotiation texts. A review of the websites of most groups that signed the 'Shrink or Sink' petition revealed that most of them did not develop their own analysis of the WTO or international trade issues; instead, they reproduced or relied heavily upon the analyses supplied by these leading organizations. The organization for which I worked at the time, the Canadian Council for International Co-operation, drew heavily from the analysis prepared by the Third World Network and Focus on the Global South for the brief it presented to the Canadian parliamentary hearings on the WTO negotiations.

Although such a process had little in common with traditional collaborations or strategic planning, it was a real collaboration; indeed, I would argue that in the complex environment in which the NGOs were operating – characterized by uncertainty and much heterogeneity among key stakeholders – there was practically no way to operationalize the collaboration other than to let it emerge.

This collaboration is based on 'generative relationships.' This concept, advanced by Lane and Maxfield (1996), suggests that strategy and direction emerge through interactions among many stakeholders instead of being set after an analysis of the environment and the development of future scenarios (Zimmerman and Dart 1998). All the right conditions existed for building generative relationships.[3] Even though there wasn't much in-depth interaction among the collaborators, there existed some *aligned directedness,* that is, basic agreement about a general set of principles and interests. There was also much *heterogeneity* among the potential collaborators, specifically, diverse ideas and areas of competence (environment, labour issues, intellectual property, and so on). There was an interest and ability of potential collaborators to engage in recurring interactions (even if most were rather superficial). Finally, there was an ability and willingness of groups to engage in joint actions. The protests in Seattle provided a key focal point on which energies could be concentrated. Commitment to collaboration (however loose) could also be demonstrated.

The *aligned directedness* was clear. The objective was best captured by the slogan, 'No New Round: Turn Around.' Beyond this and the 'Shrink or Sink' petition, the collaboration focused on opening many more lines of communication among NGOs worldwide within the limits of language and the barriers mentioned above.[4] This allowed the emergence of strategies that informed each other as interactions were multiplied. I would argue that these strategies became so influenced by one another that they blended into what became a single NGO strategy by the time of the Seattle WTO meeting. The International Forum on Globalization carried this generative-relationships strategy into the Seattle actions, with a massive teach-in.

Public Citizen, labour unions, and other leading groups encouraged people to form small groups, create their message, and come down to Seattle. The labour-sponsored rally brought together 50,000 demonstrators (including 41 busloads of Canadians). 'People came with the most amazing creativity ... It resulted in a very good picture of the widespread impacts of world trade, everything from people dressed up in turtle costumes to indigenous rights groups to people from faith-based organizations who formed prayer circles,' said Public Citizen organizer Juliette Beck in a magazine interview (EcoWorld 2000). Banners and sound bites alone don't change the world, but they shape perspectives. One such slogan generated by the collaboration was *'Le monde n'est pas une marchandise'* (the world is not for sale), which appeared on a banner carried by French farmers. Such messages have left an imprint on people's attitudes, and have been repeated often since Seattle.

More than 3,000 journalists came from around the world to cover the Seattle conference. But instead of reporting on the liberalization of trade for the business sections of their newspapers and broadcast networks, they sent home stories of butterflies, turtles, Roquefort cheese, impoverished coffee growers, and sweatshops. As one commentator observed, 'Most of the world went to bed one night not even knowing there was such a thing as the WTO and woke up the next morning filled with curiosity about it' (Barlow and Clarke 2000, 1).

The battle since Seattle

In the spring of 2000, the leaders of the Seattle protests held a key four-day meeting in Boston, which brought approximately one hundred

NGO representatives from around the world. While the meeting provided opportunities for debriefing, reflection, and some forward planning, participants were not entirely satisfied with the level of focus and direction.

In Canada, a similar attempt was made to bring more clarity to NGO strategy. The Polaris Institute and the Council of Canadians acted as conveners for a series of meetings that brought together some thirty Canadian NGO representatives. Even though a group called 'The Common Front on the WTO' was established, with its own staff co-ordinator, the meetings amounted to little more than information-sharing sessions. There were only very limited attempts to build a dialogue among attending groups. One participant privately described the encounters as a 'series of debriefings and statements about people's specific concerns.' These information exchanges remain useful, but it is hard to see how they will bring the collaboration to another level. NGOs must continue to work towards a common analysis of the threats and opportunities arising from trade agreements. So far, there is still little unity in terms of analysis and future strategy.

In the summer of 2006, the Doha Round of WTO negotiations collapsed. For civil society organizations, the Doha Round became the focal point for much activity after Seattle, cementing a campaign for economic rights and social justice, despite the disparate specific objectives pursued and differences in strategy. The Doha Round collapse offers a unique opportunity for civil society organizations to come together to propose new approaches to building a more just international trading system. This will require deliberation processes and consensus-building skills, something quite different than what was required during the pre-Seattle phase.

Collaboration during the period leading up to Seattle centred on information sharing and dialogue. As the participants' credibility was high, there was very little discussion of priorities for the filtering of information. Basic means of information sharing, such as email, were adequate. In the upcoming phase, which calls for work on choices and consensus-building, there will be a greater need for facilitation and negotiation. This phase also calls for more in-depth interactions, including face-to-face meetings, among NGOs; but such interactions seem unlikely; travel is still outside the reach of most southern NGOs, and many northern ones as well. Nor does technology solve the problem. One of the most technology-savvy NGOs working on trade issues is the Institute for Agriculture and Trade Policy (IATP), which has developed and maintains a website and a number of LISTSERVs that are supposed to facilitate the exchange of information about agricultural trade. However, a scan of the website and LISTSERVs reveals that almost all the postings are from IATP, although an effort is made to post analysis produced by other organizations from around the world.

It might be that to get to an increased level of intensity of interactions, the collaboration will have to be more clearly focused. Clearer objectives will need to be identified, and practical demands and alternatives put forward. To do this, the collaboration may need a more properly resourced coordination function, and facilitators who can legitimately convene groups and encourage dialogue. The current leaders of the anti-WTO protests do not necessarily fit the bill, given the particular interests they represent, their somewhat rigid ideological concerns, and their perceived ability to dominate the agenda. It seems to me that more appropriate facilitators would be individuals or organizations that appear to be less dogmatic, and are focused on positive outcomes for people more than a particular ideology. However, it remains to be seen if the current key actors are willing to risk losing control of the 'alternative agenda' by letting others step in and play key roles.

Because the trade agenda is varied and complex, moving to this next phase is not an easy task. The dominant presence and resources of labour and environmental groups means that specific complex issues will remain a key part of the NGO agenda, even though establishing common ground between trade and labour rights, or trade and the environment can be among the most divisive issues for northern and southern NGOs.

What will be accomplished if the collaboration still allows disparate messages to be projected to a broad mass of people? Some NGO leaders have suggested that the protesters risk becoming satisfied with their oppositional stance, without proposing clear alternatives. 'The absence of discipline, professionalism and co-ordination revealed a movement that is in a sense self-indulgent; a movement for whom, perhaps, the protest is more important and satisfying than that which is being protested about, its outcome and those most seriously affected,' argued Jubilee 2000 UK Director Ann Pettifog (2000, n.p.).

It is hard for NGOs that are focused on action to justify spending a lot of energy and resources on the process of collaboration, but this effort seems unavoidable. How can NGOs build on previous work and avoid reinventing the wheel? How can NGOs working on different issues concretely coordinate their activities better? A more deliberate exploration of norms and mechanisms that can foster more intense cooperation could identify avenues to pursue.

Experience has shown that this 'process' work probably should not be done in isolation from substantive issues. NGOs have shown limited interest in working on structures and processes separate from concrete issues.

Leaders of existing NGO networks have also suggested that NGOs seek new resources (or allocate existing resources) to experiment with new consensus-building and decision-making approaches. The idea of developing basic cooperation agreements among NGOs has also been proposed. This would not necessarily mean writing a code of cooperation or criteria for membership in a new international NGO secretariat, but rather initiating a conversation about the ways in which NGOs might better cooperate on research, capacity building, and participation by the southern NGOs (which tend to be under-represented in the UN and other global forums). Using computer-based technology or physical space to house key resources on which NGOs could draw for research and advocacy has also been deemed desirable.

3. Which Way Forward?

Organizing to bring together various social movements for systemic change is certainly a challenge. Korten (1995) says that one of the key challenges of civil society is to further build the capacity to quickly and flexibly link diverse and dispersed individuals and organizations motivated by voluntary and values-based commitments. Korten doesn't seem to be worried about what some perceive as a lack of structure in the movement; rather, the fact that the leadership of civil society is diffuse is a source of strength. Effective citizen networks have many leaders who are able to function independently, but are nonetheless informed by one another's ideas and activities. The diversity of the members of citizen networks allows them to consider problems from a variety of perspectives, and this is more likely to bring about innovative solutions. Korten argues that although the lack of defined structures makes such networks incoherent and difficult to sustain, it also gives them the ability to surround, infiltrate, and 'rattle' much larger organizations.

Many NGO leaders and commentators think that the movement needs structure that will allow for the development of more inspiring long-term goals and progress towards a short-term program. Michael Albert (2000) believes that social movements would benefit from further unification and structuring: 'We haven't combined our forces around a suitable subset of all the many possible immediate aims ... As a result, people enter our movements and after a time they become disenchanted with the lack of focus of people's energies, and thus with the lack of power to win gains.' Albert asks why NGO solidarity about a shared program could not be coupled with mutual respect for continuing differences in priority and in focus with regard to other issues. 'Our demonstrations should not be the centrepiece of our movement work.' He argues that activists need to provide venues where people can participate peacefully. His argument seems to point to a new type of rainbow coalition, whose work would reflect the sum of the diverse parts (programs) of the coalition, rather than the lowest common denominator. Each group would continue to exist and would maintain its identity while being part of this broadly structured coalition in which analysis, technical support, and constituencies would be pooled. The leadership for a particular activity would go to the organization(s) closest to the issue. The leadership would thus rotate over time (Albert 2000).

What isn't clear in this scheme of things is what happens when two opposing views on a particular issue are represented within the coalition. One can suppose that both views could coexist within this structure (as two alternatives to be considered by governments and other decision-makers). Activists belonging to such a structure would have to 'water down their wine' on specific subjects. But this could become acceptable if the power relation or leverage of such a coalition is increased, and if such a coalition helps gain more credibility and legitimacy.

The People's Summit processes are a good basis to start from, even if some find them too institutionalized. Another potential model is the World Social Forum (WSF), which was held for the first time in Porto Alegre, 25–30 January 2001, in the same time period as the World Economic Forum in Davos. The World Social Forum is conceived as 'an open meeting space designed for in-depth reflection, democratic debate of ideas, formulation of proposals, free exchange of experiences and planning of effective action among entities and movements of civil society that oppose neo-liberalism and a world dominated by capital and any form of imperialism and that are engaged in building a planetary society centered on the human being' (IGTN 2005).

The first World Social Forum involved three types of activities: (a) a series of daily plenary sessions with several invited speakers; (b) presentations of current initiatives and exchange of experiences; and (c) strategy meetings to develop networks and strengthen ties among groups that engage in similar forms of organization. WSF organizers scheduled the plenary sessions in accordance with suggestions from

NGOs. Concurrently, workshops and thematic sessions were organized in response to participants' various interests and requests. Groups that wanted to organize a workshop on a particular topic contacted the organizing committee, which then added the workshop to the official program. What is most interesting about the World Social Forum is the idea to create a space away from the events of the multilateral institutions such as the WTO, G8, IMF, and World Bank. This allows NGOs to focus their energies on building alternatives and growing the movement as a democratic alternative to the present economic order, rather than a romantic anti-capitalist reaction.

The forum was a bit chaotic, however. Canadian journalist Naomi Klein (2001) has described the free-floating, contentious, and sometimes disorganized deliberations. The forum faced many issues related to decision-making. The tensions that arose from the diversity of participants and different expectations during the forum raised a number of questions for Klein: How are decisions made in this movement of movements? Who decides which 'civil society organizations' dialogue with leaders inside the walled enclaves at Davos, Quebec City, or Doha? The need for more process and structure is apparent. The comments of participants after the forum seemed to indicate that what is desirable is some higher degree of consolidation of agendas, but not the development of a single agenda or of a particular structure. The core idea of the movement is its opposition to a certain homogenization of thought; civil society cannot merely turn the tables and propose a different kind of uniformity.

The organizers of the first forum worked hard to turn it into a permanent, worldwide process. An International Committee was formed to oversee preparations for the World Social Forums held the next two years in Porto Alegre, Brazil, before moving to Mumbai, India, in 2004. The International Committee is not an authority in a power structure, and to date no mechanisms exist to address representation issues. There are no clear voting rules and procedures. The composition of the committee strives for balance in terms of representation, but it doesn't conceive of itself becoming a bureaucratic structure. It is also very careful not to claim or be seen to represent global civil society.

The World Social Forum remains an open space. Anybody interested can come; there is no accreditation process, no screening of participants. Any individual or organization can organize a workshop, discussion, or event. The only (unwritten) expectation is that participants will have read the Charter of Principles (WSF 2006) prepared by the forum's main organizers, and share the broad values and ideas contained in it. There is probably no better way to move forward than to start from shared passions around certain issues, and then link social movements together so as to achieve greater coordination.

The 2004 Mumbai World Social Forum had all of the features of its predecessors: more than 1,000 self-organized events that brought together anywhere from half a dozen to a few thousand people, with leafleting, banners, street demonstrations and parades, music and exhibits. The most notable change was that a sizeable majority of participants in Mumbai came from movements of domestic indigenous peoples (Adivasis), and from poor people's movements. The presence of these movements may well have contributed to a shift in the culture of the World Social Forum by forcing new issues on the agenda, such as the survival of tribal people, land rights, and subsistence livelihoods, and by making the World Social Forum less of the middle-class and northern NGO affair that the previous ones had been (Conway 2004). The 2005 World Social Forum returned to Porto Alegre, and in 2006 there was a 'polycentric' WSF held in Bamako (Mali), Caracas (Venezuela), and Karachi (Pakistan).

Where the World Social Forum seems to continue to fall short is in not allowing itself enough time and space and not having developed processes to work through differences, priority-setting, and the determination of choices. It might be utopian to make many key decisions during short forums, bringing together thousands of people, but time must at least be set aside to specifically discuss strategy and decision-making. Technology also allows for sophisticated online work and even decision-making through email voting, which would permit large group decision-making. If the forum process truly becomes an ongoing one, there is the potential for increased intensity of exchanges and coordination. Perhaps driven by concerns about the lack of strategy and priorities, the 2005 World Social Forum featured some changes, including a 'Wall of Proposals' (*100 propositions* 2006). One International Council member actively urged participants to propose and support the Assembly of Social Movements' endorsement of a specific campaign.

4. Conclusion

NGOs are in a long-term learning process of experimenting with structures and norms to link diverse social movements. Over the next ten to twenty years, this process may well bring about a truly global civil society and significant global change.

However, there are still major differences among NGOs about the best way to move forward. Some feel that the People's Summits and the World Social Forum are too structured and rigid. Many others, however, think that the current methods of working together are not adequate. It is true that a lot has been achieved over the last twenty years. There are more connections among NGOs from around the world than at any time before. The information sharing among NGOs has led to parallel efforts, and to the emergence of synergies that have had significant impact. However, many feel that it is now time for more deliberate attempts to collaborate across borders and cultures, and seek to link the energies and forces of civil societies wherever they are.

Many factors need to be assembled for collaborations to be effective. A powerful and engaging vision is probably the most decisive factor. I believe the anti-economic globalization movement has this. Its specific objectives may be somewhat indefinite, but the overall vision of a world where democracy is upheld, where people can lead dignified lives, and where the spiritual, social, and cultural facets of our lives have their place alongside the economic aspects is a very engaging one. Proper leadership, of the nurturing kind, is required. Timing – recognizing opportunities to collaborate – is also key. So are the processes and organizational structures the movement gives itself. Too little attention has been paid to this aspect by NGOs. One of the challenges of writing this essay was the dearth of NGO documentation on the processes they use to work with one another. NGO websites and documentation centres are full of analyses of the ills of the world on which they are working. Campaign documents include statements, fact sheets, and long policy papers, but usually very little practical information about how to cooperate with the other members of the campaign – sometimes not even a short statement recognizing other collaborators.

Whether there is really a need for more structure and process remains hard to answer. If the present efforts to create a more just global society are envisioned as labour activism – a movement of working people and organizations seeking to gain more just relations with their employers – then it may be necessary to create more structure and process. In other words, if civil society sees itself as a sphere fairly separate from that of governments and the private sector, then it should consider further structuring itself to strengthen its voice and increase its power in relation to the transnational structures that the public and private sectors have already established. But if civil society sees itself as a space for dialogue and action outside the constraints of sometimes-narrow government debates and the short-term vision of most private-sector interests, maybe the need for more structure is less pressing than the need to foster more and better conversation and dialogue.

There certainly seems to be a need for more reciprocating conversations. Bombarded by data and knowledge from specialized disciplines, our societies seem to have forgotten the value of the wisdom gained by dialogue with others. We appear to be stuck in conversations that quickly turn into arguments. The tendency is to criticize others and their opinions, rather than engaging them in constructive conversations.

Perhaps the most appropriate next step for the movement should be an appreciative one. Perhaps what is especially needed right now is simply to affirm and encourage the emergence of a diversity of groups and individuals that have a critique of the power and influence of large corporations and political powers that derive disproportionate benefits from a particular type of globalization, to the detriment of the majority. Perhaps the movement should take more time simply to acknowledge and celebrate the fact that thousands of organizations and hundreds of thousands of individuals are taking time away from their busy lives to work towards creating a more just and human world.

Although this is easier said than done, what might be needed is to recast the conversation in a way that makes an even broader segment of the population feel included. Right now, many groups and individuals feel that it is difficult to become part of these conversations because it seems to be dominated by particular rhetoric, or because of the costs to participate. The movement could gain from a shift away from a 'conversion' model of communication, where people try to dictate things to others or convince them that their agenda is the right one, to an 'engagement' model, where others are asked to join in an exploration of issues and to work through the development of alternatives.

With regard to structures, there is no particular organizational form that should necessarily be followed by the pro-democracy movement. However, there are key strategies that seem to have more potential. The informal, flexible structures generally favoured by NGOs should be kept. They are culturally appropriate and the most suitable to bring about innovative alternatives. Asset-based community development and community mobilization strategies (pioneered by Saul Alinsky and later by John McKnight) are appropriate for the movement. What could now be done more proactively is to identify groupings that exist and let people work issues through their own groups instead of creating new groupings or structures. The key would then be to create dynamic links and relationships among various groups to promote cross-fertilization and an even richer exchange of views and ideas. The idea would be to let people work in settings that are accessible and in which they are comfortable.

It is also assumed that computer-based communication will be central to working effectively across national boundaries. Although there is the problem of lack of access by developing country NGOs, any groups with access can now share databases, work plans, and priorities, schedule meetings, and hold online discussions. Websites can house libraries of NGO documents. Email-based voting is possible, which would allow for decision-making that could involve most, if not all of the participants in a given collaborative effort. Computer-based communication can also make easier and more democratic the drafting of statements and public declarations.

Ideally, local, regional, and issue-based campaigns should be linked, potentially reinforcing each other's messages. It could also make single-issue campaigns more far-reaching by allowing links to be made with related topics, leading to the tackling of more general and systemic issues.

Without diminishing all that has been accomplished by transnational NGO collaboration, the very basic organizational forms and collaborative processes used by NGOs have probably taken the movement as far as it can go in terms of increasing the intensity of cooperation and achieving systemic changes.

What is needed is a commitment to more intense cooperation. While respect for various perspectives and ideas is required, they are not all equal. The way forward seems to be for NGOs to further identify and develop processes to work through issues, to weigh the pros and cons of options, eliminate wrong ideas, dismiss unclear thinking, and refine ideas that have the most potential.

This is how the diverse groups that make up the anti-economic globalization movement can go beyond its slogan 'Another world is possible,' and agree on what that 'other world' will be.

NOTES

1 In July 2000, the McGill-McConnell Program invited leaders from the Council of Canadians, the Canadian Labour Congress, the Direct Action

Network, the Canadian Federation of Students, and the Vancouver-based NGO 'Check-Your-Head' to Montreal, to discuss their collaboration efforts.

2 The organization I worked for at the time, the Canadian Council for International Co-operation (CCIC), signed on to the statement without much of an internal approval process. The statement seemed general enough to be acceptable to the vast majority of our one hundred members, and it seemed the right thing to do, given that it was supported by our members' key Southern partners.

3 Lane and Maxfield's (1996) preconditions for generative relationships are *aligned directedness, heterogeneity, mutual directedness, permissions,* and *action opportunities.*

4 With a few exceptions, the language of communication used was English. This meant that several key people were not reached, and that certain analyses and viewpoints that could have reinforced the NGO collaboration were not considered.

PART FOUR

The Collaborative Mindset

9 Embracing Donor Involvement

CHARLOTTE CLOUTIER

It is no longer enough to do nice things with your philanthropy – it is time to do the important things.

Peter Goldmark, former president, Rockefeller Foundation

Some Startling Figures

According to the third annual *Chronicle of Philanthropy*'s survey of gift funds, assets held by many of the biggest donor-advised funds in the United States quadrupled in value in just six years, rising from $2.4 billion in 1995 to $12.3 billion in 2001 (Lipman 2001; Larose 2002). Over the same period, overall giving grew from approximately $122 billion to $203 billion (Fix and Lewis 2001), less than half the growth rate of donor-advised funds.

A startling example can be seen in Fidelity Investments, which launched a commercial gift fund in 1992. By 2001, this fund held assets valued at $2.6 billion (*Chronicle of Philanthropy* 2002). That same year, the three largest community foundations in the United States, all founded before 1925, had assets totalling $1.7 billion, $1.5 billion, and $1.3 billion, respectively (Foundation Centre 2002).[1] In other words, in less than a decade, Fidelity's gift fund had grown to become not only the largest public foundation, but also the fifteenth largest foundation (in terms of assets) in the U.S., putting it in the same league as the well-known Rockefeller ($3.1 billion) and Annenberg ($2.9 billion) foundations (ibid.). It distributed $735 million in grants to charities in 2001, which makes it the third largest grant-maker in the U.S. as well. Overall, in 2001, it is estimated that grants totalling $2 billion were made from donor-advised funds – approximately 13 per cent of all grants made by U.S. foundations (ibid.).[2] Kitchen-table charity, this is not.

What is particularly remarkable about donor-advised funds, however, is not the extent of the assets they hold – after all, assets held by community and other public foundations in the United States represent only 15 per cent of assets held by private foundations overall – but rather their astonishing growth rate.[3] A decade ago, donor-advised funds were practically unknown and were offered quietly by community foundations to a handful of involved and generous donors. Today, they represent one of the fastest growing segments of philanthropy in the United States. Is this a passing trend or a lasting phenomenon that reflects the new demographics and profile of donors today?

A Heated Debate

Much controversy surrounds donor-advised funds; the reasons are complex and stem from various schools of thought and philosophical perspectives on philanthropy itself. Some of the controversy focuses on the question of donor involvement, and whether or not such involvement is desirable. Proponents argue that donor involvement encourages philanthropy, citing studies that show consistently that involved donors typically give more than uninvolved donors (Ostrower 1997). Opponents question donors' motives and experience, claiming that donor involvement tends to cause mission drift, if not mission shift, and often gives undue preference to popular causes (Burns 1998; *Advancing Philanthropy* 2000; Billitteri 2000). Intermingled in these debates are culture and religion, and their influence over social perspectives on what is considered a 'good' or a 'bad' gift. To complicate things further, the inception of commercial gift funds has been perceived by many (with all the usual negativity and suspicion) as yet another invasion of commercial interests into the non-profit environment. Accusations of unfair competition abound.

This essay seeks to throw additional light upon many of the issues currently being debated within philanthropic circles around high involvement giving vehicles. By looking at current giving trends, exploring giving practices throughout history and across cultures, and examining some sociological studies of giving and philanthropy, I hope to provide non-profit leaders with a sense of the opportunity that donor involvement might harbour for their organizations. Finally, I will suggest a simple approach for embracing donor involvement in the context of a major gifts fundraising program.

1. Analysing Donor Involvement

The context

From just about every perspective – the legalities of donor control, the risk of mission shift, the invasion of turf, unfair competition, or the effects of bad donor choice – the discussion on donor-advised funds boils down to one question: the pros and cons of donor involvement.

Donor involvement is not new; it has always existed, at least to some extent. Today, however, those philanthropic vehicles, such as donor-advised funds, which support and encourage donor involvement, have multiplied. Never before has the sector had to deal with donor involvement on such a large scale.

Donor involvement is not a passing fad. The growth of donor-advised funds over the last decade is one indication of this. The astronomical growth of private foundations over the same time period is another (Byrne 2002),[4] as is the growing popularity and success (with donors, mainly) of the many new high-involvement approaches to philanthropy, such as giving circles, strategic philanthropy, social entrepreneurship, social-purpose business, and venture philanthropy.[5]

It is no accident that these new initiatives have developed at a time when many Americans are sitting on an astonishing amount of accumulated wealth, a large part of which, given the right incentives, has the potential to be converted into philanthropic capital: never before has the number of 'mega wealthy' Americans been higher. In 2000, it was estimated that the United States was home to some 276 billionaires, more than 2,500 households with a net worth exceeding $100 million, 350,000 individuals with a net worth of $10 million, and some 5 million millionaires (TPI 2000). Despite the dot-com meltdown in that same year, with trillions lost on the stock market and the ensuing economic contraction, the number of billionaires had risen to 298 by 2004; the accumulated wealth in the U.S. remains staggering. What will it take to turn at least part of this wealth into resources dedicated to the public good?

Recent giving surveys show the total dollar amount of donations is growing at a slower rate than previously, and it appears that the higher figures for giving are due more to population growth than to increased penetration (i.e., more people giving more money, in real figures). When inflation is factored in, total giving has actually decreased (Epsilon-Barna 2002). Furthermore, giving continues to be concentrated among a minority of donors. Not only do individuals account for 75 per cent of donations made to charity overall, with the remaining 25 per cent coming from foundations, bequests, and corporations (AAFC 2000), but also according to some surveys, only 15 per cent of households give 2 per cent or more of their household income to charity (1996 figures), and 25 per cent of individuals account for 60 per cent of all contributions (TPI 2000). Wealth is growing, but giving has not followed suit at the same rate. Why are Americans not giving more?

Much of the wealth in the United States is new money, held by individuals who are for the most part still young and who have little, if any, experience with philanthropy. They are the 'new wealthy,' and traditional ways of giving, whether reactive[6] or at arm's length, do not inspire them.

The new wealthy have many traits in common. Most have made their money very quickly, through Initial Public Offerings (IPOs), or as a result of the boom in the stock market. They are young (many are only in their thirties) and most come from modest or middle-class backgrounds (TPI 2000). Wealth is still relatively new to them. They prefer a hands-on style and like to be actively involved in their philanthropic initiatives. Traditional 'chequebook philanthropy'– giving in response to a formal solicitation, without further involvement – is not for them. They like to innovate and experiment with new ideas, think big, take risks and move fast – in short, to take the same approach that helped them succeed in business. They want impact and accountability, and are suspicious of the 'establishment' and large institutions. They are the perennial entrepreneurs and, like most entrepreneurs, are ambitious, strategic, global, and focused on results (Byrne 2002). They are not mere ribbon-cutters, but individuals who become actively engaged in projects that quickly become passions. The emergence and popularity of new giving vehicles, such as donor-advised funds or venture philanthropy initiatives, are a direct result of the desire of the new wealthy for hands-on control – an involved, results-oriented approach to philanthropy. For these donors, involvement is not a preference, but a requirement for giving.

Even traditional philanthropists are slowly edging toward more involved ways of giving. They are moving away from chequebook philanthropy and up along the 'philanthropic curve' to ever higher levels of involvement, becoming more engaged, strategic, and focused in their giving (TPI 2000).[7] Fed up with the never-ending 'fundraising cycle,' where a donor's gift one year serves as a base for the next year and where solicitations come in, year after year, affected by peer pressure and, as one professional put it, 'the continuing case presented by the charity that its financial needs have increased yet again' (Myerberg 1989), donors today are looking for a different kind of relationship with their favourite charities: they want to be more involved.

Donor involvement is clearly the key for tapping into the phenomenal accumulated capital of today's wealthy. Yet most charities shun donor involvement and fear its consequences. At one extreme, they find that many donors are 'cocky,' parachuting themselves into situations they know nothing about, convinced that with their business savvy (why else would they be rich?) they can instantly set to rights social problems that have resisted solution by professionals working full-time over decades. At the other, charities see donor involvement as a nuisance, creating extra work and curbing their freedom to meet the needs of their constituencies in the way they see best.

A closer look at donor involvement throughout history suggests that culture, religious beliefs, and even social habits sometimes make it difficult for those on both sides of the donor-charity relationship to view donor involvement as anything but interference. Nonetheless it is possible, as we shall see, to propose a framework for embracing donor involvement in a way that respects both the desires of donors and the needs of charities.

2. Donor Involvement throughout History

Donor involvement has existed throughout the history of philanthropy. In fact, almost every social program that we take for granted today began as the vision of a committed and involved philanthropist who decided to act, sometimes against great odds and contrary to the beliefs of the majority at the time.

A notable example is John D. Rockefeller's campaign to eradicate hookworm in the southern United States, at a time when most people felt that the notorious lethargy of Southerners was simply due to inborn laziness (Chernow 1998). Or Andrew Carnegie's commitment to build public libraries in thousands of towns across the country in an effort to turn America into a meritocracy, at a time when many, if not all, members of the upper class still thought that poverty was God's punishment for sin (*The Economist* 1998). Stories abound of philanthropists whose generosity changed the shape of society for the better. Clearly, donor-driven philanthropy can be strategic, bold, and visionary.

History also shows us that before philanthropy became as organized and institutionalized as it is today, effective charity was a very hands-on activity. Giving money was not enough; one also had to carry out the activities for which the money was being given. Private donors founded and managed their own workhouses, schools, hospitals, and orphanages. A great many of these privately established institutions still exist, in some cases several centuries after their founding.

Donors in the past have, indeed, frequently and clearly articulated their desire to be involved in their giving. During the 'Benevolent Empire' period in the second quarter of the nineteenth century, American donors 'took to their causes, made generous contributions and exerted a dominant influence on their policies and programs' (Bremner 1960, 47–8). In the seventeenth century, Thomas Fuller was quoted as saying, 'The charitably minded should be left free to do what, when, where, how, to whom, and how much they choose' (Bremner 1994, 40). And in 1853, William Appleton, an eminent industrialist, declared, 'I part with money in various ways of charity but much like to do it in my own way and not be dictated to, or even asked but in a general way, to give with others' (Bremner 1960, 46).

Even high-involvement giving vehicles such as donor-advised funds are not particularly revolutionary. In substance, they seem to have been in existence for a very long time; the earliest formal examples appear to be Islamic *waqfs*, which date back to the sixth century. *Waqfs* were 'endowments' established from gifts of agricultural or commercial property by wealthy Muslims. Revenue from the properties supported various organizations of social benefit such as schools, hospitals, mosques, or orphanages. Although *waqfs* were officially under the control of public authorities, donor-founders usually maintained considerable administrative control over the organizations supported by the *waqf* they established, not only deciding how money should be spent, but also often maintaining tight personal control over general administration, including, in the case of schools, the appointment of professors (Arjomand 1998).

This is also true of venture philanthropy, which in reality is little more than the application of business principles to the funding and management of charities. Many of America's most generous philanthropists of the eighteenth and nineteenth centuries, including Carnegie, Rockefeller, the Tappan brothers, and Isaac Hopper, were fervent believers in the need to manage this 'business of benevolence' efficiently and effectively (Bremner 1960, 117). Of Leland Stanford it is said that he 'went about his task [of building Stanford University] with the same businesslike fashion he employed in building the great stock farm where his fast horses were bred' (ibid., 110). In his essay 'The Gospel of Wealth' (1889), Andrew Carnegie wrote: 'business is society's best hope for progress and philanthropy is desperately in need of reform by men with business abilities' (cited in Fox 1992, 94–117). And Rockefeller's 'were not free gifts, but hard-headed investments, made on condition that the recipient raise an equal or larger sum from other sources and instill improvement in facilities and instruction' (Bremner 1960, 136).

For centuries, the only forms of organized charity were those managed by religious institutions. As the first philanthropic intermediaries, religious organizations encouraged 'undesignated' giving as much as possible; if gifts were designated, the priorities tended to be those defined by the church: the construction of a cathedral or an orphanage, support for pilgrims, relief for the poor. However, society's most spectacular examples of generosity have not been made to philanthropic intermediaries (e.g., community foundations, United Ways, or religious organizations). Rather, the biggest gifts to society, both in the past and now, have come from individuals intensely involved in their giving. Generosity and involvement appear to be linked.

In short, modern society has invented nothing new. The only difference today is that philanthropy is no longer the preserve of the very rich; it is now accessible to all and has become everybody's business. Its problems are not those of content or approach, but of scale. Just as community foundations did at the turn of the twentieth century, donor-advised funds have democratized philanthropy, providing a way for people of moderate means to go beyond cheque signing and become active participants in building society.

Donor involvement as a driver of philanthropy

In a survey of New York City's elite donors conducted in the 1990s, Francie Ostrower made a convincing case that donor involvement encourages giving, and that a desire for involvement is a primary motive for philanthropy: 'Involvements and identifications with organizations become a central focus of donor loyalties and concern, which in turn foster and perpetuate their donations' (Ostrower 1997, 9). Her study showed that the affluent who give money are also involved with non-profit organizations in other ways. Over 90 per cent of all the donations in her survey were made to organizations with which the donor had some involvement, or grew out of a donor's relationship with persons who had some involvement with the organization. As one donor said,

'You get connected with things that you get caught up in, and respond to their needs as you get to know them' (ibid., 31–2). Another said: 'The opportunity for individual involvement is for me the most important feature of philanthropy' (ibid., 108). Donors typically prefer giving during their lifetimes rather than by bequest, as 'it allows them to stay involved with their giving and the organizations that they give to and to wield some control over how their money is spent' (ibid., 102). Ostrower concludes by confirming that, 'giving perpetuates itself, for donations lead to a greater sense of involvement, identification and obligation toward organizations, which in turn promotes more giving' (ibid., 35).

The true meaning of giving

What is a gift? When asked, most people respond using adjectives such as 'spontaneous,' 'unilateral,' and 'generous.' Yet those who have studied the act of giving both culturally and historically observe a very complex social mechanism that, in reality, is rarely spontaneous, unilateral, or generous.

Ever since Marcel Mauss wrote his groundbreaking work *The Gift* (1923–4), anthropologists and sociologists have tried to learn more about the social phenomenon of giving. What Mauss first observed formally was that the act of giving is present in almost every society and in almost every culture, whether archaic or modern. It is almost always surrounded by ritual, and its meaning goes far beyond the act of giving, or the gift itself. Put simply, his conclusions led him to believe that giving is an activity done essentially to establish and sustain relationships. Jacques Godbout, a sociologist who has written extensively on giving, maintains that this relationship is the 'spirit' of the gift, for without it a gift is nothing more than an exchange of goods (Godbout and Caille 1998).

The notion of reciprocity is firmly anchored in the notion of gift. Although this concept has provoked considerable debate between idealists and pragmatists, if we accept that a gift is the means by which a relationship is established or sustained, then it follows that to accept a gift, one *must* reciprocate, since reciprocating means accepting the relationship that is offered. It does not matter *what* is reciprocated, as this is very much influenced by social norms, culture, and habits, and varies considerably depending on context (for example, one can reciprocate with something intangible, such as recognition, friendship, or understanding). Reciprocation in one form or another, at some point in time, is necessary if the relationship is to evolve. By normative definition, gifts leave a residual sense of obligation, which binds the parties to a gift transaction together (Gouldner 1960). If giving is to continue, there must be a relationship and there must be involvement. In the words of Mary Douglas, 'the gift serves above all to establish relations, and a relationship with no hope of return, a one-way relationship, disinterested and motiveless, would be no relationship at all' (Godbout and Caille 1998, 7). Because giving is deeply linked to relationships, it must also be an act that is deeply personal, and somehow reflects the nature of the donor. If it does not, the gift becomes a tax, and the spirit of the gift, the relationship behind the gift, is lost. The donors whom Ostrower asked to define the meaning of philanthropy said that it 'grows out of the donor's sense of identity' and is 'a channel through which individuals can express various personal experiences, attachments, and relationships with other people' (Ostrower 1997, 6, 19).

The influence of religion

Why is it that an involved donor is so often considered to be a 'lesser' donor than an uninvolved donor? Why is a disinterested gift better than a gift in which the donor has an interest? Why do we harbour these beliefs?

The concept of detachment from one's giving seems to appear primarily in religious texts. Religious beliefs have had a profound influence over how people feel about and carry out their philanthropic activities. Every major religion, including Judaism, Christianity, Buddhism, and Islam, recognizes and encourages the duty of materially well-off individuals to aid the less fortunate. Gifts with strings attached are generally considered to be less 'worthy' than gifts made without expectation of a return. The gift that is given generously, unhesitatingly, spontaneously, and unconditionally is seen to be a better gift than the one that is given grudgingly, hesitatingly, or conditionally.

The Dharmashastras, the body of Hindu religious law, define different types of gifts, and rank them according to their worthiness. A gift is considered to be more worthy if it requires no reciprocation, if the donor has no ulterior motives and if it is given at the proper time and place to a worthy person. Gifts that are given meritoriously, in return for hardship or for a favour given, or that leave the donor with a certain degree of control, are not considered to be bad per se, but are deemed to be less 'honourable' than those gifts given freely, unconditionally, and with no expectation of return. It is furthermore recognized that this 'ideal' gift is also very difficult to realize. Another Hindu text, the Vedayasa, expresses it thus: 'Amongst a hundred men, one may be found to be brave, among thousands a learned man, among hundreds of thousands an orator, but a donor may or may not be found' (Andersen 1998).

Buddhism is firmly anchored in the notion of renunciation. Various Buddhist stories recount how giving (and by association, renunciation) is one of the requirements for attaining enlightenment. The story of Anathapindinka, for example, tells of how the hero's 'giving without thought of reward allows him to attain the higher paths toward liberation.' In another story, the hero Vessantara gives away everything he possesses 'to show that total non-attachment represents both the highest form of generosity and a crucial virtue for the attainment of liberation' (Guruge and Bond 1998, 79–96).

We also find this ranking of gifts in Judaism. The twelfth-century philosopher Maimonides, in *Mishneh Torah* (ca. 1175), describes eight degrees of charity. Gifts given grudgingly are ranked lowest in the scale, while gifts given anonymously rank high (Bremner 1994, 85).

Christianity in all its forms speaks extensively of giving: giving of one's self (following the example of Jesus, who gave his life to redeem humanity), giving with love, and giving generously without question. Bremner, citing Saint Paul's discourse on charity (Corinthians 1:13), even argues that 'as a result of the linkage of charity and love in Christian thought, the motivation of the donor is subject to such intense scrutiny that the equally important and no less debatable issue of the effect of the gift on the recipient is completely overlooked' (ibid.).

The way in which philanthropy articulates itself and is understood in a theological context is, of course, far more complex than what the brief outline provided here might suggest. What remains however, even from this simplified perspective, is that the major religions have idealized some definition of a 'true' gift that is pure, and made without any strings attached. There is no question that this ideal is well anchored in our collective minds, making it sometimes difficult to fully embrace the concept of an 'involved' gift as a truly generous act.

3. Some Caveats

Despite many of the positive aspects of donor involvement and its prevalence throughout history, it is important to underline the caveats. Throughout history, many people have expressed reservations, even cynicism, with regard to donor involvement, similar to those raised about donor-advised funds.

In the 1920s, questions were raised as to whether foundation-financed research could be objective, and whether institutions accepting aid from foundations and corporations would maintain their integrity (Bremner 1960, 138–9). In 1936, Eduard C. Lindeman wrote:

> Taken as a group, the trustees of the great philanthropic foundations represent social prestige, financial success, and middle-aged respectability. These are exemplary attributes, but are they adequate or proper qualifications for leaders of organizations supposedly dedicated to pioneering, path finding, and opening-up of new frontiers of social well-being? (ibid., 160).

In a more recent commentary on Carnegie's 'The Gospel of Wealth,' Karl Barry criticizes this approach to philanthropy as being 'a system built on a certitude by small groups of Americans … of knowing what all Americans need, a paternalism that rests inevitably on the choice by some of the directions that all are to follow' (Burlingame 1992, 42).

There is also the question of motive, and to what extent it influences donor choice. Motives can be positive or negative – altruistic or self-interested. Society has never been completely naïve about self-interest as a charitable motive. The seventeenth-century philosopher Thomas Hobbes 'could not conceive of anyone practising philanthropy except to enhance the esteem or honour in which he was held in the community or to promote his own security and power.' In the early eighteenth century, Bernard de Mandeville summed up the cynical view of philanthropy: 'Pride and vanity have built more hospitals than all virtues put together' (cited in Bremner 1994, 42). In an article on philanthropy in America, *The Economist* (1998) boldly states that 'in general, a high proportion of supposedly philanthropic giving goes to gratifying people's egos rather than to genuinely helping the poor' (19).

Perhaps the issue of donor involvement is not so much about how much is too much, but rather what is the difference between *positive* and *negative* involvement. Positive involvement, which is constructive and supportive, and encourages giving and dialogue, can be helpful in any organization. But what about negative donor involvement that is disruptive and controlling? What causes it? How do we contain it? It appears that the bridge that can lead donors from bad to good involvement is trust.

The issue of trust

Trust is the glue that binds society and all of our relationships within society. Trudy Grovier (1997) writes that 'there is considerable evidence to support the idea that attitudes of trust and distrust affect the nature and quality of our social reality' (35).

Much of what spurs negative donor involvement revolves around issues of mistrust: the donor's doubts over whether the charity will use the donation appropriately, or as agreed; or the charity's doubts over the donor's motives or ability to understand the real issues at hand. To resolve these means turning negative involvement into positive involvement; in other words, building trust.

Trust is critical, but it appears to be declining. A poll conducted by the *Chronicle of Philanthropy* a year after the terrorist attacks of September 11, 2001, revealed a striking erosion of confidence in charities among many Americans, with 42 per cent claiming that they have less confidence in charities in 2002 than they did previously, and 29 per cent stating that they were less likely to give to charities in that year (Greene 2002). A joint study by Epsilon and the Barna Research Group in 2002 concluded that donor confidence was at an historic low, particularly among seniors, who are traditionally the most generous segment of the population, with 33 per cent claiming to have less confidence in nonprofit organizations than they did in 2000. Although trust in the voluntary sector as a whole remains relatively strong, compared to most other sectors, and is still strong in Canada (Muttart Foundation 2000),[8] the potential negative effects of declining trust are large enough that even a small or temporary decline is worrisome. Trust is slow and difficult to build, but notoriously easy to destroy.

Much of the public discourse on trust in charities focuses on issues of accountability and transparency. Although these are important issues, they address only half of the equation. Trust cannot be one-sided, and the onus of being 'trustworthy' cannot fall only upon charities. Donors also have a responsibility. 'Trust,' Godbout writes, cannot arise between individuals who act out of self-interest only.'[9] Just as a charity that is not accountable forfeits a donor's trust, so a donor who thinks only about his or her own interests forfeits a charity's trust.

Finally, and perhaps most importantly, trust cannot be taken for granted. It must be earned, and efficiency alone is not enough to earn it. An organization that is run efficiently is not necessarily trustworthy. According to Susan Berresford, president of the Ford Foundation

(2000), 'Trust requires a personal basis. Trust often comes from caring about something, being engaged with it, and becoming so familiar with it that you feel you have a personal stake in it' (n.p.). In a speech at the Canadian Centre for Philanthropy Symposium in 2002, Paulette Maehara, president of the Association of Fundraising Professionals, said, 'When we talk about building trust ... what we are really talking about is how to create opportunities for involvement, connection and understanding in the charitable sector.' Involvement nurtures trust. And so we have come full circle.

4. The Challenge Ahead

The emergence in recent years of donor-advised funds and other high-involvement giving vehicles, such as giving circles and venture philanthropy, has forced non-profit and charitable sector practitioners to give serious thought to donor involvement and its potential impact on the way charities operate.

Like it or not, donor involvement is here to stay. History tells us that this is not a bad thing. Religious beliefs sometimes get in the way of our ability to embrace donor involvement completely and, yes, there are caveats, but these should not blind us to the tremendous opportunities and potential offered by donor involvement. Peter Karoff (1997), in a speech presented at the Indiana University Center for Philanthropy, said: 'It is time we sought to lift the bar on the articulation and the practice of philanthropy to new and exciting levels.' Donor involvement is a means for doing just that.

To do truly great things requires vision, leadership, and passion. If we want our donors to participate in our vision, and even – why not? – share their visions and their passions with us, we must embrace donor involvement. True vision requires heart. If we want our donors to have a vision for social good, we have to let them put their hearts into it.

By asking to be 'more involved,' what are donors really saying? Do they want to be more involved or better informed? Much of what we call involvement is, in many ways, simply a call for more personal and believable information – the kind of information one gets from a conversation with someone they trust, not the kind of information one gets from an ad on television.

Commenting on Martin Buber's statement that 'life itself is a form of meeting, and dialogue is the ridge on which we meet,' Karoff (1997) says the gift process itself is 'a form of meeting and dialogue' – one that most of us cut short at the first opportunity. One of the most important characteristics of dialogue is that it is two-way. Neither side does all of the listening nor all of the talking. This means that although charities may have to do a better job of lending an attentive ear to their donors, donors also have to do their share of listening. They must begin by not underestimating how truly difficult it is to give away money. Philanthropists and philosophers alike have acknowledged this. Aristotle says that 'to give away money is an easy matter, and in everyone's power. But to decide to whom to give it, and how large, and for what purpose is neither in everyone's power nor an easy matter' (Burlingame 1992, 51). Andrew Carnegie (1889/1992) said that 'the sins of millionaires in this respect [giving] are not those of omission, but of commission, because they do not take the time to think, and chiefly because it is much easier to give than to refuse' (14). Bill Gates has argued that 'anybody can give away money, the point is to give it away intelligently, which means doing it yourself' (*The Economist* 1998, 19). Giving away money is no easy matter. Perhaps donors can summon the courage to turn to charities for help.

Most people are not aware that giving responsibly so as to create an appropriate impact is a matter of skill and art. Some families have formal processes for giving, in which they involve their children; but these are few and far between. Nor is responsible giving the preserve of the very rich, many of whom are just as likely to give 'reactively' as people of modest means. Most donors tend to respond to direct solicitations (by mail, telephone, or in shopping malls) or organized appeals (such as telethons); or they may participate in walkathons or other philanthropic events (usually because a friend has talked them into it). They may buy products for which a small amount of the profit is said to be directed to a charity. In all these cases, helpful as they are, there is little or no forethought involved. The donors make no judgment as to which philanthropic causes are important to them, or how they might prefer to make a difference.

Where, then, does one learn the art of philanthropy? Given the overall increase in wealth in Western societies, and the proliferation of vehicles such as donor-advised funds, perhaps it is time truly to *democratize* philanthropy: to develop some broadly based awareness program that would sensitize people to the impact they might potentially have as donors, large or small. Each of us, in our own small way, has the potential to be a change agent; how do we build broadly based awareness about this potential?

Buber stresses the significance of open, receptive relationships between people as necessary to fostering trust (Grovier 1997, 7). Perhaps, instead of asking how we can raise more funds, charities should be asking what they are doing to foster more trust. Charities can, and should, encourage donors to engage in dialogue that will help them achieve philanthropic goals that reflect their values.

Helping donors to become better philanthropists may even encourage many donors to go beyond giving to established causes like the arts and education. As one of Peter Karoff's clients told him, 'I know how to give $100 million to Stanford [University]. I don't know how to give $100 million to the kids in the city, and that is what I would rather do' (Karoff 2000, 89). Fundraising should not just be the act of presenting a case statement to a donor, but rather a learning experience for both the donor and the charity.

Finally, it is critically important to realize that the entrepreneurial nature of philanthropy means that mistakes are inevitable. Donors will experiment, and they will make mistakes, even mistakes that we in the charitable sector could have warned them about. In the long run, this does not matter; if enough donors invest themselves in their causes, great good will come of it in the aggregate. If we can ignore Carnegie's (1889/1992) paternalistic tone, we may admit the wisdom of his statement that 'it is not expected, neither is it desirable, that there should be general concurrence as to the best possible use of surplus wealth. For different men and different localities there are different uses. What commends itself most highly to the judgment of the administrator is the best use for him, for his heart should be in his work' (26).

There are no simple answers. But neither are the questions simple. Because philanthropy touches us so deeply, and because it is so public, it is a very complex matter. There are deep tensions between the realities of fundraising, and the ethical and religious values that ground us. It is a constant challenge to try to find balance between each. But as Robert Payton (1992) concludes: 'If we embrace both these perspectives, we embrace the matrix of the spiritual and the material, of the religious and the economic, of the ethical aspirations and the practical techniques that are the defining characteristics of philanthropy' (138).

Some practical considerations

In the world of fundraising, 'getting the gift' is often the main, if not the sole, concern of the fundraiser. At times, as Dr Roy W. Menninger (1981) has so eloquently stated in a well-known speech, 'the qualities of honesty and sincerity that ought always to be at the heart of the process seem to slip away, making it seem that fundraising is a bit of a con game.' Whether a gift is fundamentally useful to the organization seeking it, whether it has the potential to make change for the better, or whether it is really what the donor wants is of secondary importance; 'getting the gift' is all that matters. This is quite unfortunate, as our too-frequent inability to engage donors in truly meaningful exchanges with our organizations not only leaves much on the table, but also has probably brought upon us, at least in part, many of the woes that today we and our organizations so aptly complain and groan about: designated gifts for non-priority projects, program funding with no contribution for core operating, frequent and complex reporting requirements, and little, if any, multi-year or renewed funding.

Engaging donors in meaningful exchanges with the organizations in which they are most interested should be the fundraiser's main task. It is these exchanges that develop and nurture involvement, the only way that leads to the sort of meaningful giving that will yield the greatest benefit to the charitable organization and the donor alike.

5. A Primer of Major Gift Fundraising

One way of understanding how fundraisers get donors involved in a major gifts program is to consider the principal shortcomings of current approaches.

Most fundraising professionals would agree that there exist essentially two types of giving: sustained giving, which is the donation of a relatively modest gift on a recurring, often annual, basis (in response to mail or phone campaigns, for example); and major giving, which is the donation of a large, usually exceptional, gift on a one-time or occasional basis (for example, in response to solicitation during a capital or endowment campaign). More recently, some groups have introduced a third type of gift, frequently called the 'ultimate' gift, which is an exceptionally large gift, often representing a significant portion of an individual's fortune, and the largest gift that the donor will make during his or her lifetime. These latter two types of gifts (major and ultimate) can be made during a person's lifetime, or after his or her death, or as a combination of both: hence the reason for not including planned giving or bequest giving as a separate 'type' of gift in this context.

The whole point of major-gift fundraising is to convert promising 'sustained' givers into 'major' givers. The most popular and enduring technique for doing so is commonly known, in fundraising jargon, as 'moves management' – a process whereby fundraisers 'move' prospective donors (donors who have the capacity and interest to make a major gift as determined by research, most often) along a 'giving cycle.' A 'move' is a specific activity, such as a meeting, a phone call, or a letter. The giving cycle represents the various stages a donor goes through before making a gift. These are, most typically: awareness (learning about the cause), cultivation (building a relationship), solicitation (asking for the gift), and stewardship (thanking the donor for the gift). This technique, often attributed to David Dunlop, is now mainstay practice in major-gift fundraising (Sturtevant 1997). Its major shortcoming, however, is that it all too frequently becomes a mechanical process. 'Moves' are often generic and standardized; the focus is on 'getting the gift,' while stewardship is barely touched upon, if not completely overlooked. Over time, the effectiveness of the technique wears thin for lack of interest and humanity in the exchange that occurs. Donors feel manipulated, and as they gain experience, they shy away from the process entirely.

It is true that one of the reasons the process fails is that it is not properly followed. Seasoned experts will say that novice fundraisers are poor listeners. They do not try hard enough to get to know their donors, so as to plan 'moves' that are genuinely meaningful to the donor. Others will maintain that the pressures to bring in the dollars are so high that there is no time for all the 'soft' stuff. This is all true. But even if fundraisers listened more, and were given more time to meet objectives, I am convinced that still this would not be enough to circumvent donor fatigue and cynicism. Relationships might be better and donors might feel happier, but it isn't likely that they will give more due to the lack of a fundamental element which the first part of this essay has sought to explain: the means for involving the donor in the organization in some deep and meaningful way.

What is involvement?

What does it mean for a donor to be 'involved?' Attending a gala, appearing at a presentation, or visiting an organization are not good examples of involvement. Nor is a meeting with a potential donor in his or her office, all of which are standard 'moves' in the fundraising world. In these situations, if well done, there is information exchange and relationship-building, which is always positive (the building of interest and awareness on the donor circle), but in none of these activities is there real involvement. Having a donor listen to what an organization has to say about itself, or listening to a donor explaining what his or her philanthropic interests are, are passive activities – seeing, not doing. They do not encourage action.

Other sorts of activities call for more thoroughgoing and stimulating involvement on the donor's part. It may be a helpful exercise to engage the donor in a meaningful dialogue over the draft of a strategic plan or program outline, while the ideas are still fluid and exchanges of opinion may suggest unforeseen solutions. In fact, presenting a complete and comprehensive plan for discussion is a waste of the donor's time; what difference will it make what he or she thinks? In any case, trying to accommodate the donor's demands for major revision can only make the organization look unprofessional and unsure of its purpose. On the other hand, encouraging the donor to volunteer on a program, or sit on the board, or (better still) an advisory committee, or participate in a brainstorming session, are all valid and effective ways of fostering meaningful involvement: a process where the donor is seen not merely as a 'funder,' but as a partner or ally in achieving some greater, mutually defined good.

Perhaps it is time to stop seeing the relationships between non-profit organizations and funders as mere exchanges, and to start seeing them as forms of collaboration: or in other words, as a coming together of two or more stakeholders that pool their understanding and tangible resources to solve a set of problems which neither can solve individually. From this perspective, fundraising success is a function of collaborative success, which depends on whether or not the participants can negotiate a framework for action based on a shared understanding of the issues, and agreement as to the interests and identities at stake. Here, involvement is no longer a threat to funder-fundee relations, but an inherent part of their nature.

Managing interference

Does involvement mean saying yes to each and every suggestion a donor makes? It may be tempting to do everything possible to please a potential donor, in the hope of securing a gift. Ultimately, however, routinely exaggerating the importance of a donor's opinions or invariably doing what he or she asks will be counterproductive. The fundraiser's willingness to bend over backwards may be flattering at first; but it ultimately calls into doubt the donor's intelligence and capacity for critical thinking. An even greater danger is that it may seriously undermine the charitable organization's credibility. A more convincing show of respect is to encourage the donor's involvement in a personal, sincere, and meaningful relationship with the organization.

It is true that donors' motivations vary widely. Some donors may give in order to gain entry into a social circle, or to gain esteem and public recognition; others may give in order to see their names in print or on a plaque, or to earn a spot on a prestigious board, or simply to obtain a tax break. Others yield to peer pressure. The reasons are numerous. A good many fundraising techniques focus on how to approach donors by identifying the motivation that appears to be driving their interest. In my own experience, however, I have found that apart from a few exceptional cases, such motivations are largely superficial. Usually there is some deeper, more essential reason for giving.

More often than not, when people are ready to give at the major level, something that usually occurs later in life, what they are most often looking for is meaning: a way of giving back or of making a meaningful contribution to society, and they feel that philanthropy might be a means of doing this. They start by taking a few tentative philanthropic steps. They might, for example, start by giving at a slightly higher level to an organization they have been supporting regularly for a period of time. In so doing, they may follow their friends' example or take their cue from well-known organizations. They may name a building, endow a program, or establish a scholarship fund. Too often, however, the satisfaction they hope to experience in making the gift is elusive. It seems that the organization forgets about them – until it is time, of course, to ask for another gift. They are unsure whether their gift has made a difference, or whether the money is being used as intended. They wonder if they themselves are at fault: did they not make themselves clear? They end up signing memorandums of agreement that look and feel like contracts, and the magic of the gift is lost. More solicitations pour in. And after a few more attempts, fatigue and cynicism set in.

The point of a fundraising process that leads to high-involvement giving is *not* about minimizing or managing interference. It is about engaging a donor in meaningful dialogue, which is the creative exchange of ideas and opinions undertaken in a 'safe' context, where everyone is on equal footing, feels respected and recognized, and feels that their input counts. The intended outcome is synergy, a meeting of the minds and ultimately, the building of partnership. As Menninger (1981) puts it, 'The giving/receiving process is fundamentally a relationship, one which deserves to be respected in its own right ... Because it is based on relationship, a great deal turns on the qualities of the interaction, and the extent to which the donor is willing to be involved ... It is (in effect) the refusal to be involved in, concerned about, and committed to the relationship that contributes to some of the less attractive aspects of the philanthropic business' (8).

6. Conclusion

We have seen here that donor involvement in non-profit organizations encourages giving, and that one way of nurturing donor involvement is to engage donors in meaningful dialogue and exchange, and ultimately to view the donor-recipient relationship as a real partnership or collaboration characterized by listening and respect. Not fully involving potential donors in the lives of our organizations does not mean that our fundraising efforts will fail. Money will come in. Many organizations may exist for years on little more income than derives from sustained giving and raffle earnings, and the windfalls of serendipitous major giving or planned gifts from time to time. Non-involvement of donors, however, represents opportunities lost. The major intergenerational transfer of wealth that will occur in the near future suggests that the opportunity cost in this regard is likely to be quite high.

NOTES

1   In order: the New York Community Trusts (founded in 1924), the Cleveland Foundation (founded in 1914), and the Chicago Community Trust (founded in 1915).
2   Grants made by the top 1,000 foundations in the U.S. totalled approximately $15 billion in 2001. As there are some 56,000 private foundations in the U.S., this figure is probably a low estimate.
3   In 2000, $408 billion was held by approximately 50,000 private foundations, compared to $61 billion held by some 4,000 private and operating foundations.

4   The number of private foundations more than doubled between 1987 and 2002.

5   Many of these giving practices require a high level of donor involvement. At the lower end, giving circles bring a group of donors with similar interests together to pool their resources for impact in a common area. The group meets regularly to make giving decisions, and follow up on grants made. At the higher end, venture philanthropists will carefully choose the organization they wish to work with, and will then proceed to help it build capacity, by investing in infrastructure (technology, IS, etc.), and leadership (support for hiring good management, or to provide training or direct involvement themselves in management), the objective being to give the organization the means of achieving tangible, measurable results toward some clearly defined goal. Venture philanthropists often expect a position on the board of the organizations they support. See www.minnesotagiving .org, www.givingnewengland.org (giving circles); www.svpseattle.org, www.venturephilanthropypartners.org (venture philanthropy); and www .tpi.org (various vehicles and trends).

6   A reactive gift or donation is made, without forethought, in reaction or emotional response to a solicitation (possibly itself based upon an emotional appeal), as opposed to a gift that is made thoughtfully as part of a wider individual philanthropic program with established priorities, identified areas of interest, etc.

7   At stage one of the 'philanthropic curve,' a donor's responses to philanthropy are primarily reactive. They are considered to be low-involvement. Donors who move to stage two begin to get engaged and start organizing their giving in a more systematic way. They might set up a donor-advised fund, or even a foundation. They are considered to be moderate-involvement. Stage three donors are highly committed. Philanthropy has become a major part of their lives. They are active learners and have become very professional about the way they handle their giving. They are considered high-involvement.

8   Public trust in charitable organizations in Canada appears to be quite high. Seventy-seven per cent of respondents to a study conducted by the Muttart Foundation in collaboration with the Canadian Centre for Philanthropy on trust and confidence in charities reported having some or a lot of trust in charities.

9   'La confiance ... ne peut naître entre des individus qui n'agissent qu'en fonction de leur propre intérêt' (Godbout and Caille 1998, 164).

10 Can't We Be Friends? An Ethical Exploration of the Nature of the Relationship between Fundraisers, Donors, and the Charities They Support

ROBERT RYAN

At no time in history has fundraising been a more socially pervasive – some might say, aggressive – phenomenon. From door-to-door canvassing to telephone calls, letters, even visits with donors, fundraising is in your face, front and centre, and ever-present in people's daily lives. Yet it is also a curiously isolated phenomenon, remote from most people's imaginative lives. Among the 25,000 or more members of the Association of Fundraising Professionals worldwide, the majority probably dreamed, as children, of becoming doctors, teachers, astronauts, or firefighters. Perhaps when children start dreaming of becoming fundraisers, we will know the fundraising profession has 'arrived.' And perhaps this arrival will be slow in coming, given the ethical quandaries in the relationships between fundraisers, donors, and charitable organizations – problems that continue to challenge even the experienced fundraiser's moral imagination.

I do remember that in my elementary school years, every so often I would be called upon to sell cookies on behalf of the local YMCA, or collect dimes for the March of Dimes. Even then, I remember thinking that it was strange how the neighbours could be so different. The nice people were the ones who would greet me at their door, smile at me, and open their pocketbooks or wallets and give. But there were others who would actually hide from me, or answer the door with what looked to be a very scary face to a little boy. They usually were not interested in giving anything; or if they did give, they made it abundantly clear that giving away a dime was something quite serious. (Of course, this was long ago, in 1966, when organizations like the March of Dimes were still in the habit of collecting dimes.) The door-to-door fundraising drive was actually called the 'Mothers' March' campaign. I guess my mother was either too busy to march or too timid to fundraise. So I was the one who got stuck having to ask our neighbours for money. I think she also knew that if I went alone, and if I looked and sounded really pathetic (I had a chronic stutter until high school), I could probably get more dimes than she ever could. Little did she know what seeds were being planted in her child's garden of career choices.

Forty years later, that same small boy, now grown up, is still knocking on people's doors and asking them for money, though the techniques he uses are far more sophisticated. He is now very intelligent (or thinks he is), and the causes and charities he represents are more urgent, important, and pressing. He won't settle for dimes anymore; in fact, his techniques have become so sophisticated and focused that he's interested only in large gifts, preferably in the millions – for example, when someone leaves an entire estate to a favourite charity in their will. But he wonders, sometimes, whether things have really changed that much.

Admittedly, I am still put off by the people with scary faces (and there are plenty of them); but I also still take delight in the people with kind faces who give with joy and without hesitation, and who usually spare far more than just dimes to help charitable causes. More often than not, the faces that are the most kind are the ones that come with wrinkles, dentures, and failing eyesight. But these faces also come with something that is worth its weight in gold to any fundraiser: generosity.

In the following pages I would like to share two stories that describe donors with very kind faces.[1] Perhaps these stories will begin to highlight some of the problems fundraisers face as they develop relationships with older donors.

One donor recently told me, before he told his family and friends, that he had been diagnosed with terminal cancer and that in all likelihood, he would be dead in six months. There may have been a practical reason for this, as the charitable organization I represented at the time had been included in the donor's will for a large sum of money. But it was also true that over the five years I had known him we had developed a very close friendship. I knew that he wanted to tell someone about his illness, and I was the person he felt most comfortable with. But why me? On the surface it made sense: he was afraid of telling his family the bad news, and somehow I fit the bill. But let's dig a little deeper.

To begin with, I was a person he did not really know well, whatever he may have thought at the time. Most of the relationships I develop with donors are by nature one-sided: donors tell me a great deal about themselves, while I reveal practically nothing about myself. This was certainly the case with Mr Schmidt. The only person I let him see was a very caring, intelligent, sympathetic man who was always there to listen to him, pick up the phone and say hello, drop in for a friendly visit, share a cup of tea and, above all, be attentive, polite and courteous – on the surface, a friend and confidant.

My other story concerns a note I once received from a donor whom I shall call Mr Blackstone. I knew practically nothing about him, though I had sent him numerous notes and letters over the years, thanking him for his gifts and making friendly inquiries about his health, his family, and other common matters of courtesy. His wife had recently died, and in her honour he sent my employer at the time, Humanitarian Relief International (HRI), a donation of $5,000. Along with the cheque was a personal note addressed to his 'dear friend, Robert Ryan.' To this day, I am disturbed by the notion that this man considered me to be his dear friend. When his wife was still alive, I had visited them once, and spent a very exasperating hour trying to draw them into polite conversation. He was tired and she was very ill, and I could tell that my visit was going nowhere. I tried to leave their house with good grace before they both fell asleep on me.

In my follow-up, I would send them thank-you notes, birthday cards, and published articles about the organization. When Mr Blackstone informed HRI that his wife had passed away, I wrote a beautiful, carefully crafted sympathy letter, in which I recalled the very pleasant afternoon I had spent with them a few years ago.

Why was I doing all this? Because before I was hired by HRI, Mr Blackstone and his wife had notified the organization that it would be the beneficiary of a six-figure bequest. My job was to keep the bequest to the organization in their will. How had doing my job transformed me from an amiable functionary to a 'dear friend'?

What exactly are these relationships between fundraisers and donors? Are they business relationships, professional relationships, personal friendships, or something in between? If one devotes one's life to raising funds for good causes, then these notions of friendship do take on a deeper meaning.

According to standard fundraising theory, there was absolutely nothing wrong with my cultivating Mr Blackstone's friendship. His record of giving indicated he was pleased with the attention I gave him. But I still say something was not quite right. How is it, now that I am no longer working for Humanitarian Relief International, that my friendship with Mr Blackstone has lapsed? But perhaps there was never a friendship to begin with.

A serious exploration of the ethical implications of the relationships between fundraisers and donors requires not only an open mind but also an open heart. This is all the more true in that much of what a fundraiser actually does is quite emotionally charged – so much so, that often I cannot separate my thoughts from my emotions. This, in short, is the problem I propose to explore.

In the first section, I shall discuss the nature of friendship from a classical perspective, drawing upon the ideas of Aristotle and applying them to current fundraising theory. Section two follows a hunch that my reluctance to engage in deeper friendships with donors may have to do, at least in part, with a certain confusion about my identity. Where exactly does Robert Ryan the person end and Robert Ryan the fundraiser begin? This requires an examination of the role and identity of both the fundraiser and the donor. In section three, I explore the different types of behaviour that charities and their representatives display around the elderly, particularly when it concerns planned giving. I am particularly concerned with the notion that the elderly are rendered vulnerable by the attention and kindness that charities and fundraisers devote to them, and that charities may deliberately exploit this vulnerability. Finally, in section four, I will focus on the idea of trust, for that is the underlying key to what makes any of these relationships meaningful, enjoyable, and successful.

1. Defining the Nature of Friendship

> To give away money is an easy matter, and in any man's power. But to decide to whom to give it, and how much, and when, and for what purpose is neither in every person's power nor an easy matter.   ·
> Aristotle, *Nichomachean Ethics*, 1109a27–9

These lines from Aristotle are familiar to many fundraisers, and have even inspired a rule of thumb in fundraising circles. The most familiar version is known as the 'five rights': To make a good solicitation for a major gift, ask the *right person* at the *right time* at the *right place* for the *right amount* for the *right purpose*. The 'five rights' rule is probably the first thing a fundraiser learns when he or she begins to read about major gifts fundraising. Many of my successful major gift solicitations come about because I align all of the 'rights' before I 'ask.' But when it comes to ethics, and especially the ethics of planned giving, I think it gets more complicated than just following the 'rights.' By the time someone reaches the stage in life when they have to seriously consider disposing of a lifetime's worth of accumulated assets, the stakes become higher for the donor, the fundraiser, and the charity to get things right ... in every sense.

In my introduction, the concerns that I raised about the relationships and friendships I've experienced with donors indicate a need to define our terms. In the realm of ethics and fundraising, there are a few players and themes that remain constant. A *fundraiser* is the representative of a charitable organization, who is seeking funds in support of the mission of the charity. 'Most fundraisers are compassionate, fair-minded people. These character traits are "habit-skills," already built into their personalities from a lifetime of experience. But sometimes ethical dilemmas are too complex for these moral habits to deal with spontaneously' (Fischer 2000, 9). I think Fischer may be far too kind when she describes the moral makeup of a fundraiser; but I do agree that in matters of ethics and morality, spontaneity and complexity often don't mix. A *donor* is the person who financially supports the mission of the organization. In fundraising circles there is a standard saying: 'A charity has no needs.' What this actually means is that a charity has no right to ask for money without having a mission, and it may ask for money only in order to fulfil its mission. The words *need* or *needs* refer to the issues that are addressed by the charity in carrying out its mission. In short, a charity doesn't have needs; it meets needs.

Let me begin this discussion by exploring the nature of friendship mainly through the ideas of Aristotle. I trust professional philosophers will allow me a certain leeway in making sense of Aristotle's ideas outside of a historical or academic context. Nonetheless, it seems that between Greece, fourth century BC and twenty-first century North America, certain habits in human relationships have changed very little, if at all.

In Book VIII of the *Nicomachean Ethics* (NE), Aristotle defines friendship broadly as a situation in which two or more people have goodwill towards each other, and each one knows this to be the case and reciprocates with goodwill (NE 1156a1–5). Aristotle also divides friendship into three broad categories. Friendships based on *usefulness* (or utility) are based on some mutual benefit to be gained (NE 1156a11–14). Friendships based on *pleasure* are based on expectations of short-term enjoyment and emotional satisfaction (NE 1156a33). And finally, complete or *perfect* friendships exist between those who are good or virtuous, and who desire the good for each other. Each loves the other for what the other is in himself or herself (NE 1156b8–9).

From a fundraiser's point of view, friendship with a donor is usually based on some type of need, and would therefore be a friendship based on utility. However, on rare occasions, more often by accident than by design, a fundraiser actually develops a meaningful and pleasurable friendship with a donor, with whom he or she shares certain likings and interests. Underlying both of these friendships, however, is the similarity of beliefs and values towards the mission of the charity held by the fundraiser and the donor.

A friendship between two people that is based on need is certainly different from one that is not based on need. This is not such a truism as it may seem, when we consider friendship between the fundraiser and the donor, since the only reason they come together in the first place has to do with the needs the charity's mission represents. Without this need, the friendship would not·exist. However, as Aristotle says, 'wealthy people and those who have acquired authority and power seem above all to need friends. For what is the use of that sort of prosperity, once one excludes the good one can do for others, which attains its greatest degree and becomes most praiseworthy when directed at friends? Or how could that prosperity be safeguarded and maintained without friends? For the greater it is, the more precarious. And in poverty and in every other sort of misfortune, people regard friends as their only refuge' (NE 1155a6–12).

Aristotle appears to be making a straightforward case as to why friends are important, especially for wealthy people who desire to make good use of their prosperity. But perhaps the real question, according to translator Michael Pakaluk is, 'Why does Aristotle suppose that great prosperity has no use, unless employed in the most significant and praiseworthy sorts of action?' (Aristotle 1998, 46). What Aristotle might be saying is that 'many virtuous actions are typically done only in the course of doing something else. For instance, courageous actions are done only in the course of action to repel some mortal threat or danger (ibid., 47).

Given that friendship based on need is the usual sort of friendship between charities and donors, one could argue that in this day and age, donors, by giving money to causes they support, don't necessarily have to take *courageous action* (apart from the courage, when called upon, to write a cheque for six figures). Regardless of whether donating to a charity is a courageous action, it is an action based on the fulfillment of a need. Suffice to say that what motivates donors to give (to fulfill the needs of those whom the charity and its mission represent) sometimes has very little to do with philanthropic intent. The donor may prefer to give to a charity rather than pay out money in taxes. He or she may wish to exclude an antagonistic relative or a greedy child from an inheritance. Whatever the donor's motive, the sole link between the donor and the charity is the matter of need or utility. When the need changes, the relationship between the donor and charity changes, and *the relationship between the donor and the fundraiser* changes accordingly. In some instances, I have ceased being a friend to the donor, either because the gift was rescinded on the part of the donor or because the gift had been made under circumstances that led me to believe there were no further gifts to be had. As Aristotle says, 'People who are friends based on usefulness break up as soon as profit ceases: for they were friends not of each other, but of their profit' (NE 1157a). This is what happened to my friendship with Mr Blackstone: when I left Humanitarian Relief International, our relationship ended. On the other hand, when we consider a friendship that is not based on need, we see that virtuous action can still occur, but as Pakaluk points out, it would not be *on account of something else* (i.e., the need). Instead, it could be on account of love, caring, or the enjoyment of like-minded activities, much like the notion of friendship for the sake of friendship (see NE 1157b).

Aside from need as a condition for certain types of friendship, Aristotle gives many shades of meaning and definition to friendship: 'Those who love on account of usefulness, love on account of what is good for themselves; and those who love on account of pleasure, love on account of what is pleasant to themselves – and not so far as the beloved is (what he is), but rather in so far as he is useful or pleasant' (NE 1156a15–17). For Aristotle, friendship can be based on usefulness, pleasantness, or virtue (NE 1156b7). Most relationships developed between donors and fundraisers are based on usefulness. Pleasantness may eventually flow from these relationships, but usefulness is the operating principle; rarely can a fundraiser ever maintain a friendship with the donor for friendship's sake alone.

We have explored need as a factor in these types of relationships, and the fact that friendships between donors and fundraisers can and often do come with many strings attached. Is there, perhaps, the possibility that a friendship between a donor and a fundraiser can be complete? According to Aristotle,

it is through loving their friend that people love what is good for themselves, since a good person who becomes a friend becomes a good for the person to whom he is a friend; so each of them, then, loves what is good for himself. And they give what is equal in return, both in their wish and in form, since 'Friendship is Equality,' as the saying goes. (NE 1157b)

This is the 'complete' friendship mentioned above, in which there appears to be reciprocity with no expectations other than the enjoyment in what Aristotle characterizes as friendship for friendship's sake. What is intriguing, if you look at the friendships established between fundraisers and donors, is that (a) there is very little equality in the relationship, and (b) the relationship, as earlier stated, is usually based on something that exists outside of the friendship (i.e., the needs that the charity and its mission represent, and the charity's need to raise money in order to carry out its mission).

It may be difficult to argue that one type of friendship is better or worse than the other, but in terms of equality, a complete friendship leans more towards friendship that is derived from self-love and self-worth versus an external cause or need. Aristotle continues: 'Only infrequently are these friendships combined (friendship for usefulness and friendship for pleasure); and only infrequently do the same people become friends for usefulness and friends for pleasure, since accidents are only infrequently coupled together' (NE 1157a). Could this be what happens when a fundraiser meets a donor whom he or she genuinely likes, apart from the fact that the donor happens to support the organization the fundraiser represents?

I can safely say that after five years of working with the HRI, I developed a close friendship with one donor, mainly because I admired his intellect, integrity, and humour. More to the point, I simply enjoyed his company. The fact that Mr Schmidt reciprocated my interest by sharing the story of his grave illness before he told his family exemplifies the great trust he placed in me. Out of the hundreds of donors I have worked with over the years, I can safely say that besides Mr Schmidt, there was no other person with whom I developed a complete friendship that went beyond our affiliation with the organization.

Now I must ask myself: if I've never shared a complete friendship with any donor except Mr Schmidt, then what's been going on all these years? Besides drinking more Earl Grey tea than I care to remember, listening to hundreds of people share their life stories, and arranging some rather special planned gifts, what have I been doing? Aristotle writes, 'To be friends with many people in a complete friendship is not possible, just as it is not possible to be in love with many people at the same time … Yet on account of usefulness or pleasure it is possible to please many people; for many people are like that, and the favours require little time' (NE 1158a10–11, 16–17).

I wonder if Aristotle wasn't at one point in his life a planned-giving or major-gifts officer working for some philanthropic society in ancient Greece. On average, an experienced major gifts officer may need to manage between 150 and 200 donor relationships per year. Conversely, a good planned giving officer needs to balance his or her time between 75 and 100 close relationships per year. Sending out birthday cards, making phone calls, dropping little notes in the mail, providing people with gift plans that illustrate tax savings – it's all in a day's work. It's easy to be pleasant to a number of people, but most of these 'pleasant' actions take place on a superficial level.

But aside from these activities which revolve around the fundraiser staying in touch with the donor and providing a service to the donor, maybe the question we need to ask is: what is the reason behind all this activity? Or to get back to Aristotle, what is the 'usefulness' of these friendships? According to Aristotle, 'Friendship on account of usefulness is businesslike' (NE 1158a20). So maybe it is about business: a good planned giving officer needs to facilitate future gifts to his or her charity, but must bear in mind that the majority of these gifts or bequests come from a person's lifetime accumulated assets. Most of the gifts that I arrange with donors now will not be realized by the charity for many years to come.

Along with dealing with large amounts of capital, cash, stocks, and real estate, a planned giving officer must also deal with the donor's spiritual side – the meaning of the gift, and what it represents to the donor. When donors leave a bequest or make a planned gift to a favourite charity, it's not just a matter of money; they are making a very personal statement about who they are and what they value. To some donors, their gift sums up or crowns the work of a lifetime. This is the reason why fundraisers must respect a donor's philanthropic wishes. The final exchange of money between the donor and the charity is charged with meaning; the exchange, in this sense, differs from a straight business transaction. What is more, the gift is meaningful to all three parties: the donor, the charity, and the fundraiser.

But if there is meaning to the gift, there is still a person making the gift. Whatever I do as a fundraiser, and particularly as a planned giving officer, I certainly will heed Aristotle's advice: 'It is especially among the elderly that this sort of friendship (usefulness) seems to occur since it is not what is pleasant that people pursue at that age, but rather what is beneficial'(NE 1156a25). The word 'beneficial' here implies what is immediately useful and advantageous, as well as benefit in the literal sense of doing or receiving good.

In my introduction, I touched upon the ethical tensions between the philanthropic intent of the donor, the integrity of the fundraiser, and the charitable organization he or she represents. By nature we are human, and it is common for human beings to derive advantage from one another. Personal make-up on both sides has a lot to do with how fundraisers and donors interact. In the cases of Mr Schmidt and Mr Blackstone, the only thing they were trying to derive from me was friendship. And I do believe there was authenticity as to how we related to each other. Each of us, and of course the organization, benefited from our relationships with each other. In the case of Mr Schmidt, I am saddened by the fact that our friendship is most likely over, now that I have left HRI. As for Mr Blackstone, I can only conclude that for my part, there was never much of a friendship there to begin with. Nonetheless I consider being kind to good people part of my mandate as a planned giving manager. I'll explore the idea of kindness later in this paper. For now, I'll leave you with one question: can the nature of the friendship between the donor and the fundraiser be solely defined by an eventual business transaction, or is there something more?

2. The Who and What of Fundraising

> Do you live off or do you live for philanthropy? Are we truly dedicated in service to the organization that has hired or retained us and to the donors who want to serve the organization with their gifts? If we are, our primary duty is to serve the donors responsibly. By doing so, we are serving the organization well.
>
> Hank Rosso, *Rosso on Fundraising* (1996, 169)

In today's hectic world of not-for-profit fundraising, the words of the late Hank Rosso, an acknowledged master fundraiser in North America, attest to an ideal. What exactly is the nature of fundraising work? Is it just a job, or is it a profession, a calling, a ministry, or a vocation? And if fundraising is the 'servant to philanthropy' as Rosso maintains (ibid., 170), then just how far are fundraisers willing to go in pursuit of a gift – or rather, how far should they go? However, I will begin with a few words about planned giving.

Planned giving has more to do with securing gifts for the future, mainly bequests, which are gifts made through a person's will. Most of the people I work with tend to be older, aged 65 and up, and most of their gifts have to do with deciding what is to become of their accumulated assets once they are deceased. Generally speaking, self-interest has very little to do with gifts to a favourite cause or charity, because the results of these gifts won't be witnessed or experienced by the donors during their lifetime. For this reason, in some respects, planned giving tends to be a more altruistic form of giving. From the charity's point of view, it represents a very specialized, highly personal form of fundraising.

According to calculations by John Havens and Paul Schervish of the Boston College Social Welfare Research Institute (SWRI), in North America, 'More than $41 trillion will be transferred to heirs over the next 55 years, of which, at least $6 trillion will go to charities as people die' (Sczudlo 2002, 17). A charity that does not have planned giving or major gifts officers out in the field will lose a huge share of these funds – or so the current common wisdom goes. This statistic is even more striking when we consider that 'one third of the current Canadian population was born between 1947 and 1966' (ibid.).

In Canada, planned giving may be perceived as being something new, but it is actually one of the oldest forms of charitable giving. Over the past fifty years, a body of fundraising knowledge has developed into theories that have been more or less accepted as fact by those practising the profession. One axiom of fundraising theory is that people give to people. Another is that proper donor cultivation leads to larger gifts. In this case, fundraising is actually the end product of friendship-raising. What is *not* axiomatic (and is in fact a new phenomenon, which I have witnessed in my ten years doing gift planning work) is the 'winner take all' principle that seems to inform the mentality of certain Canadian charities currently pursuing bequest fundraising. But let's stop for a moment and consider the actual role of the fundraiser.

At one time, I was an authorized fundraising representative for a large urban university. As such, I had been given authority by the president and board of governors to build friendships with alumni and friends of the university. This was obviously a worthy cause, and I was certainly committed to securing a financial future for this institution of higher education. The question was, however, to what extent would I go to build and sustain these friendships with the donors and alumni? As I mentioned earlier, I am not entirely comfortable, at times, with the thought that I may be unduly influencing donors, even for causes

I personally consider to be important. Indeed, I believe that as our population ages and the field of gift planning expands, and as charities become increasingly competitive, fundraisers will have to become even more aware of the roles they play as confidants and advisors to donors.

Even today, for fundraisers, the fanfare and publicity we attach to people making donations – the unveiling of a plaque, followed by staged handshakes and smiles with the CEO and the board of directors – are matters more of style than of substance. The most meaningful moments I share with donors are not the public recognition events, but rather the quiet walk, the intimate cup of tea, even the knowing smile. It is simply the point when the donor lets you know they feel happy about making a gift, for in reality, gift-giving can often be a simple gesture. On a practical level, the disconnect I sometimes sense in my job is the compartmentalization that occurs when I am working in the office: the routine, the interaction with my colleagues. Even the software programs I use transform these amazing personal experiences I have into standard, three-page biographies that are ready to print any time I need to see the latest address change, or most recent gift. I spend a lot of time with the elderly, and due to ill health and circumstances beyond their control, chaos frequently rules. However, along with the chaos comes the wonderful mystery of being human. And for me, the greatest 'mystery' is why people decide to leave money to a certain charity, and what motivates them to do so.

In my work as a fundraising professional, I try my best to honestly represent my institution, honour people's philanthropic goals, and help them achieve these goals. The question I ask myself is, 'Does the donor's philanthropic mission match the mission of the organization I represent, and if so, how can I best combine both sets of objectives?' I can only do so as long as I respect the fact that 'the role of a professional fundraiser is, indeed, that of a servant to philanthropy' (Rosso 1996, 174). If the answer is negative, it may be because the donor's interests are not fully in line with the mission of the charity. On the comparatively rare occasions when this has happened, I have offered to help the donor find a more suitable cause or charity to support.

By and large, I think anyone who enters the field of charitable fundraising does so out of a deep motivation to help build community and improve society. But let's suppose, for a moment, that fundraising is really about making money (albeit for good causes). Why, then, do we have to be so concerned about doing the right thing? Why do fundraisers, in order to join the AFP, have to sign a membership pledge card stating they will abide by a code of ethics? What exactly makes fundraising so different from any other form of business we conduct in society today?

3. The Heart of the Matter

> God could have made all men rich but he wanted there to be poor people in this world, that the rich might be able to redeem their sins.
>
> Saint Eligius

The importance of ethics

I once had a debate with a professor at the university I was associated with. I consulted with many friends and associates in the field of fundraising or non-profit management about some key concepts presented in this paper. Among my fundraising colleagues, with whom I spoke a common language and shared a common understanding, not one person questioned me as to why ethics is so important to fundraising. The professor, however, challenged me at a fundamental level:

> What makes you any different from a good car salesman selling a good car? You've both got a product – the car versus the cause. You're both ethical and honest. You're both in the business of customer relations and customer service. How do you distinguish your approach to the donor, ethically, from any other selling activity in business?

I had to think about that question, because I truly don't see myself as a businessperson. But if you look at the laws governing how charities are formed and operated in Canada and the United States, there is certainly room for a great deal of interpretation about where business ends and where charity begins.

Most successful charities are run like businesses, and a great deal of attention is paid to the bottom line. Fundraisers are responsible for revenue generation, helping the charity meet its bottom line so that it can continue to fulfil its mission. However, we must remember the 'non' in 'non-profit.' Charities are not in the business solely of making money, nor are they in the business of paying taxes to the government or dividends to shareholders. What, then, is the appropriate relationship between the fundraiser and the elderly donor? And do ethics have a role to play in defining this relationship?

Planned giving and the elderly

Earlier, I mentioned that I prefer working with people with the smiling, kind faces. Those faces usually come with wrinkles, wisdom, and knowledge. Often, those faces have seen a lot of difficult things and have suffered through some very difficult times. I prefer not to use the term elderly because I think age is something that is relative. I've met fifty-year-olds who act like they are in their nineties, and ninety-year-olds who act like they are in their fifties! I remember once having a spirited discussion with an eighty-five-year-old woman who still quite hadn't gotten around to making her will, because she had 'more important things to do,' such as going out with her friends and having a good time. When I raised my usual arguments about the disadvantages to her heirs, the government, and society in general were she to die without a will, she reminded me that she 'wasn't planning on checking off the planet anytime soon.' At the time, I finally gave up with a chuckle, and said, 'Call me when you're ready to accept your mortality!' I also remember thinking to myself that I would probably be waiting a while before she called again. She seemed to be in great spirits and good health. And she's in good company.

In a survey by Statistics Canada in the mid-1990s, seniors across the country were asked to describe their health. For those 65 and over, 77.6 per cent rated their health as being good to excellent, while 22.4 per cent rated their health as being fair to poor (Statistics Canada 1996–1997, 73). I'm not worried about the group that rated their health good to excellent. They can make up their own minds about how they want to spend their money, what they want to donate to, and how. Indeed, a large percentage of today's seniors are savvy when it comes to donating, especially those who grew up during the Great Depression; saving money is something they take quite seriously. And there are more and more of these people. In 1995, there were an estimated 3.6 million people, or 12 per cent of the Canadian population, over the age of 65. By the year 2041 this number will increase to 23 per cent of the population (Statistics Canada 2002). Another trait these people have in common is a hatred of paying taxes, which they seem on principle to consider excessive. Anything they can do to save on taxes is considered good, and they tend to welcome the tax breaks generated by contributing money to a charity.

But what about the 22.4 per cent of seniors who rated themselves in poor to fair health? Or the 27.6 per cent of Canadians over the age of 65 who reported having some type of memory problem (Statistics Canada

1996–7, 77)? Memory loss can become a serious issue when you are talk-·
ing about estate planning. I am using very broad definitions here, but I
think the seniors most 'at risk' are those who are personally inclined to
give to charity, in poor health, and lonely. In the field of planned giving,
we sometimes spend a great deal of time trying to arrange visits and
meetings with people who really don't want to meet with us in person,
but feel obliged to do so out of politeness or duty. Some donors who
agree to see us may express real interest; others are merely lonely or
bored with their own lives. In 1991, 92 per cent of all Canadians aged 65
and over lived in private households. A substantial number of these
seniors live alone. In 1991, 28 per cent of all people aged 65 and over
lived alone, compared with just 8 per cent of those aged 15 to 64. Senior
women, especially those in the oldest age groups, are particularly likely
to live alone. In 1991, 38 per cent of all senior women, and *53 per cent of*
those aged 85 and over, lived on their own (Statistics Canada 2002).

In my career, I've visited hundreds of donors, many of them older
women; more than one-quarter of these visits happened because I offered a diversion in their day. Most of these visits, in themselves, are very
pleasant: I learn a lot about the person, and I manage to impart important information about my charity, which is the purpose of the visit, from
my point of view. As I mentioned earlier, it is said that 'fundraising is a
contact sport,' and that 'people give to people.' This is true: people prefer
to give to causes and to *people they like.* Nonetheless, fundraisers visit
people for specific purposes, and with specific objectives in mind.

I once had a revealing conversation with a colleague who manages
one of the largest and most successful planned giving programs for a
prominent disease charity in Canada. Due to the nature of the disease,
she and her staff spend a great deal of their time visiting the very frail
and the very old. I once asked her, just as a point of clarification, how
much time she spent visiting with a donor. On a typical visit, I try to
spend no more than an hour with the donor, though it is never easy to
predict how long any particular visit will last. I was surprised when my
colleague said that she quite often spent half a day with one of her
planned giving donors, and that she didn't mind at all taking part in
the donor's daily activities – grocery shopping, taking a walk, playing
a game of cards. My first impression was how pleasant it must be to do
things of a personal nature with people, rather than sit in a stiff chair
and discuss the tax advantages of various planned-giving vehicles.

At first, I couldn't imagine what it must be like to give so freely of
oneself and one's time, and mix so much of my personal life with

someone else's. Perhaps a very skilled fundraiser can gently steer the conversation around a routine activity so as to include a discussion of their charity, its mission, and the services it provides. If that can be done, a long visit may be time well spent. But if the fundraiser must set aside the 'business' of the charity, then perhaps the time and the visit are wasted. One reason I try to limit my own visiting time is precisely in order to strike a balance between conversation about the donor's personal interests and discussion of the charity I represent. And yet, when I see what a powerhouse my colleague's charity has become, especially in the field of planned giving, I wonder whether I should be thinking about how to spend more time with my donors after all.

One obvious advantage in spending so much time with a single donor is that, in due course, the donor comes to know the fundraiser personally, so that the fundraiser is in a position to give purpose and meaning to the time spent with the donor. But for all the reasons I have previously discussed, their friendship is still based on need; once the needs of either party change, the friendship is bound to change, and may dissolve entirely.

But for now, let's give my colleague the benefit of the doubt. Maybe what is going on here is more than just a visitor from a charity spending quality time with a donor. Perhaps these acts of kindness to the elderly are an integral part of a planned giving officer's job. According to Robert Wuthnow, 'kindness also means combating the indifference and personal insufficiency created by institutions' (1995, 224). Because so much of what a planned giving officer eventually accomplishes comes directly from face-to-face meetings with donors, we do spend a lot of time outside of the office visiting with donors in settings where they are most comfortable – usually in the donor's home, or at some convenient restaurant or coffee shop nearby.

When I was working for Humanitarian Relief International, I would often wonder what exactly I was doing visiting donors in small towns and large cities across Canada, flying all over the country, being thoughtful and kind to so many people. I never thought of it in terms of kindness, but that's exactly what I was doing: being kind. 'Kindness is, after all, elementary, and by cultivating it in small ways and in ordinary circumstances, we can carry it with us even in the midst of institutions that encourage us to be indifferent and to simply do our jobs' (Wuthnow 1995, 228). This recalls Aristotle's remark mentioned above, that in terms simply of being useful or pleasant 'it is possible to please many people; for many people are like that, and the favours require little time.' I could argue about the time it takes to be pleasant (it can take a lot of time) but certainly being kind to donors is very useful to the fundraiser and the charity.

As I mentioned earlier, it's easy to be pleasant to a number of people, but most of these 'pleasant' actions do take place on a superficial level. So perhaps being kind and spending time with donors helps fundraisers go beyond the superficial level with a donor. But bear in mind that being kind to donors also serves a vital purpose to the fundraiser. It helps us gather important personal information about the donor, and his or her financial circumstances. Another person from the same disease charity once told me a story about spending a lot of time with one donor who, at the time, was very ill in a nursing home. The planned giving officer boasted that the donor, just before she died, wanted to be with the planned giving officer and not with her immediate family, because she felt closer to the planned giving officer. Where, in such a situation, do the bonds of personal friendship leave off and the interests of the charitable organization begin? In fact, the planned giving officer seemed to represent the outcome as a personal victory over obvious rivals – as if she had won a contest of affection between herself and the donor's family members. In this case we have a right to ask: who got the bulk of the deceased woman's estate – the charity, or the family?

Perhaps this charity needs to take a hard look at how much time their planned giving officers are spending with their donors, and on what activities. One could say that if the 'ends' of the charity are to realize significant bequest gifts, then the 'means' are less important. But what if word ever got out that their fundraiser behaved in this manner? What if the public found out that the last person to see the donor alive was the fundraiser and not the family, and what if the charity got all the money? I question how boastful the planned giving officer would be under those circumstances.

Fortunately, in this instance the charity and the family received an equal share of the woman's estate, and both parties were pleased with how the estate was settled.

Evidently, then, the relationship between the donor and the fundraiser is a bit of a hybrid, incorporating some elements of a business relationship, and some elements of a utilitarian friendship. In most circumstances, the ethical dilemmas that arise with fundraising can be addressed by thoughtful, considered actions. In certain instances, however, the answers will not readily appear. But if the fundraiser and the charity are willing to address difficult issues head-on, and use existing codes of ethics[2] as guidelines, solutions can be reached. Often the most difficult challenge is to accept the truth that the ends do not always justify the means. Simply put, a fundraiser has no right to employ unethical means or make false claims of friendship when asking people for money. On the contrary, fundraisers should continually examine their methods and conduct, with regard both to the interests of the charitable organization they represent and to the personal relationship they cultivate with each donor whose contributions they hope to secure.

4. Conclusion: It's All about Trust

Earlier I said that relationships between the donor, the charity, and the fundraiser are largely based upon the needs associated with a charitable organization or cause, and the monetary transaction with the donor. In order for the end to justify the means, one must remember, respect, and honour the meaning behind the gift. Perhaps now we need to combine these two concepts, go beyond the limitations of money, tax laws, and gift contracts, and focus on the heart of the matter – the principle of trust.

In 2002, Arthur Drache, the respected Canadian tax expert, published the article 'The Necessary Trust Factor' in the *Canadian Not-For-Profit News,* in which he writes:

> Unlike most other agreements between the parties in the commercial world, where we are dealing with donations, the parties (the charity and the donor) must be prepared to trust each other, given that there is no recourse to the courts to enforce an understanding. What is notable, of course, is that in Canada there is a high level of trust, which has been established by exemplary conduct on both sides over generations. That is as it should be and much of the fundraising done in this country depends on maintaining that high level of trust. This is one area where 'morality' and 'good business sense' operate hand in hand. (39)

Drache is certainly right to make the connection between morality and good business sense. Over the past twenty years, fundraising theory has led fundraisers to believe that they ought to encourage donors to become more involved with the charities and causes they support. The act of involvement leads to larger and larger gifts. In fact, interest and involvement are now considered to be almost as important as the criterion of financial capacity when rating a donor's potential to give. But as donors choose to become involved with charities, we run the risk of blurring the lines between a charity's moral and legal obligations to the donor. It is also a fact that what goes on between donors and charities impacts society at large. People give money to charities in order to change society for the better. Charities are merely the conduits by which these good intentions unfold. I would argue that without breaking the letter of the law, fundraisers must give equal weight and credence to the moral obligations that bind us to those who support us.

I think back to one example, where it was only the humanitarian aid agencies that were ready to listen to a family who felt they had been betrayed by an elderly uncle when he passed away, having willed the bulk of his estate to be shared among eight charities but leaving his widowed sister penniless. When the family decided to test the waters and seek non-legal redress from the charities (they asked that each charity give up 2 per cent of its intended share to create a nest egg for the widowed sister), it was only the planned giving officer from another humanitarian aid agency, and myself, who decided to give the family the benefit of the doubt and at least send a representative to meet with them and hear their side of the story. I was surprised that the other planned giving officers representing universities, hospitals, and disease charities were perplexed and annoyed that two humanitarian aid agencies would have the audacity to meet with the family, and thereby stall the distribution of the estate funds. They took the line that from a strictly legal standpoint, the will was valid; if Uncle Henry left his sister without a penny, then that is what he wanted. In the end, it turned out the family had actually received several loans from Uncle Henry, all of which were forgiven at the time of his death. Learning this, I had no qualms whatsoever about graciously accepting Uncle Henry's bequest. But I still shudder to think sometimes of the public relations nightmares that are just looming if charities hide behind their lawyers and forget why they exist in the first place.

We have seen enough articles in the newspapers about both charities and donors reneging on promises and contracts once made in good faith. With the passage in November 2000 of the McMichael Canadian Art Collection Amendment (Bill 112), the Government of Ontario took a strong position on the importance of charitable institutions honouring donor intent. As the charitable sector grows in stature and complexity, honouring donor intent will become an even more important moral issue.

Certainly, one important way to honour donor intent is for charities and donors to engage in activities that promote trust. According to

Marilyn Fischer (2000), 'We want our organizations to be structured and operated so that people of ordinary decency and courage can do well. Agency trust, based on responsible and responsive policies, and system trust, linking trustworthy agencies, provide an atmosphere in which trusting interpersonal relationships can breathe easily' (85). Because I have audited, implemented, and managed several planned giving programs for both large and small charities, I understand what Fischer means about 'breathing easily,' especially when it comes to developing sound policies and procedures.

When I look back at my own career, I see that what has guided me many times, in the absence of explicit policies or procedures in the organizations I have represented, has been my own common sense and integrity. But is this enough? Unlike the United Kingdom, and to a lesser extent the United States, the Canadian charitable sector is still very much a self-regulated industry.

I would propose that the charitable sector should begin to develop policies around the idea of a charity's institutional capability of honouring donor intent and put in place procedures that encourage all parties concerned to act with integrity and trust. Imagine if early on in my career I had worked for a charity that said I could develop friendships with donors, up to a point. I am thinking in particular of my encounters with elderly donors who belong to the 22-per cent poor-to-fair health category. It would have been helpful to have had guidelines to follow, even if those guidelines stated that all I had to do was consult with the director of development if I encountered a donor who, in my view, was either too mentally or physically incapacitated to make decisions alone.

I can think of one instance when I encountered a donor, Mr Booth, who was obviously mentally unstable. The only problem was that I discovered the true extent of his mental illness only after he had given our charitable organization two $50,000 cheques. After we received the first cheque (a considerable sum, for a first-time donation), I phoned to thank Mr Booth. We had a very polite conversation, and afterward I arranged for both the CEO and the chairperson of the board to send personal thank-you notes. Two weeks later we received the second cheque from Mr Booth, also for $50,000. I thought to myself, 'Hey, I'm on a roll!' Again, I phoned the donor, and this time I asked if I could thank him in person for his very generous donation. Mr Booth said that he would be delighted. The following week, I made a visit to his home.

After five minutes of conversation with Mr Booth, I could tell that something was very wrong. He kept referring to various 'spirits' who were telling him what to think and do, and he was having difficulty putting together cohesive sentences. Every time I tried to steer the conversation in a 'safe' direction, the 'spirits' would begin speaking to him again. (This was one of the few times in my life that I felt unsafe in a donor's home.) During the next sixty minutes, I did my best to be attentive and polite, and not to betray my worry and discomfort. When I finally left the house, I believed that I had managed to end the visit without offending Mr Booth. I have no idea what impression I made on the 'spirits.'

I immediately called my manager and alerted him to the situation. The next day, we called a meeting with the senior management team to discuss the situation. We then alerted the chairperson of the board about the donor's condition and explained that we were removing Mr Booth from our donor database. I also wrote a carefully worded note to his 'hard' (paper) file, clearly stating that after my visit on such and such a date, it was determined that due to the donor's ill-health, the charity would never ask this donor for money again. We basically made up this procedure as we went along. But in retrospect, it would have been much easier to refer to an existing policy.

To round out the story, when Mr Booth wasn't conversing with the 'spirits,' he did indicate that his mother had recently died, and that his closest living relatives were in Switzerland. I could only assume that the two sums we received had probably come from his inheritance, and I wondered how quickly Mr Booth would run through the rest of the money. In fact, he had indicated that the 'spirits' had instructed him to make sizeable donations to other charities, though I was the only representative who had actually come to see him. In this instance, our charitable organization didn't do anything legally wrong by accepting the money; but I question the moral integrity of the decision to keep the donation, once we had discovered the donor's mental condition. I did my best to protect the charity's interests. But I wonder to this day what the other charities would have done, had they found out what I found out.

Until this experience, I had always assumed that visiting with donors was an opportunity for me to get to know the donor from a fundraising point of view. It had not occurred to me that I might be required to determine whether or not a donor had the mental capacity to decide about making a gift to the charity I was representing. In the future, as more and more donors age, and more and more planned giving officers knock on the doors of the elderly, charitable organizations will almost certainly have to ask these sorts of questions, and/or design policies that address matters of donors' mental or emotional competence.

According to Dr Paul Pribbenow, vice-president for Institutional Advancement at the School of the Art Institute of Chicago, 'the real secret to building an ethical culture in an organization and in managing the moral life of the work place, is to focus only on one thing – developing trust. A commitment from the top and specific policy guidance are essential in creating a moral culture' (Courtis 1995, 1). I would add that if charities do their utmost to build moral cultures from within their organizations, the impact will prove beneficial to society on a broader level.

Aside from policy development, what else can charitable organizations do to foster a moral culture in their institutional environments, especially around the issue of friendships and fundraising? The fact is that fundraisers come and go; donors, it is to be hoped, will stay with the charity all their lives. It is not uncommon for a certain donor to establish a friendship with a particular fundraiser, only to have that fundraiser leave the organization. From the charity's perspective, it is much better for an important donor to have two or more solid, personal links ongoing with the institution. Unfortunately, for reasons that have more to do with ego and territory, some fundraisers prefer to control their relationships with individual donors rather than manage these relationships in the charity's interest.

It would be better to have a policy that encourages fundraising staff and other key representatives of the charity to establish multiple institutional relationships with donors. Under such a policy, the donor might get to know a senior manager, a board member, or a volunteer, as well as the designated fundraiser.

Unfortunately, it is much easier for the fundraiser to meet his or her short-term goals by establishing proprietary donor relationships. I question how effective these private strategies really are, in the long run. I've left enough jobs now to realize that I am only doing my job correctly if the donors I've befriended continue to contribute to the institution after I've left.

Last but not least, a few words about kindness: fundraisers and charitable organizations alike must learn to care and be kind to the donor. The ancient Chinese philosopher Lao Tsu summed it up best when he wrote over 2,400 years ago:

Kindness in words creates confidence.
Kindness in thinking creates profoundness.
Kindness in giving creates love.

By maintaining our integrity – listening, trusting, and honouring the generosity of the donor's heart – the donor, the fundraiser, and the charity can all participate in and benefit from the rudimentary and life-affirming joy of giving. Lastly, I wish to acknowledge and thank all of the donors I have worked with in my career. Without their love for humankind, there would be no philanthropy; may their spirits live on forever in the gifts they make today and in the gifts they plan to make tomorrow.

NOTES

1 Names of private donors, charitable organizations, and institutions in this essay are pseudonyms. I have altered discreetly the circumstances and details of real-life events so as to protect my subjects' anonymity.
2 In order to become a member of the Association of Fundraising Professionals, each member must agree to abide by the AFP Code of Ethical Principals and Standards of Professional Practice.

11 Health Communication, Collaboration, and Ethics: Working with the Private Sector to Influence Consumer Behaviour

ELIZABETH MOREAU

Most major national health organizations include education of patients and the public as part of their mandates, and the information they provide is both vast and varied, covering disease prevention and management as well as health promotion, patient and family support, and self-help. This kind of education targets people with particular diseases or conditions, as well as healthy individuals, health professionals, and the general public.

Over the more than ten years that I have managed communications for a children's health organization, one of the greatest challenges has been to adequately fund our public education programs. Getting credible health information to parents and caregivers is central to the Canadian Paediatric Society's (CPS) mission; yet finding the resources to do so effectively has been difficult.

That doesn't mean the private sector is not interested in working with the CPS. Companies that market to parents or child health professionals want to align themselves with the only national organization representing Canada's paediatricians. Over the years, I've watched pharmaceutical companies and manufacturers of consumer goods – along with their public relations agencies – go to almost any length to sell us their creative partnership projects. Yet only rarely do these proposals result in collaboration. Most are thinly disguised vehicles for marketing products, usually with an implicit message of CPS endorsement.

For these companies, decision-making about such funding priorities is often in the hands of marketing staff, who must demonstrate a link between their communications budgets and increased product sales. Yet many important health communication messages have no product links. And even those that do often raise difficult ethical questions. When does a 'win-win' situation become blatant product promotion? Is health information with industry involvement still in the public's best interest? Is it ethical for a voluntary sector organization to work solely with one corporation in a given area, to the exclusion of its competitors?

Collaboration between the voluntary health sector and the private sector – in particular, pharmaceutical companies – is quite common in consumer health communication. The two sectors have a mutually vested interest in communicating health information to the public. After all, certain products do enhance or maintain health. For people with diseases or chronic conditions, some therapeutic products are essential to survival. Other drugs help prevent disease and maintain health. The CPS, for example, is a vocal advocate for childhood immunization, which saves lives and protects children from disease. If we are successful, vaccine manufacturers will sell more products.

Conversations with the private sector have caused me many uncomfortable moments during my time with the CPS, and the potential for perceived product endorsement is just one issue. Other concerns arise from the cultural differences between the two sectors, the imbalance of power arising from the difference in resources, and questions of trust, all of which can make it difficult to have equitable relationships. Part of the CPS response to these issues was to develop an organizational code of ethics.

For voluntary health organizations, working with the private sector at any level raises ethical questions. But when that collaboration involves delivering health messages to the public – information that people use to make decisions about their well-being – there is an added ethical dimension that must be first acknowledged, and then thoughtfully explored. These same questions arise in other areas where the public's well-being is at stake, including safety and consumer advocacy.

This essay explores some of the questions raised by collaboration on health communication, and offers practitioners in the voluntary health sector some suggestions for building and managing relationships that are in the best interests of both their organizations and the people they serve. It examines the primary dilemmas involved in intersectoral collaboration for health communication, and discusses how they might be resolved. Finally, the need for a policy, code, or set of guidelines on ethical partnerships for health communication in the Canadian voluntary sector is considered.

1. Feeding the Public Appetite for Health Information

Health communication is everywhere. No longer are health profession-als the sole or primary conduits through which North Americans get information about health promotion and disease prevention. As public interest in health care continues to grow, most newspapers have desig-nated health reporters, and print and broadcast media regularly feature articles and segments about getting and staying healthy. Canadians with Internet access seek health information more often than any other topic. Two-thirds have visited a health website, and two-thirds of these Canadians do so monthly (Ipsos-Reid 2002). At the same time, the depth of available information has increased: medical journals and ori-ginal research, once available only to health care providers, are now easily accessible online.

Yet health communication is not just a public service or a media story. It is also a commodity, increasingly used as a marketing tool by manufacturers and retailers. On the Internet, a host of commercial sites combine health information with product promotion and brand-ing. Pharmacies use health information to add value to the consumer experience and to help build store loyalty. Pharmaceutical companies are major producers of patient information, found in waiting rooms, public health clinics, and other health care centres. Companies that produce baby formula have 'clubs' for new mothers, ostensibly to pro-vide information on parenting, but also to market the formula product with coupons or free samples. Health magazines abound, with major retailers publishing their own digest-sized health magazines sup-ported by advertising.

In fact, 'health communication' is a broad term that refers not only to information available through media but also to a wide variety of strat-egies designed to communicate information, and influence the public's decisions about disease prevention and health promotion. It includes both interpersonal communication (e.g., between patients and provid-ers) and mass communication (brochures, television, journalism). The Health Communication Unit at the University of Toronto defines five broad types of health communication (HCU, n.d.):

1. *Persuasive or behavioural communication* (including social marketing) aims to convince consumers to adopt certain healthy behaviours, such as increasing physical activity.
2. *Risk communication* conveys information about public health hazards, such as the link between smoking and lung cancer.

3. *Media advocacy* uses print and broadcast media to promote policy change.

4. *Entertainment education* is more prevalent in the United States, where agencies like the Centers for Disease Control work with the entertainment industry to integrate health messages into television and film storylines.

5. *Interactive health communication* primarily involves the Internet, and allows messages to be tailored to specific users. On the Heart and Stoke Foundation's website, users can determine their risk for developing high blood pressure or heart disease.

Health communication may aim to increase compliance with medical regimens, such as taking blood pressure medication, increase compliance with protective legislation, such as wearing seat belts, or increase individual health-promoting behaviours, such as eating more fruits and vegetables (Guttman 2000). At its essence, health communication has a persuasive quality. It aims to influence consumers to make decisions that should positively influence their health, which involves not just the absence of disease but also physical, mental, and social well-being (Ratzan 1998).

Health communication in the voluntary sector

The voluntary health sector in Canada is a large, diverse group. Made up primarily of charities, it also includes not-for-profit associations and coalitions working to promote and improve the health of Canadians. The Health Charities Coalition of Canada (2000) reports that about 5,500 of the 80,000 registered charities in Canada place a strong emphasis on health. These voluntary sector organizations are significant providers of health information for consumers.

Almost all national organizations have well-developed websites featuring patient or public education, and even fundraising appeals often have an educational, awareness-raising aspect to them. Many large health organizations are so well recognized as information providers that they are simply part of the landscape, going virtually unnoticed until an individual or loved one is affected by a disease or condition. These organizations have long promoted healthy behaviours, such as not smoking, eating well, safe sex, and physical activity.

Credible, understandable, and relevant health information is one component of a society's overall health and well-being. Voluntary sector organizations hold positions of public trust, often representing experts in a particular field, which may help explain why they are such prolific providers of health information. Many health organizations also serve as virtual self-help groups, supporting and creating communities of people affected by a specific disease or condition. For these people, information and education are critical. Still other organizations are committed to promoting good health and preventing disease, and helping consumers make informed choices about their health is part of their mandate. For most voluntary sector organizations, health information is not a marketing tool. It is a responsibility.

Voluntary sector organizations forge alliances with the private sector to communicate health information for many reasons, not the least of which is funding. The private sector offers financial resources, networks and reach, exposure, marketing expertise, and more. It is virtually impossible not to consider working with them, given the cost of delivering health communication to the public. This is complex and expensive, particularly when the target audiences are vulnerable or at-risk populations who are not receptive to health messages.

There are many different types of such alliances including social marketing alliances, donor or sponsor agreements, licensing agreements, and cause-related marketing (see table 11.1). Increasingly, corporations see the potential for added value in aligning themselves with voluntary sector organizations to deliver health information. They see they have something to deliver, and they want something in return. Unrestricted philanthropic dollars are difficult to come by, and voluntary sector organizations are under pressure to find a 'fit' between their information products and the products of a potential sponsor. Many health organizations leverage this value to help generate revenue.

The Canadian Cancer Society's website, for example, is explicit in its appeal to corporations by showing the 'bottom-line benefits' of partnerships with the Society (CCS 2006). Its sophisticated, marketing-based approach touts the benefits of being aligned with one of the country's biggest, most trusted health charities: 'A partnership with the Canadian Cancer Society will allow your company to bolster sales by enhancing your corporate image, targeting key markets and differentiating your company from the competition, while fostering customer and employee loyalty.'

The government has been another driver of intersectoral communication alliances. Health Canada enthusiastically encourages voluntary sector organizations to 'partner' with the private sector, especially to

Table 11.1
Health communication alliances

Type of Alliance	Description	Example
Social marketing	Expertise is pooled and exchanged to influence public behaviour. Partners typically are involved in all aspects of the project or program	Campaign on Sudden Infant Death Syndrome, with Health Canada, Canadian Paediatric Society, SIDS Foundation, and Pampers
Donor or Sponsor	Voluntary sector organizations develop communications (print, video, Internet) with corporate funding Donor or sponsor company's involvement (apart from financial commitment) is minimal	The Arthritis Society of Canada lists Pfizer Canada Inc. as a sponsor of its website
Licensing agreements	A non-profit logo appears on a product, often with a health message, in exchange for a fee Product may be evaluated against established criteria in order to qualify for logo placement	The HealthCheck program, administered through the Heart and Stroke Foundation, allows companies to certify 'healthy choice' products based on established criteria
Cause-related marketing	A portion of sales revenue, usually from a particular product, is directed back to a non-profit organization or charity Often there is a related health message for the consumer	Avon Canada sells a different product each year and directs proceeds to the Breast Cancer Research Initiative

raise additional funds for a program or project. In a typical health communication collaboration in Canada, the voluntary sector organization provides the content and credibility while the corporation supplies the money and marketing expertise.

On the surface, this seems like a perfect match of complementary competencies. In practice, however, such collaborations can be difficult, particularly when they involve the multi-billion-dollar pharmaceutical industry, which has a tremendous capacity to influence consumers' health and well-being.

What really happens when the corporate and voluntary sectors collaborate to influence consumers' health behaviour? What ethical questions are raised by these alliances, which have the potential for such profound implications for the consumer? Can voluntary sector organizations collaborate with the private sector on health communications in an ethical and equitable way?

2. The Nature and Ethics of Health Communication Alliances

Effective health communication: Why do we need the private sector?

Health communication is regarded as an essential element for the overall health of a society (USDHHS 2000) and, to be effective, it must be multidimensional. A single brochure or televised public service announcement is unlikely to result in positive behaviour change. Like other forms of communication, messages about health must be audience-centred in order to be effective. Communicators must understand their target audiences and become familiar with the market research techniques of their private sector colleagues. It is in part because of this marketing expertise that private sector partners can be so valuable in social alliances, not to mention the financial resources they can bring to what must necessarily be resource-rich initiatives if they are to be successful.

How consumers use health information is changing, with more and more messages available through an increasing number of channels. The systems for delivering and receiving information about health have become decentralized: where physicians were once the primary sources of health information, today individuals are responsible for finding, distilling, and using information from a variety of sources (Napoli 2001). Health messages that target consumers through a variety of channels have a better chance at success. Private-public partnerships can help leverage the resources needed for these multi-pronged approaches by 'reducing message clutter and targeting health concerns that cannot be fully addressed by public resources or market incentives alone' (USDHHS 2000).

Another important driver of intersectoral collaboration in health has been the focus on population health – promoted by the World Health Organization, Health Canada, the Canadian Public Health Association, and other leading health organizations. This 'population health approach' aims to improve the health of the entire population (rather than focus on individuals) and reduce inequities among subgroups of the population. Central to the population health approach are the 'determinants of health': a range of factors that have been shown to influence health status, such as income, social status, education, employment, social supports and networks, and physical environments. Improving the health of entire populations or subgroups is not something one organization, coalition, sub-sector or even an entire sector can do on its own. According to the Public Health Agency of Canada website (2002), 'A population health approach calls for shared responsibility and accountability for health outcomes with groups not normally associated with health, but whose activities may have an impact on health or the factors known to influence it.' So a population health approach calls for collaboration, both among organizations and agencies at a given level (e.g., community, regional, national) as well as among a range of actors in the government, private, and voluntary sectors. According to Health Canada, the potential is vast:

> Intersectoral action makes possible the joining of forces, knowledge and means to understand and solve complex issues whose solutions lie outside the capacity and responsibility of a single sector ... [It] can be used to promote and achieve shared goals in a number of areas ... policy, research, planning, practice and funding. It may be implemented through a myriad of activities including advocacy, legislation, community projects, policy and program action. (Health Canada 1999, 5)

Intersectoral action on health, a term that appears in both Canadian and international publications, refers to this range of collaborative possibilities. The question of health communication alliances between the voluntary and private sectors is just one narrow slice of this larger movement. Adopting a population health approach, which has been critical in obtaining project funding from Health Canada, requires that organizations look to the private sector to become involved in the challenge of improving and maintaining the health of Canadians.

Collaboration between commercial and voluntary health organizations

What does it mean to collaborate? While collaborating organizations maintain their own culture and structure, they also reduce their autonomy by strengthening ties with other organizations and sharing authority over certain decisions (Kanter 1989). Alliances for health communication usually involve relatively short-term, strategic collaboration on a given issue. Many health organizations, especially those concerned with populations (i.e., children, women) rather than specific conditions, are working on a host of issues at any given time, and may be linked with several corporations at once.

An opportunistic alliance, while not necessarily a desirable collaborative relationship in the context of the voluntary sector, does illustrate one of the potential pitfalls in health communications alliances. These alliances are short-term, with 'an opportunity to gain an immediate ... competitive advantage' and 'possibilities that would not have existed for either of the partners acting alone' (Kanter 1989, 185). A pharmaceutical company introducing a new drug may strike an opportunistic alliance with a voluntary sector organization to get a competitive edge in the market. Partnering with a professional or patient group to promote the benefit of a new medication offers a drug company access to a new market through a credible source. Patient and family groups, particularly those dealing with illnesses managed by drugs, are keen to inform their members about new medications being tested and released, which may give hope to people having difficulty with symptom control or side effects. But critics of the pharmaceutical industry's promotion practices point out that information produced by patient or advocacy groups is not subject to the same standards as advertisements (Mintzes 1998). And while the benefits of such an alliance for the company are clear, the risks to the voluntary sector organization may be greater. It may be perceived as a front for a pharmaceutical's agenda, especially if the relationship doesn't extend beyond the targeted promotion.

A study by Drumwright, Cunningham, and Berger (2000) coined the term 'social alliances' to distinguish relationships between non-profits and corporations from those involving just for-profit organizations. In social alliances, both parties expect the outcome to advance their organization's mission, the corporation is not fully compensated, and the project or initiative is expected to produce a general social benefit (Andreasen and Drumwright 2001). While social alliances can enhance the financial, human, and social capital of each partner, they can also lead to a host of problems, many of which have their roots in the cultural differences between the two sectors. Among those cited are misconceptions, misallocation of costs and benefits, misuses of power, mismatches, misfortunes of time, and mistrust – difficulties related in large part to fundamental differences of perspective. For health organizations, working with pharmaceuticals only amplifies these cultural differences. The resource-rich pharmaceutical industry, with its sophisticated marketing practices, is skilled at building and managing relationships with organizations, government, and individual health practitioners.

Frequently in health communication collaborations, the corporation has a financial stake in the health message that the alliance is promoting, such as a cancer organization that partners with a manufacturer of a stop-smoking patch, a heart health organization that collaborates with producers of low-fat foods, or a children's health organization that works with vaccine manufacturers. While both organizations have a stake in promoting the message, the potential for profit can call into question the voluntary sector organization's credibility. It is therefore crucial that a voluntary sector organization make ethically sound and defensible decisions before committing itself to a private sector alliance.

Questions of power and credibility

Power is frequently cited as a source of potential problems when voluntary and private sector organizations collaborate (Pryor et al. 1999; Drumwright, Cunningham, and Berger 2000; Andreasen and Drumwright 2001). Hardy and Phillips (1998) describe three aspects of power: formal authority, control of critical resources, and discursive legitimacy. When it comes to health communication, non-profit and private sector partners have different types of power. Private sector partners often control the financial or human resources (such as the marketing expertise) essential to a project, while non-profits bring reputation, credibility, and public trust – discursive legitimacy. While collaboration offers the greatest possibility for innovative change to a domain, each player needs power to be able to take part (Hardy and Phillips 1998). Successful collaborations, therefore, depend on recognizing and leveraging the legitimate power that each actor brings to the table.

Effectively using and maintaining the discursive power that voluntary sector health organizations hold is a central issue in the ethics of intersectoral collaboration. The public may perceive, for instance, that an organization is too closely aligned with a private sector partner, and is using its legitimacy to promote products. The Canadian Paediatric Society heard such criticism in 1999, when it collaborated with Merck Frosst Canada to help raise awareness of a new vaccine against chickenpox. While the CPS had a clear mandate to deliver public education in support of this new vaccine (Varicella Consensus Conference 1999), critics said the CPS was using its name to help Merck market a vaccine against a disease that many feel to be benign, despite its potential for serious complications.

The issue of organizational legitimacy was raised in the United States by a group of state Attorneys General in a 1999 report on the growing number of marketing alliances – and resulting problems – between corporations and voluntary health organizations (Pryor et al. 1999). The authors noted that, increasingly, these relationships involve substantial payment by a corporation, exclusivity (i.e., the non-profit cannot work with the corporation's competitors), and the use of the non-profit's name and logo on products – especially pharmaceuticals. The report cites surveys showing that Americans rate non-profit health organizations as among the most trusted sources of health information, while pharmaceutical companies are considered one of the least reliable. The authors raise the question of the long-term effect of intermingling highly trusted with less trusted sources of health information.

One of the organizations implicated in the report is the American Medical Association, which in 1999 adopted revised guidelines on corporate relationships that address issues such as the potential for perceived product endorsement, exclusivity, and corporate influence over AMA policy or direction. The AMA guidelines explicitly state that organizational culture is a critical element of seeking out and cultivating ethical partnerships with the private sector. The AMA does not permit exclusive sponsorships, and encourages multiple private sector partnerships for all forms of health communication, preferably from competing companies in the same product category.

The AMA didn't always discourage exclusivity and promote multiple sponsorships. In fact, its guidelines were published in the wake of a controversial agreement with Sunbeam that ultimately cost the AMA millions of dollars and threatened its credibility. In 1997, the AMA and Sunbeam reached an exclusive five-year deal that would see Sunbeam pay royalties to the AMA on sales of health-related products such as blood pressure monitors, heating pads, and thermometers. The AMA seal was to be featured in product advertising and on product packaging, as well as on written health information to be included with the products. The announcement of the deal was met with 'a blizzard of public criticism' from consumers, media, and AMA members, who focused on the exclusive nature of the deal and the fact that the AMA had not tested any of the products. Before the agreement was implemented, the AMA pulled out and Sunbeam filed a lawsuit. When it was settled in 1998, the AMA paid Sunbeam $9.9 million for damages and expenses (Pryor et al. 1999).

One risk of these alliances is that a corporation may try to exert power that is traditionally the domain of the non-profit organization. With health communication, that domain is information and expertise. When they financially support a project or program, corporations often want involvement in content development; and though many organizations have guidelines that clearly state corporate partners will have no editorial involvement, in practice this can be difficult to manage. This difficulty points to the need for up-front dialogue to make each partner's roles, responsibilities, and limitations in a given alliance clear. It also highlights the need for non-profits to retain financial independence, so as not to be beholden to their private sector sponsors, and not be too reliant on any one source of funding.

3. The Canadian Landscape

In the trenches: How Canadian voluntary health organizations manage health communication collaborations

How do Canadian voluntary sector organizations deal with the ethical issues of collaboration, power, and credibility? To help answer this question, a number of leading organizations in the voluntary health sector were surveyed in order to determine to what extent they collaborate with private sector organizations for health communication; to what extent voluntary health sector organizations perceive ethical issues to be related to such collaboration; and how such organizations deal with these issues.

The extent and nature of collaboration on health communication

All respondents reported engaging in health communication that targets the general public or a specific population, as well as targeting health care professionals. A number of organizations also produce health communication that targets policy-makers and media. The primary goals of these communications are health promotion and disease prevention, but respondents also reported using health communications to help people cope with a condition, improve the quality of care by professionals, inform about treatment options, build awareness of a disease or condition, and reduce the risk of a particular health problem. As well, all respondents reported some type of collaboration with the private sector. Most reported being involved in resource development, that is, print or electronic materials to communicate health messages. Most respondents described arrangements involving the pooling of resources that is typical of alliances (Kanter 1989), particularly those in which the voluntary sector organization contributes content expertise and credibility, while the corporation contributes expertise or resources for development and distribution through its networks.

Ethical issues related to collaboration

Respondents cited several common issues:

1. *Perceived product endorsement.* While respondents said they were careful to avoid supporting a particular product, the potential for perceived product endorsement is a concern. This is echoed by others writing about intersectoral collaboration in health (Mintzes 1998; Pryor et al. 1999; Rochon Ford 1999). In the United States, according to the state Attorneys General report, perceived endorsement by a credible organization may influence purchasing decisions:

> Many consumers may be led to believe, through the use of a familiar non-profit's name and logo in product advertising, that a product is better or superior to another similar product. Studies conducted for the American Cancer Society suggest that many consumers assume that a product advertised with the American Cancer Society's name will necessarily provide greater health benefits for themselves and their families. (Pryor et al. 1999, 14)

Although most voluntary health organizations wish to avoid the perception of endorsement, logo identification with specific products is increasingly common. The Canadian Paediatric Society, the Arthritis Society of Canada, the Canadian Dermatology Association, and the Canadian Dental Association all have allowed their respective logos to appear on products widely available in grocery stores and pharmacies. The Heart and Stroke Foundation (HSF), which runs the HealthCheck product certification program, has developed a separate logo for the program. A subtle identification remains, however, since the words 'Heart and Stroke Foundation' are part of the HealthCheck symbol.

Products that meet certain nutritional criteria can use the HealthCheck logo and program message for an annual licensing fee (HSF 2004).

Even if collaboration does not involve a particular product, there is also a question about whether working with a corporation implies endorsement of other products or practices. According to one survey respondent, 'Companies hope we will lend support to their products but we are very careful never to endorse or indicate support of any drug or product in particular. Any alliance is carefully handled to avoid that.' Still, it is clear that consumers do make many assumptions when a not-for-profit name and logo is associated with a product or company (Pryor et al. 1999).

2. *Conflict of interest.* Again, pharmaceuticals were specifically mentioned. In this context, conflict of interest is related to the extent to which a company has the potential for profit by promoting a health message or supporting a program. 'At times they do raise ethical issues,' said one respondent concerning health communications alliances, 'especially when treatment issues are involved and one of the parties is a company that is marketing a potential treatment.' Some organizations' guidelines do try to guard against conflicts of interest by specifically indicating when and how they can be involved in health information. Some guidelines also state that funds received from commercial sources must be unrestricted, and most require that the voluntary sector organization should maintain control over content.

3. *Organizational legitimacy and credibility.* Protecting the credibility of the voluntary sector organization involves maintaining a balance of power in the alliance. That is, the voluntary sector organization must ensure that its role as content expert is respected.

How organizations deal with ethical issues related to collaboration

A number of respondents said they have guidelines to deal with private sector collaborations. None of the organizations surveyed reported having an overall organizational code of ethics, though some have conflict of interest guidelines, or codes of conduct for directors. Several reported following other codes, most notably the Ethical Fundraising and Financial Accountability Code of the Canadian Centre for Philanthropy (CAP n.d.), which does not cover issues related to either collaboration or communications. In general, the guidelines are neither complex nor lengthy, and range from a simple statement of principles to detailed descriptions of scenarios that are acceptable and not acceptable. Among the most common elements are:

- *A statement about 'fit.'* Organizations want to undertake projects and programs relevant to their mission and goals.
- *A statement about editorial control.* When it comes to health communications, organizations are clear that they must maintain editorial control.
- *Provisions to avoid perception of product endorsement.* These include: permitting a corporate but not a product logo to appear on materials, avoiding projects that target users of a single product (such as users of a particular medication); specific language to be used in disclaimers and credit lines; and avoiding sponsorships exclusive to a particular product category. Despite these measures, organizations still find themselves in difficult situations. The Arthritis Society's guidelines say they 'avoid endorsement of specific products, diagnoses, treatment'; yet just a few years ago the society came under fire for newspaper advertising inserts carrying its logo and promoting the virtues of new treatments. The ad did not disclose that the society was receiving funding from the manufacturers of the products. (Johnson 2000)

For purposes of comparison, guidelines and reports from the American Medical Association, Health Canada, the World Health Organization, Health Action International (HAY-Europe), the European Public Health Alliance, and Canada's Research-Based Pharmaceutical Companies (Axed) were also considered (see table 11.2). Among the highlights:

- All organizations agree that product endorsement is to be avoided. Several have developed specific measures to avoid the perception of endorsement, such as permitting only company (rather than product) logos to appear on materials produced in collaboration.
- Most organizations also discourage exclusive arrangements, with the exception of Health Canada. Organizations cite many reasons for avoiding exclusivity, noting that is has the potential to mislead consumers, and shifts the balance of power in the direction of the company.
- One of the major differences among the guidelines is their approach to choosing potential corporate partners. The American Medical Association's guidelines (2005) reflect a commitment to upholding public trust in the medical profession and the organization. The AMA should drive the partnership agenda, both in seeking and managing alliances. The need for external funding

should be minimized. Health Canada, on the other hand, encourages strategic alliances, whether initiated internally or externally.

- The European Public Health Alliance approaches partnerships with the pharmaceutical industry almost as a necessary evil in the face of shrinking funding sources: 'Sponsorship from commercial companies could be a valuable resource but should not be entered into without careful consideration' (EPHA 1996, 1). Guidelines also differ in their objectives or stated purpose, which usually open the document. Some are straightforward guides to decision-making; others stress the organization's accountability to its consumer groups. These opening statements set the tone and approach for the entire document.

Do guidelines reflect principles of ethical health communication?

Communications practitioners will be familiar with the basic principles of ethical communication, among them truthfulness, accuracy, fairness, timeliness, and respect (IABC 2006). Honesty in health communications is paramount, to ensure that consumers have the necessary and correct information about the benefits and risks of behaviours, choices, or therapies. In alliances, truthfulness also requires full disclosure of sponsors and, if appropriate, their role in the collaboration.

Ethical health communication entails five principles: *beneficence, non-malfeasance, respect for personal autonomy, justice,* and *utility,* or the 'maximum good' (Strasser and Gallagher 1994; Guttman 2000). These principles severally and comprehensively require that audiences be given clear, complete, comprehensible messages conveying information on health and health care issues, that the messages be made readily available to as large an audience as possible, and especially to the people who are known to need the information such messages contain (see table 11.3). Accordingly, health communicators must:

- promote positive health practices and information that are in the best interest of consumers
- ensure that communications are comprehensive, without unnecessary fear or overestimations of risk (they should ensure that risk of harm is minimized, by providing information about potential side effects of treatment)

Table 11.2
Comparison of commercial and health sector partnership guidelines

	Guideline Characteristics				Key Issues	
	Public/Confidential	Audience	Objective	Exclusivity	Choice of partner	Product endorsement
American Medical Association (1999)	Public (Web)	National, U.S.: AMA staff, members, public	Protect public trust and credibility of physicians and AMA	Discouraged Encourages multiple sponsorships wherever possible	AMA should determine priorities for external funding Organizational culture should promote realistic funding objectives	Not permitted No involvement in marketing health-related products to consumers
Health Canada (2002)	Public (Web)	National, Canadian: Health Canada, other government departments, NGOs, potential partners	Help seek, secure, develop and maintain partnerships	Acceptable in some cases Helps avoid conflicts between competing companies 'Obligates chosen corporations to be active'	Based on ability and willingness to contribute to Health Canada goals	Health Canada logo not permitted where product endorsement is implied or explicit
WHO Ethical Criteria (1988)	Public (Web)	International: pharmaceuticals, with application for organizations working with them	'To support and encourage the improvement of health care through the rational use of medicinal drugs'	Exclusivity would be misleading, since not all relevant information would be available to consumers	NGOs that are not involved in activities designed to promote the sale of drugs	Direct-to-consumer ads for prescription drugs discouraged Drug promotion should not include misleading statements

Table 11.2
Comparison of commercial and health sector partnership guidelines (continued)

	Guideline Characteristics				Key Issues	
	Public/ Confidential	Audience	Objective	Exclusivity	Choice of partner	Product endorsement
HAI-Europe (1998)	Public (report)	Pharmas, NGOs, health professionals, researchers, public	Promote best possible use of medicines, if and when needed, in interest of individual and public health	Exclusivity would contravene WHO Ethical Criteria	Apply accountability and transparency guidelines recommended for all NGOs	NGOs should be aware of pharma companies' efforts to secure explicit or implicit endorsement
European Public Health Alliance (1996)	Public (upon request)	EPHA, broader European NGO community	Help NGOs deal with the need to seek additional sources of funding	Discouraged Warns NGOs against becoming too reliant on industry funding	Consider how they fit with independently derived strategic plans NGO must set the agenda	Discouraged 'If any working relationship with the industry would embarrass an organization ... don't do it'
Canadian Voluntary Sector Organization #1 (2000)	Confidential	Internal	Protect interests of client groups affected by disease (seen by companies as potential sources of profit)	Not mentioned explicitly	Consider specific scenarios rather than qualities of partner	No product logos permitted on joint work No projects that target users of a single product

Table 11.2
Comparison of commercial and health sector partnership guidelines (*continued*)

	Guideline Characteristics				Key Issues	
	Public/ Confidential	Audience	Objective	Exclusivity	Choice of partner	Product endorsement
Canadian Voluntary Sector Organization #2 (1997)	Confidential	Internal	Allow organization to respond to requests for endorsement	Not encouraged	Case-by-case, determined by CEO, legal counsel and senior staff	Case-by-case Endorsement monies go to operating fund
Canadian Voluntary Sector Organization #3 (1999)	Confidential	Internal	Avoid potential conflict of interest with drug manufacturers, especially in light of new treatment options	Exclusive product sponsorships should be avoided	Consider how the mission of the organization can be fulfilled. Review of potential partners by committee of legal counsel, medical advisor and volunteers	Perceived product endorsement cited as main risk of partnerships with pharmas Explicit "non-endorsement" statement required in some cases
Arthritis Society of Canada (2000)	Public (Web)	Internal and public	Inform public	Not mentioned	Consider compatibility with goals and objectives	To be avoided

- ensure personal choice and informed consent by telling the truth about risks and benefits, not distorting or exaggerating facts
- consider what topics should be covered and who should be targeted
- consider the best use of limited resources

Above all, health communicators, like health practitioners, should follow the precept of Hippocrates: 'First, do no harm.' The guidelines reviewed in table 11.2 reflect these principles in action to varying degrees. Perhaps not surprisingly, those most firmly rooted in these principles are the WHO *Ethical Criteria*, which promote positive, informed health choices, 'truthfulness and righteousness,' full disclosure, and moderation in information. Of drug advertisements, the criteria state: 'While they should take account of people's legitimate desire for information regarding their health, they should not take undue advantage of people's concern for their health.' Yet despite being an international standard, awareness and application of the criteria are low among health professionals and industry alike (Mintzes 1998).

The guidelines of Canadian health organizations do reflect these ethical principles to some extent:

- *Non-malfeasance or doing no harm.* While promoting the health and well-being of client groups is either stated or implicit in many guidelines, it is more difficult to find explicit reference to the risks of harm through collaboration. Even product endorsement is usually positioned as a threat to the organization's credibility, rather than as a potential health risk for consumers.
- *Respect for personal autonomy or personal freedom.* By refusing exclusivity, most organizations recognize that consumers need a range of choices and information. While most organizations provide for disclosure of industry funding – another measure to ensure consumers have truthful information on which to base decisions – they may wish to consider the benefits of making their processes or policies known to the public as well.
- *Justice, fairness, and equity.* At least one organization states explicitly that it will not work on projects that target users of a single product. While the motivation may be to avoid product endorsement, this policy does somewhat reflect the justice principle. Declining to enter into exclusive agreements which may limit the number of consumers who have access to information is also a matter of justice. On a

Table 11.3
Principles of Ethical Health Communication

Ethical Principle	Relevance to Health Communication	Implications for Collaboration
Beneficence or doing good	Promote positive health practices and information that are in the best interest of consumers	Voluntary and private sector may disagree on best interest, e.g. treatment versus prevention
Non-malfeasance or doing no harm	Ensure communications are comprehensive, without scaremongering or exaggeration of risk Ensure that risk of harm is minimized, e.g., by providing information about potential side effects of treatment	Increasing 'medicalization' of problems shifts the balance of power from consumers (and voluntary consumer-based groups) to health professionals and industry
Respect for personal autonomy or personal freedom	Ensure personal choice, informed consent by telling the truth about risks and benefits, not distorting or exaggerating facts	Persuasive or manipulative techniques that are common in industry may threaten personal autonomy Full disclosure of partners and their roles is critical
Justice, fairness, equity	Consider what topics should be covered and who should be targeted	Voluntary and private sector may differ in priorities for messages and targets Voluntary sector may target those most vulnerable, while industry looks for profit potential
Utility, effectiveness, or the 'maximum good'	Consider the best use of limited resources	By targeting those who will benefit most from information, organizations may be reaching people who are privileged to begin with (Guttman 2000)

larger scale, the question of justice in health communication merits a broader approach, ideally on a national level, to determine the extent to which information is easily available and accessible to those who need it and what, if any, gaps in information exist.

- *Utility, effectiveness, or the 'maximum good.'* In the context of collaboration, this principle involves making joint decisions on the best use of limited resources. In part, this is why voluntary sector organizations collaborate in the first place – to expand their base of resources and potential reach. None of the guidelines reviewed addressed conflicts between the partners specifically over use of

resources, though some do make reference to establishing procedures for disagreements at the outset of the collaboration.

In general, then, application of the principles of ethical health communication is, at best, implicit – and at worst, inconsistent. In part, this
points to the need for a national set of basic standards on which health
organizations can agree.

'Indirect' to consumer: Legal, but ethical?

Direct-to-consumer (DTC) advertising of prescription drugs, which is
permitted in the United States but not in Canada, has become a growing promotional tool for pharmaceuticals since it began to appear in the
late 1980s. By 1996, pharmaceuticals were spending more on DTC ads
for prescription drugs to consumers than on advertisements to health
professionals (Mintzes 1998). One of the most common criticisms lev-
elled at this form of advertising is that it aims to persuade consumers
that drug treatment is the answer to just about every ailment – from
serious emotional and psychological problems to heartburn (ibid.).

There are three forms of DTC advertising: product claim ads, which
include the product name and describe its use; 'reminder' ads, which
name the product without stating what it is used for; and 'help-seeking'
ads, which tell consumers about new treatment options without any
details (Gardner, Mintzes, and Ostry 2003). While all three ostensibly
contravene the *Canadian Food and Drug Act*, reminder and help-seeking
ads are becoming increasingly common. Ads in consumer magazines,
with no mention of a pharmaceutical company, direct readers to websites or toll-free numbers that are run and staffed by companies. Some
pharmaceuticals have established 'programs' that promote drug treatment for a particular condition. One reason why such advertising and
programs are relevant to health organizations is that they mimic a voluntary sector approach, using techniques that suggest discursive legitimacy while avoiding reference to company or product names. Program
websites focus on disease treatment with only subtle references to
products, and consumers will be forgiven if they mistake the source of
the information as a not-for-profit organization. In many cases, they'll
have to search vigilantly to find the source or owner of the site.

Pharmaceuticals also seek help from voluntary health agencies to
build support for new or forthcoming products (Rochon Ford 1999).
In 2001, a Canadian pharmaceutical company approached a number
of voluntary health organizations to develop a public awareness

campaign about certain childhood diseases. The company was seeking approval for a vaccine that would protect against certain infections. It also recruited parents whose children had suffered damage as a result of these infections. The goal was to raise awareness of these diseases and in turn build public support for their product, creating pressure for fast-track approval in Canada. Several meetings were held, but the organizations decided that – despite the benefits of parents knowing more about the early signs of these diseases – they could not support an education campaign funded by a single sponsor currently seeking Health Canada approval for its product; it was clearly a conflict of interest. In the United States, this kind of underwriting goes much further. Increasingly, organizations are created as 'fronts' for industry concerns. Public relations firms refer to these manufactured grass-roots organizations as 'AstroTurf,' after the synthetic product that replaced grass in baseball and football stadiums in the 1970s (Gosden and Beder 2001).

Indeed, there is reason to be skeptical. Beyond just influencing consumer behaviour, pharmaceutical companies have been accused of using public relations firms to influence policy agendas to promote the sale of more drugs. Gosden and Beder (2001) make a compelling case for how a sophisticated and extended public relations campaign, involving the development of consumer and family-based advocacy coalitions, funding of selected psychiatric research, and a media campaign to raise fears about untreated mental illness, has helped dramatically expand the multi-billion dollar market for schizophrenia drugs in the United States and Australia. Their theory is that pharmaceutical companies, working through public relations firms, have influenced public opinion, psychiatric research, and public policy. The results, they posit, are (a) widespread acceptance of the notions that medication is the 'gold standard' of schizophrenia treatment (and that untreated schizophrenics are a risk to society), and (b) involuntary treatment of people with the disease. The writers also charge that the growing early-intervention movement, which can involve treating people who are at risk of schizophrenia but still asymptomatic, is simply expanding the market for schizophrenia drugs. This may be a cynical view; but if there is any truth to the theory, voluntary sector organizations should take heed.

4. The Need for National Leadership

Is there national leadership on the question of private and voluntary sector collaboration for health information that can serve as a benchmark for non-profits? There are at least two potential sources to help explore this question: Health Canada, the government department with which virtually every national health organization is involved in some way (funding, policy development, research, and advocacy are just some examples); and the national voluntary health sector itself.

Health Canada

Since the late 1980s, Health Canada has been involved in social marketing efforts with the private sector. In 1996, the Partnerships and Marketing Division (PMD) published an article describing Health Canada's enthusiasm for partnering with the private sector to 'heighten awareness, change attitudes and encourage behavioural change' and extolling the power of strategic alliances to deliver benefits both to corporations – more say, more recognition – and government or nongovernmental organizations: access to marketing expertise, distribution networks, and enhanced credibility (Mintz, Hudson, and LeBrun 1996). Aside from a brief warning that potential partners should be researched to ensure a good fit and to minimize the risk of getting involved with a controversial or questionable corporation, there is little exploration of the possible pitfalls or ethical questions involved in partnering with the corporate sector on health issues.

The same can be said for Health Canada's *Guidelines for Partnering and Collaborative Arrangements with the Private Sector and Other Partners* (2003), which is essentially a 'how-to' for choosing, negotiating, delivering, and evaluating strategic alliances. It cites a number of benefits to private sector partners, including demonstrated social responsibility, enhanced image and reputation, and competitive advantage in recruiting new employees. There is no mention of the obvious marketing benefits of extended reach, association with a credible source, or potential for increased sales.

The guidelines implicitly endorse exclusive agreements, a practice cited by many (Mintzes 1998; Pryor et al. 1999) as a critical ethical issue: 'Where appropriate, PMD may enter into exclusive strategic alliances. Exclusive strategic alliances may be defined as (a) allowing the partner to be the sole project partner, or (b) that no other directly competing organizations would be accepted as partners' (Health Canada 2003, 12). Most of these partners, though manufacturers of consumer goods, are not pharmaceutical companies. As a regulatory body, Health Canada rarely forges social alliances with pharmaceuticals.

One example of an exclusive Health Canada partnership involves the Canadian Paediatric Society and the Canadian Foundation for the Study of Infant Deaths, which were partners in a social marketing campaign to reduce the incidence of sudden infant death syndrome (SIDS) by promoting the back sleeping position for babies. The campaign was supported by Pampers, which carried the 'Back to Sleep' message on its diapers (Health Canada 2005). Indeed, Pampers' involvement helped extend the prevention message to thousands of Canadian parents, but one wonders about parents who purchased other products, including lower-priced store brands. Arguably, these parents may be the ones most in need of the message, since they may be exposed to less prenatal and perinatal health information. It could also be argued that a government department promoting a health message should not be limiting it to a target group of consumers. There were, of course, other elements of the campaign designed to reach a wider range of Canadian parents, such as the distribution of posters and brochures in hospitals, but the exclusive Pampers deal still raises thorny questions.

One of the dilemmas for health communicators designing programs for the government or funded by the government is demonstrating results and effective use of resources, often over a short period of time. To do this, it is easier to target the most receptive audience (i.e., the people who are most likely to adopt the desired behaviour) than to reach the people who are not ready to change, yet may need the message most – a task that demands more resources than most communication programs possess.

The national voluntary health sector

Formed in 2000, the Health Charities Coalition of Canada (HCCC) is the only formal umbrella group for voluntary sector organizations working in health. While the primary orientation of the HCCC has been on health policy and health research funding, the organization also provides a forum for health NGOs to voice common concerns. However, the HCCC has not formally addressed the issue of private sector collaboration.

In the health sector, opinions on working with the private sector are as diverse as the organizations themselves. In the mental health community, for instance, there is debate about whether private sector pharmaceutical support is appropriate. Often, people with mental illness have difficulties taking medication, especially since many drugs used to treat conditions like schizophrenia and bipolar disorder cause unpleasant side effects. Self-help consumer or survivor groups are usually averse to partnerships with pharmaceutical companies, which they perceive to have a conflict of interest. Typically, traditional medical organizations or professional groups are more comfortable with these relationships, and community agencies fall somewhere between these two poles.

Still, there is a general view that pharmaceutical companies are an important part of health care, and that voluntary sector organizations can work with them, provided the relationship is managed wisely. Medications are among the most effective components of a comprehensive treatment program, are often essential to health care, and can allow people to live independently in the community. And with direct-to-consumer advertising becoming an increasingly greater media presence (American messages inevitably reach Canadians through television, magazines, and other media), many non-profits feel pharmaceutical companies have an obligation to help the sector ensure consumers receive balanced information, in order to make informed choices about their health care.

The market mentality described by Andreasen and Drumwright (2001), which was discussed earlier, is also pervasive in the most literal sense when it comes to pharmaceutical support of the health sector. Conditions for which there is no therapeutic product to be marketed receive little, if any support. For example, since there is little effective treatment for muscular dystrophy, there is limited interest by pharmaceutical companies in partnering with the Muscular Dystrophy Association. In fact, the MD Association's biggest financial supporters in Canada are firefighters, with whom the organization has worked since 1954. On the other hand, the size and scope of national organizations concerned with cardiovascular disease or cancer, for instance, reflect to some extent the huge number of people who are in some way touched by these diseases. But they also reflect the multimillion-dollar research and development industry behind them. This market approach to corporate giving lies at the heart of the cultural difference between the two sectors.

Clearly, there are cross-cutting issues related to private sector collaboration that affect many voluntary health sector organizations. Given its focus on research and public policy, the Health Charities Coalition of Canada may not be the ideal forum for this conversation. However, it is one of the few places where many different national health organizations come together.

5. Lessons Learned

Primary ethical dilemmas

Collaboration with industry can be beneficial for voluntary sector health organizations and consumers, and may even be necessary in times of decreased government funding. But there are both micro- and macro-level ethical issues associated with private sector involvement in health information delivery. Among them are:

Conflicting values. Because of fundamentally different cultures and motivations, there can be underlying tension between the private and voluntary sectors when working together. But in health communication alliances, there may also be tension between the desire to promote health and wellness, and the need to promote pharmacological treatment options. Companies may be reluctant to promote non-pharmaceutical methods of treatment (Rochon Ford 1999).

Exclusivity. Corporations may request exclusivity when working in an alliance to gain a competitive advantage over their competitors. If a voluntary health organization works with only one company in a given product category, there is an implicit suggestion of endorsement. Exclusivity can add financial value to an alliance, but it can also create problems in the context of delivering health information to consumers. Most organizations agree that exclusive arrangements should be avoided because they create the perception of product endorsement and thus have the potential to mislead consumers.

Power imbalances. Despite the fact that voluntary sector health organizations have the power of discursive legitimacy, their credibility and expertise are often accorded less value when compared with financial resources from the private sector. In fact, without the reputations and expertise of the health organizations, health communication alliances would have little value to the consumer. The challenge for voluntary sector communicators is to place appropriate value on their contributions to the alliance, so that there can be a fair exchange that benefits both organizations.

Market mentality. A market-driven approach to health communications can leave some causes underfunded, and can also create disparities within causes themselves. Take the children's health field, for instance. The Canadian Paediatric Society has little trouble raising funds for immunization education, particularly information aimed at the public, which is increasingly concerned about vaccine safety. The pharmaceutical industry typically invests huge sums of money in developing a new vaccine and, to recover their investments, the company or companies producing the vaccine must persuade health professionals and voluntary-sector health organizations to promote immunization, and ensure the public continues to be receptive to new vaccines. There is also the larger, international question as to whether current practices in vaccine promotion are equitable, given pharmaceutical companies' focus on growing the market for new vaccines, instead of trying to reach the estimated 30 to 40 per cent of children worldwide who lack even the most basic immunizations (Hardon 2001). In many other areas of children's health such as literacy, childcare, and mental health, private sector support is much harder to come by.

Lack of transparency. Voluntary health agencies do not appear completely transparent when it comes to their relationships with the private sector. Policies or guidelines on corporate sector alliances are not readily available. A scan of the websites of the organizations who were surveyed turned up only one brief set of guidelines (the Arthritis Society). Future research may explain why organizations feel the need to keep such policies confidential – even though they ostensibly exist to help preserve public trust.

Lack of national standards or consensus. There are no Canadian standards or guidelines for voluntary sector health organizations collaborating with the private sector. Organizations have developed their own guidelines, which are inconsistent and not rooted in any national agreement on what is best for Canadian consumers. These inconsistencies in the way voluntary sector organizations work with industry have the potential to create competition that may not be in the best interest of either voluntary sector health organizations or consumers.

In the past, corporations were more likely to give philanthropic dollars to support particular educational materials or initiatives. Today, they look for increased reach, increased relevance, and ultimately a message that will help sell products. Much of the funding for health communication alliances comes from marketing or advertising budgets rather than philanthropic areas of the company (Rochon Ford 1999). Increasingly, corporations look to voluntary health agencies to help meet their own marketing objectives, and organizations must decide whether the potential benefits to their target audiences outweigh the ethical risks when a company is essentially driving the agenda. To be involved in successful collaborations, voluntary sector organizations must leverage their own power – the credibility and expertise that draw the private sector in the first place.

While individual organizations can deal with micro-level issues specific to their own target groups, it is much more difficult for organizations alone to tackle the larger questions involved in private sector collaboration. The voluntary health sector must question the broader agenda of industry, talk to each other about the challenges of collaboration, foster national leadership, and learn from experiences in other countries. While preserving the public trust in the sector is critical, this objective cannot be regarded in isolation of the need to – above all – promote and uphold the best interests of consumers.

6. Recommendations: Putting Ethics into Action

Addressing the ethical issues related to intersectoral collaboration for health communication requires action at three levels: by single practitioners, organizations, and the sector as a whole.

Communications practitioners in voluntary health organizations

Before entering into a health communication alliance with the private sector, communications practitioners should consider asking these questions:

- What is driving the need for this project? Is it in the best interests of consumers? Would we pursue it even without private sector support?
- Have we assessed the value of what we bring to this alliance? Given the value of our name, reputation, and expertise, what do we consider to be a fair exchange?
- Are we prepared to have an upfront conversation with this company about the possible ethical issues we may encounter?
- What is this company's expertise in the area of health communication? What do they hope to achieve through this alliance?
- Are there provisions for ending the alliance should we encounter ethical issues that cannot be resolved?
- What is the likely public perception of this message and this collaborative relationship? Is there any potential for misleading consumers?

- Does this alliance present a conflict of interest for either us or the private sector organization? If so, can the issue be managed?

Voluntary health organizations

Voluntary sector organizations should look at their policies and procedures to determine whether they have the necessary tools to support meaningful discussion and action on health communication collaborations. Among the questions to be considered at the organizational level are:

- How do we choose the companies with which we collaborate? Do we have adequate screening procedures in place?
- Do we have guidelines on collaborating with the private sector? If so, do these guidelines specifically address projects that target consumers?
- Will our guidelines help us manage the possible ethical issues that may arise from such collaborations?
- Are these guidelines or processes available to the public? If not, why not?

Organizations may want to consider going beyond the specific issue of private sector collaboration, examining its overall ethical performance. The Canadian Paediatric Society did just that in 2003, partly to address the issue of intersectoral collaboration but also to take a broader look at the ethical foundation of its policies and procedures. The result was an organizational Code of Ethics that provides guidance to everyone working on behalf of the organization – board, staff, and volunteers – to help make decisions and deal with ethical issues (CPS 2004).

The voluntary heath sector

Voluntary health organizations play a crucial role in delivering credible health information to Canadians, and alliances with the private sector can help improve the quality and reach of this information. By working together, voluntary health organizations can strengthen their ability to leverage collaborative relationships. The sector, and ultimately consumers, would benefit from a discussion among health organizations on the ethics of collaborative projects targeting consumers. The sector might establish some basic guidelines on the ethics of these collaborations, which could serve to create consistency as well as reduce unnecessary competition among organizations. The question of market-driven messages should also be addressed at the sector level, to find ways of gaining more support for causes that have little or no commercial appeal for sponsors. This specific discussion could lead to a broader exploration of the ethics of intersectoral collaboration in general. The sector would be strengthened if there were some agreement on how to resolve the basic issues faced by all organizations that seek to work with the private sector.

NOTE

Because of the small sample size (N = 24) and low number of respondents (N = 7), the findings from the survey cited in this essay are presented not as comprehensive picture of the current situation but rather as a snapshot of how some voluntary sector health organizations handle private sector collaboration on communication projects, and as a gauge of issues that may demand further exploration.

12 Bridging Strategies for Amnesty International

1. From the Personal to the Organizational

I am a 'hyphenated' Canadian: a Chinese-Canadian. I am what the Chinese community refers to, often in a derogatory sense, as 'bamboo': yellow on the outside but hollow on the inside. That is, while I have the physical features of a Chinese person, I lack the culture and inner essence of 'Chineseness.'

I grew up in the small town of Brooks, Alberta. Our family was the only Chinese family in the town. At home, we maintained a Chinese way of life. I spoke Chinese at home and English at school. In order to survive at school, I had to quickly adapt to the dominant Western Anglo-Canadian classroom culture. Thus, I would say that on the inside I'm not 'hollow' but rather 'rural Albertan Canadian.'

At an early age I also became an 'intercultural bridger': a person who is able to function within two very different cultures and who is often called upon to translate or mediate between the two. This often requires a delicate juggling act. As my parents spoke limited English, I became the translator in the family – the go-between who helped interpret the English business world to my parents and who could explain their views to the outside world.

It is very difficult to develop a sense of belonging in two different cultures at the same time. I started to question my own cultural identity. In the words of Lyse Champagne (1990), who wrote of her experience as a French Canadian growing up in anglophone Ontario, 'it's not about the two solitudes not understanding each other, it's about understanding the two solitudes. Knowing both of them intimately – too intimately, perhaps. And not wanting to choose between them' (5).

Ironically, this dilemma has followed me to my present work setting. Amnesty International, the organization that I work for, is considering the possibility of assuming the role of go-between or 'intersectoral bridger' between the human rights domain and the corporate domain. Amnesty's objective is to bring the human rights message to the corporate sector, not merely to forge friendly relationships or translate the two domains to each other. To carry its message, however, Amnesty needs to understand both domains so as to find the common ground where dialogue can take place. In the course of doing bridging work, Amnesty needs to resist the pressure to choose one side over the other. Moreover, throughout the bridging process, Amnesty needs to maintain its own unique organizational identity.

Is there a connection, I wonder, between the phenomena of individuals as intercultural bridgers and organizations as intersectoral bridgers?

From the organizational to the personal

Formed in 1961, Amnesty International is a non-profit organization that works to promote human rights worldwide. Amnesty's vision is of a world in which every person enjoys all of the human rights enshrined in the Universal Declaration of Human Rights (UDHR 1948) and other international human rights standards. To this end, Amnesty's members campaign to stop torture, end political killings and 'disappearances,' free prisoners of conscience, protect refugees, abolish the death penalty, and prevent other grave abuses of human rights. Amnesty is known for the quality of its accurate, persistent, and timely research and for its ability to mobilize people across the world to pressure governments and others to prevent or stop human rights violations.

Amnesty has more than a million members and supporters in over 140 countries and territories. I work in the Anglophone Branch of Amnesty Canada, which has 65,000 members, 100 community groups, and 450 youth groups. A democratic movement, Amnesty is governed by a nine-member international executive committee (IEC) whose members are elected every two years by an international council representing the different sections. Decisions on Amnesty's overall vision, mandate, strategic plans, and constitution are made by the international council. Independent of all governments, political persuasions, and religious creeds, Amnesty is funded by its worldwide membership and through donations. No funds are sought or accepted from governments.

In the 1960s and 1970s, Amnesty's main mission was to mobilize international pressure on behalf of individuals imprisoned for their beliefs and in violation of the civil and political rights of the UDHR. Since then, the world has changed significantly. The simplicity with which Amnesty approached its work in the 1960s – 'adopting' a prisoner and writing letters of protest to the government on that person's behalf – is no longer adequate today. Amnesty has had to broaden its human rights work so as to encompass the issues of massive human rights abuses (genocide, ethnic cleansing, mass killings), the prevalence of refugee flows, the proliferation of armed conflicts, human rights abuses committed not only by governments but also by non-state actors (guerrilla forces, terrorist groups, corporations, and individuals in their community and household contexts), and the human rights implications resulting from the extreme concentration of poverty and wealth in an increasingly globalized economy.

The 2001 International Council Meeting in Dakar, Senegal, made a key decision to enlarge Amnesty's mandate so as to 'prevent and end grave abuses of the rights of physical and mental integrity, freedom of conscience and expression and freedom from discrimination' (AI 2002). This allowed Amnesty to campaign in the area of economic, social, and cultural rights (ESC) within the UDHR, and, in particular, on the role of corporations in promoting and defending human rights.

Amnesty feels that the area of business and human rights has become one of the most important and challenging new fronts in human rights activism. Amnesty's work in this field is based on the recognition that companies and other economic actors have significant power to perpetrate human rights abuses directly or indirectly, as well as great potential to promote and protect human rights.

There are many good things that a business can do to enhance human rights in the world. The influence and reach of multinational corporations (MNCs) is immense. Many companies operate with budgets far in excess of many of the world's states. They operate all over the world. They have dealings with government officials at national, regional, and local levels. Thus businesses can, both directly and indirectly, promote and improve the basic rights of millions of people worldwide, if they choose to include the promotion of human rights as one of their areas of concern. They can also play a powerful role in human rights reform by raising human rights issues with their host governments.

On the other hand, some businesses have done a lot of harm in the course of their operations. Mining companies, for example, have violently forced communities off their traditional land to make way for resource extraction (for example, Conquistador Mines in Colombia).[1] Rivers may be poisoned by the run-off from mining operations, harming the environment and endangering the lives of the people who rely on the rivers for safe, clean water (consider Placer Dome in the Philippines and elsewhere).[2] Workers may be threatened, beaten, or killed when they seek to organize in order to assert their basic labour rights (Unocal in Myanmar).[3] Citizens living in surrounding areas and employees working in a large international company's facilities may be injured or become sick as a result of unsafe working conditions (for example, the Union Carbide disaster in Bhopal, Madhya Pradesh, India).[4] Tax revenues and royalties from resource development may help prop up undemocratic governments and be used to buy weapons that lead to human rights violations (Talisman Energy in Sudan).[5]

There are many ways that a company can exercise influence for human rights in the course of its operations. Amnesty International's 'Human rights principles for companies' (2001b) raises three areas of responsibility in contributing to the promotion and protection of human rights. First, Amnesty calls on MNCs to be responsible for their own operations. Human resources practices and policies must meet international standards on labour rights, including health and safety, freedom of association and the right to collective bargaining, non-discrimination, disciplinary practices, and avoidance of child labour and forced labour. Any security forces that a company hires must, like its own personnel, be properly trained in and committed to respect international guidelines and standards for the use of force (in particular, the United Nations Code of Conduct for Law Enforcement Officials and the UN Basic Principles on the Use of Force and Firearms by Law Enforcement Officials). Secondly, Amnesty asks companies to help create an environment where human rights are understood and respected. This means that MNCs should adhere to international human rights standards even if the national laws under which these companies operate do not specify or comply with the inherent rights in the UDHR. Companies can improve their ability to promote human rights by developing explicit company policies on human rights; providing effective training for their managers and staff in international human rights standards; consulting non-governmental organizations (including Amnesty) on the level and nature of human rights abuses in different countries; and establishing a clear framework for assessing the potential impact on human rights of all the company's and its subcontractors' operations. Thirdly, companies should implement and monitor their policies and practices for compliance with their voluntary corporate codes of behaviour. This monitoring should be done credibly and monitoring reports should be independently verifiable.

Companies often claim that the fault lies not with themselves but with the local security forces: military and police, paramilitary groups or private security firms hired to protect the companies' interests. Amnesty holds that the companies themselves must take responsibility for these actions, whether they are carried out by company employees or by others working on behalf of the company. Companies often assert that it is inappropriate for them to intervene in matters of human rights reform, as they prefer not to intrude on the politics of the countries where they operate. Amnesty argues, on the contrary, that the failure to intervene in a situation where human rights abuses are taking place is, in itself, an inappropriate political act. The preamble of the UDHR clearly obliges all 'organs of society,' which includes businesses, to work to promote human rights (UDHR 1948).

The question for Amnesty is that of strategy. How should Amnesty approach the corporate sector? Should Amnesty join other human rights and social justice NGOs in confronting businesses? Conversely, should Amnesty find ways to cooperate with businesses to help them become better corporate citizens? A third possibility is for Amnesty to take on the role of strategic bridger between the international business world and the world of human rights and social justice NGOs.

If Amnesty were to take on a strategic bridging role, what risks would it take? What would the opportunities be? How would Amnesty develop its competency in this area? How would Amnesty help its staff and members, who are comfortable and familiar with their role as oppositionists, take on new roles as intersectoral bridgers? Could Amnesty draw on the experiences of intercultural bridgers to increase its leadership skills in this area?

Should and could Amnesty take on the intercultural alternator role that I have been grappling with in my own life? Are there parallels between an individual who is a bridger and an organization that is a bridger? And so, this essay will take me full circle from the personal to the organizational and back to the personal.

Initial personal reflections

Lyse Champagne (1990) writes: 'Expect contradictions, because living two lives is a contradiction. Expect compromises, because living in two cultures requires compromise. Expect the unexpected, because living a double life brings much that is unexpected' (5).

My father, who had immigrated to Canada in 1911, brought my mother and my sister from their little Chinese village to live in rural Alberta in the winter of 1950. The *Chinese Exclusion Act* of 1923 had effectively stopped all Chinese immigration to Canada. When it was repealed in 1947, Chinese men already living in Canada were allowed to send for their wives and unmarried children (under the age of 18) from China. This made a small but noteworthy impact on the little towns in Western Canada where the Chinese had chosen to settle after the construction of the railway. The townsfolk were used to seeing aging Chinese men running the laundries, restaurants, and market gardens and working as labourers in the coal mines. The early 1950s, however, brought an influx of Chinese women and children to these isolated towns. The Chinese families were largely ignored and left on their own to cope, living very separate lives from the white community.

Our family settled in Brooks, Alberta. My father ran the local restaurant, which offered Canadianized 'Chinese' food (chop suey, chow mein, and sweet-and-sour chicken balls) to a population raised on Alberta beef and mashed potatoes. I grew up in rural, conservative, white, Anglo-Saxon, Christian, gun-toting cowboy country. It wasn't difficult to embrace the dominant culture. In fact, I envied my classmates and often found myself wishing that my own family was 'normal.' Why wasn't my dad a rancher? Why couldn't my mother make macaroni and cheese for supper instead of exotic, strange-smelling Chinese food? Why couldn't they speak English? Why couldn't I own a horse? Why did we have to live on top of the restaurant? I desperately wanted to be assimilated, to be absorbed into the dominant culture.

My parents were afraid that I would lose my culture and they put a lot of effort into making sure that I didn't forget my roots. They purposely taught me Chinese as my first language and were very strict about speaking Chinese when at home. We followed Chinese customs. My father had been a political activist, and he wanted me to develop an appreciation for Chinese history and culture, as well as understand the hardships of pre-1947 immigrant life in Canada.

Living two almost separate lives – the Western English-speaking school life and the Chinese home life – I learned how to adapt my behaviour to the social or cultural context of the moment. It was tension-filled. Finding my identity became a quest. At one point, I decided to become Japanese, as there was another Japanese family living in the area. The name 'Sen' in my last name sounded very Japanese to me, so I started to call myself 'Lily Sen.'

Ironically, thanks to the racism that pervaded Brooks in the 1950s, I was prevented from assimilating with the dominant culture, no matter how much I wished that I were white. Growing up, I was acculturated into the majority culture, but was always defined by others as Chinese, mainly because of my outward appearance. I began to think in English. I lost my ability to dream in Chinese. In fact this was a typical acculturation experience, as described by Teresa LaFromboise and her colleagues (1993).

After graduation from university, I lived overseas for two and a half years, teaching school in Papua New Guinea and travelling and visiting numerous development projects in south-east Asia. These experiences had a most interesting effect, for living and working overseas not only helped me to discover what it is to be 'Canadian' but also gave me a new appreciation of what it is to be Chinese.

On my return to Canada, I enrolled at York University in Chinese studies and rediscovered all those things about 'Chineseness' that I had tried so hard to ignore when I was growing up. At first, I approached my studies with a sense of outrage at the treatment that Chinese immigrants had endured in Canada. I became 'more Chinese than the Chinese' and chastised my own parents for reverting to English words in the middle of their sentences. Luckily, I had some wonderful white Canadian friends who helped put some perspective into my life. Gradually, that indignant, puritanical outlook mellowed into a more accepting and trusting mode. I was learning how to alternate (LaFromboise et al. 1993).

The process of working oneself through the different phases – rejecting assimilation, embracing acculturation, and then, finally, finding a solution in alternation, is not unique to me. It is a process that many 'hyphenated' Canadians have lived through. For me, the ability to alternate between and bridge two cultures has helped me find a new sense of groundedness and balance to replace my feelings of cultural schizophrenia growing up in, and alternately accepting and then rejecting, two different worlds. I can see the strengths and shortcomings of both cultures, yet I can also actively seek and enjoy the best of both worlds; above all, I understand the role that I can play to mediate between these two worlds. I now feel at ease with my duality.

2. Amnesty's Potential as an Intersectoral Strategic Bridger

Is a version of my personal transformative experience possible in the work world? In other words, can Amnesty, as an interorganizational bridger between the domains of international human rights and multinational corporate enterprise, play a new creative role as a catalyst for transformation? What are the risks? Would Amnesty find itself being assimilated or acculturated by the corporate sector? Or would Amnesty be able to find the organizational equivalent of alternation?

Bridging with the for-profit sector is a new area for most NGOs. Strategic bridging is a promising approach for non-profit organizations. Yet if this approach is poorly managed, if it is not adequately explained to colleagues and workers within an organization as well as to NGO allies, the organization may lay itself open to being branded as a 'sell-out.' What, then, are the 'limits of the acceptable' (Murphy 2002, 2)?[6]

Because Amnesty is privately funded (as mentioned above, Amnesty accepts no government funding whatsoever), it has the freedom to publicly chastise governments, including the Canadian government, for their violations of, or failure to uphold, the principles of human rights. Amnesty also has strict corporate donations guidelines, which prevent its accepting any funds from companies known to be involved in human rights violations. Amnesty can thus play a unique role in promoting human rights in the corporate sector, without fear that its funding sources might be jeopardized if it raises its voice too loudly.

Amnesty has the reputation of being 'a voice crying out in the wilderness' against human rights abuses, no matter how unpopular the cause. With a very strong mandate to fight for human rights everywhere, Amnesty has defended heinous murderers from being deported to countries where the death penalty is being used. Amnesty raised an outcry against the prison conditions and treatment of Taliban and al-Qaeda prisoners at the U.S. facility in Guantanamo Bay. The organization took a principled, but unpopular stand when it refused to consider Nelson Mandela as a prisoner of conscience because he advocated violence in overthrowing the apartheid regime in South Africa. Thus Amnesty's foray into the world of business, taking a collaborative bridging strategy instead of an oppositional strategy, has raised a few eyebrows. Has Amnesty gone soft? Is it 'sleeping with the enemy'? This question is being asked not only by sister human rights and social justice organizations but also by Amnesty members and staff.

Arguments against a bridging strategy

Corporations are driven by the profit motive – to obtain the highest returns on investment for their shareholders. Social justice, if it comes into play at all, is very much a secondary motive. Instead of helping corporations make changes to meet minimum standards, Amnesty should be advocating for the *transformation* of corporations and of society itself into a more equitable and just world. Amnesty's scarce resources would be co-opted into the creation of a 'human face' for corporations, which, fundamentally, believe in the maintenance of the prevailing social order. According to Murphy (2002, 21), 'If market capitalism is predicated on injustice, how can we talk of corporations as a factor in promoting justice? The critical question should not be: "How can we convince corporations to promote justice?" Rather, the question should be posed: "How can we activate to eradicate the injustice of corporate behaviour and the profit logic and the unjust effects of corporate actions?"' On these terms, Amnesty ought not to undertake the role of a strategic bridger, nor perhaps should it entertain any form of collaboration with the private sector.

Taking on a bridging role would place Amnesty in a highly visible position, opening Amnesty to even greater political and economic pressures, thereby increasing its organizational vulnerability. Moreover, the corporate sector is so much more powerful and has so many more resources than Amnesty that Amnesty could find itself on the losing side in asymmetrical relationships.

Arguments in favour of a bridging strategy

According to Amnesty's research, the human rights situation around the world is getting worse, not better, with very few viable or sustainable solutions in sight. Waiting for some other organization to come forward and assume a collaborative role with international business could be seen as being irresponsible; Amnesty cannot become morally mute at this critical juncture (Bird 1996). If Amnesty, therefore, has a responsibility to engage the business sector in a collaborative human rights strategy, Amnesty should draw on its strengths, namely, its reputation for timely accurate research; its high level of name-recognition and credibility in the eyes of the media and general public; and the high regard that human rights activists and sister social justice organizations have for its skills, capabilities, and record of achievement.

There are three compelling reasons why an organization should consider a collaborative strategy (Trist 1983):

1. The problems are too large for any single sector to address on its own.
2. Collaboration can foster new innovative strategies.
3. Collaborative strategies are necessary in a situation of increased environmental turbulence in the domain.

All three reasons can be used by Amnesty to justify a foray into collaborative efforts. Most businesses would rather not have to think about human rights at all if they aren't pushed to do so. Persuading Canadian business leaders to embrace respect for human rights as a cardinal business principle is a bigger challenge than any one organization or one domain can tackle. Amnesty has found that tried-and-true oppositional methods (writing letters of protest, sending petitions, expressing our views to the media, lobbying key government officials, etc.), which have proven to be effective when raising human rights abuses perpetrated by governments, do not produce the same results when applied to the corporate world. From talking to company insiders, Amnesty found that many CEOs had refused to meet with Amnesty because they feared they would be the target of confrontational tactics. A common reaction of businesses, when faced with a deluge of protests from different interest groups, each with its own special 'take' on the issue, is to retreat rather than to engage. Thus, the conditions are ripe for Amnesty to try new strategies, including collaborative strategies.[7]

On the positive side, a bridging organization can be an influential force for positive development (Brown 1991). If Amnesty can bring businesses on side, especially those that operate in countries where human rights abuses take place, there is great potential for making a positive impact on conditions in these countries. Bridging strategies, especially those motivated by altruism, can bring about a transformation towards a better society (Westley and Vrendenburg 1991). Bridging could create a unique opportunity for Amnesty to develop new cutting-edge strategies that will be transformative and generative and which will, in the long run, make the world a better place.

Conditions

Identification of stakeholders. Amnesty is currently researching the human rights records of Canadian businesses, with a special emphasis on identifying companies that strongly support human rights principles and have the potential to act as role models for other businesses – for example, by using their economic leverage to demand that host governments respect the human rights of their citizens. At the same time, Amnesty is starting to network with other human rights and social justice organizations in this domain.

Understanding stakeholder values, motives, and expectations is a key challenge for Amnesty. Westley and Vredenburg (1991) distinguish between *altruistic* bridging, which has been designed or mandated and is problem-focused and transformative, and *egoistic* bridging, which is voluntary, self-serving, and maintenance-oriented.

Collaboration with the international business sector therefore entails both sorts of bridging strategies. Amnesty seeks to engage with businesses for an altruistic reason: to promote its vision of a world in which every person enjoys all the rights enshrined in the UDHR. Businesses, on the other hand, are required by their shareholders to make profits. Attention to compliance with international human rights standards can enhance safeguards for corporate investments, employees, assets, and reputations. Proper attention to health and safety and environmental performance can likewise pay dividends for the business. Thus a given company might well collaborate with Amnesty for egoistic reasons – as a matter of 'enlightened self-interest.'

On the surface, organizations should be able to work together, even if they are motivated by very different reasons, as long as these motives are transparent and acknowledged by all the parties at the table. What often happens, however, is that the different parties' underlying expectations are not explored fully and are not fully understood by either side. Amnesty starts from the position that 'no Canadian corporation wants a dollar tainted by the misery of a fellow human' (AI 2001a). A hard-nosed business executive, on the other hand, might say: 'We don't want our company tainted because it would bring us bad publicity, which could lower our share value. If, in the process, human misery is being relieved, then that's a bonus.' When unexplored expectations come to the surface (and, especially, if this occurs during crisis points), the resulting clash could quickly tear apart any collaborative venture. Understanding the values, motives, and expectations of the key players will go a long way to help the stakeholders arrive at mutually agreeable goals and directions.

Another issue to address is the need for Amnesty to make sure that its own members are clear about the rationale and expectations for work with the private sector. Amnesty members need to understand that Amnesty is not 'selling out' its own altruistic values but rather is using egoistic arguments in order to get businesses to become involved in protecting human rights.

Degree of recognized interdependence. The question of the level of interdependence between the corporate domain and the human rights domain is still hotly debated within Amnesty. Some members, who are strongly against international economic globalization, feel that Amnesty would just be used by the MNCs as a public relations tool to help them further their own ends. On the other hand, some multinational corporations see Amnesty as a thorn in their side rather than an ally to help them achieve their goals. The notion of interdependence between the two domains needs a lot more exploration by both Amnesty and the businesses involved.

Legitimacy of the stakeholders. Amnesty's well-established legitimacy in the human rights milieu does not necessarily guarantee or shield from criticism the 'good' companies that work with the organization. For example, embarrassing questions were raised when Amnesty collaborated with The Body Shop, in the light of accusations made in the media about The Body Shop's production practices in Southern countries and the treatment of its employees in the North. Some corporations may have an excellent environmental and human rights record in one country and an abysmal one in the next. Other companies, because of their relatively small size, or their reputations as 'lightweights' in the industry, may not be very influential as role models for the corporate sector, so that working with these companies may produce very little impact. It is very easy to identify and target the companies that have had bad human rights records – the Talismans and Unocals of the corporate world; it is much harder to find companies that have the potential to do good.

Legitimate authority. Amnesty needs to be transparent in sharing its goals and objectives with sister social justice and human rights organizations. These organizations must feel confident that Amnesty's work will benefit, not undermine, their own work, and they must feel a sense of ownership of the larger strategy of improving human rights conditions around the world for all.

Differences of power and resources. In the human rights domain, Amnesty is seen as a large, stable organization with substantial resources; but it is a small player in terms of the immense resources controlled by the corporate sector. According to the United Nations Conference on Trade and Development listing of the largest transnational corporations and world economies in 2000, 29 of the world's 100 largest economic entities are transnational corporations. Exxon, for example, with a value-added figure of $63 billion, ranked forty-fifth on the list, making it comparable in economic size to the economy of Chile or Pakistan (UNCTAD 2002).

It can be tempting to succumb to the material comforts associated with the corporate lifestyle. For example, Amnesty had been trying to meet with a Vancouver-based Canadian mining company for many months. The company had cancelled a number of appointments, some at the last minute. When Amnesty accused the company of deliberately evading its commitment, the CEO sent a personal apology and set up a special meeting for the end of the week. Because of the high cost of travel from Ottawa to Vancouver and the optics of ensuring donors that Amnesty would not misuse their donations on perks, Amnesty's staff always travel by the cheapest airfare and ordinarily schedule a number of events during a visit in order to make best use of the trip. It would have been very expensive to fly from Ottawa to Vancouver for a last-minute meeting, and so Amnesty declined the invitation. The CEO then sent Amnesty free first-class airline tickets and vouchers for first-class hotel rooms for the night. The temptation to accept these tickets was great. However, would this have been perceived as a bribe? Even if Amnesty felt that there was no bribery involved, and even if the tickets were for economy fares and accommodations, the bad optics that this could create for its members, the media, and the general public prevented Amnesty from accepting.

There are power differences as well. Corporations, especially MNCs, wield immense financial and economic power on the world stage. Amnesty, on the other hand, has *discursive* power, which it can wield strategically and widely. This discursive power derives from three sources:

1. Meticulous and thorough research: every public statement is carefully researched, discussed, checked by the legal department for possible liability and further researched if necessary, before Amnesty releases the statement.

2. Amnesty's operating principles, which state that no allegations against perpetrators of human rights violations shall be made public by Amnesty without verifiable information to back up its claims.
3. Amnesty's adherence to the values of non-partisanship, fairness, even-handedness, and transparency.

Given its discursive power, Amnesty can quickly raise public attention to human rights abuses perpetrated by a particular company. This bad publicity may have a negative impact on the company's reputation and may even result in financial setbacks.[8] However, any mistake on Amnesty's part, or a variance in the interpretation of events by one party over the other, could result in Amnesty being sued for libel. Amnesty would not have the finances and stamina to sustain a long drawn-out court action.

It is, therefore, in the interests of Amnesty and MNCs alike to exercise their respective strengths and competencies in favour of collaborative strategies.

Alternative approaches

Are there other ways for Amnesty to engage the corporate sector besides collaboration? Amnesty has considered two approaches at opposite ends of the spectrum: *confrontational activism,* which calls for Amnesty to emphasize its oppositional role and employ more confrontational tactics; and *consultancy,* which calls for Amnesty to work directly with companies in the hope that change might come from the inside.

Confrontational activism: the oppositional approach. Some Amnesty members feel that the organization has been too slow to react to fast-breaking human rights situations. Amnesty's exhaustive research process can take a great deal of time, and 'the heat of the moment' may have long passed before a public statement has been issued. The media may have lost interest or another organization may have jumped into the fray, creating publicity for itself and even exploiting the research work that Amnesty has already done.[9] Amnesty, in trying to be non-partisan, may come across as too 'polite,' 'middle of the road,' or 'wishy-washy.' Other members may feel the organization is dominated by too many cautious 'mandate conservatives,' who have created too many rules that stifle member activism. An organization such as

Greenpeace, in contrast, has the reputation for always taking a strong, adversarial, 'in your face' stance on issues, never compromising its positions on the environment, regardless of the cost or the possible long-term advantages that might be gained through a more restrained approach. This, the confrontationalists argue, is exactly how Amnesty should behave in the human rights field, as lives could be lost if Amnesty takes too long to react.

The consultancy approach (sometimes known euphemistically as the 'solution partner' approach). In Norway, Amnesty has set up human rights training seminars for business people. Amnesty Norway has worked with Norsk Hydro and GN Great Nordic, two of the country's largest multinational corporations. Both Norsk Hydro and GN Great Nordic are involved in large hydroelectric projects in the People's Republic of China and in Indonesia – countries with abysmal human rights records. The funding for Amnesty's work comes from the two Nordic MNCs. The premise is that, by playing a direct role in human rights education within the business sector, and in a setting that is not only approved by but also funded by major Nordic MNCs, Amnesty can effect change from within. I feel that this is *not* a collaborative strategy; rather, Amnesty Norway is acting as a paid consultant to the two companies.

Bridging strategies

The typology of bridging organizations developed by Lawrence and Hardy (1999) is a useful tool for examining different bridging strategies proposed by three different Amnesty sections: Amnesty Canada, Amnesty Sweden, and some members of Amnesty USA. Lawrence and Hardy's typologies are based on the degree to which a bridging organization shares the values of other organizations with which it is collaborating. A 'centre extension bridger' holds similar values to the centre organizations. It plays a key role in transmitting values of the centre to the organizations on the borders. A 'border federation bridger,' on the other hand, closely aligns itself with the organizations on the border, and sees its role as bringing the views of the periphery to the centre as well as negotiating on behalf of border organizations. The 'pure bridger' attempts to incorporate values from both the centre and the border.

CENTRE EXTENSION BRIDGING: TWO APPROACHES
Corporate social responsibility (CSR) approach (Amnesty Canada). This approach emphasizes the use of corporate codes of conduct to govern the

FIGURE 12.1
Typology of bridging organizations

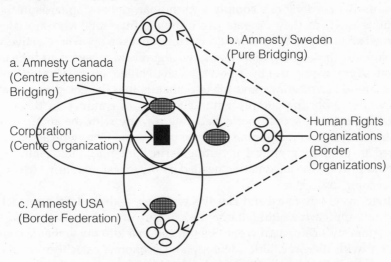

a. CENTRE EXTENSION BRIDGING (Amnesty Canada)
b. PURE BRIDGING (Amnesty Sweden)
c. BORDER FEDERATION (Amnesty USA)

Adapted from 'Figure 1: The Structure of Activist Domain,' *Building Bridges for Refugees: Towards a Typology of Bridging Organizations* by T. Lawrence and C. Hardy (1999).

actions of corporations, which they voluntarily adopt. Accordingly, Amnesty Canada would try to meet the business sector on its own turf. Using vocabulary and categories familiar to the business world, Amnesty would frame the issue of human rights in terms of good business practice. Ethical business practices should generate better public relations and more positive publicity for the company, which would lead to increased consumer confidence, greater employee satisfaction, stronger name recognition for the company's products, and better sales and increased profits.

Amnesty's chief role would be to help frame the codes of conduct, to ensure that these codes are standardized, and to help disseminate information about these codes to the general public.

Socially responsible investment (SRI) approach (Amnesty Canada). This approach calls for individual investors to use their investment power to ensure that corporations comply with human rights standards in the countries where they operate. Accordingly, investors who are concerned about human rights would use their investing power selectively to support those companies that have a good track record in human rights. They would use their power as shareholders to raise questions at shareholder meetings and make demands that the companies that they are supporting comply with CSR codes of conduct. In this approach, Amnesty would not collaborate directly with the companies themselves but with the small group of investment firms who are interested in promoting ethical investments in their portfolios. Amnesty would provide the information needed by the investment firms to conduct company audits.

In terms of Lawrence and Hardy's typology, both the CSR approach and SRI approach would fall into the category of *centre extension bridgers.* Amnesty's campaign would be pitched in a 'discourse that is consistent with the prevailing ideology and economic catechism' of the business world (Murphy 2002, 2). Amnesty would not question the fundamental values of the corporate sector. Rather, the CSR approach would focus Amnesty's attention on boundaries, rules, benchmarks, and operating procedures.

One limitation of this approach, however, lies in the fact that CSR codes are voluntary. Unless there are methods by which signatories can be held accountable to the code, this type of strategy has very few teeth. A case in point is Enron, which for three years before its 2001 collapse and bankruptcy scandal had been listed by *Fortune* magazine as one of the '100 Best Companies to Work For.' Enron had great policies on climate change, human rights, and anti-corruption; its CEO gave speeches at ethics conferences. Milton Moskowitz, the co-author of the annual *Fortune* list and a contributing editor to *Business Ethics* magazine, points out that '[m]uch of the [CSR] movement has been a public relations smoke screen ... It appears that much of the corporate social responsibility movement has dealt in peripheral matters, in language, in mechanical social screens. Behind the scenes, the dirty work went on as usual. I am sorry to be cynical. But you have to admit, it's depressing' (Moskowitz 2002, 36).

The SRI approach is completely within the realm of the corporate world. According to *Keeping the Right Company,* an SRI document prepared by Amnesty Canada's Francophone Section, 'Amnesty

International considers that the profit motive is compatible with human rights. In fact, for AI, financial interest is inseparable from these rights. By guaranteeing political stability, a constitutional state protects investments. In the same way, a healthy and educated population increases economic productivity. AI calls therefore on all economic actors, including investors, to ensure respect for these rights' (AI 2001c).

CSR and CSI strategies are reformist in nature. Lawrence and Hardy (1999) point out that a centre extension bridger can be perceived by those in the periphery as having 'sold out' to the centre (65). Murphy, who is highly critical of this type of strategy, takes this caution even further: 'We risk becoming an intrinsic part of the system that we should be committed to transform. Our role as advocates often becomes "to ameliorate the worse effects."'

Since Amnesty does not take a stand for or against any particular economic system, a CSR or CSI strategy would be still feasible under its mandate. In order for such a strategy to succeed, however, Amnesty needs to clearly explain the motivation for choosing such strategies to its staff and membership, as well as hold discussions with other voluntary organizations in the human rights and social justice fields.

BORDER FEDERATION BRIDGING: THE WATCHDOG APPROACH

Many Amnesty activists, especially some of the more vocal members of Amnesty International USA, feel strongly about this approach. Amnesty's role, they feel, is to help bring about changes in corporate operations through citizen action at the local level. Amnesty would play a watchdog role, researching the human rights records of various corporations and publicizing its findings widely. This would bring offending corporations to the attention of opposition forces within the country and around the world – environmental groups, trade unions, indigenous groups, civil society organizations, and political parties – with the overall objective of forcing the offending businesses to either change their practices or close their operations entirely. Given Amnesty's international reputation and high profile in the media, this approach may have considerable potential.

There are many arguments against taking this approach as well. As Lawrence and Hardy have pointed out (1999, 66), the 'border federation' type of bridging organization shares and promotes the values of the periphery, forcing the centre to be more receptive to periphery demands. However, two critical risks for a border federation are membership fractionalization and loss of credibility. Some positions taken by

periphery organizations may become so convoluted or excessively nu-
anced (with different periphery organizations taking different slants on
an issue) that the border federation may spend most of its time trying
to prevent infighting, or seeking a common position that it can espouse.
(In Amnesty's case, periphery groups might question its right to speak
on behalf of their organizations.) The border federation risks losing its
own membership as well: many Amnesty members may choose to go
and work directly with the voluntary organizations at the grass-roots
level, rather than through Amnesty as an intermediary. Lastly, there are
many other organizations, including those that specialize in different
corporate sectors (such as Mining Watch and the Taskforce on the
Churches and Corporate Responsibility) that can fill the role of industry watchdog.

PURE BRIDGING: THE PROMOTIONAL APPROACH

Amnesty Sweden is engaging in dialogue with the Swedish business
sector to raise its consciousness about the role that businesses can play
in promoting and upholding human rights standards. Training tools,
educational pamphlets, and workshop outlines have been produced to
help corporations exercise due diligence in examining their own human rights records and to train their key decision-makers to take human rights into account. These tools are being put together by a team of
academics, human rights advocates, and businessmen and business-
women. Swedish businesses are invited to attend special educational
forums, where they will hear from both businesses and human rights
advocates. Amnesty plays an advisory or consultative role to the team
and also acts as a convener for public forums. The costs of the project,
workshops, and forums are being covered by the different parties involved, including Amnesty.

In adopting a 'pure' bridging approach, Amnesty Sweden must
spend a lot of time bringing the different players to the table and helping them put together standardized educational materials that respect
their various perspectives and still carry a consistent message. One of
the risks for Amnesty Sweden could be a domain change in the corporate sector, which could undermine Amnesty's position as the centre-
approved bridging organization. If the materials produced are not seen
as useful, if the workshops are seen as a waste of employees' time, and
if the forums end up in acrimonious debate, then there will be very few
incentives for companies to continue with this project. Another risk is
the possibility of discord arising among the human rights organizations

involved, many of which will withdraw their support if they see little or no change in the behaviour of the Swedish companies as a result of this project. Thus, Amnesty Sweden risks either being deemed irrelevant by the centre or losing its legitimacy with the periphery.

An opportunity or a risk?

How will Amnesty deal with the doubts that are being raised by its own members and staff and by other human rights organizations about this type of work? For an organization to be a successful bridger, its members must understand the diverse perspectives that the organization is trying to integrate; the bridging organization is thus obliged to 'sell' its position to its own members as well as to its allies among human rights organizations. How likely is it that all members and stakeholders will be able to understand Amnesty's new role?

THE COMPLEXITY APPROACH

The complexity approach views organizations as 'complex adaptive systems' (CAS) that are analogous to living organisms and consisting of independent parts that share a common life. The greater the ability of the organization to adapt to its environment and to change and learn and adapt as the environment changes around them, the more effective the organization. Complex adaptive systems are multifaceted, non-linear, and interactive (Zimmerman, Lindberg, and Plsek 1998). Effective management decisions in a CAS are highly dependent on the degree of certainty and the level of agreement on the issue in question.

Ralph Stacey proposed that managers use an 'Agreement and Certainty Matrix' to help identify the type of decisions that need to be taken. Decisions are fairly simple to make if the people in an organization are close to agreement on an issue and if the issue or decision itself is close to certainty. The key is to search for best practices and to repeat what has worked in the past. Decision-making can be complicated if the people in the organization are in disagreement but the decision is close to certainty (in which case you would concentrate on consensus building or negotiations to arrive at agreement), or if the people are close to agreement but the issue is far from certainty (in which case you would go back to the organization's mission and vision and make decisions on which strategies would help the organization achieve its mission). On the far side of the grid, a situation of anarchy would exist if both apply: the people are far from agreement and the issue is far from certainty. Stacey points out that there is a large area in the matrix diagram that lies between anarchy and the traditional management approaches. Stacey calls this the 'zone of complexity' (or 'edge of chaos'). While this zone does not respond very well to traditional management decision-making, it is a zone of high creativity and innovation (Stacey 1996).

When we use the Stacey Matrix to gauge the level of certainty in Amnesty about the decision to undertake a collaborative strategy and the level of agreement of Amnesty staff and members on choosing this particular strategy, we see that this situation falls exactly in the *zone of complexity*.

Traditional management strategy views complex situations as problem areas that need to be fixed rather than as opportunities to innovate (Zimmerman, Lindberg, and Plsek 1998). Amnesty may perceive its members' and allies' doubts as problems that must be resolved. Taking a traditional management stance, Amnesty might place so many conditions on what is or is not permissible (maximum specifications) that this would effectively block any new initiative. Another traditional solution would be to revert back to conventional techniques such as letter-writing, petitions, silent vigils, and small demonstrations in front of corporate headquarters, even though Amnesty has already concluded that these methods have limited impact on the corporate sector. Amnesty could also defer having to make the decision to go ahead by diverting the discussion to engage its members in protracted debate on whether or not responding to human rights abuses by non-state actors is a priority within Amnesty's present plans.

However, if Amnesty chooses to view its complex situation as an opportunity to be explored, then Amnesty must work with the paradoxes and tensions that exist. Realizing that it cannot control outcomes from the centre, Amnesty may encourage the 'fringes' (staff and members who want to try collaborative methods with the corporate sector) to test and experiment with one or two projects and to learn from these experiments. The Amnesty board of directors and management could develop a 'good enough' vision and minimum specifications ('min specs') instead of maximum specifications (which is the usual way that Amnesty works) for collaborative work (Zimmerman, Lindberg, and Plsek. 1998).

What would a 'good enough' vision look like? Traditionally, before Amnesty embarks on any new venture, the whole movement must take up the discussion. Various studies and pilot projects are undertaken

FIGURE 12.2
Zone of Complexity: Intersectoral bridging strategies for Amnesty

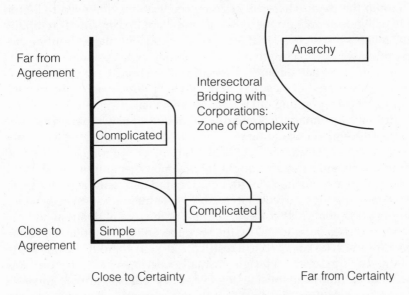

Adapted from 'Stacey Agreement and Certainty Matrix,' *Edgeware: Insights from Complexity Science for Health Care Leaders*, B. Zimmerman, C. Lindberg, and Paul Plsek (1998).

and recommendations from these studies and projects are then taken to the international council meeting, which is held once every two years, for a decision. If the issue is controversial and if a significant number of Amnesty sections seem reluctant to take a definitive vote, then the recommendations could be referred to subcommittees for further deliberation and study. It is estimated that Amnesty holds member consultations for four to eight years before major changes to its work can be made. A 'good enough' vision would set aside the need for full organizational agreement on Amnesty's precise role (for example, not to try to answer definitively whether Amnesty's role should be one of advocacy, watchdog, whistle-blower, constructive critic, or 'solution partner' before anyone can proceed) and let different Amnesty sections develop the roles that seem the most appropriate in the circumstances. The 'good enough' vision can simply be to minimize the harm and maximize the good that businesses can do in this area of human rights.

In terms of 'min specs,' Amnesty needs to loosen its tight boundaries and to resist the temptation to overdesign the program before venturing into the work. There are certain specifications that need to be followed. For example, Amnesty would not want to damage its credibility for reliable research, so that any public statement made about a company's business practice that violates human rights principles must be verifiable. Another minimum specification would be that Amnesty's work in the area of business and human rights should not prevent Amnesty from pointing out human rights violations that take place.

In Amnesty Canada, it is a requirement that all new program areas be vetted through the planning process, and usually, only those programs that can demonstrate concrete linkages to other program areas (for example, different programs might cover similar geographic or thematic areas, or planned actions might be presented in a multifaceted way, so that one campaign can cover a number of themes or issues) become the top-priority items. Other ideas, because of the lack of financial and human resources, tend to fall by the wayside. In this situation, a facilitative approach (as opposed to a restrictive design approach) would be to allow small groups to engage in small experiments and try out new ways of working with businesses, even if the linkages are not apparent from the beginning. Linkages, if any, will arise organically as the work proceeds. Members and staff who are interested in working in the area of business and human rights should be encouraged to proceed (albeit slowly and with caution), even though Amnesty may not have thoroughly diagnosed all the risks or put into place all the necessary systems and safeguards to cover these risks.

In order to learn as much as possible from these different experiments, Amnesty needs to develop a method for facilitating learning exchanges and dialogue among the various project holders, as well as between the business and human rights program and the other programs that Amnesty conducts. Growth in the sector of business and human rights would evolve in stages, as different components become integrated after they have been tested, refined, proven, and accepted by Amnesty as being viable.

An inherent flaw?

Westley and Vredenburg speculate that organizations that are innovative and flexible enough to attempt bridging strategies are hampered by the inability of their democratic decision-making processes to build internal commitment to a bridging strategy (Westley and Vredenburg 1991). Is it an inherent flaw for Amnesty, a decentralized membership-based voluntary human rights organization, to attempt to strategically collaborate with hierarchical profit-driven multinational corporations?

Strategic bridging works best when an organization is flexible and entrepreneurial as well as disciplined and strategic. Entrepreneurial organizations, according to Henry Mintzberg (1981), are characterized by their simple, informal, and flexible structures and their centralized, personalized, and sometimes charismatic power. Such organizations are quick, responsive, dedicated, and directed. On the other hand, innovative and flexible organizations – what Mintzberg calls 'adhocracies' – are characterized by organic team structures, fluidity, and selectively decentralized power. While an adhocracy organization would be the one most likely to try innovative strategies such as strategic bridging, the adhocracy organization would have to act more like an entrepreneurial organization in order for these strategies to succeed.

Enbridge, a Canadian company headquartered in Calgary, Alberta, is one of the major partners in OCENSA (Oleoducto Central SA), the second-largest crude oil pipeline being built in Colombia. (Other partners include Ecopetrol from Colombia; TotalFina-Elf from France; British Petroleum from the UK and Triton/Amerada Hess from the U.S.) Amnesty has been particularly concerned about the high incidence of human rights abuses, many of them perpetrated by the paramilitary and some by the guerrilla factions, on Colombians living in the areas of oil exploration and pipeline construction, especially in the states of Puttamayo and Barrancabermeja. Amnesty wanted to raise the matter of human rights in Colombia with Enbridge; in particular, to urge Enbridge to play an active and positive role in the protection of human rights in the areas where its operations were underway.

A couple of Enbridge shareholders had tried to raise the Colombian human rights issue at an Enbridge shareholder meeting but were persuaded to withdraw their resolutions if Enbridge promised to meet with socially responsible investment fund managers along with another mutually agreed-on third party. Amnesty was quite pleased to have been selected as the third party. The first thing that Enbridge did at the meeting, however, was to hand out a tightly worded confidentiality agreement, which they insisted that all parties sign. This would have effectively neutralized Amnesty's core competency – its ability to raise its voice against human rights abuses around the world. In situations such as this, the decision to sign or not to sign had to be made on the spot; fortunately Amnesty was able to withdraw from the forum in an amicable way. Nonetheless, it is easy to imagine the consequences if Amnesty had signed the confidentiality agreement – especially as the Amnesty staff person attending the meeting would not even have been able to fully explain his actions to his colleagues.

Let us consider another possible scenario. This scenario has Amnesty sections in Canada, the U.S., France, and the UK working with the key partners in Consortium 'ABCD,' which is mining for gold in an African country ('Country X'). The French Amnesty Section works with Company A, the UK Amnesty Section with Company B, the American Amnesty Section with Company C, and the Canadian Amnesty Section with D in a collaborative effort to encourage the Consortium members to comply with a code of ethics (a CSR strategy). However, human rights abuses continue to occur in Country X. Members from Amnesty Canada's Human Rights Defenders Network are approached by a re-spected trade union with the information that a key trade unionist in Country X has 'disappeared' and other workers have been threatened. The trade unionists feel that the probable perpetrators were Country X's security forces, possibly in response to complaints made about the trade union by one of the companies in the Consortium. How quickly can Amnesty deal with this situation? How will the decisions be made? Who should be involved?

If Amnesty were to follow normal protocol, this issue would need to be discussed by the four sections concerned. Within the Canadian Section, Amnesty staff would need to discuss this with key members involved in the Human Rights Defenders and the Business and Human Rights programs – two separate teams with some overlapping mem-bership. The Canadian Section's secretary general and possibly the media director and the chair of the Amnesty Canada board of directors would be involved if Amnesty decided to make a public statement. Amnesty Canada would also need to consult with the other Canadian NGOs and groups it works with on Country X, including church groups, solidarity groups, and the trade unions. Throughout this pro-cess, the four different sections (Canada, France, UK, and the U.S.) would need to be in contact with one another, as well as with Amnesty's research and campaigning staff at the international secretariat in London. The international staff would also consult with staff involved in business and human rights work at the international level. Recommendations would need to be vetted by the legal department, the editorial board, and senior management, including the international secretary general. In politically sensitive cases, the staff would present a recommendation to the international executive committee for a decision. Amnesty's long and cautious process for consultation and decision-making would definitely be a liability in this scenario.

Does this mean that, because of the conflicts that can arise between the nature of the work and Amnesty's present organizational structure and culture, Amnesty should abandon the idea of assuming a strategic bridging role with corporations? Not necessarily. According to complexity theory, Amnesty could view the dilemma not as a problem to be solved or else avoided, but as an opportunity to apply innovative techniques to change its own structure and processes in response to various situations. This could mean involving the key staff and board members (at both the international level and the section levels) in developing 'good enough' visions for Amnesty's collaborative work and 'min specs' to provide a level of control and guidance as experimentation takes place. Amnesty would need to set aside the traditional lines of authority and control to experiment with emergent structures and processes, learning from each experience and building new policies and procedures by drawing upon the best experiences (Zimmerman, Lindberg, and Plsek 1998).

In reference to my earlier discussion about using complexity tools, Amnesty could decide on the 'min specs' for this particular case. For example, 'min specs' could be:

1. The disappearance is verified.
2. The urgent action released on behalf of the missing trade unionist is written by the urgent action coordinator, using the correct tone and language and following Amnesty's usual protocols.
3. Every section involved uses the urgent action as the basis for an urgent letter-writing campaign.
4. Amnesty publicly calls upon Country X's government to investigate the disappearance, identify those responsible, and hold them accountable for their actions.

Each section could then decide on the appropriate methods for working with their business leaders and with the human rights and social justice organizations in their communities on this issue. One section might wish to involve the business and union people in their own country to work together on a joint union-management campaign to promote the safety of labour advocates. This could involve putting together an action plan that the affiliate's management staff and trade union leaders in Country X could use in case of possible future threats to the company's employees, including trade union leaders. Another section might wish to ask the corporation to make quiet inquiries about the disappearance with high government officials in Country X. A third section might wish to involve their Amnesty members working on the human rights defenders program to join the business and human rights members in mounting a socially responsible investment campaign aimed at companies that do business in Country X. An important element is that, as each section engages in its work, information is being exchanged among the sections and Amnesty is learning from this experience. This would, eventually, lead to re-examining traditional Amnesty practices and policies and either refining these policies or changing them, if necessary.

Making the experience truly transformative

Both individual alternators and bridging organizations are confronted with issues concerning identity and loyalty, which can be very stressful. Can this experience be transformative?

Lyse Champagne (1990) describes her experience as an intercultural bridger between the francophone and anglophone cultures in Canada as sitting between two chairs:

> *Assise entre deux chaises.* The trouble with sitting between two chairs is that you end up on the floor – which is not the most comfortable place. You like both chairs, although for different reasons. One is elegant, a little ornate; the other, practical and versatile. You get to spend time on each chair, although you're never allowed to stay for very long. Something always happens and you end up on the floor again. And while you're on the floor, you can see the underside of the chairs, the way the material is fraying on this one, the slightly crooked frame and unfinished underside of the other ... (141)

According to Westley and Vredenburg, 'Bridging, as a form of collaboration, in a sense has the worst of both worlds' (1991, 81). No doubt, then, that because bridgers can more clearly see the flaws in both worlds, whether they be individuals involved in intercultural bridging or organizations involved in intersectoral bridging, they are more vulnerable to the problems and risks and may more easily lose themselves along the way, especially if the distinction between the agent and broker roles is blurred. Champagne (1990) has stated, 'In always trying to understand two cultures, I have run the risk of not understanding myself. By living in two cultures, I have learned not to belong in spite of the fact that I come from a culture where belonging is everything' (147). On the other hand, bridgers can see the *best* of both worlds. The potential for creating a positive impact on the world is very exciting. Bridgers can bring together the best and brightest from both sides to work together on transformative solutions. Successful projects can mobilize local energies and resources to sustain activities over the long term. The experience from successful linkages can be used to influence, enhance, and expand collaborative efforts in other domains and areas of work. As the grass-roots become involved with the centre in successful collaborative efforts, new vertical linkages will develop on a broader scope – a scope that will enable grass-roots activists to influence regional and national policies that shape long-term world political, social, and economic systems (Brown 1991).

What would make the experience truly transformative and not just reformist? I feel that, at the heart of the matter, is the need to reconceptualize the *problématique* – away from the traditional problem-solution frameworks – and into transformative frameworks. A bridging organization should also be aware that there is a time to creatively challenge as well as a time to foster cooperation; and that conflict in itself is not necessarily bad (Brown 1992). At the very least, engaging in courageous conversations and viewing conflict as an opportunity for dialogue will, over the course of time, lead to more openness within Amnesty.

3. The Options

Amnesty has a number of choices to make. First, whether or not to collaborate with the business sector; and if Amnesty were to collaborate, to what degree and at what level should it do so? There are both positive and negative reasons for choosing either of these strategies. With a 'no involvement' strategy, Amnesty risks being left behind as other organizations seize the opportunity to work with the corporate sector. On the other end of the spectrum (taking a greater oppositional role), Amnesty would need to change its stance of non-alignment and to openly state its identification with radical grass-roots social justice organizations. While this may attract a younger, more activist-oriented audience, Amnesty could lose much of its credibility with the mainstream sectors of society (the media, governments, corporations) as well as lose support from its more conservative members. A bridging strategy, which is in the middle of the spectrum, brings with it both risks and opportunities.

Table 12.1 summarizes the risks and potential outcomes of these three major options for Amnesty International. Reviewing this table, I conclude that the middle option, that of choosing a strategic bridging strategy, looks the most promising. The 'no involvement' option is obviously no option at all; it is contrary to Amnesty's raison d'être. A greater oppositional role would be extremely risky and would be the role furthest from the status quo; to take this option, Amnesty would have to make major changes in the way that it operates. It is highly unlikely that the majority of its members would want this to happen. The bridging strategy role also has risks, but I feel that, given some hard work and dedicated commitment to this work by key staff and members, Amnesty could meet the conditions that need to be in place to ensure that a good bridging strategy is operational.

4. Conclusion

On reflection, I feel strongly that alternation is the best way for an individual to deal with the sense of dislocation and uncertainty when forced to live in two worlds. Becoming biculturally competent allows the individual to turn a potentially negative experience into a positive transforming experience.

As for Amnesty, I feel that Amnesty certainly ought to adopt a strategic bridging strategy for its dealings with the corporate sector, first of all because the work is vitally important and must be done; second, because the work will transform Amnesty into a dynamic and innovative organization that will be well equipped to respond to a changing human rights context worldwide; third, because Amnesty has the financial, human, and technological resources to meet the challenges as they arise; and finally, because the potential for creative, generative, and transformative solutions is high.

On balance, it would seem that the most advantageous bridging strategy for Amnesty is that of a 'pure bridger.' This would allow Amnesty to maintain its unique identity while keeping within the boundaries of its overall mandate. In order for this to work, key Amnesty staff and members would need to clarify – and agree on – Amnesty's core values. Amnesty's goals for bridging should be

Table 12.1
Strategies for Amnesty International

	No Involvement	Bridging Strategy	Greater Oppositional Role
Positive Outcomes	Amnesty would not need to deal with the many complex problems and dilemmas posed by working with the business sector. This allows Amnesty to devote its resources and energies to other areas of work and to continue to build its core competences in the programs that it is already undertaking.	The work, if lodged in the zone of complexity, can be innovative, generative, and transformative. Links formed are long term. Amnesty is able to advance the articulation or crystallization of the problem domain. Corporations become committed to human rights. Significant impact can be made on improving human rights around the world.	Amnesty would build closer relationships with other periphery organizations working on the same issues. Amnesty can learn new action-oriented tactics. There is a greater potential for coalition building among allied organizations. The 'in your face' actions might generate more media coverage and, as a result, attract younger, more enthusiastic members.
Negative Outcomes	Nothing ventured, nothing gained. The organization may be left behind by other organizations in its own field if it cannot respond to changing environmental contexts. This could result in a net loss in members and in the number of financial supporters. The organization may become moribund, sticking to traditional structures, methods, and processes.	Amnesty cannot meet the conditions that must be in place to ensure good bridging. Amnesty will not be able to deal with the challenges as outlined in this essay. The bad experience causes Amnesty to lose credibility among its members and supporters.	No real impact is made on changing the corporate sector, whether to stop human rights abuses or to act as advocates for human rights. Amnesty may be perceived as belonging to the radical fringe and will have very little credibility in the corporate sector. Amnesty's key strengths (thorough research; well-thought-out, non-partisan approaches) would be questioned by the mainstream media and the corporate world.

clearly articulated. The values and goals of the centre organizations (the businesses involved) and the peripheral or 'island' organizations (human rights and social justice groups) must be clarified and shared. The motives (altruistic or egoistic or something in between) and the expectations of all the parties involved must be made transparent. Differences of power and resources between the corporate sector, the voluntary human rights sector, and Amnesty must be explored, addressed, and accommodated. Intra-organizational mechanisms for managing difficulties (including conflict) need to be developed.

Waddell and Brown (1997) provide ten guiding lessons about developing intersectoral relationships through a six-stage process. In order to make this experience a transformative one, I would suggest the following for Amnesty:

1. *Increase the level of buy-in* from Amnesty staff and members by facilitating educational and open-sharing sessions and developing and using effective communications tools to keep everyone continuously informed.
2. *Work collaboratively* with allied organizations in the human rights domain. Protocols should be established for continued information sharing, communications, and joint decision- making.
3. *Do not rush to resolve setbacks,* or even failures. Take the time to reflect and learn from them.
4. *Know the best time to foster cooperation* and the best time to raise challenges. Learn from experiments in intersectoral bridging. Learn from other organizations that are engaged as intersectoral bridgers such as the Pembina Institute, Participatory Research in India (PRIA), and the Highlander Education and Research Center.[10] Liaise with academics and learn more about cutting edge research in this area.
5. *Bring in staff and members with alternator experience* to help lead the bridging work. Provide skills training to the alternators to enhance their leadership skills (negotiations, conflict management, facilitation, consensus building, decision-making, etc.). Find ways to foster intercultural exchange and dialogue (management exchanges, joint values clarification meetings, team building).
6. *Select a bridging approach* that is appropriate to the leadership of the organization, the organizational context, the issue at hand, and Amnesty's culture. Instead of viewing a strategy as 'either/or' (either collaboration or confrontation), consider a continuum of approaches.

Although Amnesty's experiments in developing bridging strategies to link the organization with the international corporate sector may engender scepticism in some quarters of the human rights movement, there is room for optimism. The role that Amnesty can play as an intersectoral bridger may yet make significant changes towards a world where the human rights of all individuals are fully respected.

NOTES

I would like to express my deep appreciation to the faculty and staff of the McGill-McConnell Program as well as to my classmates for their support in making this a true learning experience. Special thanks to my tutor Jan Jorgenson, who challenged me to write with clarity, and to my professors Frances Westley, Frederick Bird, Harrie Vredenburg, and Brenda Zimmerman, whose animated and dedicated teaching inspired us all. Within Amnesty International, I am grateful to our managers, who supported me throughout my course of studies in the program – with special thanks to Jeff Flood, Amnesty's former business and human rights program officer, who reviewed several drafts of this essay and provided me with a wealth of information and advice.

1 Prior to 1998, Conquistador Mines, incorporated in British Columbia, ran its gold mining operations in the Marmato mining district of western Colombia through its subsidiary, Corona Goldfields SA. In January 1998, Corona declared its interest in exploiting a gold mine in the town of Simiti. The mine was claimed by both the Higuera-Palacios family and 35,000 poor miners who had worked the mine for 30 years; 30,000 of the miners were affiliated with Agromining Association of the South of Bolivar (ASOGROMISBOL). When Corona indicated its interest in Simiti, paramilitaries started a campaign of terror in the area. Death squads captured and killed miners, including ASOGROMISBOL vice-president Luis Orlanda Camacho. Union representatives and displaced villagers from Simiti (in July and August some 5,000 people had fled to the city of Barrancabermeja to escape paramilitary action in Bolivar State) met with President Andres Pastrana and charged that multinational mining companies were funding the paramilitaries that had forced them to flee their homes (Ismi 2000).
2 Placer Dome group was one of the world's largest gold producers, operating fourteen mines in five countries. A number of industrial accidents causing major environmental damage can be attributed to Placer Dome's

faulty operations. These include a tailing spill into a major river system at Marcopper in the Philippines in March 1966; cyanide leaching at Golden Sunlight Mine in Montana; pollution of the Lagaip River by tailings dumped from the Porgera Mine in Papua New Guinea; and acid mine drainage problems at the Buckhorn mine in Nevada (TCCR 2002).

3   Thirteen Burmese villages filed a lawsuit against Unocal, a California-based oil company, for human rights abuses perpetrated by the Burmese military, including rape, forced labour, and murder, in connection with the Yadana gas pipeline project. The U.S. Federal District Court determined that Unocal knew or should have known about the abuses committed, but found that Unocal could not be held liable because it did not control the Burmese military's actions. On 18 September 2002, the Ninth Circuit Court of Appeals reversed the Federal Court ruling, stating that the plaintiffs need only demonstrate that Unocal knowingly assisted the military in the perpetration of the abuses. The court found that forced labour such as that employed by the Burmese military on behalf of the Unocal pipeline is the 'modern equivalent of slavery,' and it stated that corporations 'that aid and abet egregious human rights abuses can be held accountable' (United States Court of Appeals for the Ninth Circuit in the Case of *Doe v. Unocal*, filed 18 September 2002).

4   Union Carbide India Ltd. (UCIL) set up a fertilizer plant in Bhopal in 1969. The process involved the use of MIC (methyl isocyanides). In 1984, a dangerous chemical reaction occurred when large amounts of water seeped into the MIC storage plant and 40 tons of lethal MIC gas leaked into the surrounding community. Thousands of people were killed and hundreds of thousands were injured (Trade and Environment Data Base 2003).

5   Talisman Energy, a Calgary-based oil company, was involved in developing oil reserves in civil-war-ravaged south-central Sudan. Critics claimed that the revenue from the oil production was used to help the military regime commit human rights abuses against the people in the area. Amnesty International pointed out the link between massive human rights violations by the security forces of the Government of Sudan and various government-allied militias and the oil operations by foreign companies. 'Foreign companies are involved in this lucrative oil production, and they expect the Sudanese government to provide a secure environment, which includes the use of security forces to protect oil company staff and assets. Thus, Amnesty International believes many foreign companies tolerate violations by turning a blind eye to the human rights violations committed by the government security forces or government-allied troops in the name of protecting the security of the oil-producing areas' (AI 2000).

6   Murphy (2002) raises the dilemma that social justice advocates, including
    the Corporate Social Responsibility Movement, could be co-opted into
    becoming integral parts of the system, instead of transforming the system.

7   Amnesty's first request to meet with 'XYZ Inc.' was refused. Company
    officials later told Amnesty that they were at first reluctant to meet
    because they feared that all they would hear would be unfair accusations.
    XYZ had been approached by a number of NGOs within the same period,
    and management was worried that the company might be the target of an
    orchestrated campaign. (Name withheld for reasons of confidentiality.)

8   Negative publicity about Talisman Energy's role in the Sudan created
    considerable problems for the company, in terms of its reputation and the
    impact on share prices. In June 2001, the U.S. Congress passed the *Sudan
    Peace Act*, which threatened to delist companies doing business in the
    Sudan from the New York Stock Exchange. In October 2002, Talisman
    Energy sold its interest in the Greater Nile Oil Project in Sudan. In
    announcing the sale, CEO Jim Buckee stated: 'Talisman's shares have
    continued to be discounted based on perceived political risk in-country
    and in North America to a degree that was unacceptable for 12 percent of
    our production. Shareholders have told me they were tired of continually
    having to monitor and analyze events relating to Sudan' (CNW News
    Release, 30 October 2000).

9   A good example is the Landmines Declaration, which Amnesty did not
    sign until many months after the historic agreement was forged in Ottawa.
    The internal debate within Amnesty went on for many months. By the
    time Amnesty signed on, the story was 'old news.' Many Amnesty
    members were upset that it had taken the organization so long to get on
    board.

10 The Pembina Institute is an independent, not-for-profit environmental
    policy research and education organization based in Drayton Valley,
    Alberta. Pembina's Corporate Eco-Solutions Program includes the
    provision of a consulting service to corporations to help them make their
    businesses more environmentally sustainable (Pembina 2006).
    Participatory Research in India (PRIA) is a non-profit voluntary organiza-
    tion that promotes initiatives for the empowerment and development of
    the poor and marginalized. A key objective is to contribute to the area of
    social development by creating effective networks and partnerships and
    providing space for institutions, local government, and individuals to
    interact and dialogue (PRIA 2002). The Highlander Research and
    Education Center is a non-profit centre that works with groups struggling
    against discrimination, racism, and poverty in the United States

(specifically in Appalachia and the deep South). Highlander brings people together to work collectively on strategies and activities to confront and change unjust policies and structures (F. Adams 1986).

PART FIVE

The Catalytic Mindset

13 A Snowball's Chance: Children of Offenders and Canadian Social Policy

SHAWN BAYES

> North of the 49th parallel, we treasure equality ... Canadian morality tran-
> scends traditional religious definitions; it can be characterized as a secular,
> pluralistic and ecological morality, a greater responsibility for the other.
>
> Michael Adams, *Sex in the Snow* (1997, 192–3)

Most Canadians believe their country is second to none in the ways it
treats its citizens and the quality of life it provides. They expect that
Canada's children will receive the help they need to grow and be able
to participate in society. To that end, Canadians invest in the care and
treatment of children with illnesses, handicaps or disabilities, as well as
other problems. They believe that Canadian children in need of medical, educational, and social services should receive them, even if the
prognosis is not certain. The premise has been that children should
have the opportunity to reach their potential.

That premise, however, is being reconsidered, as governments and
voluntary agencies grapple with fiscal restraints and develop criteria to
ration services. Although the emphasis has been to ensure that the door
remains open, what were previously considered the rights of Canadian
citizens (such as health care and welfare) are now being discussed as
privileges, and often predicated upon assumptions of likelihood of
'successful' intervention. In such a climate, it can be difficult to argue
for the expansion of services, or even for the refocusing of attention to
include those considered 'less worthy.' Thus, Canadians stand in delicate tension between believing that their country is the best in the
world, feeling responsible for others, and at the same time wanting to
step back from many of the burdens of responsibility. Consequently,

governments discuss reducing personal income tax and offering families 'choice and freedom' to manage difficulties so that people can be 'responsible for themselves.' Just such examples are cited in a report by Mike Harris and Preston Manning for the Fraser Institute that calls for governments to offer choice and opportunity to Canadians to take responsibility for themselves through measures like welfare reforms – as BC, Alberta, and Ontario have done in the past ten years (Harris and Manning 2005).

In this environment, there is a brooding undertone of fear. Canadians demand to be safe from crime, and they want measures such as increased policing and longer sentences to deter crime and guarantee safety. Canada has one of the highest incarceration rates in the industrialized world, and yet its citizens report a growing incidence of fear of victimization. Canada continues to fill its prisons, even though it has a decreasing crime rate (Statistics Canada 2005b, 1; Statistics Canada 2006b, 1).

Cultural theories abound with explanations of the triangulation of the aging of Canada's population (a growing sense of frailty and mortality makes the aged more fearful), the marketing of crime (through lurid fiction, music, and even gangster clothing), and the politics of crime (all major political parties have platforms on 'getting tough' with criminals). Other theorists frame the issues of crime and prison in the context of social exclusion: that those excluded from society because of poverty, racism, fear of difference, or lack of political influence express their exclusion through criminal acts, violence, and fear of others. These two perspectives provide differing large-scale explanations of the phenomena. Both, however, frame the discussion around the common assumptions of community development: that is, each takes for granted that the answer to crime prevention lies within the community rather than the individual. Who would not want to believe that? Who wants to believe that certain people are born to be criminals? The idea is reprehensible. And so the wide net of social development and inclusion is used as a model for crime prevention.

However, there is a particular group of children whose involvement in crime is epidemic, and whose circumstances and risk factors are diminished when viewed through the broad net of social development. The lives of these children are all too often narrowed within the confines of prison bars and the correlated problems of crime. They are invisible within the broader issue groupings of poverty, addiction, family problems, and neighbourhoods of lower socio-economic indicators. Canada, unlike such countries as the United States, the United Kingdom,

India, and Australia, has not recognized this particular group of children for whom the risk of criminal involvement and incarceration is exorbitant. These children, the children of prisoners, have become socially invisible. For all its compassion and good intentions, Canada has diminished their opportunities and done little or nothing to prevent them from leading barren lives.

In order to assist the children of prisoners, it is necessary not only to consider who their parents are and the issues these children face, but also to understand that within the group itself, there is a particular subgroup at even greater risk: the children of imprisoned mothers. While the response that is required must come from both the government and the voluntary sector, the latter has a pivotal role to play in ensuring these children have a place within society.

1. Prisons and People

The unwritten history that we, as Canadians, carry in our collective unconscious tells us that, while anyone can go to prison, certain groups within our society go to prison more frequently than others. The Canadian public is aware that the people who go to prisons are overrepresented by the poor, Aboriginals and those with family histories of abuse, neglect, and correlated problems such as addiction. Furthermore, the public is aware that more men than women go to prison and that most prisoners will return to their communities.

Correctional Service Canada (CSC), along with other sources, provides the following description for prisoners in CSC care serving sentences over two years:

- 18 per cent of prisoners are Aboriginal (though Aboriginal people make up only 3 per cent of the Canadian population) (CSC 2005, 2–4)
- 4 per cent of prisoners are women (ibid.)
- 80 per cent abused alcohol and/or drugs (because of their substance abuse, the physical and mental health of prisoners is generally worse than that of the overall Canadian population) (ibid.)
- 84 per cent of all those charged with violent crime are men; only 16 per cent are women (Statistics Canada 2006c, 169). Women are consistently more likely than men to be charged with property offences rather than violent offences
- 20 per cent of prisoners have been previously hospitalized in a mental health facility (11 per cent have a current psychiatric diagnosis) (CSC 2005, 2–4)

- prisoners have a high incidence of infectious diseases, particularly AIDS and hepatitis C. The proportion of prisoners with HIV is 6 to 70 times higher than the proportion of all Canadians with HIV. The proportion of prisoners with the hepatitis C virus (HCV) is at least 30 times higher (and in some prisons, 100 times higher) than that of Canadians who are not in prison (Lines 2002, 4)
- Almost all prisoners will be released back to the community, most in less than five years (CSC 2004a, tables 1, 4; CSC 2006b, 7)

There is one other crucially important distinguishing trait of prisoners. A disproportionate number of prisoners come from families where at least one other family member was incarcerated. In the United States, the Center for Children of Incarcerated Parents conducted a study of incarcerated women and found that 33 per cent of the women had a parent who had been incarcerated, approximately 80 per cent had a member in their immediate family who had been incarcerated, and 59 per cent had multiple family members who had been incarcerated (Gabel and Johnston 1995, 47). The center also reported that over one third of incarcerated men also had an immediate family member who had been incarcerated (ibid., 4).

It should be said that there now exists only limited research regarding children of prisoners. Most studies are small and are of male prisoners and their children. Of the studies that do exist, few are longitudinal. Adult prisoners and their children face multilayered problems, and it can be difficult to isolate the impact of incarceration from other factors such as abuse, poverty, limited education and addiction (to name only a few). Thus, as A.E. Kazdin (1998) has noted, 'over time several risk factors become interrelated because the presence of one factor can augment the accumulation of other risk factors' (68). Nonetheless, the existing research literature demonstrates unequivocally that the risk factors mentioned above significantly predispose a child to criminal behaviours, and that the accumulation of risk factors only exacerbates the likelihood of criminal justice involvement.

2. Gender Differences

Although females account for roughly half of the total Canadian population, their rate of incarceration is much lower than males, and their collective profile differs significantly. In 2004, of all offences committed, 18 per cent were committed by women. Women are consistently more likely to be charged with property offences than violent offences (such as homicide, assault, or robbery). In 2004, 32 per cent of women prisoners were charged with a property offence, in contrast to 22 per cent of men. Furthermore, the large majority of property crimes that women were charged with involved either theft under $5,000, or fraud. Men were more likely to be charged with breaking and entering, and other types of personal theft. Women represented only 16 per cent of those charged with a violent crime, and the majority (62 per cent) of the charges of violence against women were for common assault. The proportion of women charged with other forms of violent crime such as sexual assault (2 per cent) or robbery (11 per cent) was very low (Statistics Canada 2006c, 168–9). By contrast, a full 81 per cent of all male prisoners have committed a violent offence such as homicide, assault, or robbery (CSC 2005, 2).

So it is fair to say that female prisoners commit less serious crimes than men, for which they are incarcerated for shorter periods of time. In the fiscal year ending March 31, 2004, 70 per cent of women admitted to sentenced custody spent 31 days or less in provincial or territorial institutions, compared to 54 per cent of sentenced men (Statistics Canada 2006c, 172). Thus, based upon the daily count data provided by Adult Correctional Services in Canada (Statistics Canada 2006a, 3), 9,830 people were serving sentences of less than two years (excluding those held without bail on remand). The incidence of women serving a sentence, however, was 10 per cent (Statistics Canada 2006b); in other words, only 298 women in the entire country, on any given day, would be serving a sentence between 31 days and 2 years less a day.

The average male offender also has a higher level of education, a better standard of living, and a lower incidence of mental illness, addiction, and historical abuse than his female counterpart. In contrast, according to a special Canadian Human Rights Commission report (2003):

- The average female offender is between the ages of 20 and 34.
- Two-thirds of female prisoners have children, and a full two-thirds of those women are the sole caregivers of their children.
- 50 per cent of these women have not exceeded Grade 9 in school. According to another report, in May 1995, 40 per cent of incarcerated women were illiterate.
- Over two-thirds have unaddressed physical or mental health problems. Incarcerated women have the highest rate of HIV

infection for women in Canada, and the highest rate of mental illness in women.

- Over 80 per cent have been physically and/or sexually abused.
- 80 per cent were unemployed at the time of their incarceration, compared to a general female unemployment rate in Canada of less than 10 per cent.
- Most female prisoners report transient and unstable housing.
- More than 32 per cent of female prisoners are Aboriginal, in contrast to over 18 per cent of male prisoners. (Sapers 2006, 1)

Another overwhelming difference between male and female prisoners concerns their children and the implications of parenthood. Studies in the U.S., Canada, and the UK all report that a significant proportion of prisoners have children. Female prisoners have more children than other women; and for their children, their incarceration has huge implications. These mothers, in contrast to male prisoners, tend to be the sole caregivers for their children. Thus, when men are incarcerated, their children's lives are disrupted far less than in the case of women prisoners, whose children are frequently placed with immediate or extended family members, instead of in foster care (S. Gabel 1992; Bloom and Steinhart 1993; Sheridan 1996; Healy, Foley, and Walsh 1999; Mumola 2000).

'I tell'

'I tell 'em to make sure Grampa keeps his pecker in his pocket. He's old now. He won't ... I don't ... I don't suppose I have to worry.'

Mother, serving three years, with two children (ages 5 and 7) who live with her parents[1]

A U.S. survey reports that 90 per cent of the children of incarcerated fathers live with their mothers. In contrast, approximately one-quarter of the children of incarcerated women live with their fathers, half live with their grandparents, and the remainder live either in foster care or familial (or otherwise arranged) housing. Thus, children of female prisoners live in circumstances (including the extent of their financial support) that go largely unrecognized by social agencies (U.S. Department of Justice 1992, 10). Families providing kinship care for children are not usually eligible for additional funding, such as that provided for

Source: CircleVision.org.
Credit: Tom Bottolene/CircleVision.org. Reprinted by permission.

children in foster care. Thus, the families taking the children, and often the children themselves, feel the impact of a drop in family income. These children come from living in poverty into situations with additional pressures. For example, grandparents who are retired or are nearing the end of their working lives are faced with increased financial burdens, and the responsibility of raising children. Not surprisingly, studies across three-quarters of a century (since the late 1920s at least) have documented the financial impact of parent incarceration, and found severe problems of adjustment in the face of reduced family income (Bloodgood 1928; Sacks 1938; Morris 1965; Ferraro et al. 1983).

Due to the limited number of female prisoners, there are few prisons for women in Canada. Thus, incarcerated women are often transported away from their homes and children. For example, women sentenced in Alberta, Saskatchewan, and Manitoba are sent to the federal prison in Edmonton or the one provincial women's prison in each province; yet those three provinces have fifteen provincial and twelve federal prisons for men. The numbers are similar across Canada. Thus, in addition to the disruption of caregiver continuity initiated by a parental prison sentence, most children of incarcerated women will be unable to visit their mothers, frequently because of the long travelling distances. In their 1993 study, Bloom and Steinhart reported that distance between the child and the correctional facility in the U.S. was the main reason given by mothers for infrequent or non-visitation by their children (Bloom and Steinhart 1993, 26). Cunningham and Baker (2003) also found it to be a significant factor in Canada.

There is evidence that disruptions of the parent-child relationship are predictive of later violent behaviour of children (Hawkins, Farrington, and Catalono 1998). Moreover, research shows that children suffer intensely from their parents' incarceration (Hostetter and Jinnah 1993). The children suffer from separation anxiety, expressed through isolating behaviours and sleep disorders, as well as displays of aggression and excessive anger. They experience other emotional problems, including feelings of fear, abandonment, shame, and guilt. Additionally, children whose mothers have been incarcerated are subject to peer ridicule and mockery, exacerbating their feelings of loneliness and alienation (McGowan and Blumenthal 1978). And they have an increased risk of lower academic performance, truancy, gang participation, and substance abuse (Stanton, S. 1980; Baunach 1985; Gabel, S. 1992; Dressel and Barnhill 1994; Seymour 1998; Ascione and Dixson 2002).

'I don't talk'

'I don't talk about it.
What would you say?
My mother killed my dad?
I tell them my aunt is my foster mom.'

Boy, age 13

In view of the data, it should come as no surprise that substantially higher levels of delinquency occur among children of incarcerated parents, compared with other children (West and Farrington 1977; Gabel, S. 1992; Moses 1995; Rowe and Farrington 1997). One study found that children of inmates are five to six times more likely to be incarcerated than peers without incarcerated parents (Bloom 1995, 60–8). A recent study by Joseph Murray and David Farrington (2005, 1269–78), using data from the Cambridge Study in Delinquent Development, one of the most respected longitudinal studies that has followed children since the 1960s, found that children with an incarcerated parent were 3.3 times more likely than their peers to be convicted between the ages of 17 and 25.

Most alarmingly, the number of children affected by incarceration is increasing in Canada – particularly for children of incarcerated mothers. CSC research on the number of women incarcerated between 1981 and 1998 (serving sentences over two years) indicates that there are approximately one and a half times as many women incarcerated now as then. By 2009, CSC anticipates that the population of incarcerated women will have increased by 31 per cent (CSC 2001, 6).

3. Female Prisoners and Their Children

The profile of a female offender and the reasons for which she is incarcerated are important factors in the composite of circumstances that affect her children. More women than men have incomes below the poverty line. Indeed, the rate of poverty for single female-headed families is higher today (56 per cent) than it was thirty years ago, when the Royal Commission on the Status of Women issued its groundbreaking report calling for change (Townson 2000, 2).

For women who are the sole caregivers for their children, it is virtually impossible to raise children on a low-paying job. They are often forced out of employment completely, and onto social assistance. Women consequently face the prospect of cycling through welfare, poverty, and the erosion of employment skills while absent from the labour market for a period of time. They are then further impoverished by the denial of job opportunities. For example, in British Columbia, where the minimum wage in June 2006 was eight dollars an hour – which was among the highest in Canada (Government of Manitoba 2006) – a single parent with two children living in Kamloops or Victoria would have to work over 65 hours per week, every week of the year, at minimum wage, in order to reach the poverty line of $27,386 (Canadian Council on Social Development, 2006). Women on welfare in BC are

Source: Lincoln Clarkes from the Heroines Series, portraits of women in the Downtown Eastside of Vancouver, 1998–1999.
Credit: Lincoln Clarkes/Heroines series (www.anvilpress.com). Reprinted by permission.

even more disadvantaged, and live well below the subsistence level. As of January 2005, a woman in Kamloops or Victoria with two children would receive $10,566.96 per annum – a full $16,819 below the poverty line (Government of British Columbia 2005).

Single-parent families live in the midst of numerous stressful and disruptive circumstances. Children who live in a household with one parent are considerably more likely to live below the poverty line than are children who live in a household with two parents (Moore and Halle 2000). In addition, single parents move more often than intact families

(Caldwell 1998, 7–17), and studies show that children who move frequently are more likely to have problems at school. Moves are even more difficult if accompanied by other significant changes in the children's lives, such as death, divorce, loss of family income, or the need to change schools (AACFAS 1999). Even when their mothers are employed, children of single mothers suffer economic disadvantages because women in Canada still earn less than men (Statistics Canada 2006c, 135). Weak social supports and programs further erode a parent's ability to cope with stress, while highly stressed parents tend to be psychologically unavailable to their children. According to the American Psychological Association (2004), single-parent families deal with many more pressures and potential problems than the nuclear family does.

The environment of children in single-parent households often correlates with a life of poverty and crowded dwellings, conditions that have been demonstrated to be significant predictors of juvenile criminal involvement (Weatherburn and Lind 1997); these same factors frequently correlate with parental substance misuse. The incidence of prenatal exposure to drugs or alcohol among children of prisoners appears high. In her 1992 Children of Offenders study, Denise Johnston found that 'over half of the children of women who had been arrested, and 77% of the children of currently or previously incarcerated women, had been exposed prenatally to drugs or alcohol' (Gabel and Johnston 1995, 68–9). Because of their lower body weight compared to men, women experience a slower dilution of drugs within their bodies. Typically, increased drug concentrations result in related heart disease, hypertension, gastrointestinal hemorrhage, anemia, and malnutrition, all of which can further affect fetal development. Parental substance abuse therefore multiplies the dangerous factors already affecting a child. When mothers go to prison, the effects on their children can be profound, and the consequences more severe than for the children of male prisoners (Richards and McWilliams 1996; Caddle and Crisp 1997). Maternal incarceration, specifically the abrupt and prolonged separation of a mother from her children, has been found to be detrimental to both mother and children (McGowan and Blumenthal 1978; Henriques 1982; A.M. Stanton 1978; Hunter 1985; Fessler 1991, Fletcher, Shaver, and Moon 1992). Disruption of the attachment bond between mother and child is particularly detrimental to children between the ages of six months and four years (Fuller 1993, 41–7). As well, it is recognized that the impact of the separation of mother and child is particularly profound for older children (Johnston 1995, 68).

These effects can be long lasting or temporary, depending on the child's age, the relationship of the mother and the child, the caretaker's relationship with the child, and the way in which the mother's incarceration has (or has not) been explained to the child.

The experience of parental incarceration is only one of many factors that may influence children of prisoners. The literature suggests that the children of incarcerated parents may have been exposed to other risks, such as poverty, parental substance abuse, or mental health problems prior to their parent's incarceration. How children respond to those circumstances is also affected by their personal resilience, where they are placed when their parent is incarcerated, the nature of their relationship with the substitute caregiver, and the multiplicity of traumas. The most important point is that parental incarceration serves to flag the risks and the accumulation of factors most likely to plague children of prisoners in the future.

'I know'

'I know I could be somebody. I want to go to school ... It's my sixth one.'

Girl, age 10

A strong social bias against women who have gone to prison presumes that they cannot be good parents (Aboriginal Justice Implementation Commission 1999; Dickon 2005). Nor does identifying children of incarcerated parents assist in identifying all the children who will be affected. As Loeber and Dishion argue, 'the very fact that a father possesses a criminal record, one established before the birth of a child, will enhance the child's prospect of developing his or her own antisocial career' (1983, 94).

4. Canadian Solutions

Despite being an 'advanced industrial society,' Canada imprisons people at a notably high rate. In 2004 and 2005, Canada's rate of imprisonment was 129 inmates per 100,000 population (Statistics Canada 2006a, 8), making it one of the highest incarcerators in the Western world. Canada's rate of incarceration is 40 per cent higher than those of

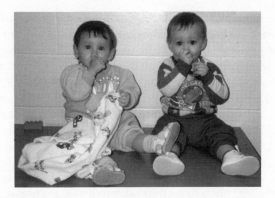

Source: CircleVision.org
Credit: Tom Bottolene/CircleVision.org. Reprinted by permission.

most Western European countries. Iceland has the lowest rate in this group of nations, at 39 per 100,000 population, or 30 per cent of Canada's rate (Walmsley 2005, 5). Canadians, however, tend to compare themselves to their neighbour to the south – the country with the highest incarceration rate in the world, with almost six times Canada's rate – rather than to the traditional benchmarks of other Western democracies.

As most incarcerated people are jailed for relatively short periods, the number in prison at any one time gives a better picture of that part of the justice system. On an average day in Canada in 2004–5, there were approximately 152,600 adults in custody or under community supervision – a higher rate than a decade ago. Of these, some 35,098 per day were under some kind of community supervision order, such as probation, or some other form of conditional release; the remaining 54,410 adults were held on remand (Statistics Canada 2006a, 1–2).

The same study reports that nearly 357,200 people were admitted to correctional services in 2004–5 in Canada – more than the combined populations of Prince Edward Island, Nunavut, the Yukon, and the Northwest Territories (Statistics Canada 2005c, 1).

No one knows for certain how many children have incarcerated parents, or how many children have been affected by incarceration. The question has only been considered within the last decade in other countries, and more recently, and only partially, in Canada. It is, however, an important question, and one to which it is possible to give a fairly clear, if approximate, answer.

As previously cited, in 2004–5, 150,024 people were imprisoned in Canada. Given their incidence of having children (56 per cent of men, and 67 per cent of women), and their birth rates (2 children for men and 2.4 for women), it is possible to do a rough calculation predicting the number of children they have: 173,605 children (see Seymour 1998, 469–94).[2]

Now consider that 10.93 per cent of Canadians have a criminal record.[3] If children of prisoners have at least a 3.3 times greater likelihood of incarceration than their peers, then it is possible to predict that 62,498 children will follow their parents to prison; in other words, that 85,470 parents will be replaced in prison by 74 per cent of their children.

Even more disturbing, however, is the fact that almost every incarcerated woman gives birth to a child who will replace her in prison. It is here that the legacy of parental gender is truly expressed: because more women than men have children, and because they have more children, women will replace themselves in the prison system at a higher rate.

The grim reality is that approximately 206,051 children in Canada under the age of 19 have a parent who has been to prison.[4]

Malcolm Gladwell, in *The Tipping Point* (2000), describes how even the slight manipulation of one factor in a complex system can radically change outcomes. He uses the example of a flu epidemic, in which the strain of flu is contagious for 24 hours and carries a 2 per cent probability of transmission per contact. Each person carrying the flu virus meets, on average, fifty people per day. In this scenario, the disease is in equilibrium: 1,000 flu carriers will meet 50,000 people each day and infect 2 per cent of them, or 1,000 people. But if the variable changes slightly, the outcome will change greatly. If each person meets 10 per cent more people per day (for example, in busy pre-Christmas shopping), the slight change in this one variable – only five more people – affects the infection rate exponentially. The number of infected people doubles every eight days, and the flu-suffering population will continue to double until the epidemic is controlled by intervention to reduce one of the parameters of contagion. Changes made at the 'tipping point' can have enormous impact because it is a moment of great sensitivity. A 10 per cent *decrease* in the number of people becoming flu victims (from 50 to 45) would reduce the number of victims from 1,000 to 478, and at that rate the flu would die out in a couple weeks. Alternatively, if each person with flu was infecting 70 people per day, a drop of five contacts from 70 to 65 (or any number above that required to maintain equilibrium), would allow the flu to continue spreading, and the epidemic would not end.

Table 13.1
How many children of prisoners incarcerated in 2004–5 will enter the Criminal Justice System?

Number of children with incarcerated mothers:	
Approximate number of incarcerated women (7.62% of total)	11,430
Number of women in prison with children (67%)	7,658
× 2.4 (average number of children per incarcerated woman)	18,380
(a) Percentage of Canadians with criminal record	10.93%
Increased rate of incidence for children of prisoners	36%
(b) Number of children likely to acquire a criminal record	6,617
(36% of 18,380)	
Thus, the replacement ratio for female offenders by their children is 86.4% (6,617children with criminal records born from 7,658 women)	
Number of children with incarcerated fathers:	
Approximate number of incarcerated men	138,594
Number of men in prison with children (56%)	77,612
× 2.0 (average number of children per incarcerated man)	155,225
(c) Number of children likely to acquire a criminal record (36% of 155,225)	55,881
Thus, the replacement ratio for male offenders by their children is 72% (55,881 children with criminal records born from 77,612 men)	

As previously noted, Canadians have more than a one-in-ten likelihood of having a criminal record (10.93 per cent). In reality, however, certain groups are significantly overrepresented. Aboriginal people constitute only 3 per cent of the population, but 20 per cent of incarcerated males, and 31 per cent of incarcerated females within provincial and territorial prisons (Statistics Canada 2006c, 171). Aboriginal people are almost 18.5 per cent of the total federal prison population; Aboriginal women represent 32 per cent of women in federal prisons (Sapers 2006, 1). Blacks make up 2 per cent of the population, and yet represent 6 per cent of federally incarcerated inmates (CSC 2004b, 29).

Add the factor of a parent incarcerated and, unless changes are made, it is possible that the number of inmates who are second-generation prisoners will continue to grow substantially. For women, the small variable increase in the number who are parents, coupled with their higher birth rate, makes a huge difference. Crime replicates itself through the children of male prisoners at the rate of 72 per cent of the population base, while female prisoners replicate their number at the rate of 86.4 per cent of the population base. This does not even consider prisoners coming from the rest of the population.

Next, consider that Aboriginal women have a birth rate of 1.5 times that of the average Canadian female (Statistics Canada 2005d, 25), and it is possible to see that this small variable increase will result in substantially increased numbers of Aboriginal children entering the criminal justice system and, moreover, subsequently being replaced on more than a one-to-one ratio by their own children. Using the previous formula, and factoring in Aboriginal women, who make up approximately 31 per cent of all women provincially and federally incarcerated, and among whom the birth rate is 1.5 times the Canadian average, we arrive at an exponential replacement rate of 103 per cent.

According to a 2006 report from the office of the Correctional Investigator, 'While the federal inmate population in Canada actually went down 12.5% between 1996 and 2004, the number of First Nations people in federal institutions increased by 21.7%. This is a 34% difference between Aboriginal and non-Aboriginal inmates. Moreover, the number of federally incarcerated First Nations women increased a staggering 74.2% over this period' (Sapers 2006, 1–2). This reported increase conforms to the replacement model of incarcerated prisoners by their children. And this increase will continue to occur unless changes are made.

Using Gladwell's analogy of the tipping point, assisting the children of women prisoners can have substantive impact because the number of women is relatively small, but forecast to grow because of their higher birth rate and their frequency of being parents. Further, the issue of children of prisoners is largely a gender issue – involving incarcerated mothers or caregivers of children whose fathers are incarcerated.

Incarcerating women for the sorts of crimes the majority of them commit and are incarcerated for, such as a variety of property offences, serves neither the Canadian public nor their children. The Canadian public is no safer because of their incarceration. Nor does this incarceration serve any other purpose. Wherever individuals stand on the question of prisons, their position is likely premised either on a concern for public safety or on a belief that a prison sentence will positively change the offender's behaviour. If the intended effect is deterrence – to stop or slow the rate of crime in the community – it is ineffective, because the sentencing of the women, as the figures above show, is effectively increasing future crime. If the intended result is rehabilitation, it is likewise ineffective. Most women commit minor crimes and serve short sentences. These short sentences provide no opportunity for a woman to acquire the skills that would allow her to address problems of education, mental health, addiction, unemployment, and other factors that

Table 13.2
Aboriginal female prisoners and their children

Approximate number of incarcerated women	11,430
31% Aboriginal Women	3,543
Number of Aboriginal women in prison with children (67%)	2,374
Number of non-Aboriginal women	9,056
Number of non-Aboriginal women in prison with children (67%)	6068
(a) Number of children per incarcerated woman (from table 13.1)	18,380
(b) The 2,374 Aboriginal women have twice the birth rate of non-Aboriginal women	
(c) Equation for determining number of children of incarcerated Aboriginal women: $(2,374 \times 1.5B)$ (birth rate) + $(9,056 \times B)$ = 18,380 children where B (birth rate) = 1.908817	
(d) Increased rate of incidence for children of prisoners	36%
(e) Average number of children of Aboriginal prisoners	6,797
(f) Number of Aboriginal children likely to acquire a criminal record (36%)	2,447
The replacement ratio for Aboriginal female offenders by their children is 103.1%	

have led her to incarceration. It is also worth noting that studies on children who were provided with help or intervention all reported better outcomes for the children who remained in the family home – even where there was substances abuse, neglect, or physical abuse present – than for those children who were removed from their home (NCASA 1999; USDH 1999).

This is where the theory of the tipping point suggests strategies for intervention that could contribute to Canadians' long-term goal of safe communities and improved life outcomes for the children of prisoners. Some are relatively straightforward alternatives such as house arrest or community service rather than incarceration for short sentences (for example, less than thirty days). These strategies would make a substantial difference and could, in fact, reduce the number of children affected by 31 per cent.[5]

Other strategies that lower the likelihood of criminal involvement for the children of prisoners can also make a difference in arresting the 'contagion of incarceration' – an epidemic cycle that sees prisons being planned for Canadian children not yet born.[6]

These strategies involve the management of prisons to mediate some of the more detrimental aspects of imprisonment for children, such as stopping body searches of children visiting their parents, allowing children and parents to speak on the telephone, and providing visiting space that encourages parent-child relationships. Significant research speaks to the benefit of parental contact and the impact of systemic barriers to children visiting their parents (Bloom and Steinhart 1993; Gabel and Johnston 1995; Caddle and Crisp 1997; Cunningham and Baker 2003; Blanchard 2005).

Additional resources could allow programs to assist parents to increase their parenting skills and support their children from prison. This is particularly important for the children of women, since the majority of female prisoners intend to return to parenting their children upon release.

'I wonder'

'I wonder what my life would have been if I had normal parents.'

Boy, age 9, both parents imprisoned

---

5. The Financial Costs

Imprisoning people is expensive. According to Statistics Canada, in 2002–3 federal, provincial, and territorial governments spent $2.7 billion on imprisoning adults (Statistics Canada 2005a, 1). In 2004–5 that figure had climbed to $2.8 billion (Statistics Canada 2006a, 1).

The federal government's figures offer further insight. In 2002–3, the CSC planned to spend approximately $1.5 billion on federal corrections, that is, for people serving sentences of over two years (CSC 2002, 25). According to CSC, the average cost of maintaining a male federal prisoner in 2002–3 was about $176 per day or $64,464 per year. The cost of maintaining a female prisoner for the same time was about $464 per day or $169,399 per year (CSC 2004c, 14). Clearly, the smaller number of female prisoners, about 5 per cent of the total population, does not provide economies of scale, as is the case with men.

Thus, it took roughly the entire combined taxes of five Canadian families of two or more persons to pay for the incarceration of one man for one year with Correctional Service Canada. It took the combined personal income taxes of roughly thirteen families of two or more to incarcerate one woman for one year[7] (Statistics Canada 2004, 28). Put another way, in 2002–3 alone, the $2.7 billion spent on imprisoning adults required the combined personal income tax revenue of Newfoundland, Nova Scotia, Prince Edward Island, and the Yukon for those years (Statistics Canada 2003b, 31–2). With the predicted increase in prison population anticipated under current legislation, the costs can only be anticipated to increase as more individuals enter the criminal justice system.

Jack's troubled career: The costs to society of a young person in trouble (National Crime Prevention Strategy 2001) traces the costs of providing for one fictional (but typical) youth from his early years through adolescence. A pattern of troublesome behaviours is calculated as his mother, child welfare, school, and the criminal justice system struggle to cope with Jack's increasingly challenging and rowdy behaviour, shoplifting, and vandalism, resulting in Jack's entering into the care of the child welfare authority and undergoing periods of incarceration. By the time he reaches the age of seventeen, the care for Jack totals $511,500 – and Jack himself is now a young offender.

If even one-third of the previously estimated 206,051 children currently under nineteen and with a parent in prison (or previously in prison) followed Jack's path, the cost can be estimated at almost $35 billion by the time those children reach age seventeen.

Canada, one of the highest incarcerators in the world, is investing in a solution that is disproportionate and building a future prison population, while at the same time failing significant numbers of its children even as it invests resources into them.

The legacy of incarceration for children of prisoners commits Canada to costs for years to come within the child welfare, education, and criminal justice systems. Thus the question is one of allocation, since these monies must remain on the table in order to support the incarceration of those already convicted and those to come.

Other countries use different means. A number of studies have examined this question. The most recent, published in November 2006 by the Crime and Society Foundation (Downes and Hansen 2006), examined research from across the United States, and then replicated it across eighteen countries in the Organisation for Economic Co-operation and Development (OECD). The study found that there is an intimate link between a country's amount of welfare spending and level of imprisonment. The seven countries with the highest rate of imprisonment have the lowest rates of welfare spending, while the eight with the highest welfare have the lowest imprisonment rates. The overwhelming indication is that welfare cutbacks imply penal expansionism, and the

Source: Correctional Service Canada Photofile http://www.csc-scc.gc.ca/text/photofile/
index_e.shtml.
Credit: Correctional Service Canada. Reprinted by permission.

relationship between the two has become stronger over the past fifteen
years. This can be seen most clearly in the U.S., where the trend towards mass imprisonment over the past two decades has been accompanied by ever-greater restrictions on welfare rights for the poorest
families. In a 2004 study of the fifteen countries of the European Union,
Hanns Von Hofer found that, following a post-war increase, crime rates
fell in the Scandinavian countries. By the 1990s, this decrease had resulted in stabilized theft rates, the lowest rate of personal victimization
in the EU, and similar rates of homicide and other crimes to those of
other EU countries. The Scandinavian countries are also characterized
by relatively low rates of police to citizens, high rates of crimes solved
by police, above-average conviction rates, the imposition of fines in a
high proportion of criminal cases, relatively low prison populations,
and short periods of incarceration.

The author argues that shifts towards punishment, 'getting tough' on
crime and criminals, and political frameworks that believe individuals
determine whether or not they fail, and that the 'welfare society' produces individuals with no incentive to raise themselves out of poverty,

will not decrease the incidence of crime. 'It will with certainty increase the size of prison populations and is also very likely to increase the public's feelings of insecurity' (Von Hofer 2004, 162).

Thus, it is clear that while the solutions we have chosen fail to take into account the generational legacy of those we imprison, they also will not improve the lives of Canadians. If our goal is to prevent crime, other avenues are required. If Canada is to live up to its (now largely mythical) standards of universality and inclusivity, it needs to recognize children of prisoners as invisible victims of our correctional system and legitimize their problems through the provision of appropriate services.

6. Recognizing Children of Prisoners

Over a period of three months (September to December 2002), the author conducted a series of interviews with child welfare policy advisors for each Canadian province and territory (Bayes 2002). These interviews revealed that no province or territory in Canada keeps any statistics on the number of children under guardianship care who have a parent in prison. No province or territory officially recognizes the problems for children related to parental incarceration. None of them recognizes that the child of an incarcerated parent is at increased risk of criminal justice involvement. None provides any training for social workers regarding the risk profile for these children.

Within Canada, the children of prisoners and the risk they face is minimally acknowledged by the CSC and the National Crime Prevention Council (funded by the Department of Justice). There are a number of small programs funded; however, there are none outside the criminal justice system in the domains of education, medicine, and child welfare, where the services to children are provided (ibid.). Outside of the correctional system, the risk to children of prisoners has not been recognized.

Countries such as Australia, India, the UK, and the U.S. formally recognize the children of prisoners, and provide funded programs and systemic supports, including educational strategies and manuals for teachers, and courses on the subject in university curricula for teachers and social workers. Australia also considers the caregiver role for prisoners and their children when determining appropriate sentencing sanctions.

According to the report summarizing a criminal justice round table on youth justice renewal in February 2000,

There is a major problem group out there that's impacting our penal systems and it's children of offenders. In Calgary there is a school with 240 children, all under twelve; 60% of those children are children of offenders. When they looked at statistics from CSC, they found that 59.7% of adult incarcerates are children of adult offenders. Somehow these kids have to be reached. This is a group that we should really work at finding because the likelihood is that 6 out of 10 are going to end up in the system. At Chaudière House, quite a few young offenders are children of offenders. There are statistics that show that young offenders are over 50% children of offenders. We need to find a way to address that target group, because that's the feeding ground apparently for a majority of future offenders. (Ruest 2000, 4)

For over twenty-five years, there has been research conducted regarding prisoners and their families. However, the focus has remained on how to support and enable released prisoners in making successful transitions to the community. It is only in the past ten or fifteen years that the needs of the children of prisoners have been seriously discussed; and that knowledge has not infiltrated the Canadian ethos within the educational, medical, child welfare, and correctional systems. Nor has this knowledge reached the voluntary sector, where children come in contact with recreational, cultural, mentoring, faith and child-development programs and services. These avenues have been shown to be particularly ameliorative for the factors directly related to criminal involvement. As the Ontario experience reported in the Early Years Study (Mustard et al. 2000) has shown, the transfer of understanding within the policy machine of government is a difficult task, given the nature of government departments and the politics of society. It is extraordinarily difficult for governments to establish policies in areas that cut across government departments. Many of the service programs of these departments are involved in important remedial functions (services for children with difficulties), but they are not directly involved in preventative activities. Integration of these functions at the community level is sometimes very difficult (Mustard et al. 2000, 76–9).

As governments represent all citizens of their constituency, the services they provide for children are, of necessity, broadly based. The responsibility of caring for children is left to their parents, except where the child is at imminent risk. Governments design programs and services upon models of universality to counteract or prevent poor life outcomes that are deemed to go against the social good – for example, by establishing programs that reduce physical and social risks so as to allow children a healthy start in life. These programs have included prenatal screening, nutrition, and recreation and community programs for disadvantaged youth. Yet these programs, with the exception of those for disadvantaged youth, are available equally to children or their parents across income classes. However, as Dr Dan Offord of the Canadian Centre for Children at Risk has often stated, not all groups of Canadian children or their parents participate in and benefit equally from universal programs: disadvantaged children consistently participate at substantially lower rates than their middle-class counterparts, and thus are not afforded the protective ameliorative benefits (Offord, Lipman, and Duku 1998). Thus, the provision of programs is not enough.

Voluntary sector organizations (VSOs) do not operate within this model. While government is concerned at the macro level, the voluntary sector has the specific ability to focus its attention and resources at the micro level. More importantly, the voluntary sector can interact with people without the mandate of legislation. VSOs provide programs across the continuum of service, support, advocacy and fundraising in order to achieve better outcomes. What is more, they can seek out their clients: they are not founded upon a public guarantee of delivering access for all, but rather upon the recognition that access does not exist for all. Governments may try to ensure that there are no barriers for those in need; but the voluntary sector recognizes that access sometimes must be adjudicated in order to reach those in need who may be entitled to support but are not receiving it, or for those whom governments don't recognize as being in need of service. Sometimes the courts have been used to ensure that privilege is not secured through the denial of rights to others.

The children of prisoners deserve more than the proverbial 'snowball's chance in hell.' The systemic issues they and their parents have faced, and continue to face, exacerbate their struggles: the institutionalization of poverty through minimum wages set far below the poverty level, welfare rates set below levels at which people can survive, and child poverty rates that are higher than sixteen of the twenty-three richest countries in the world (UNICEF 2005, 4).

In addressing the children of prisoners and dismantling the multigenerational legacy of criminal justice involvement, we must take a two-pronged approach, involving the criminal justice system and government services along with the voluntary sector. Leading the social innovation and adaptation required should be organizations such as the Elizabeth Fry and John Howard societies, which understand the need for convergence of social assistance, child welfare, criminal justice, and social policy, and have the knowledge to assist others to adapt their practices to recognize and assist the children of prisoners.

Federal and provincial governments must live up to the United Nations Convention on the Rights of the Child, to which Canada is a signatory, and ensure such measures as a child's right to know their parent, have contact with them, and for the child's best interests to be considered in decisions affecting them. The judiciary must:

- sentence more convicted offenders to community alternatives (particularly persons who would otherwise be incarcerated for short periods, or for whom there are no concerns of grievous harm to others)
- consider parental roles and responsibilities at the time of conviction (weighing the separation of parent and child and the creation of a generational legacy against any perceived benefit of incarceration)

The correctional system must:

- enable parents and children to have phone contact without charging the prisoner prohibitively high phone charges per minute
- provide visiting space that is developmentally appropriate for children of various ages and that allows a more normal interaction between parent and child
- alter entrance procedures to the prison for visiting children, such as body searches, pat-downs, and the restriction of food items, so as not to traumatize or intrude upon a child's sense of self, and allow the child to feel relatively at ease
- provide parents and children with family counselling in order to facilitate offender re-entry into the family and to reduce potential parent-child conflict created by the child's experience of parental incarceration

Government services must be sure that:

- universities and colleges incorporate a curriculum about the children of prisoners for social workers, teachers, probation

officers, criminologists, lawyers, and youth and child workers, and
that members of the judiciary, legislature, and parliament are
educated
- foster-parent training programs are developed
- child-welfare authorities provide adequate resources to kinship
  families caring for the children of a family member (comparable to
  those received by non-relative foster families caring for children)
- parental incarceration is considered a risk factor for children in
  planning for care management by child welfare authorities
- where necessary, funding be available to enable children to travel
  periodically to prison to visit their parents
- school guidance counsellors recognize current or previous parental
  incarceration as an indicator of likely lower academic achievement
  by a child and provide additional support and tutoring where
  possible
- residential addiction services in the community accept women and
  their children together to enable women to seek treatment while
  maintaining custody of their children
- adequately funded programs for Aboriginal women and children
  living on reserves are provided by Indian and Northern Affairs
  Canada; programs for urban Aboriginal women and their families
  must be increased, and the Department of Indian Affairs must fund
  services off-reserve
- the cycle of poverty, addiction, homelessness, crime, and incarceration is broken; provincial and federal governments must fund
  specialized agencies such as the John Howard and Elizabeth Fry
  societies so they can provide support to prisoners after they
  complete their sentences. Currently these organizations are not
  funded for this purpose, even though ex-prisoners need help to
  rebuild their lives with the specialized expertise these agencies
  offer. Ex-prisoners often have multiple issues compounded by
  being institutionalized, criminalized, and marginalized. Many
  organizations will not work with the multiple complexities of
  clients, particularly those who have a history of violent acts or
  active mental illness, addiction, and infectious diseases
- funding be reallocated from imprisonment to sentences in the
  community for those people who pose no community risk. These
  offenders may then serve their sentences in the community and be
  provided assistance, while beginning to renew or build skills to
  succeed

The voluntary sector must:

- provide programs for the children of prisoners, particularly arts, sports, and community programs with mentorship and child-development opportunities that make allowance for family instability and changing locations
- develop a process of follow-up contact for children enrolled in programs who attend sporadically to encourage their participation
- provide single mothers with respite care and community support programs that address their isolation and increased stress
- ensure that parent-support help lines understand the issues related to women, crime, and their children

Citizens participating in social justice organizations must:

- advocate for minimum-security prisoners to serve their sentences in halfway houses (which, by law, meet the standards of minimum-security prisons) rather than prison if the offender is not a risk to the community
- advocate for effective services and programs for Aboriginal people and for parents affected by poverty, crime, and generational issues
- expand diversity and anti-racism training to include training on the impact of poverty, racism, and colonization of Aboriginal peoples in Canada

Basic interventions are required to restore the implicit promise of Canadian citizenship that equal access to services exists and that all children can grow and advance according to their abilities rather than through station or privilege. The expertise exists in Canada to address the issues. The solutions required are not novel. We need to identify the children of prisoners in order to inform the government and the voluntary sector about their lives, and develop programs to meet their needs and those of their parents.

NOTES

1 All quotations in text boxes are from confidential sources.
2 According to Statistics Canada (2006a), in 2004 and 2005, 357,200 adults were incarcerated. Twenty-three per cent (78,584) were sentenced to

provincial or territorial responsibility (less than two-year sentences) and 20 per cent (71,440) to federal sentences. Of those sentenced to custody, 10 per cent of provincial or territorial prisoners and 5 per cent of federal prisoners were women. The average rate of women incarcerated was therefore 7.62 per cent of all prisoners.

3   The RCMP Criminal Records Division is cited as advising there were 3,282,193 Canadians with a criminal record in 2001 (Public Safety and Emergency Preparedness Canada 2004, 99). The 2001 Census of Canada estimated the population of Canada at 30,007,094 (Statistics Canada 2002). Thus 10.93 per cent of all Canadians have a criminal record.

4   A rough estimate was calculated using the same information previously cited on the 2001 Canadian population and the number of Canadians with a criminal record (see note 2). The incidence of those with a conviction was apportioned 19 per cent to women (Quann 2003, 10). The incidence of parenthood and the number of children that men and women have changes over time. However, for the purpose of gaining a perspective, the conservative birth rate of 2001 was applied to those with a criminal record in Canada.

Secondly, not all people with a criminal record will go to prison. According to Statistics Canada (2003a, 1), approximately 21 per cent of people involved in the correctional system were imprisoned. Lastly, using the same data source, it is possible to calculate from the 9 per cent of women sentenced to provincial or territorial prisons, the 5 per cent sentenced to federal penitentiaries (ibid., 11), and the Offender Count in the Correctional System (ibid., 3) that the average rate for incarceration for women is 6.8 per cent of the total prisoner population for the fiscal year ending 31 March 2002. Thus, the total number of children can be calculated.

With the additional information from the 2001 Census that 7,778,865 children were aged nineteen and under (Statistics Canada 2001), it is possible to calculate a rough estimate of the number of minor children today who are affected – an astonishing 206,051, or 2.6 per cent of all Canadian children!

5   An estimate was calculated based on the fact that 22 per cent of those incarcerated served provincial or territorial sentences; that 10 per cent of those individuals were women (Statistics Canada 2006a, 1), of whom 70 per cent served sentences of less than 30 days versus 54 per cent of men who served sentences of less than 30 days (ibid., 10). The formula presented in table 13.1 was used to determine the revised number of children, and their reduction numerically and in proportion.

Table 13.3
Calculation of total number of children

	Men	Women	Total
Canadians with a criminal record	2,658,576	623,617	3,282,193
Numbers in prison (21% of those with a record: men, 93.2%; women, 6.8%)	642,391	46,870	689,261
Total number of children in Canada aged 19 and under			7,778,865
Rate of incidence in total population; number of children/Canadian population (30,007,094)			0.259234200
Total prisoners with children (men: 0.56 x.642,391; women: 0.67 × 46,870)	359,739	31,403	
Number of children (2.4 women; 2.0 men)	719,478	75,367	794,844
Number of children aged 19 and under (based upon Canadian population distribution rate)	186,513	19,538	206,051

6 In a Canadian Senate debate of 4 May 2006 on the expansion of prison facilities, the Hon. Lorna Milne, Deputy Chair of the Standing Senate Committee on Legal and Constitutional Affairs, cited a Correctional Service of Canada estimate published during the 2004 election campaign that placed extra prison spending at somewhere between $5 billion and $11.5 billion over the next ten years, depending on the number and types of facilities needed. Milne also cited Simon Fraser University criminologist Neil Boyd, who estimates that up to twenty-three new prisons will have to be built in order to meet an expected influx of prisoners.

7 These amounts are calculated using CSC figures for the average cost of incarceration for men and women, divided by the average personal income taxes collected for families of two or more for 2002. Canadian families of two persons or more paid an estimated $12,800 on average in income taxes in 2002 (Statistics Canada 2004, 28).

14 Public Dialogue: Bridging the Gap between Knowledge and Wisdom

JACQUIE DALE

In recent times, the concept of dialogue has had great resonance. It occurs today in many different settings and contexts: personal relationships, labour relations, community development, organizational behaviour, management and policy-making – to mention just a few.[1]

This essay will explore the concept of *public dialogue*: its meaning and use, and its connection to the ideas of citizen engagement and democracy. It also will explore the social and political malaise to which public dialogue is called on to respond, and offer some reflections on how well the process of public dialogue can meet this challenge. To do this, the essay offers three concrete approaches to citizen engagement that use public dialogue processes. The essay concludes by examining some of the opportunities and challenges in implementing public dialogue and the roles various societal actors can play, with particular emphasis on the voluntary sector.

Throughout the essay, I will make reference to my own work with the Canadian Council for International Cooperation, and more recently with One World Inc. Much of this work has focused on deliberative dialogue: a structured, essentially values-based form of dialogue that is very useful in exploring various approaches to a given issue. Two other important forms of dialogue are also examined: Citizens' Panels and participatory budgeting.

1. What Is Public Dialogue?

According to the Oxford English Dictionary, dialogue is 'a conversation carried on between two or more persons ... a verbal interchange of thought.' To the ancient Greeks, the literary form of conversation known as *dialogos* was essentially a debate – an attempt to reach agreement about an experience or statement or hypothesis; and it is in this sense that Plato uses the word in the seminal exchanges of ideas between Socrates and his followers.

However, Plato, in a sense, leaves plenty of room for an open-ended meaning of dialogue, for his philosophical give-and-take seldom reaches a firm conclusion on any topic. And perhaps this did not escape the notice of the physicist and philosopher David Bohm, when he proposed a daring new formulation of the meaning of dialogue:

> *Logos* means 'the word,' or in our case we would think of 'the meaning of the word.' And *dia* means 'through' ... The picture or image that this derivation suggests is of a stream of meaning flowing among and through and between us. This will make possible a flow of meaning in the whole group, out of which may emerge some new understanding. It's something new, which may not have been in the starting point at all. It's something creative. And this shared meaning is the 'glue' or 'cement' that holds people and societies together.
>
> The object of a dialogue is to listen to everybody's opinions, to suspend them, and to see what all that means ... Dialogue is the collective way of opening up judgments and assumptions. (Bohm 1992, 16)

We may think, therefore, of dialogue as being a shared inquiry – a way of thinking and reflecting together (Isaacs 1999). It is something we do *with* others, not *to* others: a conversation in which people build on each other's ideas, listen to and make an effort to understand what each person is saying, and in so doing explore the assumptions underlying the participants' ideas. (See appendix 14.A for contrasting meanings of dialogue and debate, a word whose root sense is 'to beat down.') It can be a dynamic, exciting, and empowering activity, but it takes discipline. Yankelovich (1999), who talks about the 'magic' of dialogue, suggests three principles that are essential for genuine dialogue:

1. *Establish equality among participants and exclude all coercive influences.* In genuine dialogue, there is no room for arm-twisting or threat of consequences once people leave the room – no hint of sanctions for expressing unpopular or politically incorrect views. There is a ground rule in dialogue that covers this aspect: 'In dialogue, everyone is an equal. Leave status and stereotypes at the door' (see appendix 14.B: 'Ground Rules for Dialogue').

2. *Listen with empathy.* The ability to think someone else's thoughts and feel someone else's feelings is crucial to dialogue. This doesn't mean that dialogue is necessarily emotional (although emotions are certainly not discouraged), but it does mean that participants are listening in order to understand, and are listening with understanding. 'Maintain an open mind and listen carefully to others' is a ground rule that helps to reinforce this idea.

3. *Bring assumptions into the open.* Often when we talk to others, we skim the surface of our ideas. We do not delve deeply into our thoughts in an attempt to really understand what we ourselves are saying, and why we are saying it. Dialogue takes 'deep dives' in which participants uncover the assumptions and values behind their views and perspectives. Here is the ground rule I use to help people remember this principle: 'Ask clarifying questions. Help to develop one another's ideas.'

To these three principles, I would add a fourth, which is particularly relevant to public dialogue:

4. *Encourage a diversity of perspectives.* In my experience of facilitating dialogues, the most helpful exchanges occur when there is a diversity of people and perspectives in the room. In part, this is because diversity helps to fulfill the three principles of dialogue stated above. Diversity also helps move people out of their usual ways of thinking about an issue or idea. It encourages us to break out of our mental habits and break down the stereotypes we hold about other people's perspectives. How often do people neglect to listen because they think they already know what an 'environmentalist' or a 'business leader' will say? When people are exposed to a range of perspectives in genuine dialogue, it shifts their views of other people's views.

One of my favourite stories comes from an early dialogue I conducted with a group of citizens in a small town in Cape Breton, Nova Scotia. For several months they had been wrestling with a community issue – the closing of the local fish plant – and it had polarized the town. I arrived on a frosty night, into a rather frosty environment – people were staring coldly at each other across the room. By the end of the dialogue, people were excitedly speaking to each other with new energy and insights about their community issue. Two things contributed to the empowerment of the group that night. One was that the dialogue was on globalization – a topic quite different from the issue they had been wrestling with. This allowed people to open up and listen to one another. The second was that the organizer had done a great job at getting out a diversity of people. There were people sitting at the table who had never talked together, even though they all thought they knew each other's views – the fish plant manager, the people who did the fishing, the local councillor, and the ex-mayor. Through the dialogue, many of them really listened to each other for the first time, first-hand. The dialogue broke down the stereotypes they held of one another, released new energy, and generated the possibility for new understandings and insights.

Dialogue is about creating meaning together, finding a shared understanding of an issue, and discovering what values are most important in resolving it. There are various textures of dialogue: *deliberative* dialogue, the weighing of different approaches or choices regarding an issue; *reflective* dialogue, the exploration of underlying causes, rules, and assumptions in order to arrive at deeper questions and frame the problems more effectively; and *generative* dialogue, through which participants invent unprecedented possibilities and build on new insights.

Types of dialogue

Public dialogue can be deliberative, reflective, or generative, depending on who the participants are and what's being discussed.

PARTICIPANTS

In very broad terms, public dialogue may involve stakeholders who are external to the sector or milieu hosting the dialogue. It could also involve citizens – members of the public who are engaging in dialogue in their capacity as citizens. Public dialogue, however, does not include dialogue among individuals, families, or internal staff in organizations (including business and government). It does not include dialogue across or between governments, or dialogue within sectors (e.g., voluntary sector groups or business associations).

One of the most frequent uses of public dialogue is to initiate interaction between government and stakeholders (including the voluntary sector) or between government and citizens.

CONTENT

Public dialogue is about public issues at any level, from community to international. Public dialogue can occur when citizens come together to make decisions or reach an understanding about a local issue that they can resolve without calling on or interacting with the government.

However, public dialogue often focuses on issues of public policy and programs. This links public dialogue to government and governance. Often organizers of public dialogue – whether it is government, voluntary sector groups, or citizens themselves – are hoping to connect the outcomes of the dialogue to public policy processes. Because public dialogue is about public issues and public policy, it is often resorted to as a response to the problems people see in today's democracy and system of governance.

2. The Malaise

Many citizens in Canada (and in many other parts of the world) are cynical about government and politics today. Often when I begin a dialogue with citizens on behalf of the government, there is negativity in the room that has to be overcome. Distrust in governments (at all levels) and the related feeling that there is insufficient accountability and transparency are a recurring theme expressed by citizens in dialogue after dialogue. The pressure is on for governments to be concerned with the process by which decisions are arrived at and implemented, and whether that process is truly democratic, as well as with the competition of opinions and programs regarding those decisions (Rebick 2000). In an era of 'new public management' (Phillips and Orsini 2002), where government's role is to steer the boat and not row, citizens may still want some say about the way the boat is being rowed – or how close a watch the government keeps on the oarsmen (Stein 2001; Gregg 2002).

Many of the issues citizens grapple with today – issues like globalization, climate change, and security – are extremely complex. They are beyond the capacity of any single research team, public policy department, local or even national government body to solve. At the same time, our technology has moved forward by leaps and bounds. Many of today's advanced technologies – cloning, biotechnology and new weaponry, to mention just three areas – pose huge ethical questions. In this context, some level of agreement, or at least mutual awareness as to the values of a society, is essential in determining wise public policy. These values are best expressed and determined not by government or media elites but by citizens exercising opportunities to think and work through public issues collectively and arrive at a shared understanding of how to move forward.

Added to this is the rapid pace of social and technological change, to which local communities, no less than national governments and international businesses, must adapt at an unprecedented rate. As Kenneth J. Gergen (2000, xxiii) puts it, 'In such a world our traditional problem-solving resources scarcely apply. By the time alternatives are tested, the world has moved on. It is not "the answer" that we must seek but rather a continuous process of answering. Required are cease-less conversations.'

To make these conversations public means recognizing the diversity of knowledge that citizens bring to the process. In the Western world, science, from its pre-eminent position, has influenced our areas of de-velopment, leading us to become 'technological giants but sociological midgets' (Yankelovich 1999, 191). Yankelovich argues that wise policy comes from the combination of facts and values. It is not helpful to treat facts as if they come from a world of abstract knowledge and values as if they belong to an inaccessible or unverifiable world of private experi-ence. Wisdom – the ability to judge soundly and to deal sagaciously with the facts, especially as they relate to life and conduct – requires both.[2]

3. The Challenge of Public Dialogue

Fundamental to the idea of public dialogue is the interaction between governments and citizens in the determination of what is in the public interest and how to achieve it. Gregg (2002) paints a rather disturbing picture of this relationship in Canada. He suggests that over the past dec-ades, Canadians have stopped asking government to guide the public interest, settling instead for mere efficiency and accountability, while avoiding the crucial dialogue on the public good or discussions about the kind of community we want and value. In the absence of dialogue on social values or on what will generate the greatest good for the greatest number, the public good is overtaken by regional, religious, and ethnic loyalties, or else by common self-interest. Public dialogue can respond to this challenge. It is a way to get at the heart of what people value and de-termine common ground about what the public good(s) should be.

When I conduct public dialogues on behalf of governments, it is very common for participants to question whether or not they are taking part in a true consultation process – that is, whether their advice will really be considered. There is much scepticism among the public about government consultation, which is often seen as a 'tell and sell' public relations exercise around a decision which for all intents and purposes has already been made.

Organizers of true engagement processes find they must overcome the barriers these past consultations have created. For example, in late fall of 2006, we began doing public dialogues on an issue related to pandemic preparedness in Canada – specifically whether the use of antiviral drugs for prevention should be publicly funded by government. This was a serious question, which posed a dilemma for scientists and policy-makers, because the science was not clear as to the effectiveness and safety of the drugs if used in a pandemic situation. It also raised significant ethical concerns, as governments could not afford to provide such drugs for all Canadians. This raised yet another dilemma: which groups should have priority to receive the antiviral drugs?

Citizens in the dialogue responded to these challenges and did a remarkable job at finding common ground and working towards a sound public judgment. However, in every dialogue I facilitated, the participants first needed to be assured that a decision had not already been made, and that their advice was indeed needed. On the other hand, the citizens had no objection to the fact that advice from scientists and other stakeholders would also be sought and duly considered; they understood that they were not making the decision alone, and many were indeed relieved not to have that weight on their shoulders.

While not wanting to minimize the effort many committed civil servants are making to bring these kinds of authentic consultations to fruition, the reality is that it is still an uphill battle. The fact that these people need to be courageous and determined in order to succeed in pushing through innovative processes illustrates that the standard template of consultation, with all its inherent problems, is still dominant (Phillips and Orsini 2002). Government chooses what policy issues will be discussed and what questions will be asked. Agendas and invitation lists are proposed and controlled by government. Information flows in one direction. There is little time for local citizens or groups to prepare. And the style of interaction follows the safe and predictable format of a presentation, followed by a question-and-answer period. There is little opportunity for engagement and public dialogue.

Public dialogue is a challenge for government, but one full of promise – perhaps too many promises. In my years of working on public dialogue, I have heard it suggested that the process could

- reconnect governance and citizens
- determine the public good based on values and what is in the broad community interest, rather than political, stakeholder, or career interests
- produce wiser policy
- reinvigorate democracy

- produce new alternatives/solutions
- engage citizens in civil life
- stimulate our collective intelligence
- develop citizenship skills

This is a huge mandate. So, what does public dialogue actually look like in practice, and what would a few concrete examples show us about its potential?

4. Three Approaches to Public Dialogue

Three approaches to public dialogue will be examined. In doing this, the following nine questions will be asked about each approach:

1. *Is it genuine dialogue?* Does it meet the four features of dialogue presented earlier: treat the participants as equals; encourage active listening; uncover assumptions and values; and encourage a diversity of perspectives?
2. *How well does the dialogue include minorities or marginalized groups?* Does the participation reflect the diversity of the population, including those that are often harder to reach?
3. *Who determines and frames the issue?* Are citizens involved or are they only being asked to respond to issues and choices that have been identified and developed by government officials or elite social groups?
4. *Is there political commitment to the process?* Are the results listened to?
5. *What types of knowledge are included?* Is preparation or training required in order for meaningful involvement to be possible?
6. *How is the process of dialogue encouraged?* Are there facilitators – people whose focus is on the process, not the content and who, ideally, have been trained in moderating productive dialogue? Since a facilitator must be objective, it is common for the facilitator to be a neutral third party.
7. *What are the expectations in terms of the dialogue outcomes?* Here it is useful to consider the following possible goals for engagement. Metaphorically, these can be viewed as rungs on a ladder. For example, one must have climbed the rung 'Sharing of ideas' before one can reach 'Common ground' (see figure 14.1).
8. *How are participants found and selected?* Do participants receive payment or other compensations? Are their expenses reimbursed? Who pays for this?

Figure 14.1: Ladder of engagement[2]

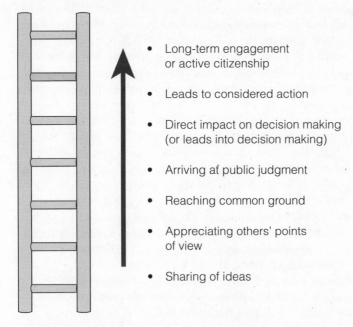

- Long-term engagement or active citizenship

- Leads to considered action

- Direct impact on decision making (or leads into decision making)

- Arriving at public judgment

- Reaching common ground

- Appreciating others' points of view

- Sharing of ideas

9. *How does the dialogue balance breadth versus depth?* For example, is there intensive involvement of fewer people over multiple sessions versus a large number of people in a single intensive session?

Deliberative dialogue

Deliberative dialogue engages participants in policy discussion. This form of dialogue, which has been used several times in Canada over the past five to ten years, is a robust process that can be adapted to a variety of issues and to both stakeholder and citizen processes. Citizen processes are those in which people participate in their capacity as individuals. Stakeholders, in contrast, usually participate as representatives of a certain interest group and therefore may feel constrained to stay within the bounds of that interest group's perspective. Experience, however, demonstrates that deliberative dialogue can provide a space and process for stakeholders to move beyond their stated positions.

The earliest Canadian deliberative dialogues took place in the mid to late 1990s, and included a project called 'The Society We Want,' conducted by the Canadian Policy Research Networks (CPRN 1999), and the initiative 'Choices in Common, Communities in Common: Canadians Deliberate about Globalization,' conducted by the Canadian Council for International Cooperation (CCIC 1999a). Since then, deliberation has been used on topics as diverse as health care, disaster mitigation, trade and food security, private sector–NGO relationships, diversity in the workplace, climate change, and post-secondary education.

These dialogues or forums are generally structured, facilitated processes that are based on a 'deliberation guide' prepared specifically for the issue at hand. The guide is a workbook that generally provides background information and lays out three approaches to the issue (for samples, see CCIC 1999b). During a forum, participants reason and talk together about basic policy directions in a way that goes beyond a debate, the presenting of positions, or casual discussion. As a collaborative engagement, deliberative dialogue encourages people to break out of habitual viewpoints and stimulates new ideas or ways to think about an issue. It builds on participants' knowledge and experience to find common ground from which alternative strategies or policies can be developed. Deliberative dialogues are values-based processes, in contrast to being agenda- or position-driven.

HOW IT WORKS

One of the earliest deliberations to take place in Canada was conducted by the Canadian Council for International Cooperation (CCIC) under the theme 'Choices in Common, Communities in Common: Canadians Deliberate about Globalization.' An umbrella organization for groups active in international development, CCIC and its members wanted to find a way to engage a broad range of Canadians in dialogue on global issues. It ran a national pilot in 1999 on the topic of globalization. The starting point of the process was the framing of the concerns about globalization and the production of a deliberation guide, which presented three choices or perspectives on the issue (CCIC 1999b). The choices resonated with the public but were not aligned with political party perspectives or polarized views (e.g., environmentalists against developers). The choices were tested in focus groups made up of everyday citizens to be sure the choices had been framed appropriately. A readers' group, made up of people who had in-depth knowledge of the issue but also understood the need to present the issue and choices objectively, reviewed the guide for bias.

Four CCIC member organizations hosted deliberative dialogues in their communities: the Centre for International Studies (CIS) in Cape Breton, Nova Scotia; the Manitoba Council for International Co-operation (MCIC) in Winnipeg, Manitoba; the Marquis Project in Brandon, Manitoba; and the Association Québécoise des Organismes de Coopération Intérnationale (AQOCI) in Montreal, Quebec. Their role was to solicit and recruit a variety of participants and to select people willing to be trained as moderators and recorders for the dialogues. In total, over 130 people were trained. They facilitated the dialogues and took notes on the main themes of discussion.

Each dialogue was three hours long. It began with participants completing a pre-forum questionnaire. Then the topic of globalization was introduced and people were asked to provide examples of how they (or people they knew) had been affected by globalization. This validated people's experiences as an entry point for dialogue. With the support of the moderator, the participants then reviewed the choices, exploring the values underlying each and the trade-offs that existed within and between choices. At the end, they explored any common ground they had arrived at from which new alternatives could be developed or from which action could be taken. Finally, participants completed a post-forum questionnaire.

Over the last few years, more than fifty forums on globalization were conducted across Canada and over 600 people participated. Those who took part attended as citizens, not as representatives of any particular group or affiliation. However, the range of people invited to participate was broad enough to ensure the diversity of perspectives needed for a good deliberation. Some forums spanned three generations, and included people from a range of ethnic and professional backgrounds. One particularly memorable dialogue brought together high school students with community business leaders and blue-collar workers. An important element of this work was to bring the results of the forums – the public judgments participants had arrived at – to government and other interested 'influencers,' including the CCIC membership. This was done in several ways, including inviting government officials to attend the forums and take part in a wrap-up event and panel discussion with the participants. However, most of this work to bring the results of the deliberations to the attention of decision-makers was done after the results were compiled, through wide dissemination of a final report (CCIC 1999a) and numerous presentations and meetings with policy-makers, civil society organizations, and others.

The effects of this work since 1999 have been extraordinary. The CCIC dialogues have won two national awards for contributions to citizen engagement and public discourse: the Suzanne Peters Award for Citizen Engagement in 2000, and the Arthur Kroeger College Award for Public Discourse in 2002. Today, the process has spread right across the country, with organizations in every province now involved and trained in the approach. Groups in Atlantic Canada have organized their own deliberations on the topic of climate change. CCIC has worked with its counterpart in the United States to organize similar deliberations on global issues there. CCIC and its sister for-profit, One World Inc., has continued to use and expand on the deliberative dialogue work, including its use in government-sponsored processes with both stakeholders and citizens.[3]

ANALYSIS

This subsection will assess both the concrete examples and the findings for the nine questions described above.

1. Is it genuine dialogue?
Finding: There is no doubt that deliberative dialogue can be genuine dialogue. It treats participants as equals; it encourages active listening; it uncovers assumptions and explores values; and it thrives on diversity.

2. How well does it include minorities and the marginalized?
Finding: Because it is important to have a diversity of perspectives, it is usually a priority to encourage minorities, or those not usually engaged in policy issues, to participate.

3. Who determines and frames the issue?
Finding: Framing issues has proven to work best when a sample group of citizens (or stakeholders, if they are the anticipated participants) engages in the framing process – presenting it in a way that citizens can relate to. The question of who determines the issue is more difficult. Typically, whoever is hosting the dialogue decides on the issue.

4. Is there political commitment to the process?
Finding: It is a major challenge for voluntary sector-led processes to be listened to by the government. However, this does not lessen the importance of the sector itself listening to the input.

One of the more extensive Canadian examples of deliberative dialogue was for the Commission on the Future of Health Care in Canada (the Romanow Commission) in 2002. These dialogues took place in twelve locations across Canada and approximately 40 citizens participated in each day-long session. Participants deliberated on four scenarios (approaches) for reforming the health care system in Canada. Those working on the final report say that the citizen input figured very prominently in the final set of recommendations.

5. What types of knowledge are included? Is preparation or training required?

Finding: As a values-based dialogue, deliberation draws on people's experiences and what they value in their lives, families, and communities. However, having an information session up front helps citizens focus more clearly on the given issues. Although training citizens how to participate in dialogue is not required, the training of moderators is essential to ensure consistent and comparable results across several sessions.

6. How is the process of dialogue encouraged?

Finding: In the globalization dialogues, as in most deliberative dialogues, the idea of the dialogue is presented at the beginning of the session. Ground rules are established, which help the participants work towards building a discussion. The moderator, who is trained in deliberation, is also central to a dialogue's success. (For the rules used in the globalization dialogue, see appendix 14.B.)

7. What are the expectations in terms of the dialogue outcomes?

Finding: In most deliberative dialogues, participants make every effort to provide their best advice to decision-makers. The participants themselves are not involved in decision-making. The expectations are normally clear in this regard. Some sessions have resulted in individual or collective action, though this is not necessarily an intended outcome.

8. How are participants found or selected?

Finding: In some cases, people are randomly selected and paid to attend in much the same way as they are invited to participate in a focus group. This is usually done for dialogues where it is crucial that the participants form a representative sample of the various stakeholders. For the globalization dialogues, targets were set for the type and level of diversity being sought. However, people still chose to come and to participate without payment.

9. How does the dialogue balance breadth versus depth?
Finding: Many deliberative dialogues in Canada have been single events, where participants attend a half-day or full-day dialogue process. Organizers have opted for including more people, thus obtaining a more representative sample of participants than would be possible if resources were devoted to conducting multiple sessions with a much smaller group.

This opting for breadth in the range and number of participants fits with the objectives of arriving at some areas of public judgment and providing these to decision-makers. However, if other goals become important, like using a dialogue to begin a process of community development, encouraging action, or working through long-standing situations of conflict, multiple sessions would be essential.

Citizens' Panel/Consensus Conference

A Citizens' Panel brings together a group of lay people to explore a complicated issue (often of a technological nature) that is also socially controversial. Used successfully in Europe, where it is known as a 'consensus conference,' its use in Canada has been more limited, although the recent Citizens' Assemblies in British Columbia and Ontario formed to examine issues of electoral reform use an approach very similar to Citizens' Panels (British Columbia Citizen's Assembly on Electoral Reform, 2004). (In the United States, a very similar approach is called a 'Citizens' Jury.') A Citizens' Panel's premise is that the general public can make sense of complex issues and provide thoughtful, deliberated input on policy when given the time and resources to do so. A Citizens' Panel involves a panel of ten to twenty-four citizens who are both representative of the general public and well informed about the given issue. Considerable time is spent in both selecting the panel participants and in bringing them up to speed on the issue (often one that is considered to be the province of experts only). Citizens' Panels have dealt with issues such as the use of genetically modified organisms in agriculture, xenotransplantation, food irradiation, infertility, local governance, and solid-waste sites.

HOW IT WORKS
One of the first tasks in a Citizens' Panel process is to establish an advisory group, often consisting of various stakeholders who bring a range of perspectives to the issue. The advisory group helps select the

participants, define the scope of the dialogue, and draw up a list of experts and witnesses. Advisory group members also work with panel staff to avoid bias in the project, making sure all sides of an issue are treated fairly.

There is usually an open call for panellists, and the participants are chosen to represent a diversity of views and experiences. Through preparatory meetings, the participants get to know each other, learn about the various aspects of the issue or technology in question, develop key questions to be addressed, and select experts or witnesses from the advisory committee's list to form the 'experts' panel.' This phase of the work is often moderated by objective professional facilitators, who are contracted by the sponsoring body, and often requires two or three weekends so that the participants have time to reflect on what they are learning.

The Citizens' Panel culminates in a public session, sometimes called a Citizens' Conference, lasting two or three days. The session is professionally moderated. Participants engage with the experts' panel, hear presentations, ask questions, and then (often on the second day) cross-examine the experts in order to fill in any gaps and to probe the issue further. Members of the citizens' panel then retire to develop their recommendations and conclusions, which they present publicly, often in the form of a preliminary report. In some cases the expectation is that a consensus report will be delivered; in others, the panel's conclusions need not be unanimous, as long as minority positions or statements are acknowledged in appropriate detail. Over the course of the following few weeks, a final report is prepared, printed, and distributed. There is often media work done through public communiqués and announcements to bring the results to a wider audience.

For a Citizens' Panel to work successfully, it is essential that the process be, and be seen to be, objective. It must provide the conditions for an open and constructive dialogue. The process will lose all credibility if participants think they are being presented with biased or incomplete information or with only certain perspectives and not others. Thus the resource material, the experts, the facilitators and recorders, and the members of the advisory committee must all be carefully selected to ensure that overall there is a balanced and impartial presentation of ideas and information.

One of the first Citizens' Panels in Canada to use the consensus conference format was held at the University of Calgary in 1999. The topic was food biotechnology, and the Citizens' Panel was convened in the context of the Canadian Biotechnology Strategy, which included public participation as one of its goals.

The first step was to set up an advisory committee representing various stakeholder interests: people from regulatory agencies, industry, and civil society groups (primarily environmental and consumer organizations).

The conference organizers decided to adopt a regional rather than national focus. Participants were therefore drawn from the four Western provinces. Over 356 people applied in response to advertisements and press releases inviting volunteers to sit on the panel. From these, the committee selected fifteen panellists – students, a heavy equipment mechanic, a letter carrier, an engineer, a rancher, and businesspeople. The panellists' ages ranged from 17 to 59. Members of the experts' panel came from across Canada.

The Citizens' Panel members were given a package of background materials and took part in two preparatory weekends, during which they drafted questions to ask the expert panel and conducted further research. The culminating session, referred to as the Citizens' Conference, was a three-day event open to the public. The format was based on six key questions formulated by the panellists. Experts responded to these questions and then the panel retired to prepare its conclusions and recommendations. The report was made public and was sent to several federal and provincial ministries and other interested parties. Media coverage was also arranged; although, interestingly, the panel participants felt that the commercial media distorted their recommendations (Health Canada 2000, 130).

ANALYSIS

1. Is it genuine dialogue?
Finding: A Citizens' Panel approach enables citizens to participate as equals and puts them on a more level playing field with the experts. The experience of citizens' juries supports the idea that genuine dialogue does occur in the process. Jurors are able to deliberate together as fellow citizens. They gain understanding and empathy for those who think or feel differently. Everyone's concerns and questions are considered. Jurors are asked to grapple with the serious trade-offs and the need to set priorities, inherent in so many complex issues. The thoughtful and constructive nature of a jury's recommendations is a result of a respectful and deliberative process (Nethercut 2000, 5).

2. How well did it include minorities or marginalized groups?
Finding: In a panel of a dozen or two dozen citizens, the capacity to include minorities is limited. However, one can assume, in the effort to make the panel representative of the community demographics, minorities would be included.

3. Who determines and frames the issue?
Finding: The group hosting the process chooses the issue for the panel's consideration and the advisory group refines it further. In the Citizens' Jury process, this group also prepares the 'charge' – typically a series of questions addressed to jurors. In the Citizens' Panel process, the participants develop their own set of questions for experts to respond to, but still within an overall mandate framed by the hosts and the advisory group.

4. Is there political commitment to the process?
Finding: In processes hosted by non-governmental groups, there is the same problem as in deliberative dialogue when it comes to connecting the results to government policy. Even sessions initiated by the government have sometimes run into problems when policy-makers attempt to interfere with the process rather than allow the panel to challenge widely accepted 'expert' policy assumptions head on. In March 1998, for example, a Citizens' Panel reviewing local governance models for the Ottawa-Carleton Region disbanded, citing 'immensely destructive interference in the Panel's process by numerous municipalities' (Health Canada 2000, 130).

5. What types of knowledge are included? Is preparation or training required?
Finding: A Citizens' Panel is based on the proposition that citizens can contribute their experiential and value-based way of knowing on an equal footing with technical and information-based knowledge, and that this will result in wiser public policies or action plans. A great deal of time is devoted to informing participants about the technical aspects of the issue on which they will confer. Some researchers have noted that Citizens' Panels can influence the attitudes, training, and day-to-day work of experts, particularly in how they bridge the communication gap between themselves and lay people. This is a tremendously important result, because it can help to overcome one of the most serious challenges in making public dialogue work: the 'technological fix.'

6. How is the process of dialogue encouraged?
Finding: Professional facilitation is an important component of the Citizens' Panel process.

7. What are the expectations in terms of the dialogue outcomes?
Finding: The expectations of the Citizens' Panel process are clearly expressed as wanting the participants to arrive at a public judgment on the issue in question, and that this judgment be framed in recommendations that can be inserted into the decision-making process. The panel is not, however, the decision-maker unless the host (e.g., government) has given it that mandate and sticks to it.

8. How are participants found or selected?
Finding: Participants are generally found through an open call (e.g., using the media) or through random selection by phone. Respondents who agree to receive additional information are entered into a pool from which the final panellists are selected. A selection grid reflecting key demographic variables is drawn up. It often includes a variable related to people's attitudes towards the issue at hand. Panel selection is done anonymously by choosing candidates in the pool according to their numbers on the selection grid.

9. How does the dialogue balance breadth versus depth?
Finding: This is clearly an approach that chooses depth over breadth. It is an intensive process, both for the citizen panellists and for the experts.

Participatory budgeting process

The participatory budgeting process involves citizens in a series of meetings that are designed to determine development priorities for a government budget. Since it was first piloted in Porto Alegre, Brazil, in 1989, it has been used in nearly 100 other cities in Brazil, as well as cities in Peru, Uruguay, Ecuador, El Salvador, and Venezuela, to help develop municipal budgets. The meetings tend to be organized according to neighbourhoods and themes. The citizens decide on a portion of the budget, often as much as 20 per cent – usually funds not allocated for ongoing programs, and have an opportunity to look at the previous year's expenditures and assess the community's progress. Each district of the city draws up its investment budget priorities and then chooses delegates to convey them to the city administration. While the municipal council can review the proposals for overall planning and budgeting purposes, it cannot change the priorities or the allocation of funds.

The goal of participatory budgeting is to re-engage citizens in democracy by opening up the space for citizen dialogue and input into municipal decision-making. Backed by a strong vision of 'social citizenship,' the process involves ordinary citizens in making planned choices through popular participation in order to improve the standard of living and the quality of life for the majority. In countries like Brazil, where the majority of people are poor, this means, first and foremost, improving the lives of those living in poverty.

HOW IT WORKS

The municipal administration (either the planning or the finance department) divides the city into districts. A schedule of meetings (sometimes called neighbourhood assemblies) is publicized through the media, civil society groups, and so on. There is at least one meeting in each district. These tend to be large meetings with well over 100 people in attendance. During a meeting, the participants determine the priority problems for consideration in the budget. They also elect their delegates. Sometimes the number of delegates for each meeting will vary according to the number of people who attend. The delegates from the several districts then meet with the municipal council to determine the overall priorities for the portion of the budget open to citizen input. These priorities are then presented to the municipal council (Sucupïra and Mello 1999).

Often there are additional meetings of the neighbourhoods. Civil society groups often organize preparatory meetings to begin the work of identifying and prioritizing local concerns. There are often two rounds of official meetings: the first, to hear the results of the previous year and elect delegates, and the second, to determine the new budget priorities for the district. There are also often thematic meetings, which overlap with the neighbourhood meetings. These generally address city-wide priorities such as public transportation or health care.

The participatory budgeting process began with the Partido dos Trabalhadores or Workers' Party (PT) winning the municipal election in Porto Alegre, a city of over 1.3 million inhabitants, in 1989. In each of the city's sixteen districts, two official rounds of district and thematic meetings were held annually. There were five themes open for discussion: public transportation and traffic; health care and social assistance;

education, culture and leisure; economic development and taxation; and city organization and urban development (De Sousa Santos 1998).

Before the official process begins, preparatory meetings are held for citizens, which are convened and chaired by popular councils or community organizations, during which the demands and claims of the citizens and groups are collected. These meetings begin the process of community mobilization to select the district delegates. These meetings can be quite heated, with clashes taking place between different political factions during the formulation of demands.

A schedule is posted of the official meetings, which the mayor and members of his or her staff attend. All district meetings are open to the public, but only those living in the particular district can vote. However, at the thematic meetings, any citizen who attends can vote. The mayor's office organizes the process and encourages widespread attendance with the help of neighbourhood groups that help to mobilize people, especially those living in poverty. At all the meetings, flyers providing a financial report that explains major expenditures are given out. A video is shown that demonstrates projects approved in the previous year's budget that are either in progress or have been completed. Plays, including popular theatre, present community issues through the medium of drama, and other cultural activities are sometimes presented before the official meeting gets under way.

At the first meeting, which could be attended by 500 to 700 people, the results of the previous year are presented, citizens do an evaluation, and the first delegates to the Forum of Delegates are elected. Then there is a series of intermediate preparatory meetings, organized by community or thematic groups, or by the elected delegates. At these meetings, participants rank concerns and demands according to the priorities that they have established or else against a set of general criteria used to set priorities city-wide. Through this period the remaining delegates to the Forum are elected.

The second round of official meetings is then held. Each district and thematic meeting elects two councillors and two alternatives to the Participatory Budget Council (COP). They serve for one year and can only be re-elected once.

Members of the Forum fulfill consulting, controlling, and mobilizing functions and are responsible for supervising the work and acting as the intermediary between the COP and the districts or thematic areas. The COP is the main decision-making body, where the regional and thematic priorities are discussed and measured against a set of criteria. COP delegates receive training in municipal finances and operation of the participatory budget.

Once choices are made, the COP prepares an investment plan, which includes a detailed list of the works and activities prioritized by the council, with appropriate allocations. This is then presented to the mayor and the municipal council, which formally adopts the budget. It is understood that the municipal council will make minor changes to the COP proposal.

The results of the participatory budgeting process have been striking. In 1989, only 49 per cent of Porto Alegre's population had water and sewage. In 1996, 98 per cent of households had water and 85 per cent were served by the sewage system (compared to 42 per cent in Brazil as a whole). Streets have been paved at the rate of 30 kilometres per year. Despite the fact that fifteen wealthy families own most of the land of Porto Alegre, housing for the marginal populations has improved. The entire city has garbage collection and school enrollment has doubled since 1989. Ninety-eight percent of the city has electricity, compared to 88 per cent in Brazil as a whole.

Many of these achievements were a result of increased revenue through tax increases, which citizens advocated for through the participatory budgeting process. The former mayor, Tarso Genro, believes that the transparency in municipal spending brought about by participatory budgeting increased the motivation to pay taxes (De Sousa Santos 1998).

The effects of the participatory budgeting process in Porto Alegre have been far-reaching. The process has been extensively studied and replicated, and has been acclaimed for both the efficient and the highly democratic management of urban resources. Indeed, the participatory budgeting process of Porto Alegre was selected by the United Nations as one of the 40 urban innovations worldwide to be presented at the Second Conference on Human Settlements in 1996.

Participatory budgeting has also begun to make its mark in Canada. For example, since 2002, tenants in Toronto Community Housing have engaged in a participatory budgeting process to determine priorities on a discretionary portion of the housing authority's budget for capital improvements on the buildings and grounds it manages. Participatory budgeting exercises have taken place in other cities as well, including Guelph, Hamilton, Sudbury, and Vancouver.

ANALYSIS

1. Is it genuine dialogue?

Finding: It is difficult to know if genuine dialogue is occurring. Certainly the attempt to equalize participants and give all a voice would seem to indicate a dialogue process. According to De Sousa Santos (1998), results are achieved through a network of democratic institutions geared to reaching decisions by deliberation, consensus, and compromise. However, he also argues that the pattern of participation and institutionalization can produce conflict.

2. How well does the dialogue include minorities or marginalized groups?

Finding: Participatory budgeting prioritizes involvement of the poor and the marginalized. In fact, one of the reasons that the thematic meetings were added was that there was very limited participation of the middle and upper class in the regional meetings.

3. Who determines and frames the issue?

Finding: Participatory budgeting is an emerging process, adjusting itself to multiple demands as it tries to balance objective criteria with the politics of popular participation. In general, it has been a responsive process open to negotiation; the addition of the thematic meetings is one example of its adaptability.

Voluntary sector and popular organizations, many of which are closely connected to political parties, have had a very significant role in the participatory budgeting process: mobilizing people to attend, helping to define priorities, and so on. These groups themselves have evolved from a political culture based on protest and confrontation to a culture of negotiation.

4. Is there political commitment to the process?

Finding: Participatory budgeting was introduced by the Workers' Party (PT) upon its election to government, and its commitment to the process has remained strong. Changing the actual decision-making structures has been essential to the success of the process. Political commitment at the citizen level has likewise been strong. Over 85 per cent of those surveyed gave the municipal government a strong approval rating in 1996 (De Sousa Santos 1998). However, the political commitment at the level of the community groups is less certain. Those not actively engaged in the participatory budgeting process argue that the government has co-opted the popular movement and distorted its agenda.

5. What types of knowledge are included? Is preparation or training required?

Finding: Participatory budgeting is based on citizens' knowledge – their experiences, their knowledge of their communities, their values, and their passions. This is fundamental to the process. However, it also involves technical and financial knowledge. The use of criteria based on what people would like to achieve through the budget allocation helps people to weigh their decisions and certainly choices are made in the meetings.

6. How is the process of dialogue encouraged?

Finding: The opportunity for dialogue is encouraged through the democratic space opened up broadly for citizens. There are much higher levels of interaction between people of different perspectives and views, as they come together in both the official and the neighbourhood-run meetings – some of which have developed sophisticated processes for assessing priorities.

7. What are the expectations in terms of the dialogue outcomes?

Finding: Participatory budgeting is clearly a decision-making process, and is not set up to create dialogue as such. As Yankelovich (1999, 127) argues, it is important to maintain the distinction between dialogue and decision-making as processes that require different styles of interaction. Nonetheless, dialogue is an important forerunner to decision-making, and perhaps an indispensable precondition for achieving wise decisions.

8. How are participants found or selected?

Finding: The meetings are open to all and are widely publicized. Community groups are very active in mobilizing people and ensuring that all have the opportunity to attend the meetings if they wish. Delegates are elected in a democratic manner, though it is difficult to get enough votes to be elected if the candidate is not already active in community organizations and has the backing of some of the associations. No one is paid for his or her participation or service as a member of the Forum or the COP, despite meeting weekly for five months in the case of the COP. Delegates must even pay their own transportation.

9. How does the dialogue balance breadth versus depth?

Finding: In the Porto Alegre example, 14,267 people participated in the official meetings in 1996. If one adds the preparatory and intermediate meetings, total participation comes close to 100,000 people, or 8 per cent of the population. At this level of engagement, the choice is clearly for breadth. However, through the electoral system, depth is achieved also as the elected delegates have an opportunity for intensive training, discussion, and decision-making.

5. Public Dialogue as a Social Process: Challenges and Ways Forward

The example of the participatory budgeting process from Brazil was included in this essay not so much because it models good public dialogue (although citizen engagement is certainly a paramount objective) but because it demonstrates the real-life complexity of bringing new social processes into being.

In Canada, most of the experiments in public dialogue have been relatively small scale, focused on specific issues and within limited time frames. If we Canadians are to meet the challenge of being more than 'social midgets,' we will need to expand our experiments in social processes like public dialogue so they become authentic forms of ongoing civic interaction. There is every reason to feel optimistic about the possibility of creating a habit of deliberation, where people, communities, and governments would turn to processes such as deliberative dialogue, instead of heading automatically into debate and win–lose scenarios.

Baiocchi (2001) argues that the Porto Alegre experience has proven to be a school of 'deliberative democracy,' because it has fostered new and more intermeshed institutions in civil society, renewal of civil society leadership positions, and greater adherence to deliberative procedural rules. Despite the problems it has worked through and the ones still facing it, the participatory budgeting process has shown that an alternative way of doing things is possible.

Several factors will be important if we are to bring public dialogue up to the level of social process in Canada. This section explores four of them.

Ability to work out complex issues

The world of public interaction requires that we be tolerant of ambiguity when it comes to results. One doesn't really know if something will work until one tries it. When faced with complex issues or even incomprehensible events, 'there is often no substitute for acting your way into an eventual understanding of them' (Weick 1998, 550). Instilling public dialogue as a social innovation may require a leap of faith – one that understandably will be difficult for some people to take (including certain government leaders and social activists). In my experience, citizens have proven time and again that they can take on complex, sometimes opaque, issues like fiscal federalism and provide useful advice by applying their values and common sense.

Creating meaning together

As members of a society steeped in the language of technology and science, it is hard for us to communicate ideas about complex processes that don't follow simple formulas. It is even harder to connect those processes to ideas of social transformation. However, there are many people looking for ways to talk about new forms of democracy, civic life, social capital, collective intelligence, and the power of dialogue.

Dialogue is about making sense and creating meaning together. It seems strange to talk about the need to communicate *about* dialogue. Yet, in my experience, I find it is difficult for people to understand the idea of genuine dialogue until they have experienced it. Public dialogue is a process of transformation – the creation (or re-creation) of an alternative way of working on public issues. Howard Gardner (1996) talks about how difficult it is to communicate the idea of transformation; he suggests that one needs to create new stories and images from which people can begin to build a picture or understanding of what this new possibility is.

If people have a range of experiences to which they can connect an idea, the process of transformation moves more quickly. To illustrate this point we only need to look at Canada's Atlantic provinces where deliberative dialogue has been picked up and expanded on more quickly than in other parts of the country. Many people there have said that it reminds them of the Antigonish Movement when people came together around a kitchen table to talk about what was going on in their community, identify the needs to be met and how to meet them.[4] Social memory lingers long in Atlantic Canada. When Nova Scotians begin to hear about the ideas of public dialogue, it has immediate resonance with them; there is a way to weave it into their understanding.

This points to the reality that experiments in public dialogue are crucial and we need to have more of them. The more people who can directly experience public dialogue, the better. Certainly, the participatory budgeting process has built stories and images that resonate in Brazil and, increasingly, in other parts of Latin America and beyond. However, we still need to get better at expressing the nature and dynamic of public dialogue itself so that it becomes a social idea that resonates with more of the public. Canada took a first step in this direction in October 2005, when the first national conference of the Canadian Community on Dialogue and Deliberation was held in Ottawa (C2D2 2006). About 300 people – dialogue practitioners, community and business leaders, policy-makers, academics and students, researchers, elected officials, and citizens from across Canada and abroad – came together to establish and nurture a growing network of people interested in promoting and furthering public dialogue in Canada. Two more conferences have since been held (in 2007 and 2009).

Voluntary sector roles

As can be seen from the participatory budget process, the role of the voluntary sector and civil society in these processes is not always clear cut. However, voluntary sector groups are essential contributors to public dialogue and can fulfil at least three key roles:

1. *Incubators for active citizenship.* Voluntary sector organizations have always played a central role as places where citizens can work together in response to a community need. Through community involvement and action, people have the opportunity to connect to broader social issues. In the future, voluntary sector groups could enhance their role in this way by offering training and capacity building in policy development and budgeting. Time and time again, dialogue processes fight an uphill battle as they move from the exploration of values to policy considerations – when what has been explored and discovered in terms of values is translated into terms or options that can work at a policy level.

Voluntary sector organizations build citizenship capacity through practice – a learning-by-doing approach. When people become members of voluntary sector boards, they can develop skills in governance and policy development, provided that their organizations have active memberships and democratic practices. When these are in place, voluntary sector organizations can be powerful incubators for individuals, teaching them how to be more active citizens.

2. *Community convenors.* Voluntary sector organizations have never had such legitimacy in Canadian society as they have today. An EKOS poll in 2005 found that citizens trust voluntary sector groups more than

any other 'institution.' It is hardly surprising to me that, in Canada, it was primarily voluntary sector organizations like CCIC and CPRN that were at the forefront of experimenting with public dialogue processes.[5] Many other voluntary sector groups have the capacity to serve as neutral convenors for public dialogue. The Community Foundations of Canada (2001) has recognized this role and includes 'Creating Opportunities for Dialogue' as one of its ten key principles.

Of course, not all voluntary sector groups fit this bill. Many are formed around strong ideological perspectives and are more interested in convincing others of the 'rightness' of their perspectives than in providing opportunities that would encourage people to think for themselves. This doesn't mean that groups with a strong social cause can't convene dialogues; CCIC, for example, has a strong social justice focus. However, the convening organization must be able to reserve its own views, trust in the wisdom of citizens, and provide space for genuine dialogue. The community, in turn, must believe that the organization can convene a public dialogue in good faith. Otherwise, those who disagree with the perspective of the hosting organization will not get involved because they will assume that the host is intent on promoting a particular perspective about the issue being discussed.

Interestingly, activists and advocacy groups are often highly resistant to the idea of public dialogue. Despite the rhetoric about the 'right of the people' to decide, in reality there is often much distrust that citizens will make the 'right decision.' Here again, in my experience, citizens have proven their wisdom in reaching sound public judgments about social issues. The problem of 'political correctness' and the resulting stagnation in activist organizations is nothing new. As the Porto Alegre example illustrated, either these groups become increasingly conflicted or confrontational, or they become submerged and new entities are formed with fresher perspectives.

3. *Connectors between citizens and government.* One of the key roles that voluntary sector organizations can play is connecting government and citizens. Voluntary sector organizations know their communities; they know how to reach out to people and how to mobilize them. These are essential skills to successfully engage citizens in dialogue.

R.D. Putnam (2000) suggests that voluntary sector organizations play a crucial role in building social capital – the horizontal networks produced by voluntary action that generate trust in our fellow citizens and our government. This networking capacity makes voluntary sector organizations ideal connectors. For example, besides lobbying government for recognition of the need for broad-based consultation, voluntary sector organizations can use their networks and their knowledge of their communities to ensure that those people who are most affected by the issue participate.

The technological fix: 'Elites know best'

One of the major obstacles to public dialogue is the scientific and professional elites' conviction that the public cannot make any significant contribution to policy because the average citizen does not possess the knowledge that professionals bring to the table. There is a legitimate side to this argument, especially when government is charged with ensuring the safety and security of its citizens. I see this problem regularly in my work with Health Canada, which has a mandate to engage the public on 'key federal decisions that affect health' (Health Canada 2000, 11), but which also acts as a regulator with a central role in determining what is safe for Canadians. There is a daily struggle between the mandate to engage and the need to ensure safety, much of which is based on scientific knowledge.

However, this is not an either/or choice. Both the experts' knowledge and the citizens' common sense are crucial to the formulation of wise policy. Wisdom is the union of values and information. Policy based solely on technical or scientific knowledge is not necessarily wise policy. Sometimes we don't have clear science to go on, as in the case of pandemic preparedness mentioned above. Nor is science itself necessarily free of values. In my experience, researchers and scientists, like the rest of us, best remember ideas (and research) that support their own perspectives or biases.

Citizens have the capacity to become well informed, just as experts have the capacity to better appreciate the everyday concerns of citizens. Consider, for example, the health-related issues we face as a society today that cannot be resolved by technical knowledge alone – biotechnology, cloning, and euthanasia to name a few. Dialogue on the crucial questions of ethics and values is integral to the formulation of wise and enduring policies to monitor these issues.

Increasing the opportunities for genuine dialogue between experts and citizens is a way to narrow the divide. It is crucial therefore that public dialogue should gain in credibility as a means of enhancing technical or scientific knowledge through publicly shared wisdom.

6. Conclusion

Public dialogue has a huge potential for reshaping Canada's democratic communities. There is the possibility of marrying values to information to produce wiser policy that is in the interest of all communities, however large or small that community may be. In the words of J.G. Stein (2001, 225), 'The legitimacy of this conversation rests on recognised, fair, inclusive, and open procedures for deliberation and persuasion, where those who join in reflective discussion are neither intimidated nor manipulated.'

Will citizens participate if these deliberative processes and procedures are there? In this age of consumerism and a rapid pace of life, there is a great deal of scepticism about that. However, the examples in this essay indicate citizens' willingness to engage, especially if they know that their engagement will make a difference – in short, that they will be listened to. Thomas Paine, the democratic champion of the American and French revolutions, wrote about there being a genius, 'a mass of sense lying in a dormant state – which good government should quietly harness' (Paine 1791/1987, 240). If nothing brings it forth to action, it lies dormant. Our challenge is to draw out the genius of everyday citizens and unleash the energy and creativity that lies there to move our societies socially as well as technologically forward. Public dialogue has a crucial role to play in that endeavour.

NOTES

1 Since this paper was written, the use of dialogue in Canada has expanded and there are now many experiments and initiatives going on across the country. An organization dedicated to linking people interested in dialogue and deliberation, the Canadian Community of Dialogue and Deliberation, was established in 2006. In 2009, it held its third national conference. For more information on this organization and dialogue in Canada, visit www .C2D2.ca.

2 The idea of a ladder was inspired by the classic article by Sherry R. Arnstein, 'A Ladder of Citizen Participation' (1969, 216–24).

3 A more recent use of deliberative dialogue on global issues has been organized by the *Canada's World* initiative. For information, visit www .canadasworld.ca.

4   The Antigonish Movement was a social action venture that encouraged
    people to work through community issues and take action on these issues.
    Using adult education methods, the movement's organizers encouraged
    fisherman, farmers, miners, and others to establish study clubs. From these
    sprang credit unions and cooperatives that gave working-class people more
    control over their social and economic destinies (Lotz and Welton 1997, 9).

5   Since this paper was written, CPRN has closed its doors and CCIC has
    down-scaled and lost its public engagement capacity. Both these decisions
    were largely the result of financial constraints.

Appendix 14.A
Deliberative dialogue versus debate

DELIBERATIVE DIALOGUE	DEBATE
Collaborative	Oppositional
Common ground	Points of divergence
Listening to find meaning	Listening to find flaws
Listening to find agreement	Listening to find points to argue
Openness to being wrong	Determination to be right
Weighing alternatives	Winning
Assumes that others have pieces of the answer and all can find it together	Assumes there is a right answer and someone has it
Involves concern for the other person	Involves countering others

Appendix 14.B
Ground Rules for Dialogue

1. The purpose of dialogue is to understand and to learn from one another (you
    cannot 'win' a dialogue).
2. All dialogue participants speak for themselves, not as a representative of others'
    interests.
3. In a dialogue everyone is treated as an equal: leave status and stereotypes at
    the door.
4. Be open and listen to others, especially when you disagree. Suspend judgment.
5. Identify and test assumptions (even your own).
6. Listen carefully and respectfully to the views of others: acknowledge you have
    heard the other, especially when you disagree.
7. Look for common ground.
8. Express disagreement with ideas, not with personalities or motives (disagree
    without being disagreeable).
9. Respect all points of view.
10. The moderator guides the discussion, yet remains objective.

Source: Public Health Agency of Canada (2006) (adapted).

15 Social Entrepreneurship: The Power and Potential of Mission-based Businesses

JENNIFER FLANAGAN

The practice of social entrepreneurship (SE) – currently the umbrella term for the myriad business activities being undertaken by voluntary sector organizations (VSOs) – has gained significant momentum over the past several years. Although various definitions exist, social entrepreneurship is, essentially, an approach that brings money and mission activities closer together in order to leverage opportunities for new and more diversified funding, with the end goal of delivering more missions. I encounter examples of social entrepreneurship on a daily basis, from the fundraising newsletter I receive from a non-profit in Calgary (and which I pay for), to the company that cleans my office (a company that the hospital has spun off to generate revenue for the hospital), to the gym at the YMCA where I pay a fee to exercise (one of the oldest non-profits still around). The context for adopting SE activities can vary, but the motivation is based on the current competitive and funding-strapped conditions in which increasing numbers of voluntary sector organizations are operating in Canada. Exploring innovative ways to become more self-sufficient is not simply an option; it is becoming a matter of life or death for some organizations. Organizations that have successfully adopted SE approaches have recognized the value of their organizational assets and have leveraged these assets so as to pursue new and exciting opportunities to fund more missions. The voluntary sector is in need of new models, new freedom, and new energy, and social entrepreneurship is one method that is making this happen, with very positive results.

This essay explores the opportunities and risks involved when voluntary sector organizations adopt a social entrepreneurship mindset that results in the development of new revenue-generating innovations.

Throughout this essay, I give due consideration to individual organizations in context and to the possible negative repercussions of adopting SE approaches and activities. My interest in this topic stems from the potential I see for my own organization, Actua, to adopt a more aggressive SE approach, and I have used it as a testing ground for exploring the implementation and execution of SE. An analysis of Actua's history, challenges, and assets shows that, with careful business planning and detailed risk analysis, there is unmistakeable potential for implementing SE activities that will foster more financial independence and more mission delivery.

In my research and interviews with representatives of organizations currently involved in SE, I have developed a more detailed sense of the external context that is fuelling the emergence of SE activities, and of the internal processes and leadership characteristics that are making SE possible within voluntary sector organizations. The first section of the essay discusses these factors and details some of Actua's history and context in order to set the stage for exploring its SE potential. The second section expands the discussion of SE activities beyond Actua, and I propose five categories by which to structure the various ways in which SE is being implemented. The third section outlines several themes that I have observed among Canadian practitioners. The fourth section details Actua's SE potential.

1. Social Entrepreneurship and Actua's Context for the Emergence of SE

Dees (1998) defines social entrepreneurs as 'one species in the genus entrepreneur.' Since social entrepreneurship shares the underpinnings and characteristics of traditional entrepreneurship, it is therefore helpful to understand the original concept. Two economists, Jean-Baptiste Say (in the nineteenth century) and Joseph Schumpeter (in the twentieth) elaborated the concept of the entrepreneur from the elementary notion of the initiator or undertaker of a business enterprise to that of a heroic figure: a self-aware catalyst and innovator, a coordinator of resources and generator of economic growth. Dees (1998) pushes this historical definition even further. Using the work of Peter F. Drucker and Howard Stevenson, he defines entrepreneurs as business people who not only identify and develop opportunities but also are undeterred by any apparent lack of resources, taking risks to mobilize the required resources through aggressive strategy, creative financing, and opportunistic alliances. These characteristics are critical for SE activities, but social entrepreneurs (and their organizations) face the added challenge of having to balance both a financial and a social bottom line. On the other hand, the idea of social entrepreneurship is compelling and attractive because it suggests the possibility of combining the ethical satisfaction of creating or promoting social benefits with the material advantages of generating profit and building assets through the innovative, proactive business approaches of entrepreneurship.

The increasing momentum of social entrepreneurship is due to a host of social, political, and economic factors. Among these factors are the increasing demands and needs for social services and support that are placed on VSOs as a result of government restructuring and cut backs. The level of these demands continues to rise, especially with the increase in the gap between the rich and the poor; and the level of public-sector support seems to be decreasing at an equal if not greater rate. Corporate and individual giving is inconsistent, making it even more difficult for non-profits to sustain themselves and plan over the long term. In addition to this tightening of resources, an increasing number of non-profit organizations are feeling the impact of competition with more than 80,000 registered charities in Canada competing for the same dollars. This increased level of competition has resulted in new demands for VSO organizations around accountability, return on investment, and public profile. All these factors have shaken people's confidence in the sustainability of non-profit organizations, and are making many non-profits rethink their approaches and their way of doing business.

In a 1999 Kellogg Foundation study documenting the impact of economic change and globalization upon philanthropy, Tom Reis found that there are two strong forces driving social entrepreneurship (Reis 1999). The first is that most social change missions may actually benefit from a more innovative, entrepreneurial approach. The second is that the sustainability of most non-profit organizations now depends on the diversification of their revenue streams, often so as to include earned income streams or revenue-generating partnerships with the private sector. Taking a more entrepreneurial approach is no longer a matter of choice but rather a matter of survival. I believe that an organization like Actua is in an excellent position to gain further independence and greater capacity through its entrepreneurial activities.

Actua: Overview and history

Incorporated in 1993, Actua is a national charitable organization that is dedicated to implementing a national strategy to raise the level of science and technology literacy among Canadian youth. The mission of the organization is to provide young Canadians with positive, hands-on learning experiences in science, technology, and engineering. Actua is a membership-based organization, with 28 member organizations operating out of universities and colleges across Canada. Actua members reach over 220,000 young people per year, through summer camps, school workshops, community outreach activities, and specialized initiatives to under-represented groups. The national office (of which I am the CEO) provides support, resources, and training to members, in the form of cash, equipment, training and professional development, online collaboration and learning tools, and national promotion.

Actua has always thought of itself as a very entrepreneurial organization. We have prided ourselves on taking a new and innovative approach to science and technology education, in which we connect science to what is important in the lives of kids. We have had a very flexible structure that is capable of adapting quickly in response to the changing environment. For example, in 1998, because technology had become more of a focus in the education and economic communities, the original Actua entity, Youth Science Camps of Canada, merged with another national organization, Virtual Adventures Camps of Canada, which was more focused on technology. This was one of the first instances of a non-profit merger in Canada. The following year we were faced with the loss of over half of our revenue, due to the termination of Industry Canada's Science Culture Canada program, through which we were receiving funding. We quickly positioned the organization to take advantage of new funding opportunities and partnerships with private sector companies such as Nortel Networks, Hewlett-Packard Canada, and Celestica. Through a combination of project funds, contracts, and sponsorships, we were able to double Actua's revenue in less than two years.

The entrepreneurial spirit with which we run our organization and our programs makes us unique and inspires many of the people that work for Actua. As the organization grows in size and complexity, the danger of becoming more traditional and less entrepreneurial is a very real one. At Actua, we are tackling a series of concerns.

Challenges. Actua faces many of the same challenges other non-profit organizations face, the largest being the lack of sustained funding. Lacking any large, long-term sponsor, Actua starts from almost zero funding each year. Other significant challenges include increased competition for funding and clients, increased demands for accountability and recognition from corporate sector partners, limited growth potential of our current member organizations (due to limited infrastructure), and a lack of profile at the national level.

Motivations. I want Actua to be on the cutting edge of the non-profit world, both in the programs that we offer and in the way we run our organization. My motivations for pursuing social entrepreneurship are to increase Actua's financial independence, to explore opportunities to leverage our competencies, to increase the quality of our service delivery, and, most importantly, to reach more Canadian youth with Actua programs.

Objectives. In considering the pursuit of social entrepreneurship, Actua's objectives, in addition to gaining more financial independence, include strengthening our overall fundraising efforts by considering fundraising as a business venture. This has required us to package and put a dollar figure on what we can offer to potential partners. As this leads to a better understanding of Actua's core competencies and assets, it has the effect of solidifying our mission, vision, and values.

2. What Is Social Entrepreneurship? Categories of Implementation

Social entrepreneurship can be defined in various ways. The various forms of SE activities differ mainly in how financial and social returns are integrated and whether the emphasis is placed on the financial or social aspects. Two Canadian examples that demonstrate some of this variance are Social Capital Partners and Ashoka. Social Capital Partners,[1] an organization that funds social entrepreneurs, is focused on the financial aspects, believing that socially entrepreneurial organizations must implement earned-income structures before they can become truly self-sustaining. Ashoka, an organization that has been identifying and investing in leading social entrepreneurs around the world since 1981, defines social entrepreneurs as those individuals with unique, system-changing solutions for the world's most urgent social problems.[2] As these examples show, one SE definition may be strongly focused on the financial bottom line, while another may focus on the innovative nature of social change.

The current research on distinguishing forms of SE is limited. Boschee (2001) distinguishes between two categories of social entrepreneurship. One involves starting a new separate business venture; the other involves identifying and pursuing new earned income strategies within the existing non-profit structure. Fowler (2000) distinguishes three categories of social entrepreneurship. The first is called 'integrated' social entrepreneurship and refers to situations in which income-generating activities are designed to produce positive social outcomes. The second category is 're-interpreted' social entrepreneurship, in which existing non-profit capacities are utilized so as to diversify the organization's income sources. The third is 'complementary' social entrepreneurship where a non-profit organization adds a for-profit business venture that does not produce a direct social benefit but generates profits, which are used by the organization to deliver its mission. After comparing Canadian examples to the categories described by Fowler and Boschee, I expanded these categories to five instead of three, which I believe supplies a more useful means of describing the diversity of mechanisms by which social entrepreneurship is implemented.

The five categories that I propose apply to non-profit organizations that have existed for an appreciable period of time before undertaking a social entrepreneurial venture. Three characteristics, each with two possible types, are used to describe the five categories. The first characteristic describes where the market-driven activity is located: either inside the organization as an earned income stream (integrated) or outside the organization as a separate business unit (parallel). The second characteristic is what is being sold or marketed, and whether it is based on an existing organizational competency or asset (related) or a completely new competency (unrelated). The third characteristic is how the activity relates to mission delivery: whether the activity directly delivers mission (profit as a means) or allows for income to be generated that is then used to deliver mission (profit as an end).

Category 1: Integrated; related; profit as an end

A non-profit organization (NPO) may decide to leverage an existing competency or asset on a fee-for-service basis, by making one or more of its services available to a new client base, which pays for the service instead of receiving it for free. For example, an organization that provides a meals-on-wheels service for elderly shut-ins might also offer a meal delivery service to wealthier clients in order to generate additional income. A non-profit may also leverage assets such as its own audience reach, reputation, or profile in order to generate sources of new income in the form of sponsorships by private sector corporations interested in cross-marketing and public relations opportunities. In this example, the service provided to clients is an organizational asset that is leveraged in a way that is not directly related to the non-profit's mission but still allows new income to be generated for use in expanded mission-related activities. Most NPOs participating in this form of social entrepreneurship also fundraise from other sources.

These activities leverage assets that have been developed by the non-profit organization in the course of delivering its mission. Even if very few of the organization's basic resources are diverted from mission delivery to developing a new SE asset, the organization must still make sure that it can afford to undertake the SE activity without compromising its mission. It should be made very clear from the beginning, both internally and externally, how the new activities are integrated into existing workloads. If poorly managed, this can easily lead to confusion, internal tension, and overall negative impacts on the organization's mission.

Category 2: Integrated; related; profit as a means

Some non-profits have used their existing competencies and services to develop earned-income strategies that deliver mission-driven products and services directly to clients. The ways in which organizations accomplish this may include fee-for service offers, contracts, and product sales or consulting. The income is provided by third parties: individuals, government departments, or companies who find it cheaper to pay for the service rather than provide it for themselves. In-home nursing care to keep elderly people in their homes and out of hospitals or full-care facilities, after-school programs for at-risk youth, hospice care for terminally ill patients, and water irrigation management for governments in developing countries are just a few examples. The non-profit must effectively package and market its products or services and the clients must be able to see the value added components. This approach reduces the risk of competition between income and mission (since one cannot be delivered without the other), but it does not eliminate it completely. There is still the risk of focusing too heavily on what is necessary to sell the service (e.g., promotion costs, staff time for client relations), which could have a detrimental effect on the quality of services being provided. A careful balance must be maintained and monitored to ensure that the services provided are focused on the needs of the users while still marketable.

Category 3: Parallel; related; profit as an end

A non-profit organization may decide to take its Category 1 earned-income activities a step further and create a separate business venture that is able to grow beyond the confines of the non-profit entity. This means that the social entrepreneurship entity can have its own staff and operate separately from the day-to-day operations of the parent organization. An agreement for profit sharing is developed to detail how the non-profit will continue to benefit financially from the new SE entity.

A successful Canadian example is One World Inc., a for-profit spin-off of the Canadian Council for International Cooperation (CCIC). One World Inc. leveraged core competencies around deliberative dialogue and public consultation as a successful business venture that now provides services to the Canadian federal government and other non-profits. One World Inc. has returned a dividend to CCIC in three of the last four years (with the largest dividend, $35,000, in 2005–6. One World Inc.'s CEO, Jacquie Dale, expects even larger returns to CCIC in future years now that the organization has successfully developed its own contingency funds.

To minimize risk to the non-profit, the new spin-off should have a completely separate identity and legal structure. If the new entity were then to fail, the organization would be insulated from significant damage to its reputation.

Category 4: Parallel; related; profit as a means

A non-profit organization may decide to establish a separate business that leverages an existing competency and that delivers mission directly. This is taking the Category 2 model a step further. An example is CARE Canada, which, in 1995, recognized it had developed unique competencies in international human resource deployment and information technology integration. In order to allow these two core entities to grow more fully, CARE supported the creation (i.e., in principle but not financially) of a new non-profit organization called Global Development Group (GDG), which not only provides high-level HR and IT services to CARE but also provides this service to other international organizations, thus expanding CARE's mission. When GDG was first incorporated, the original intention was to return a portion of its revenue to CARE. However, GDG has evolved and launched three private sector companies; while CARE has received services without markups or profit margins, funds have not been returned to CARE directly as yet. This model has the potential for major benefits to the parent organization: on the one hand, increased mission delivery backed by shared profits; on the other, broader and more sophisticated services provided by the new entity, without the added cost. In this model, the organization must be careful not to become completely dependent on the spin-off for essential services. A back-up plan should be in place. It would be a significant undertaking to reintegrate these activities back into the organization should the new entity fail.

Category 5: Parallel; unrelated; profit as an end

A non-profit may decide to start a separate business entity that is completely unrelated to its mission. For example, some non-profits, like the Chicago Children's Choir, have started Ben & Jerry's ice cream franchises with the intention of creating an ongoing revenue stream by reinvesting the profits in the parent NGO. This was a more popular strategy in the late 1980s in the United States, with Ben & Jerry's going so far as to waive the franchise fee and provide additional support to non-profits that purchased franchises. Even with the additional support provided by the franchise, the up-front costs and time necessary to break even (up to seven or eight years), combined with the complexity of managing a profit-driven business and a social mandate, makes this model a risky one. Nor has the model been as lucrative as originally thought. The Chicago Children's Choir, which has not been running the franchise long enough to see a significant return, put a new spin on their service to customers: they sing while they scoop! They also see a social mandate – job training and skill development for youth – within the operation of the franchise. I have not found any examples of long-term success for non-profit organizations that have started completely non-mission-related ventures.

Obviously, not every method would apply to every organization. Organizations thinking about adopting a social entrepreneurship strategy should carefully consider which the best option is to pursue. The distinctions between these categories are not extreme, but they are useful in understanding the risks involved for a given organization in its current situation. If an organization cannot identify a position within one of these social entrepreneurship categories, it may not have the resources or organizational structures to pursue this type of activity. Or it may be delivering on a mission that is not necessarily marketable to a wider audience of paying clients. Methods for identifying competencies and earned income potential will be discussed later in the essay.

A legal consideration: The Income Tax Act *and charities*

The current Canadian *Income Tax Act* (ITA) allows registered charities to carry on related business activities. The definition of 'related business activity' is interpreted in many different ways. The ITA clearly states that charities undertaking non-related business activities can lose their charitable status (Canada Revenue Agency 2005). This is different from the U.S. tax law, which permits charities to run 'unrelated businesses' that are subject to unrelated businesses income tax (UBIT) at the same rate as corporate taxes. What is not completely clear in the ITA is the distinction between related and non-related business. For example, the Act says that a volunteer-run business, such as a hospital gift shop, even though not related to the purpose of the charity or NPO, is considered related because it is a business that is linked to the charity's purpose *and* subordinate to that purpose.

Most non-related business activities undertaken by charities (fundraising events, conversion of donated goods to cash, sponsorships, occasional business transactions, and business investments) are acceptable and legal, because these activities have a starting and ending point and do not carry the same level of risk as running an ongoing business. Charities that are carrying on regular business activities in a constant manner over time fall outside these exemptions, and the businesses are considered non-related. Charities are also not permitted to be partners in an ongoing business.

In the ITA, the current definition of a related business has two requirements. The first is that the business must be linked to the charity's purpose. This can include businesses that are part of a charity delivering on its mission – for example, a cafeteria in a hospital or a bookstore on a university campus. This also includes offshoots of core programs, where a charity, in the course of delivering on its mission, has created an asset that it is then able to exploit in a business. The second requirement is that the related business must be subordinate to the main purpose of the charity. The charity must be able to demonstrate clearly that the business activity does not take up a majority of the charity's resources; that it is integrated and not acting as a separate entity within the confines of one organization; that no individual is benefiting personally from the business; and that the charitable purpose continues to be the main factor in decision-making.

If a charity charges a fee for its programs in order to generate revenue, this fee must be accessible to a wide range of the population or there must be a fee structure in place that provides low-cost service when necessary.

It is clear that there is currently a lot of room for SE activities within the confines of the *Income Tax Act*. It may be just as well that charities in Canada are not permitted to start completely unrelated businesses, considering the significant risk of failure and the possible consequences for the charity. Charities undertaking any business activities must pay close attention to changes that may occur as both the Canada Revenue Agency and U.S. Internal Revenue Service guidelines evolve.

What makes a social entrepreneur?

Although the focus of this essay is on social entrepreneurship at an organizational level, the role of the individual social entrepreneur is critical. SE ventures are often started or driven forward by an individual – a social entrepreneur – who sees the potential for these ventures to provide significant return to the organization and who can articulate the actions necessary to put their vision into action.

The Canadian Centre for Social Entrepreneurship (CCSE), established at the University of Alberta in 1997, describes social entrepreneurs as leaders of social change who combine an entrepreneurial approach with a strong commitment to the 'social bottom line.' Social entrepreneurs are like for-profit entrepreneurs in that they have a higher tolerance for uncertainty and risk and they pursue their goals tirelessly in spite of initial obstacles and lack of resources. Not only do social entrepreneurs have a vision about the kind of change they want to create, they also have the necessary business acumen, problem-solving capacities, and ethics to realize their vision.

In *Social Entrepreneurship* (2000), one of the few full-length books on the subject, Peter Brinckerhoff identifies six very definite characteristics of social entrepreneurs:

1. A willingness to take risks on behalf of the people the organization serves.
2. The commitment to finding new ways to serve the organization's mission.
3. An understanding of the difference between needs and wants.
4. An understanding that all resource allocations are investments.
5. The ability to make decisions with the social and financial returns in mind.
6. An overall understanding that mission requires money. (202–3)

Ashoka, the organization that has been identifying and supporting social entrepreneurs for over twenty years, takes these characteristics one step further and defines the outcomes necessary to be considered a social entrepreneur. It looks for people who will become references in their field and will set or change patterns and policy at a national or international level.

Another element common to all these characteristics is that social entrepreneurs do not feel personally bound by non-profit norms and traditions. Although all strategies should be examined to ensure a match with the organization's values, social entrepreneurs are creative and open to considering any strategy that is likely to provide resources to their social mission.

Is your organization ready for SE?

Although many SE activities within organizations are started by individuals with social entrepreneurship qualities, the organization must itself share some of these qualities in order for the activities to be successful and sustainable. Adopting more business-like approaches is still controversial in the non-profit world. There are many people who believe that mission and money cannot easily coexist and that any focus on generating a profit will dilute the idea of the mission. This is a very real concern that should be addressed thoroughly inside the organization before adopting SE activities. However, the notion that non-profit organizations have nothing in common with for-profit businesses or that they could not learn from applying some appropriate business concepts is outdated and potentially harmful to their mission. Any non-profit organization ought at least to explore the terms on which mission and money might coexist. Brinckerhoff emphasizes that individuals and organizations pursuing entrepreneurship must learn to be comfortable with the role that money and profit can play in a non-profit mission. The non-profit organization's values need not be compromised by SE activities if the organization takes care to communicate clearly the motivations and impacts of the new business activities or practices to all stakeholders. It is crucial to have checks and balances in place to ensure that the mission is not taking a back seat to money. Making this balance clear will be important to external stakeholders, including the general public, who are interested in seeing that the priority of non-profit organizations is on its mission delivery and upholding strong values.

Another risk that has been identified in the increased blurring of the lines between the non-profit and for-profit sectors is the potential negative impact on society caused by the reduction in diversity of approaches (Zimmerman and Dart 1998, 9). It is clear that the values-based, socially focused approach of the non-profit sector is critical to the well-being and success of society. Social entrepreneurship is not about transforming all non-profits into for-profit business clones; it is about adopting successful practices that allow voluntary sector organizations' social purposes to thrive, while maintaining their values and remaining focused on their missions. Non-profits practising social entrepreneurship should continue to celebrate and promote their unique differences and competencies. The challenge for many VSOs is that they often do not realize their strengths and assets. The process of identifying these assets and strengths, which is so necessary in social entrepreneurship, allows VSOs to identify what can be leveraged. In addition, it creates an opportunity to exchange expertise and skills with the for-profit world.

3. Outcomes and Analysis of Research Interviews

To get a first-hand account of SE activities currently being delivered, I interviewed two practising social entrepreneurs. Geoff Cape (named an Ashoka Fellow in 2005) is the executive director of Evergreen, a national charitable organization with a mandate to bring nature to our cities through naturalization projects. Mike Mispelaar is the president of Global Development Group, the CARE Canada spin-off mentioned earlier. Both Geoff and Mike are career entrepreneurs who have vastly expanded the scope and success of their respective organizations. Both organizations are highly successful, and both have adopted SE as an organizational approach.

Next I interviewed two representatives of organizations that fund social entrepreneurs and SE activities. Sean Van Doorselaer is the vice-president of Social Capital Partners Enterprise Centre (Toronto). Christina Gibb was the manager of Ashoka Canada. As previously explained, SCP and Ashoka work from different SE models.

Lastly, I interviewed Rob Briscoe, then president of the Venture Institute, a consulting firm that specializes in training and support for entrepreneurs.

During the interviews, I allowed the flow of conversation to guide the focus of the discussion so as to spotlight the respondents' most important concerns. I then reviewed and integrated findings from the interviews and my literature review. This produced a set of common themes, which are broad enough to accommodate, but also clear enough to highlight certain striking differences among the interviewees, as some of the examples below will show.

Theme #1: The emergence and implementation of social entrepreneurship in Canada

The funding situation in Canada is driving the emergence of more SE activities. Many voluntary sector and non-profit organizations realize that they must acquire different skill sets to deal with the new competitive environment that demands accountability and good public relations.

In all SE activities, there is strong emphasis placed on innovation (new ideas, approaches, models) and on familiarizing people and helping them to become comfortable with the ways in which money and mission have to work together. Geoff Cape at Evergreen realized that he could effectively combine a social mission with aggressive business techniques in order to drive social change in the environmental sector after an experience he had as a student entrepreneur. In the third year of his business, he tripled his profits by partnering with a local charity to promote sales and then splitting the profits equally. Shortly after this student experience, Geoff started Evergreen and integrated much of the learning. As the organization nears its thirteenth year of operations, Geoff now believes that Evergreen has implemented a new form of institutional entrepreneurship. Although there is no start-up element and no new entity has spun off yet, there are mechanisms in place to drive constant innovation both in programming and financing.

The way in which social entrepreneurship is approached varies between organizations in a manner similar to the five categories of implementation that were discussed earlier. While Geoff Cape has chosen to build entrepreneurship throughout the Evergreen organization, others decide to generate a new venture. Global Development Group was founded because CARE Canada realized that in delivering its mission for so many years, it had developed human resource and information technology competencies that could be marketed to the private sector and to government. CARE realized that the potential for future growth of these competencies within its organization was limited. CARE had a choice. It could halt the growth of its human resources and information technology units, but in so doing it would inevitably stunt the growth of the entire organization in the future. Instead, the two units were taken out of the organization and reconstituted as Global Development Group, which then marketed the services to other organizations. This allowed CARE's HR and IT expertise to continue growing and developing, and in the process it also brought down the internal cost of these services for CARE.

Theme #2: Non-profit does not mean unbusinesslike

Every organization, regardless of whether it is non-profit or for-profit, has two sides to it. One involves running a business – financing, advertising, human resources, strategic planning; the other involves carrying out its mission. Most people do not go into business to run the 'business' side of things; they start businesses because they are passionate about their mission, whether it is coffee, emergency relief, graphic design, or educating youth. One cannot exist without the other or, in other words, a mission cannot exist without money. You can make the best cup of coffee in town but if you have unhappy staff and untargeted promotions that undermine your profitability, your good coffee won't get you very far. It is the same in the voluntary sector. Non-profit organizations may be experts at delivering their mission, but often they lack the tools, training, and resources they need to reach their full potential. In certain crucial respects, every non-profit leader and manager should be able, when necessary, to think like a business executive.

Rob Briscoe, who works with many for-profit and non-profit organizations and entrepreneurs, sees that many of the private and voluntary sector organizations face the same challenges and problems in growth and sustainability. He uses a metaphor of pushing a car up a hill to describe the challenge and potential of business as applied to non-profits. Most non-profits would surround the car with a host of staff and volunteers, who would begin slowly pushing the car up the hill. Good social entrepreneurs are more innovative, and recognize the necessity and benefit of investing in getting the car's engine up and running so that the trip to the top of the hill is much easier and much more efficient. Many organizations are so focused on pushing the car up the hill, and so exhausted by the effort, that they forget completely about the engine inside the car. The point is that investing in the infrastructure of an organization and exploring new mechanisms for financial viability will enable organizations to achieve their missions more effectively.

Theme #3: The role of innovation is social entrepreneurship

It is certain that those I interviewed viewed innovation as a critical part of their social entrepreneurial work. Not all people who start businesses are true entrepreneurs. The person who starts a hot dog stand on the corner is not doing anything different or being particularly innovative. In the same way, a company that improves a product or service is not necessarily innovative. Innovations are new approaches that stand out; they are unique and go on to set new standards and practices within their industry. Likewise, in social entrepreneurship, innovation is about finding new solutions to old problems while finding new ways to fund these new activities.

In working with hundreds of entrepreneurs, Rob Briscoe has seen the word 'innovation' overused, and he works to get people to understand the difference between innovation and optimization. Both words are important, but confusing them can lead to an organization's having false ideas about how innovative it truly is or how much focus it is putting on distinguishing itself from the competition.

Ashoka's view of innovation is focused on the idea, concept, or model for social change, not necessarily the income generation that enables it. The organization looks for people with groundbreaking ideas who have the potential to change systems at a national or international level. A good example is Mary Gordon, one of Ashoka's first Canadian fellows, whose Roots of Empathy Program for school classrooms has had dramatic success in reducing aggression and violence by breaking the recurring cycles of abuse among generations of children. Her program has parents bring their new babies into an elementary classroom every couple of weeks. The students experience the vulnerability of the baby and learn how the baby expresses its needs (crying, for example, can mean the baby is upset, or is hungry, or has another need it is trying to express). The program develops children's emotional intelligence and helps them to more accurately name their feelings – the first step in conflict resolution. The results so far have demonstrated a significant reduction in bullying, and more kids are sticking up for each other in the classroom and on the playground. Mary Gordon's vision is to build more caring classrooms with the eventual goal of building a more caring world.

Brisco contends that every organization should be open to innovative ideas coming from all parts of the organization. This is quite a challenging change, since many organizations are so focused on efficiency that there is no room for the 'luxury' of playing with new ideas within the organizational culture. In this era of rapid change, however, organizations will have to look beyond their efficiency lens, or they will perish, no matter how efficient they may be.

Theme #4: Making it happen: Diversification of revenue streams

There are various ways in which non-profit organizations are choosing to diversify their funding streams, both within the current structures of their organizations and by starting new ventures.

One way this is happening in Canada is through a more aggressive pursuit of corporate-sector partnerships. These are no longer just about handouts. Geoff Cape has secured multi-year, million-dollar deals with large corporations for programs that were packaged along with recognition opportunities and a fair market value price. Geoff and his staff put together a list of companies whose values and approaches complemented Evergreen's values and vision. The benefits and returns from both a social and a marketing perspective were communicated clearly and unequivocally to potential corporate investors. Geoff believes that the language that is used to describe these funding relationships is critical. 'They are market transactions and investments; continuing to see them as a handout only continues to put us in a weaker, more vulnerable position.'[3] When Evergreen is looking for new funding partners, it is searching for investors, and a lot of time is spent in assessing potential relationships in terms of market dynamics. For example, Evergreen is in the media quite frequently and therefore is able to enhance the media profiles of its national sponsors like Toyota Canada and Home Depot. This offers a high added value. With regard to media exposure, Evergreen is able to demonstrate to the corporation that sponsorship will deliver higher returns on its investment in Evergreen than it could obtain from regular advertising. Another innovative example from Evergreen is its $55-million Brick Works Project, a large-scale social enterprise in Toronto designed to transform the way people think about nature in their cities. The project is being funded by a wide range of partners, including various levels of government, individuals, corporations, and other non-profit partners. The objective of the environmental education facility is to be 100 per cent self-sustaining – unlike many major cultural institutions that require millions in subsidies every year to maintain their operations.

Although not involved with corporate sponsorships, Mike Mispelaar has always had more success in generating revenue for his CARE projects when he ran them as a business. One example is a local CARE project that created a water irrigation system, which CARE packaged for easy replication. He generated revenue by demonstrating to local governments that he could create irrigation systems at a cheaper rate than either the government or the private sector. Thus, in securing funding for expansion, he was able to deliver on CARE's mission to bring fresh water to communities on a much larger scale. When he took over the reins at Global Development Group in 2000, he began reapplying these business methods to generate revenue, which he then reinvested in software, infrastructure, equipment, staff training, and other assets. He has successfully led dozens of projects, using this self-sustained approach.

These two leaders have very strong entrepreneurial underpinnings, but they are not acting alone; they are being supported by entire organizations that share in their belief. At Evergreen, the majority of the staff are empowered to find their own sources of funding for the programs for which they are responsible. Entrepreneurship and innovation are thus coming from every corner of the organization and not only from Geoff. This policy has been extremely popular with corporate and foundation partners, who like hearing directly from program staff about the success of the programs they are supporting.

Theme #5: Balancing the double bottom line

One criticism of social entrepreneurship is that it dilutes the voluntary sector or non-profit organization's mission. Effectively balancing the ongoing mission with the excitement and novelty of a new social entrepreneurship venture is definitely a challenge that must be considered and planned for. The first step is for the organization to formally state its mission and core values. These statements then form the framework for decision-making when it comes to pursuing new entrepreneurial activities. The organization can be proactive about this process by devising a set of questions to be asked when evaluating a new opportunity. It is important to evaluate the mission return and the financial return on the investment each and every time a new SE venture is pursued.

When Evergreen started introducing more market-driven mechanisms to secure new revenue, tensions arose because many in the organization did not want to see the commodification of the social value they were creating. Geoff overcame this challenge through open dialogue within his staff and board. Evergreen is very careful in choosing the companies with whom it becomes involved to ensure that there is a keen understanding and respect for Evergreen's values and approaches.

At CARE, several board members with business experience knew that the cultural barriers to SE within the organization were too strong. For the new Global Development venture to succeed, it had to be separate from the parent organization. For Mike Mispelaar, balancing a social mandate with the need for profitability involves being one step ahead of the normal investor and the market. GDG must anticipate demand in the market and reposition itself to enable other market mechanisms to follow. This requires greater alertness, vision, commitment, and sophistication than a traditional entrepreneur ordinarily needs.

Theme #6: Promoting organizational readiness for social entrepreneurship

Introducing new activities and ways of approaching revenue generation will undoubtedly cause significant cultural change within a voluntary sector or non-profit organization. Organizations with cultures that are built around a charity mindset will feel the tension that is created when earned income or new revenue streams are introduced. Most organizations prefer not to step too far out of their comfort zones; yet staying inside the comfort zone may be an even greater risk over the long term. Nor is private sector commercialization alone to blame. In the present-day climate of tightly controlled and focused government funding, many organizations are already at risk of drifting away from their mission.

One of the best strategies to overcome the fear of risk is to take a scalable approach to introducing these new ways of working. Trying something on the smallest possible scale to see how it will work may make risk-averse staff and board members much more comfortable. This helps to minimize losses if the SE venture fails (as a good portion of new ventures do). This is exactly the approach that Mike Mispelaar used with his CARE projects. As he worked on his small project, he developed standard processes, systems, solutions, and templates that could easily and quickly be implemented in other areas at a low cost. As a result, CARE members were much more receptive to large-scale expansion, which was further supported by the huge investments that were usually secured from governments over the long term.

Many non-profit organizations already include income-generating activities. These activities are often run with a charitable mindset and are often not as profitable as they could be. Rob Biscoe cites the example of the church that he attends, which produces CDs of the popular lectures given each week. Due to demand, the church began selling the CDs for $5 each to cover the cost of production. Yet the vast majority of those who attend this church are upper-middle-class people who could afford, and would be willing to pay, a higher price. A small upfront investment made by the church to research an appropriate price point could lead to a modest earned income stream over the long run – simple but still effective.

Theme #7: The role of the funder

Most non-profits that adopt social entrepreneurial activities will continue to generate revenue through fundraising. With the rise of social entrepreneurship and the blurring of the private and voluntary sectors, traditional funding agencies may start to see the need for (and the benefit of) investing in capacity building and innovation. Some foundations and corporations now invest in a much more progressive fashion, but these are still the exceptions, not the norm.

Most funding agencies have generated their capital resources through successful business ventures. Their directors understand the value of longer-term commitments, innovation, and entrepreneurial spirit; yet they provide funding in a very conservative, sometimes controlling, manner. It is critical that funders see today's non-profits in the same light that non-profits should see themselves – as mission-based businesses.

Ashoka's approach is to provide each elected fellow with the equivalent of a reasonable non-profit salary for three years – enough time for individual fellows to model and develop an idea without having to worry about fundraising for their own salaries. Ashoka's success is a strong example of the minimal investment that needs to occur in most organizations in order to get new innovative programs or practices off the ground. As well, Ashoka uses scalability as the basis of its funding model: small investments in the beginning lead to sustainable growth and yield very high returns over the longer term.

Social Capital Partners takes a similar approach, but funds a different type of social entrepreneurship entirely, providing venture capital to non-profit businesses that create missions while creating profit. Specifically, their mission is delivered by hiring at-risk youth to staff these businesses, thereby fostering employability skills, income generation, and training and mentorship opportunities. Not only does Social Capital Partners invest start-up cash in these businesses, it also supports them with resources and expertise in all aspects of running the business through their Enterprise Centre.

4. Actua and Social Entrepreneurship

This section will explore Actua's approach to its own entrepreneurial activities: organizational readiness, obstacles to SE implementation, assets and capital that could be leveraged through SE.

Organizational readiness

It is critical that an organization is prepared for SE before it is implemented. The following factors will contribute to Actua's overall readiness:

Capacity. Actua is at an advantage in having a relatively small, young, and open-minded staff whose members are eager to try new things. This makes it easier to discuss potential changes. Undertaking a new venture, including the time required to develop a plan and to research options more thoroughly, will require the addition of staff and possibly the shifting of current roles. The new activity may also require an investment of cash up front. There are many options for generating this seed funding, including using a portion of Actua's contingency fund, asking one of our current funders for an additional one-time investment, or seeking a new source of funding. Several board members are eager to explore new possibilities for the organization.

Marketable Assets. Actua has developed many services, products, and technologies that could be of interest to other organizations. For example, we have invested heavily in building Actua's technological capacities. We also have a very strong and proven reputation and a significant audience reach.

Market Opportunities. There are many needs faced by other non-profits that we could potentially fill for a fee, specifically in knowledge management, training, online collaboration, survey systems, and reporting mechanisms.

Asset identification

This is perhaps one of the most exciting and eye-opening steps in the process of preparing for social entrepreneurship. Many organizations, including Actua, take the assets that we have developed for granted, when in reality many could be leveraged to generate income. In table 15.1, I have brainstormed a list of assets based on what we have, what we do, and what we know.

This is a very long list of assets. It will be important for us to look at how we can leverage all of these assets, but not necessarily as new income streams or businesses. There are, however, quite a few that have the potential to generate income.

Opportunities

Out of the list of assets, we must determine those with the most potential for being leveraged. Which assets are unique and could be competitive? Which are realistic and sustainable? Can the asset provide clear and measurable value? Again, this will require much more rigorous evaluation. As a start, I have identified certain assets that I believe have the most potential in two categories: assets that will enable Actua to pursue new and more lucrative *partnerships* with the corporate sector; and assets that could potentially develop into new *enterprises*.

Partnership assets

Wide geographic reach and excellent media profile and potential. It is much easier for corporations to get their names in the media when they are associated with a charitable cause. Actua has strong media appeal in that we work with many different youth groups across Canada. We could promote media opportunities to new potential sponsors.

Strong brand reach to pre-teen and teen markets. Many corporations are interested in gaining access to youth markets because of their vast buying and decision-making power. By choosing our partners very carefully, Actua has the potential to use this asset in a responsible, ethical

Table 15.1
Asset identification – Actua

Things we HAVE:	Things we DO:	Things we KNOW:
• Attractive office space in a desirable location	• Continuously innovate our curriculum and programs	• Building and managing tri-sectoral partnerships
• State-of-the-art equipment, including videoconferencing capabilities	• Collect and analyse large amounts of data over the Internet	• Choosing, integrating, and training on new technology systems
• Well-developed and attractive brand	• Produce programs at a low cost	• Running summer camps
• Award-winning reputation	• Deliver training and professional development	• Issues related to girls in science
• Access to large pre-teen and teen market	• Deliver national conferences	• How to reach underprivileged youth
• Trust of local communities across Canada	• Deliver kids' programs	• Managing large-scale national projects with multiple stakeholders
• References from satisfied sponsors	• Fundraise from private sector	• Mechanisms for effective reporting
• Access to low-cost, highly skilled talent	• Video conference	• How to connect science to kids' lives
• Easily mobilized network	• Connect kids across the country	• Working with private sector
• Access to national distribution network	• Connect kids with scientists and engineers	• Staff with strong technical expertise
• Large geographically disbursed membership	• Provide jobs for university students	• Strong practical research expertise
• Strong media appeal	• Provide recognition opportunities to sponsors	
	• Write excellent proposals	

way. We also have an attractive, easily recognizable brand that makes it appealing for sponsors to associate it with their logos.

Enterprise assets

Capacity to collect and analyse large amounts of data online, specifically for research or survey purposes. Actua has developed a cutting-edge survey system that enables the collection, analysis, reporting, and storage of large amounts of data. Many non-profits are struggling with the logistics of collecting impact data. Not only does Actua have the system, but we also have the training in place for successful implementation.

National project management and reporting coordination. Actua has substantial expertise in managing large-scale, multi-year projects that involve coordinating multiple clusters of geographically dispersed groups. The computerized accountability and reporting mechanisms that Actua has designed have received very high praise from funders.

Training and professional development for the delivery of youth programs. Actua has been offering low-cost, high-value conferences for over fifteen years. We have dozens of training modules and materials pertaining to the effective, high-quality delivery of educational programs for youth. These materials could apply to any sector. Many organizations that do not fit Actua's membership criteria might be willing to pay for access to the training opportunities that we provide.

Risks

Assessing the risks associated with starting an SE activity is critical. The following key risks should be considered:

Financial. How long will it take to receive a financial return on the investment? How much is Actua willing to invest in this new venture, being completely aware that it could lose money or take several years to return the investment? Is this the best investment to make with the relatively small surplus that Actual has accumulated?

Reputation. Actua has an excellent reputation for delivering on its commitments to projects. In fact, funders can count on us to deliver beyond expectations. This reputation has taken years to develop. Any new activity could have an impact on Actua's overall reputation. We must also to be very careful to clearly communicate the purpose and motivation for undertaking SE activities.

Organizational. Actua must make sure that it has the necessary resources in place to handle the additional workload that will be created. We do not want staff to feel overwhelmed.

Next steps for implementation

The analysis that I have started here will have to be deepened in order to get a true sense of the opportunities that exist and the risks involved. This would require the following steps:

1. Discussion Document: Create a discussion document on social entrepreneurship and Actua's potential to start new entrepreneurial activities.

2. Mission Statement: Solidify Actua's mission statement and ensure we have full organizational buy-in from members and from the board.
3. Discussion about Risk: Evaluate the risk factors throughout the process, with more thorough analysis once specific ideas are suggested.
4. Objectives: Make a clear and compelling case for how new activities could deliver more mission.
5. Asset Evaluation: More thorough brainstorming and discussion on Actua's assets involving staff and members of the Board. Determine which assets are unique, who would value the asset, how willing people are to pay for it, and how much social return on our mission it will provide.[4]
6. Narrow Opportunities: Identify the top opportunities for new ventures and determine revenue potential.
7. Market Assessment and Feasibility Study: Test our ideas to see if they do in fact have market potential.

Once these steps have been accomplished, Actua will be ready to embark on a business-planning process, which may change as more stakeholders become involved. However, Actua will have tools and knowledge in place that will allow us to plan and analyse our new SE ventures very thoroughly in order to ensure successful operation and maximum returns.

5. Conclusion

Many Canadian voluntary sector and non-profit organizations are having success with social entrepreneurial models. Evergreen's diversification of its revenue stream has enabled the organization to grow by 500 per cent in the past two years. The entrepreneurial approach has also heightened the attention that all staff members pay to performance and accountability. Ashoka's strategy of investing in social entrepreneurs early in their growth cycle has paid off. Within five years of their respective nominations, 64 per cent of Ashoka's social entrepreneurship fellows have gone on to have a positive effect on national policy and 88 per cent credit the Ashoka investment as being critical to achieving this success. Global Development Group is reinvesting all profit back into building capital in order to put the infrastructure in place for its next round of growth. In the meantime, CARE has already benefited tremendously from higher-quality human resources and information technology services, which GDG has provided at a very reasonable cost.

Despite the risks involved and the danger that new initiatives may fail, social entrepreneurs and organizations with SE mindsets are uniquely focused on learning from the experience and moving on to the next opportunity for leveraging their organizations to greater mission output. Careful business planning, branding the mission, and calculated risk taking will contribute to the overall sustainability and growth of Canada's VSOs and NPOs over the long term.

For non-profit leaders who want to adopt entrepreneurial activities but are having trouble convincing their boards, the key is to use a scalable approach. Creating a small working model of income generation will allow the organization to see what SE looks like and be reassured that success can be achieved. This model can then be scaled up as much as the markets will allow.

For Actua, the potential of social entrepreneurship is hard to ignore and could be the basis of Actua's next period of growth. The first and most significant step will be to solidify Actua's mission and values and secure a buy-in from all stakeholders. Our mission will then provide the guidelines within which to explore the level of risk we are willing to undertake and the investment we are willing to make in a new SE venture. What is certain is that Actua can immediately start dealing with its current programs and funding relationships in a more entrepreneurial fashion. This will also contribute to the process of identifying assets that Actua can leverage in order to diversity its funding stream for future sustainability. While I do not expect these new activities to completely replace our current fundraising model, I do believe that a greater diversification and strengthening of our revenue streams is possible.

There is no doubt that the Canadian social sector needs to be shaken up, as do the agencies that fund it. The old charitable approaches, which in the past led to chronic dependency and instability, need to be laid to rest. The time is right for new voluntary sector models to emerge. Social entrepreneurship will fuel innovation and help us find new and shorter pathways to social improvement and change.

NOTES

Please note that all facts and legislation referred to in this essay were verified at the time of writing. Changes that may have occurred since 2003 are not reflected in this essay.

1 See http://www.socialcapitalpartners.org.
2 See http://www.ashoka.org.
3 Geoff Cape, interview with author, February 2002, Toronto, ON.
4 There are a number of tools available to help with the asset evaluation process, including a very thorough grid matrix provided by Peter Brinckerhoff in *Social Entrepreneurship* (2000).

Conclusion:
The Practice of Ethics and
the Voluntary Sector

FREDERICK BIRD

It seems appropriate, in concluding this book, to say a few words about the importance of ethics in the voluntary sector. The McGill-McConnell Program did not include a separate module on ethics; instead, the five modules focused upon mindsets – reflective, analytical, global, collaborative, and catalytic – and part of each module was devoted to ethics, which thus functioned as an integrating approach or theme.

Ethics can be usefully viewed as a social practice, or rather a set of overlapping social practices. These practices include a range of activities by which we exercise judgments, initiate projects, settle disputes, cultivate habits, and voice concerns. These practices are all ethical insofar as we undertake them in relation to some kind of normative expectations. In turn, these normative expectations may be variously identified in relation to valued outcomes as well as to obligatory or desirable ways of behaving, which in turn bear a relation to personal virtues or cultural mores. Correspondingly, we engage in the social practice of ethics in a number of different ways. We do so as we uphold standards of etiquette, seek to identify and address injustices, attempt to resolve moral dilemmas, and encourage acts of charity. We are likewise practising ethics when we work at disciplining ourselves or others, exhort ourselves or others to act with courage, and ponder alternative ways of utilizing limited resources. Additionally, whether or not we invoke formal philosophical ideas or explicit moral rules, we are practising ethics when we overtly praise or blame others for their accomplishments and shortfalls, when we identify and enforce social rules, and when we pause to reflect on what values we hold most important.

The social practice of ethics assumes many forms. In this conclusion, I discuss four characteristic forms of ethics:

1. Ethics as voicing
2. Ethics as good conversations
3. Ethics as evaluating
4. Ethics as fostering charity and justice

In each case I will illustrate these forms with reference to the essays that form the chapters of this book. In the process, I will call attention to the ways people engage in the social practice of ethics through their involvements in voluntary sector organizations (VSOs). By means of this essay, I hope to provide both a fuller account of the everyday practice of ethics and a richer appreciation of the ways voluntary sector organizations are challenged by and contribute to this practice.

The reader will notice that I often use verbs rather than nouns when referring to ethics. We are often led to think of ethics as cognitive statements embodied in sets of philosophical principles, social rules, sacred maxims, revered teachings, honoured mores, and the like. As such, ethics seems to be found in these objects, which are, to be sure, particular forms of knowledge or information. This view leads to the reification of ethics, the regarding of ethics as a certain kind of 'thing.' I think it is much more fitting to think of ethics as an important kind of human activity – or rather, as I have already noted, as a set of activities. To be sure, this activity often involves consulting or invoking various revered statements. But it is important to appreciate the activity of ethics itself. It is useful as well to explore a bit further the close interrelationship between the practice of ethics and the voluntary sector.

1. Ethics as Voicing

We engage in the practice of ethics whenever we call attention to moral concerns. We are variously moved to voice moral concern as a way of pointing to problems that must be attended to and of challenging ourselves and others to work so as to realize moral ideals. We voice moral sentiments both to affirm our sense of community with others and to raise alarms when our shared mores seem to be threatened. Although we often associate ethical voicing with the protests of prophets and the pronouncements of visionaries, ethical voicing occurs as well whenever we seek to arouse attention about moral concerns – even in informal conversations. We voice moral concerns to sound alarms, invoke shared identities, and inspire excellence. We can indeed use the word *advocacy* appropriately to refer to the activity of ethical voicing.

However, we need to guard against an overly restrictive understanding of advocacy in the sense of 'verbal support or argument for a cause, policy, etc.' (according to the *Canadian Oxford Dictionary*). In ethics, we may for all practical purposes, consider advocacy as the act of giving voice to or speaking up for any moral concern.

As we speak up about moral concerns, we often feel moved in person to do so as a way of giving voice to our conscience. Not to speak out is to muffle or silence our conscience. Nonetheless, as we look around our world we can see many examples of muted consciences: that is, situations in which people with moral sentiments fail to give voice to their sense of what's wrong, to their visions of what might be possible, and to their feelings of connectedness with others. Because we feel our voices won't make a difference, or because we fear to offend others, or because we don't know quite the right words to use, we often don't voice our moral concerns, or else we speak about them by means of whispers and evasion (Bird 1996).

We have entitled this book *Voices from the Voluntary Sector*, and indeed many of the essays included here involve more than the expression of ideas relevant to effective voluntary sector leadership; rather, they are calls for action. They point to areas of concern that have been overlooked or received less than adequate attention. They direct readers to pause and rethink particular assumptions and to see other possibilities. For example, Shawn Bayes challenges readers to consider the human and social cost of the ways in which Canada's incarceration practices overlook the impact on the children of offenders. Cindy Blackstock wonders why voluntary sector organizations have not been more involved with First Nations families and children living on reserves. Marg McGregor cautions NGOs to prepare themselves to deal with unexpected crises. Robert Ryan calls upon fundraisers to respect the humanity of the people they seek to recruit as donors. Jennifer Flanagan exhorts voluntary sector organizations to think more creatively about ways they can use entrepreneurial activities with integrity to help finance and enhance their programs. In each case, these authors voice concern in hopes of moving others to act.

Many voluntary sector organizations were established in order to voice concerns effectively about a wide range of social issues. Many, like Greenpeace or Human Rights Watch, function to call attention to problems and abuses that need to be addressed. CARE, for example, was initially formed to seek help for refugee families. Amnesty International was established to seek help for political prisoners and other victims of human rights abuses. Many other organizations, especially arts organizations and religious associations, invoke ideals they think we ought to pursue and realize.

Calling attention to moral concerns is an integral feature of the voluntary sector. This activity of voicing assumes diverse forms. Voluntary sector organizations variously raise their voices to champion causes, protest against perceived problems, caution others about difficulties, arouse interest in new possibilities, and inspire extra efforts to realize ideals. As they raise their voices in broadly articulated expressions of care and engage in positive action across a wide spectrum of civic engagement, VSOs make a vital contribution to the life of contemporary societies. Voluntary sector organizations thus play a special part in keeping alive the practical calling of ethics as voicing. By speaking up and calling attention in their varied ways, VSOs enact and embody the conscience of civil society.

2. Ethics as Good Conversation

The essays in this book indicate that people face a number of critical choices as they work in and volunteer for VSOs. The authors raise a number of ethically charged questions. What kinds of leaders should they be? How do they best use their time? How should they responsibly transfer authority? How should they effectively prepare their organizations for emergencies? How do they foster a lively sense of accountability? How should they sensitively encourage donors? How do they balance conflicting concerns and interests when courting potential sponsors? How should they allocate limited organizational resources? What steps should they take to renew old and tired organizations?

One of activities people inevitably engage in as they practise ethics is to deliberate about these kinds of morally informed choices. Ethics is especially associated with efforts to determine which alternative courses of action are *right* and which are most likely to promote *good* outcomes. Ethics textbooks and primers are typically written to provide readers with useful models for figuring out acceptable responses to moral dilemmas. These works characteristically instruct readers about diverse reasons and teachings they might consult and invoke as they make up their minds. Clearly, moral deliberation is a thought-filled and thought-driven activity. One of the basic characteristics of decisions we have arrived at ethically is that we can provide intelligible and discussable reasons to account for our choices. If we cannot provide these kinds of accounts, then our choices are likely to reflect personal preferences, unthinking customary habits, or coercive influence and not ethical considerations.

It is important to recognize as well that moral deliberation is a timely activity. We morally deliberate at certain moments in time in relation to particular contingencies, possibilities, and difficulties. These timely considerations affect the character of problems as well as the resources we can bring to bear. Furthermore, the process of deliberating takes time. We cannot responsibly make up our minds until we have acquired the information we need, taken account of the positions others are likely to take, adequately assessed our own resources and appropriately considered the alternatives. Although we may make matters worse if we take excessive amounts of time to deliberate, thereby missing opportunities and aggravating our circumstances, we may also reach decisions prematurely if we do not fully explore our opportunities.

Ethics is also a social and communicative activity. We often engage with others as we deliberate. We question others in order to obtain information about conditions, risks, and precedents. We seek their counsel and advice, often probing, reacting, and asking further questions as we seek to determine the relevance of what we hear from them for the concerns we are addressing. Rarely do we seek counsel only passively; typically, we seek to work with and rework the advice we are offered. In addition, and more importantly, in most situations moral deliberation requires that we negotiate with others who are likely to be involved in or affected by the decisions we are making. If we are trying to reach agreements, establish policies, or invoke common standards as normative guides, we inevitably have to find ways of persuading others so that we can finally reach mutually acceptable common points of reference. Thus, negotiating often occurs as we attempt to establish shared moral understandings, and it typically accompanies efforts to apply these shared understandings to particular situations. In the latter settings, where we seek the active consent or the passive assent of others, we are compelled to listen and respond to their concerns as we attempt to persuade. We are more likely to reach effective agreements in these settings to the degree we have engaged with the others in two-way, interactive exchanges.

I have used the term 'good conversation' as a way of describing the deliberative aspect of ethics as an activity that is at once thoughtful, timely, and communicative. Conversations, after all, take place over time. They call for and elicit thoughtful interactions with others. The word 'good' in this phrase signals in part that these interactions are undertaken in hopes of realizing valued objectives. To be sure, this term 'good conversation' is a metaphor. Sometimes deliberating is something we do alone, at least until we need to solicit the advice or cooperation of others. Often, however, moral deliberation calls for consultations, negotiations, and applications that require communicating with others. Many of the philosophical models overlook the timely and communicative aspects of moral deliberation even while they emphasize their thoughtful character. The term 'good conversation' is a way of calling attention to all of these features.

In addition, I am using the term 'good conversation' normatively and not just descriptively. I use this term to identify ways in which those moral deliberations that involve others ought to take place. The word 'good' is thus also used in this sense to refer to conversations that proceed in keeping with particular standards. 'Good conversation' thereby invokes a set of four simple standards or norms that are particularly important because, I maintain, only insofar as people adhere to these standards can they arrive at shared moral understandings and consent to normative agreements that they will regard as morally binding. In short, these standards allow people to converse, bargain, negotiate, and collaborate in mutually respectful ways about all sorts of matters, including those about which they may well have different views and conflicting interests. Moreover, these four standards, as I will shortly indicate, are either overtly invoked or customarily assumed by all human communities:

1. As we communicate with others we should speak honestly, without any effort intentionally to deceive or mislead.
2. We are expected to pay attention to what others communicate, neither ignoring nor intentionally misrepresenting what they communicate. We are correspondingly expected to empathize enough with them so that we can gain a minimal sense both of what they are saying and of why, on their terms, they are saying it. This respect calls for us to be attentive; it does not require that we agree with them; but it does lead us to listen well.
3. We are expected to engage in these conversations reciprocally, taking turns and responding as we speak to the concerns that are raised by the others with whom we are conversing. We are called upon to avoid turning our communications with others into by-passing monologues. We are also called upon to continue the

communications until we have reached mutually satisfactory understandings with the other. As such we are called upon to avoid trying to trump the other with our last word.

4. Finally, we are called upon to keep the promises we make as a result of these conversations.

These four standards are basic. All cultures hold up the importance of not lying, reciprocity, and keeping promises. Most make some reference directly or indirectly to the importance of listening respectfully to those who address us. We might add other relevant standards, for example, that we should communicate with others civilly and in ways that are intelligible. Clearly, civility helps and so do attempts to communicate in ways others are likely to comprehend. But these are extra standards and not fundamental ones.

These four standards are useful. Adhering to them facilitates interactive communications. Negotiations and conversations become difficult, if not impossible, to the degree that any party to communicative interactions suspects the other of violating these standards. In contrast, conversations that proceed in keeping with these standards foster trust (Bird 1996).

Many chapters in this book point to the ways honest, attentive, and reciprocating communications have worked to facilitate satisfactory negotiations, initiate and strengthen collaborations, and occasion mutually appreciative relationships. In differing ways, each of the essays on collaborations (see part four) argues that these relationships are best approached as dialogues proceeding like good conversations. Ryan calls for fundraisers to listen carefully to the donors from whom they are seeking contributions and to see their relationship in reciprocating terms. Cloutier challenges fundraisers both to be attentive towards and to engage in respectful negotiations with today's growing numbers of venture philanthropists. As she examines the relationships between health care charities and various businesses in the health care field, Moreau argues that the negotiations integral to these relationships must be honest, mutually respectful, and fair. In each case the authors argue that these deliberations are likely to reach satisfactory conclusions to the extent that those involved engage in honest, attentive, and reciprocating communications.

Other essays reach corresponding points. They variously stress the importance of collaborations and they add that collaboration works best when those involved communicate forthrightly, listen attentively, interact reciprocally, and can be counted on to keep their promises. By means of such dialogues, they can 'build bridges' (Mah-Sen), cultivate and encourage youth to become leaders (Manser and Langlois), and develop global networks (Roy). This kind of honest, respectful, and responsive communication is just what makes public dialogues work (Dale).

One of the important, albeit indirect, ways by which voluntary sector organizations contribute to the well-being of society as a whole is the degree to which they foster and immediately institutionalize these kinds of conversations and debates about contemporary moral issues. As voluntary associations, they invite and arouse public discussions among their members, volunteers, and boards about all manner of ethical concerns. These range from drunk driving to the care for handicapped persons, from global trade to the status of First Nations, from the importance of ballet to global warming, from troubled youth to health care. In diverse ways they foster and facilitate the social practice of ethical deliberating as a thoughtful, timely, and communicative activity. They exhibit well the practice of ethics as a good conversation.

3. Ethics as Evaluating

In addition to speaking up about moral issues and addressing and deliberating about moral choices, we engage in ethics to monitor and evaluate, review and assess our own practices and activities, and to determine the degree to which they correspond with our purposes and our objectives. To evaluate is to exercise judgment. We are called upon to exercise judgment in the present, not just as a backward-looking way of assessing what has taken place but also, and perhaps more importantly, as a forward-looking way of preparing ourselves to fulfill our purposes in the future.

Ethical evaluating involves at least four interrelated activities:

1. Ethical auditing can be viewed narrowly (though not atypically) as a kind of policing activity that we are called upon to perform in order to see to what extent our practices comply with relevant standards. We may variously review practices for compliance. We may, for example, like the Donner Awards, develop scales to gauge degrees of compliance and awards fitting grades for these different levels of practices. We may also expose and penalize those whose practices most seriously deviate from expected guidelines.

However, it is important to recognize that monitoring and evaluating involves more than policing and grading.

2. Ethical evaluating also involves attempts to review and learn from present and past practices. Evaluating is part of a feedback loop. It is a way of gaining a lively sense of what works well (or not so well), and why. Ideally, as we audit our performances, we will gain not only information about shortfalls and mistakes, we will also gain some insights about their causes and how things might be done differently. If ethical monitoring is to foster real learning, then it is important that those who are expected to learn should be actively engaged in the process. People are likely to learn much less if they are simply handed an impersonal report than they would if they participated more fully in the process.

3. Ethical evaluating also involves efforts to identify and encourage possibilities and potentialities. We are called upon to review present and past practices in part in order to discover otherwise overlooked resources and assets. The process of evaluating is integrally linked with the process of valuing. In the practice of Appreciative Inquiry, this connection is fully acknowledged. In reviewing present situations and past experiences, AI calls upon people to fully appreciate – that is, assign value to – and build upon their strengths and the past activities about which they feel passionate. The 'asset identification' process works similarly. John McKnight, who developed asset identification as a process to deal with social problems, criticizes the way we tend to think of social issues in terms of problems, that is, deficits. Rather, he argues, we need to assess areas of concern – impoverished neighbourhoods or degraded environments – in terms of their assets, their overlooked strengths, possibilities, and resources viewed in relation to individuals, informal social relationships, as well as existing organizations. However we engage in this process, evaluating is closely connected with assessing assets, appreciating what can be appreciated, valuing what has value (Kretzman and McKnight 1993).

4. The process of ethical evaluating includes efforts to put into practice what has been discovered in the process. If the evaluating is to involve genuine auditing, then whatever has been reported must also be heard, understood, and responded to. If evaluations are to be effective, then those affected must pay attention to them, listen and comprehend, and react and respond as seems fit to them. The process of evaluating is cut short whenever it largely consists

of reporting without active efforts to engage those who by their actions can make a difference. People respond variously to evaluations. They may seek to ignore or resist them, if they think they might be called upon to make extra efforts. In contrast, ideally, we hope those immediately affected by evaluations will respond with commitment that involves learning from the past, avoiding previous shortcomings, and fostering present possibilities. They are most likely to respond with commitment if they have been actively engaged in auditing and assessing, as that is part of the process.

Overall, we engage in the ethical practice of monitoring and evaluating in hopes of fostering a lively sense of accountability or perhaps, more fittingly stated, a lively sense of responsibility. Evaluations occasion and strengthen responsibility when they incorporate all of the several activities described above. In contrast, evaluations are typically undermined in several ways. For example, many people neglect to take time to evaluate. Others undertake limited evaluations, devoting too much attention to policing and not enough to learning. Often the evaluating process is undermined when audits overlook important information, focusing, for instance, excessively on deficits and discrepancies and not enough on possibilities and assets, or attending too much to details without a lively sense of overall direction. Evaluations are also undermined when they are ignored or evaded, as they are likely to be if those meant to hear the audits are not in some ways engaged in the process of developing them (Bird 2006).

The essays in this book refer to the ethical practice of evaluating in a number of ways. In his essay on the Donner Awards, DeMarco directly asks how voluntary sector organizations ought to be evaluated effectively in order to foster greater accountability. He makes a number of criticisms of the way the Donner Awards focus on efficient use of financial resources. In the process these awards tend to overlook both how these organizations effectively realize their purposes and how they utilize other social and human resources. As an alternative, DeMarco proposes the action-oriented practice of evaluating developed by Michael Quinn Patton (1997). In several other essays in this book, the authors write about the importance of evaluating without focusing on any particular method. For example, McGregor reviews how Canadian Olympic teams responded to unanticipated crises, Roy looks over various efforts to foster global networks in response to economic globalization, and Moreau reconsiders the way health care charities have interacted with pharmaceutical businesses. These essays are all for-ward-looking: they engage in evaluations not so much as ways of grad-ing the past but as ways of preparing more adequately for the future.

4. Ethics as Cultivating Charity and Fostering Justice

We practise ethics as we speak up about moral issues, decide how to act about moral dilemmas and evaluate our practices. We practise ethics as well when we work to cultivate moral sentiments and establish morally valued institutional arrangements. Much like the classical Greeks, we variously seek to inspire courage, foster temperance, and develop prac-tical wisdom. We also value thrift, industry, respect for the aged, and good humour in the face of life's complexities. Charity and justice rep-resent two values that we especially honour and seek to cultivate. We seek both to develop them as fundamental dispositions and embed them as principles that guide our basic institutions. Charity (although it is not one of the classical Greek virtues) and justice are especially central to the work of voluntary sector organizations.

Charity has been especially promoted by religious movements. It has been associated with benevolence and altruism. Beginning in the nine-teenth century, voluntary sector organizations were popularly known as charities. This association with charity remains quite appropriate be-cause even though the wide variety of organizations that today consti-tute the voluntary sector (including non-governmental organizations, non-profit organizations, religious associations, and semi-public schools and clinics) hire thousands of workers and sometimes charge fees, they are also able to operate because they are able to encourage and persuade people to donate to their programs in multiple ways. People not only give money, property, legacies and items of financial value, but also contribute in a wide range of non-tangible ways: skills, time, interests, affections, loyalties, and love. By using the term 'volun-tary sector' to refer to all of these varied organizations, we acknow-ledge the way in which they promote and sustain their activities by fostering voluntary donations and gifts of diverse kinds.

Charity is important to voluntary sector organizations in a second way, because it is expressed not only through volunteering and donat-ing but also through caring for others. VSOs direct care towards diverse 'others': alienated children, refugees, impoverished households, polit-ical prisoners, First Nations children and families, AIDS victims, young people seeking new horizons, natural environments at risk, and house-holds needing medical care. VSOs offer services, provide benefits, and develop human contacts with hundreds of thousands of people, who might be entirely bereft of aid and assistance without their help.

Voluntary sector organizations promote charity in a third way that is not as readily recognized: that is, they promote community. There has always been a very close connection between the practice of charity and the experience of community. Charities have traditionally directed their contributions to two quite different groups of people: those on the margins of society – orphans, widows, the needy, the poor – who might well be lost to the community without assistance; and religious and cultural institutions, whose values embody, and whose leaders publicly express, the central values around which communities are organized. Care for both of these groups has been integral to sustaining the sense of community. Charity is often offered as part of implicit systems of reciprocity, in which the recipients are expected to act in ways the donors tacitly expect. If the recipients are on the margins of society, they are expected to maintain their loyalty to the community and not revolt. If they are religious and cultural leaders, they are expected to maintain and celebrate central communal values.

Today, voluntary sector organizations promote charity as community in several ways. Many VSOs, including most religious associations, create and sustain communities of identification, commitment, and mutual assistance. Many VSOs are membership associations. Their leaders typically seek to cultivate a sense of community among members, many of whom may be strangers to each other, through various activities, newsletters, and tokens of identification. Other VSOs, such as community foundations, work to foster feelings of community outside their organizations, in the larger society.

The essays in this book tend to avoid explicit discussion of charity as such. Because Ryan and Cloutier are fundraisers, they do refer to ways of promoting and responding to voluntary donations in terms of organized charity. As a leader of an organization with a strong spiritual tradition, Voyer discusses the importance of community among Taoists in Canada. Nonetheless, all the authors recognize that they work for organizations that might well be called charities. They variously discuss the means by which they most effectively care for, and care about, the projects and purposes that they regard as most important. In many ways these authors take for granted the charitable character of their work: for the most part, they assume that they work for organizations supported by gifts of time, money, and commitments. They assume as well that their organizations exist to serve and care for others, and that these various efforts help to foster and sustain feelings of community.

They then focus their thoughts in these essays on ways to realize these purposes effectively, in response to contingent developments.

This reticence about charity reflects another factor to which these essays devote more attention, namely, the importance of balancing charitable practices with a lively concern for justice. Justice can be defined in many ways. Minimally, we use the word justice to denote fairness in exchanges, distributions, and judgments such that each person or group receives what they rightly deserve. Concerns about justice are found in a number of the foregoing essays. Blackstock and Bayes point to injustices suffered by First Nations living on reserves and by the children of incarcerated offenders. Mah-Sen invokes notions of justice as she calls attention to those suffering from human rights abuses, while Roy discusses efforts to mobilize global responses to injustices suffered by developing countries. From a different perspective, Moreau argues that voluntary sector organizations do themselves an injustice in relation to their corporate partners when they fail to bargain hard enough in defence of their own interests. DeMarco invokes notions of justice when he wonders whether the mode of evaluation favoured by the Donner Awards fairly assesses the strengths and weaknesses of VSOs. Still, apart from Bayes' essay about the children of incarnated mothers, overall, the concern for justice assumes something like a leitmotif rather than a focal theme in these essays.

Despite these reticences, we can, I think, forthrightly state a number of observations about the importance of voluntary sector organizations as agencies devoted to fostering both charity and justice. The authors take for granted that these principles are different yet complementary: promoting charity without justice encourages sentimentality, paternalism, and tolerance for indefensible injustices; demanding justice without charity encourages dogmatism and resentment. Charity leads those pursuing justice to seek respectful compromises and fosters forbearance in the face of inevitable shortfalls. Justice, in turn, challenges those committed to offering charity to speak up for the people they serve and address the underlying causes of the afflictions they seek to comfort.

Final Thoughts

All humans engage in the practice of ethics. Parents are practising ethics as they seek to influence the conduct of their children by relating stories of moral exemplars, by informing them of social rules, and by disciplining and rewarding them for their conduct. Teachers, preachers, rabbis, imams, and priests engage in the practice of ethics as they exhort others how to live well. Negotiators engage in the practice of ethics as they bargain over how disputes ought to be best resolved and contracts ought to be appropriately concluded. Whenever we deliberate about alternative courses of action, whether alone or with others (and we inevitably involve others insofar as the successful completion of our actions requires the cooperation, consent, or even the non-involvement of others), we are practising ethics insofar as we are considering notions about how we ought to act.

We often associate ethics with well-known systems of ideas, rules, and arguments: utilitarian ethics or Confucian ethics, medical ethics or environmental ethics, or research ethics, the ethics of the Greek philosophers or of the great monotheistic faiths. Yet people often engage in the everyday practice of ethics without ever forthrightly invoking any organized body of ethical thought. As they exercise judgments, deliberate about possibilities, and seek the cooperation of others, many people invoke the normative ideas embedded in their ethnic traditions, in the mores of their communities, and in the ethos of their organizations, ideas which are often not formally labelled as being ethical. It is important to recognize that people often engage in the social practice of ethics even though the normative ideas that inform their deliberations and communications are not connected directly with any recognized system.

In various ways, voluntary sector organizations especially facilitate the social practice of ethics. They invite people to give of their time, interests, and talents for the well-being of society generally, although typically in relation to a particular cause or area of concern. They foster and facilitate active civic engagement in diverse social issues and public debates. They challenge people regarding overlooked injustices, forgotten oppressions, unmet needs, and unanticipated difficulties. They function to support and maintain the networks of interactions and identifications that give rise to and sustain our sense of community. In their diversity, they embody and celebrate the diversity that is constitutive of modern societies. In a fundamental way, voluntary sector organizations are indeed provocative – that is, they are *pro-voicing*: they act in ways that allow people to voice their concerns and to give voice to their beliefs.

The essays in this book are all expressions of the social practice of ethics, although none was written as a formal statement of ethics. By means of these essays the authors in practical ways raise their voices about a wide range of concerns. They deliberate about moral choices and dilemmas. They reflect upon and evaluate their own programs. And throughout, they seek to foster charity and promote justice.

References

Aboriginal Justice Implementation Commission. 1999. *The justice system and aboriginal people*. Report of the Aboriginal Justice Inquiry of Manitoba, Vol. 1. http://www.ajic.mb.ca/volume1/chapter13.html (accessed 30 November 2006).

Adams, Frank. 1986. *Unearthing seeds of fire: The idea of Highlander*. Winston-Salem, NC: John F. Blair.

Adams, Michael. 1997. *Sex in the snow: Canadian social values at the end of the millennium*. Toronto: Viking Books.

Advancing Philanthropy. 2000. Donor direction: How much donor involvement is too much? (November–December): 10–11.

Albert, Michael. 2000. The movements against neoliberal globalization: From Seattle to Porto Alegre. www.zmag.org/albertgreecetalk.htm (accessed 15 October 2006).

American Academy of Child and Family Adolescent Psychiatry (AACFAS). 1999. Children and family moves. *Facts for families* 14. http://www.aacap .org/publications/factsfam/fmlymove.htm (accessed 29 November 2006).

American Association of Fundraising Counsel (AAFC). 2000. *Giving USA*. Glenview, IL: Giving USA Foundation.

American Psychological Association. 2004. *Single parenting and today's family*. APA Help Center, Articles and Information, Family and Relationships. http://www.apahelpcenter.org/articles/article.php?id=16 (accessed 28 November 2006).

Amnesty International (AI). 2000. *Sudan: The human price of oil*. London: Amnesty International Publications. AI Index AFR 54/01/00 ERR (3 May).

– 2001a. *Human rights: Make it your business*. Ottawa: Amnesty International Publications.

– 2001b. *Human rights principles for companies: Helping Canadian transnationals promote and protect human rights*. Ottawa: Amnesty International Publications.

– 2001c. *Keeping the right company: A campaign of sensitization to responsible investment as a tool for the promotion of human rights.* Montreal: Amnesty International Publications.

– 2002. *Report from the 2001 ICM, Dakar, Senegal.* London: Amnesty International Publications.

Andersen, Leona. 1998. Philanthropy in South Asia. In *Philanthropy in the world's traditions,* ed. Warren F. Ilchman, Stanley L. Katz, and Edward L. Queen, 57–78. *Philanthropy in the world's traditions.* Bloomington, IN: Indiana University Press.

Andreasen, Alan R., and Minette E. Drumwright. 2001. Alliances and ethics in social marketing. In *Ethics in social marketing,* ed. Alan R. Andreasen, 95–124. Washington, DC: Georgetown University Press.

Andriole, Stephen. 1985. *Corporate crisis management.* Princeton, NJ: Petrocelli Books.

Anonymous. 1987. They soon forget. *Youth Exchange* 2 (August): PAGE.

Aristotle. 1998. *Nichomachean ethics.* Books VIII and IX. Translated with a commentary by Michael Pakaluk. Oxford: Clarendon Press.

Arjomand, Said Amir. 1998. Philanthropy, the law and public policy in the Islamic world before the modern era. In *Philanthropy in the world's traditions,* ed. Warren F. Ilchman, Stanley L. Katz, and Edward L. Queen, 109–32. *Philanthropy in the world's traditions.* Bloomington, IN: Indiana University Press.

Arnstein, Sherry R. 1969. 'A Ladder of Citizen Participation.' *Journal of the American Planning Association* 35, no. 4 (July): 216–24.

Ascione, W.C., and J. Dixson. 2002. Children and their incarcerated mothers. In *Women at the margins: Neglect, punishment and resistance,* ed. J. Figueira-McDonough and R.C. Sarri, 271–301. New York: Haworth.

Ashoka. Support Social Entrepreneurs. Selection Criteria. http://www.ashoka.org/support/criteria (accessed 17 January 2007).

Augustine, R. Norman. 2000. *Managing the crisis you tried to prevent.* Cambridge, MA: Harvard Business School Press.

Baiocchi, G. 2001. Participation, activism and politics: The Porto Alegre experiment in deliberative democratic theory. *Politics and Society* 29, no. 1 (March): 43–72.

Barlow, Maude, and Tony Clarke. 2000. The battle after Seattle. A working paper for strategic planning and action on the WTO. Ottawa: Canadian Centre for Policy Alternatives (privately circulated).

Barton, Laurence. 1993. *Crisis in organizations: Managing and communicating in the heat of chaos.* Cincinnati, OH: South-Western Publishing.

Bauman, Z. 1989. *Modernity and the holocaust.* New York: Cornell University Press.

– 2001. *Community: Seeking safety in an insecure world.* Malden, MA: Blackwell Publishers.

Baunach, Phyllis Jo. 1985. *Mothers in prison*. New Brunswick, NJ: Transaction Books.

Bayes, Shawn. 2002. Children of prisoners in Canada. Unpublished survey conducted through the Elizabeth Fry Society of Greater Vancouver.

Beavon, D., and M. Cooke. 2001. An Application of the United Nations Human Development Index to Registered Indians in Canada, 1996. Unpublished paper prepared for the Department of Indian Affairs and Northern Development Canada.

Bennett, M., and C. Blackstock. 2002. *A literature review and annotated bibliography on aspects of aboriginal child welfare in Canada*. Winnipeg: First Nations Child and Family Caring Society of Canada.

Bennis, Warren. 1989. *Why leaders can't lead: The unconscious conspiracy continues*. San Francisco: Jossey-Bass Publishers.

Berresford, Susan V. 2000. Social service and public trust: an antidote to indifference. Remarks at the John C. Whitehead Forum. Washington, DC, 9 February. http://www.fordfound.org/news/view_news_detail.cfm?news_index=110 (accessed 26 January 2010).

Biggart, N.W. 1989. *Charismatic capitalism: Direct selling organizations in America*. Chicago: University of Chicago Press.

Billitteri, Thomas J. 2000. A run for the money. *Chronicle of Philanthropy*, 20 April.

Bird, Frederick B. 1996. *The muted conscience: Moral silence and the practice of ethics in business*. Westport, CT: Quorum Books.

– 2006. Fostering social responsibility in business: The role of ethical auditing. In *Just business practices in a diverse and developing world*, ed. Frederick Bird and Manuel Velasquez, 157–81. New York: Palgrave Macmillan.

Blackstock, C. 2005. Same country: Same lands; 78 countries away: An exploration of nature and extent of collaboration between Voluntary Sector and First Nations Child and Family Services agencies in British Columbia. *First Peoples Child and Family Review* 2, no. 1: 130–59. http://www.fncfcs.com/pubs/vol2num1/Blackstock_pp130.pdf (accessed 26 January 2010).

Blackstock, C., S. Clarke, J. Cullen, J. D'Hondt, and J. Formsma. 2004. *Keeping the promise: The United Nations Convention on the Rights of the Child and the lived experience of First Nations children and young people*. Ottawa: First Nations Child and Family Caring Society of Canada. http://www.fncfcs.com/docs/KeepingThePromise.pdf (accessed 26 January 2010).

Blackstock, C., T. Prakash, J. Loxley, and F. Wien. 2005. *Wen: de: we are coming to the light of day*. Ottawa: First Nations Child and Family Caring Society of Canada. http://www.fncfcs.com/docs/WendeReport.pdf (accessed 26 January 2010).

Blanchard, Brigitte. 2005. Incarcerated mothers and their children: A complex issue. Correctional Service Canada. http://www.csc-scc.gc.ca/text/pblct/forum/Vol16No1/v16-a16_e.shtml (accessed 15 December 2006).

Bland, Michael. 1998. *Communicating out of a crisis.* New York: Palgrave Macmillan.

Bloodgood, R. 1928. Welfare of prisoners' families in Kentucky. In *Children's Bureau Publication,* No. 192. Washington, DC: U.S. Department of Labor.

Bloom, B. 1995. Imprisoned mothers. In *Children of incarcerated parents,* ed. K. Gabel and D. Johnston, 21–30. New York: Lexington Books.

Bloom, Barbara, and David Steinhart. 1993. *Why punish the children? A reappraisal of the children of incarcerated mothers in America.* San Francisco: National Council on Crime and Delinquency.

Bohm, David. 1992. On dialogue. *Noetic Sciences Review* 23 (Autumn). http://www.ionsnw.org/dialogue.htm (accessed 31 October 2006).

Born, Paul. 1999. The inner journey. Lecture. McGill-McConnell Program: Master of Management for National Voluntary Sector Leaders, Module 1. McGill University, Montreal. 25 August. Photocopy.

– 2003. Leadership as energy. Waterloo, ON: Tamarack: An Institute for Community Engagement.

Boschee, Jeff. 2001. Eight basic principles for non-profit entrepreneurs. *NonProfit World* (July–August): 15–18.

Bremner, Robert H. 1960. *American philanthropy.* Chicago: University of Chicago Press.

– 1994. *Giving: Charity and philanthropy in history.* New Brunswick, NJ: Transaction Publishers.

Brinckerhoff, Peter. 2000. *Social entrepreneurship: The art of mission-based venture development.* New York: John Wiley and Sons.

British Columbia Citizen's Assembly on Electoral Reform. 2004. Final Report: Making every vote count: The case for electoral reform in British Columbia. Victoria.

Brown, L. David. 1991. Bridging organizations and sustainable development. *Human Relations* 44, no. 8 (August): 807–31.

– 1992. Development bridging organizations and strategic management for social change. *IDR Reports.* Online Library at http://www.jsi.com/idr/online_lib.htm (accessed 14 February 2003).

Brown, Lester. 1995. *Who will feed China? Wake-up call for a small planet.* New York: W.W. Norton.

Bryman, A. 1992. *Charisma and leadership in organizations.* Newbury Park, CA: SAGE Publications.

Burgess, Julia. 2000. Youth involvement can be the key to community development. *Community Youth Development Journal* 1, no. 1 (Winter). http://www.cydjournal.org/2000Winter/burgess.html (accessed 19 February 2006).

Burlingame, Dwight, ed. 1992. *The responsibilities of wealth (Philanthropic studies)*. Bloomington, IN: Indiana University Press.

Burns, Lon M. 1998. Charities shouldn't treat donors like customers. *Chronicle of Philanthropy,*7 May. http://www.philanthropy.com (accessed 10 February 2010).

Byrne, John A. 2002. The new face of philanthropy. *Business Week*. 2 December. http://www.businessweek.com/magazine/content/02_48/b3810001.htm (accessed 26 January 2010).

C2D2. 2006. Canadian Community on Dialogue and Deliberation. http://www.c2d2.ca (accessed 30 October 2006).

Caddle, D., and D. Crisp. 1997. *Imprisoned women and mothers*. Research Study 162. London: Home Office Research and Statistics Directorate.

Caldwell, B. 1998. The HOME: Home observation for measurement of the environment inventory. *Zero to Three: Homes and Homelessness* 19, no. 1 (September): 7–17.

Canada Revenue Agency. 2005. Business-related business sanctions: Summary policy (revised 13 September 2005). http://www.cra-arc.gc.ca/tax/charities/policy/csp/csp-b02-e.html (accessed 17 January 2007).

Canadian Cancer Society (CCS). 2006. Corporate giving: Cancer is everyone's business. http://www.cancer.ca (accessed 2 February 2010).

Canadian Centre for Philanthropy (CCP). 2001. *Report on charitable giving and volunteering in Canada*. Toronto, ON.

– n.d. Ethical Fundraising and Financial Accountability Code. http://www.imaginecanada.ca/page.asp?id=ethical_fundraising_code_one (accessed 2 February 2010).

Canadian Centre for Social Entrepreneurship (CCSE). What is social entrepreneurship? http://www.bus.ualberta.ca/ccse/geninfo/default.htm (accessed 17 January 2007).

Canadian Coalition for the Rights of the Child (CCRC). 1999. How does Canada measure up? Ottawa: Canadian Coalition for the Rights of the Child.

Canadian Council for International Co-operation (CCIC). 1999a. Final Report: Choices in common, communities in common: Canadians deliberate about globalization. Ottawa: CCIC.

– 1999b. A World in Common: Talking about what matters in a borderless world (Dialogue guide). Ottawa: CCIC.

Canadian Council on Social Development (CCSD). 2003. *Funding matters: The impact of Canada's new funding regime on non-profit and voluntary sector organizations*. Ottawa: Canadian Council on Social Development.

– 2006. Fact sheets. Poverty lines: Before-tax low-income cut-offs, 2005. http://www.ccsd.ca/factsheets/fs_lico05_bt.htm (accessed 29 November 2006).

Canadian Human Rights Commission. 2003. A Profile of federally sentenced women: Who are they? In *Protecting their rights: A systemic review of human rights in correctional services for federally sentenced women*. Special Report to the Canadian Parliament. http://www.chrc-ccdp.ca/legislation_policies/consultation_report-en.asp (accessed 20 November 2006).

Canadian Paediatric Society (CPS). 2004. Code of ethics for the Canadian Paediatric Society. http://www.cps.ca/English/insideCPS/ethics.pdf (accessed 2 February 2010).

Canadian Policy Research Networks (CPRN). 1999. Discovering the society we want: Public dialogue kit. Ottawa: CPRN.

Carnegie, Andrew. 1889/1992. The Gospel of Wealth. First published as 'Wealth,' *North American Review*, no. 391 (June 1889). Reprinted in *The responsibilities of wealth (Philanthropic studies)*, ed. Dwight Burlingame, 1–31. Bloomington, IN: Indiana University Press.

100 propositions du Forum social mondial. 2006. Essai collectif. No. DD 151. Paris: Éditions Charles Léopold Mayer.

Cervone, B. 2002. Taking democracy in hand: Youth action for educational change in the San Francisco Bay Area. Takoma Park, MD: Forum for Youth Investment. http://www.forumfyi.org/Files/takingdemocracy.pdf (accessed 16 October 2005).

Champagne, Lyse. 1990. *Double vision: Reflections of a bicultural Canadian.* Toronto: Key Porter Books.

Chandler, M. 2002. *Stabilizing cultural identity as a hedge against suicide in Canada's First Nations.* Presentation of research findings at the Aboriginal Research and Policy Conference, Ottawa, ON, 26 November.

Chernow, Ron. 1998. *Titan: The life of John D. Rockefeller, Sr.* New York: Random House.

Choudry, A. n.d. Bringing it all back home: Anti-globalization activism cannot ignore colonial realities. http://www.arena.org.nz/globcoln.htm (accessed 26 January 2006).

Chronicle of Philanthropy. 2002. Donor-advised funds: Assets, awards, and accounts at sampling of big providers. http://www.philanthropy.com (accessed 10 February 2010).

Chryssides, George D. 2001. *Unrecognized charisma? A study of four charismatic leaders,* Center for Studies on New Religions, London. http://www.cesnur.org/2001/london2001/chryssides.htm (accessed 1 October 2002).

Clemens, Jason. 2000. Non-profit organizations need to be more business-like. *Globe and Mail* (Toronto), 3 November, B11.

Collins, Jim. 2001. *Good to great: Why some companies make the leap … and others don't.* New York: Harper Collins.

Commission on the Future of Health Care in Canada. 2002. *Report on citizens' dialogue on the future of health care in Canada.* Ottawa. http://www.cprn.org/en/doc.cfm?doc=32 (accessed 30 October 2006).

Community Foundations of Canada. 2001. *Explorations: Principles for community foundations.* 2nd ed. Ottawa: CFC.

Conger, J.A., and R.N. Kanungo. 1998. *Charismatic leadership in organizations.* Thousand Oaks, CA: SAGE Publications.

Conway, Janet. 2004. Brazil to Mumbai: A controversial move (11 February). http://www.rabble.ca/everyones_a_critic.shtml?x=30273 (accessed 26 January 2010).

Cooney, D. 2000. Xairos 2000--Opportunities and challenges at the present stage of the struggle. Presentation at the Social Welfare Action Alliance National Conference, Lansing, MI, 24 June. http://www.universityofthe-poor.org/schools/social/articles/XAIROS.pdf (accessed 12 January 2006).

Cooperrider, David L., and Jane E. Dutton. 1999. *Organizational dimensions of global change: No limits to cooperation.* Thousand Oaks, CA: SAGE Publications.

Cornell, S., and J.P. Kalt. 2002. Reloading the dice: Improving the chances for economic development on American Indian Reservations. http://www.ksg.harvard.edu/hpaied/res_main.htm (accessed 24 January 2006).

Correctional Service Canada (CSC). 2001. *Performance report for the period ending March 31, 2001.* Ottawa: Treasury Board of Canada. http://www.tbs-sct.gc.ca/rma/dpr/00-01/CSC00dpr/csc00dpre.pdf (accessed 20 November 2006).

– 2002. *2002–2003 estimates. Part III – Report on plans and priorities.* http://www.tbs-sct.gc.ca/est-pre/20022003/rCSC___e.pdf (accessed 3 December 2006).

– 2004a. *An examination of the average length of prison sentence for adult men in Canada: 1994 to 2002.* Tables 1, 4. http://www.csc-scc.gc.ca/text/rsrch/reports/r136/r136_e.shtml#t1 (accessed 6 December 2006).

– 2004b. *A Profile of visible minority offenders in the federal Canadian correctional system.* Research Branch. http://www.csc-scc.gc.ca/text/rsrch/reports/r144/r144_e.pdf (accessed 7 December 2006).

– 2004c. *Performance report for the period ending March 31, 2004.* Ottawa: Minister of Public Safety and Emergency Preparedness. http://www.csc-scc.gc.ca/text/pblct/dpr/2004/DPR_final_2004_e.pdf (accessed 22 November 2006).

– 2005. *Response from the Correctional Service of Canada to the 31st Annual Report of the Correctional Investigator 2003-2004.* Ottawa. http://www.csc-scc.gc.ca/text/pblct/ci03-04/ci03-04_e.pdf (accessed 9 November 2006).

– 2006a. *National Facility Directory. Prairie Region.* http://www.csc-scc.gc.ca/text/region/nat_facility_dir_e.shtml#p1 (accessed 20 November 2006).

– 2006b. *Women Offenders 2006.* Women Offender Sector. Ottawa:Correctional Services Canada.

Courtis, Shirlene. 1995. Building an ethical culture in an organization. *Canadian FundRaiser* (March): n.p.

Cunningham, Alison, and Linda Baker. 2003. *Waiting for Mommy: Giving a voice to the hidden victims of imprisonment.* London, ON: Centre for Children & Families in the Justice System of the London Family Court Clinic. http://www.lfcc.on.ca/WaitingForMommy.pdf (accessed 28 November 2006).

D'Souza, Anthony. 1989. *Leadership: A trilogy on leadership and effective management.* Bangalore, India: St Paul's Publications–Africa/Haggai Institute.

Dallaire, Roméo A. 2004. *Shake hands with the devil: The failure of humanity in Rwanda.* With Brent Beardsley. Toronto: Random House Canada.

De Sousa Santos, B. 1998. *Participatory budgeting in Porto Alegre: Toward a redistributive democracy.* Thousand Oaks, CA: SAGE Publications.

Dees, J. Gregory. 1998. The meaning of social entrepreneurship. The Kauffman Center for Entrepreneurial Leadership. Stanford University. http://www.stanford.edu/class/e145/materials/dees_SE.pdf (accessed 17 January 2007).

Dickon, Chris. 2005. Family ties, through prison walls. Connect for Kids (March 21). http://www.connectforkids.org/node/2916 (accessed 30 November 2006).

Dickson, A. 1976. *A chance to serve.* London: Dennis Dobson.

Dillard, Annie. 1988. *Teaching a stone to talk: Expeditions and encounters.* Revised edition. New York: Harper Perennial.

Douglass, Frederick. 1852. What to the slave is the Fourth of July? Speech to the Rochester Ladies' Anti-Slavery Society, Rochester, New York, 5 July. http://douglassarchives.org/doug_a10.htm (accessed 26 January 2006).

Downes, David, and Kristine Hansen. 2006. *Welfare and punishment: The relationship between welfare spending and imprisonment.* London: Crime and Society Foundation. http://www.crimeandsociety.org.uk/opus208/WelfareandPunishmentembargo.pdf (accessed 7 December 2006).

Drache, Arthur. 2002. The necessary trust factor. *Canadian Not-for-Profit News: The Insider's Edge on Current Developments in Canadian Non-Profit Organizations* 10, no. 5 (May): 39.

Dressel, Paula, and Sandra K. Barnhill. 1994. Reframing gerontological thought and practice: The case of grandmothers with daughters in prison. *The Gerontologist* 34 (October): 685–90.

Drucker, Peter F. 1977. Managing the public service institution. In *Managing nonprofit organizations,* ed. Diane Borst and Patrick J. Montana, 16–31. New York: Amacom.

Drucker, Peter F. 1990. *Managing the non-profit organization: Practices and principles*. Oxford: Butterworth-Heinemann.

Drumwright, Minette E., Peggy H. Cunningham, and Ida E. Berger. 2000. Social alliances: Company/nonprofit collaboration. Report No. 00-101, Cambridge, MA: Marketing Science Institute.

Dubin, Charles L. 1990. *Report of the Commission of Inquiry into the use of banned practices intended to increase athletic performance*. Ottawa: Ministry of Supply and Services Canada.

Economist, The. 1998. Philanthropy in America: The gospel of wealth. 30 May, 19.

EcoWorld. 2000. Juliette Beck and Global Exchange. Interview by Ed 'Redwood' Ring (6 December). http://www.ecoworld.com/home/articles2.cfm?tid=287 (accessed 18 January 2003).

Edwards, P. 2001. *One dead Indian: The premier, the police and the Ipperwash crisis*. Toronto: Stoddart Publishing.

Ehrenfeld, David. 1978. *The arrogance of humanism*. Oxford: Oxford University Press.

EKOS. 2005. *Rethinking citizen engagement*. http://www.ekos.com/studies/RethinkingCitizenEngagement2005.pdf (accessed 28 October 2006).

Eliot, T.S. 1969. 'Burnt Norton' (Four quartets). In *Complete poems and plays*. London: Faber and Faber.

Epsilon-Barna. 2002. *The 21st century donor: Emerging trends in a changing market*. Arlington, VA: Epsilon and Barna Research Group. http://www.epsilon.com/donor_report.pdf (accessed 25 February 2003).

Erikson, E. 1980. *Identity and the life cycle*. New York: W.W. Norton.

European Public Health Alliance (EPHA). 1996. *Commercial sponsorship and NGOs*. Brussels: EPHA.

Evernden, Neil. 1992. *The social creation of nature*. Baltimore: Johns Hopkins University Press.

Ferraro, K., J. Johnson, S. Jorgensen, and F. G. Bolton. 1983. Problems of prisoners' families: The hidden costs of imprisonment. *Journal of Family Issues* 4 (December): 575–91.

Fessler, Susan Raikovitz. 1991. Behind bars: Women's needs are unmet. *Albany Times Union*, 4 August: B1.

Feynman, Richard P. 1988. Personal observations on the reliability of the Shuttle. In *'What do you care what other people think?' Further adventures of a curious character*, 220–37 (Appendix F). New York: W.W. Norton.

Fink, Steven. 2000. *Planning for the inevitable*. New York: American Management Association Communications.

First Call. 2002. Vancouver: B.C. Child and Youth Advocacy Coalition. http://www.firstcallbc.org (accessed 16 January 2006).

Fischer, Marilyn. 2000. *Ethical decision making in fundraising*. Toronto: John Wiley and Sons.

Fix, Janet L., and Nicole Lewis. 2001. Growth in giving cools down. *Chronicle of Philanthropy*, 31 May. http://www.philanthropy.com (accessed 10 February 2010).

Fletcher, B.R., L. Dixon Shaver, and D.G. Moon. 1992. *Women prisoners: A forgotten population*. Westport, CT: Praeger Press.

Florini, Ann. M., ed. 2000. *The third force: The rise of transnational civil society*. Nihon Kokusai Koryu Senta (corporate author). Washington, DC: Carnegie Endowment for International Peace.

Flower, Joe. 1995. Building a visionary organisation is a do-it-yourself project: A conversation with James C. Collins. *Healthcare Forum Journal* 38, no. 5 (September–October): n.p.

Foundation Center. 2002. U.S. foundation giving trends. http://www.fdncenter.org/fc_stats (accessed 15 February 2003).

Fowler, Alan. 2000. NGDOs as a moment in history: Beyond aid to social entrepreneurship or civic innovation? *Third World Quarterly* 21, no. 4 (August): 637–54.

Fox, Kenneth. 1992. Comments on Andrew Carnegie's 'The Gospel of Wealth.' In *The responsibilities of wealth (Philanthropic studies)*, ed. Dwight Burlingame, 94–117. Bloomington, IN: Indiana University Press.

Fraser Institute. 2000. *Merger creates largest non-profit awards program in Canada: Only program in Canada to measure performance against peer groups* (media release), October 13. Vancouver: Fraser Institute. http://oldfraser.lexi.net/media/media_releases/2000/20001013-2.html (accessed 17 January 2003).

– 2002. *Annual report 2001*. Vancouver: Fraser Institute.

– 2003a. *Award recipient testimonials*. Vancouver: Fraser Institute. http://www.fraserinstitute.ca/donner/pdf/awards-testimonials1.pdf (accessed 10 February 2003).

– 2003b. *Donner Award ceremony and recipients*. Vancouver: Fraser Institute. http://www.fraserinstitute.ca/donner/award.asp (accessed 30 January 2003).

– 2003c. *Donner Canadian Foundation Awards*. Vancouver: Fraser Institute. http://www.fraserinstitute.ca/donner/index.asp (accessed 30 January 2003).

– 2003d. *Donner Canadian Foundation Awards for Excellence in the Delivery of Social Services 2003 application form and guide*. Vancouver: Fraser Institute. http://www.fraserinstitute.ca/donner/pdf/application.pdf (accessed 10 February 2003).

– 2003e. *Donner Canadian Foundation Awards for Excellence in the Delivery of Social Services* (brochure). Vancouver: Fraser Institute. http://www.fraserinstitute. ca/donner/pdf/brochure.pdf (accessed 10 February 2003).

Friedman, Thomas. 2000. *The Lexus and the olive tree: Understanding globaliza-tion*. Revised edition. New York: Farrar, Straus and Giroux.

Fuller, L.G. 1993. Visitors to women's prisons in California: An exploratory study. *Federal Probation* 57, no. 4 (December): 41–7.

Gabel, Katherine, and Denise Johnston. 1995. *Children of incarcerated parents*. New York: Lexington Books.

Gabel, Stewart. 1992. Behavioral problems in sons of incarcerated or otherwise absent father: The issue of separation. *Family Process* 31, no. 5 (July): 303–14.

Gardner, David M., Barbara Mintzes, and Aleck Ostry. 2003. Direct-to-consumer prescription drug advertising in Canada: Permission by default? *CMAJ* 169, no. 5 (September 2): 425–7.

Gardner, Howard E. 1996. *Leading minds: An anatomy of leadership*. With the contribution of Emma Laskin. New York: Basic Books.

Gergen, Kenneth. 1991. *The saturated self: Dilemmas of identity in contemporary life*. New York: Basic Books.

Gladwell, Malcolm. 2000. *The tipping point: How little things can make a big difference*. Boston, MA: Little, Brown.

Godbout, Jacques T., and Alain Caille 1998. *The world of the gift*. Trans. Donald Winkler. Montreal: McGill-Queen's University Press.

Gosden, Richard, and Sharon Beder. 2001. Pharmaceutical industry agenda setting in mental health policies. *Ethical Human Sciences and Services* 3, no. 3 (Fall/Winter): 147–59.

Gould, Stephen Jay. 1977. *Ever since Darwin: Reflections in natural history*. New York: W.W. Norton.

– 1981. *The mismeasure of man*. New York: W.W. Norton.

Gouldner, Alvin W. 1960. The norm of reciprocity: A preliminary statement. *American Sociological Review* 25, no. 2 (April): 161–78.

Government of British Columbia. 2005. BC Employment and Assistance Rate Tables. Ministry of Employment and Income Assistance. January 1. http://www.eia.gov.bc.ca/mhr/ia.htm (accessed 29 November 2006).

Government of Canada. 1998. Statement of Reconciliation issued by The Honourable Jane Stewart, Minister of Indian Affairs and Northern Development, in the Canadian Parliament on 7 January 1998. http://www.ainc-inac.gc.ca/gs/rec_e.html (accessed 16 January 2006).

– 1985. *Indian Act. R.S.*, c. 1–5.

Government of Manitoba. 2006. Minimum Wage Rates Across Canada. Manitoba Labour and Immigration. June. http://www.gov.mb.ca/labour/labmgt/resbr/wages/minwage.html (accessed 29 November 2006).

Granatstein, J.L. 2000. History as victimology. In *Great Questions of Canada*, ed. R. Griffiths, 3–7. Toronto: Stoddart Publishing.

Gray, Barbara. 1989. *Collaborating: Finding common ground for multiparty problems.* San Francisco: Jossey-Bass.

Greene, Stephen G. 2002. In disaster's wake. *The Chronicle of Philanthropy,* 5 September. http://www.philanthropy.com (accessed 10 February 2010).

Greenleaf, Robert K. 1991. *Servant leadership: A journey into the nature of legitimate power and greatness.* New York: Paulist Press.

Gregg, A. 2002. Wake up, Canada. *Maclean's* (April 8): 46.

Grovier, Trudy. 1997. *Social trust and human communities.* Montreal: McGill-Queen's University Press.

Guruge, Ananda W.P., and G.D. Bond. 1992. Generosity and Service in Theravāda Buddhism. In *Philanthropy in the world's traditions,* ed. Warren F. Ilchman, Stanley L. Katz, and Edward L. Queen, 79–96. Bloomington, IN: Indiana University Press.

Guttman, Nurit. 2000. *Public health communication interventions: Values and ethical dilemmas.* Thousand Oaks, CA: SAGE Publications.

Hall, Michael H., Susan D. Phillips, Claudia Meillat, and Donna Pickering. 2003. *Assessing performance: Evaluation practices and perspectives in Canada's voluntary sector.* Toronto: Canadian Centre for Philanthropy.

Hardon, Anita. 2001. Vaccination policy and the public-private mix. In *Private-public 'partnerships': Addressing public health needs or corporate agendas?* Report of a seminar held November 3, 2000. Amsterdam: HAI-Europe. http://www.haiweb.org/campaign/PPI/seminar200011.doc (accessed 2 February 2010).

Hardy, Cynthia, and Nelson Phillips. 1998. Strategies of engagement: Lessons from the critical examination of collaboration and conflict in an interorganizational domain. *Organizational Sciences* (March–April): 217–30.

Harris, Mike, and Preston Manning. 2005. Caring for Canadians in a Canada strong and free. The Fraser Institute. http://www.fraserinstitute.ca/pdf/Publication_English.pdf (accessed 6 December 2006).

Hawkins, J.D., D.P. Farrington, and R.F. Catalano. 1998. Reducing violence through the schools. In *Violence in American schools: A new perspective,* ed. D. S. Elliott, B.A. Hamburg and K. R. Williams, 188–216. Cambridge: Cambridge University Press.

Hayes, Richard E. 1985. Corporate crisis management as adaptive control. In *Corporate crisis management,* ed. Stephen Andriole, 21–7. Princeton, NJ: Petrocelli Books.

Hayes, Teresa. 1996. *Management, control and accountability in nonprofit/voluntary organizations.* Aldershot, UK: Avebury.

Health Communication Unit (HCU). n.d. *Introduction to health communication.* Health Communication Unit, Centre for Health Promotion, University of

Toronto. http://www.thcu.ca/infoandresources/health_communication.
htm (accessed 1 January 2006).

Health Canada. 1999. *Intersectoral action . . . Toward population health*. Report of
the Federal/Provincial/Territorial Advisory Committee on Population
Health. Ottawa: Minister of Supply and Services.

– 2000. *Policy toolkit for public involvement in decision making*. Ottawa: Minister
of Public Works and Government Services Canada.

– 2003. *Guidelines for strategic alliances and collaborative arrangements for social
marketing initiatives*. Marketing and Creative Services Division,
Communications, Marketing and Consultation Directorate. Ottawa:
Ministry of Supply and Services.

– 2005. Sudden infant death syndrome 'Back to Sleep' campaign. http://
www.hc-sc.gc.ca/ahc-asc/activit/marketsoc/camp/sids_e.html (accessed
2 February 2010).

Health Charities Coalition of Canada (HCCC). 2000. *Responding to the health
concerns of Canadians: Recommendations to the Standing Committee on Finance*.
1 September. http://www.healthcharities.ca/en/brief_010900.htm (accessed 1 January 2006).

Healy, K., D. Foley, and K. Walsh. 1999. *Parents in prison and their families*.
Queensland, Australia: Catholic Prison Ministry.

Heart and Stroke Foundation of Canada (HSF). 2004. HealthCheck corporate
brochure. http://www.healthcheck.ca/english/pdf/corporate_brochure.
pdf (accessed 1 January 2006).

Henriques, Z.W. 1982. *Imprisoned mothers and their children*. Washington, DC:
University Press of America.

Hesselbein, Frances. 2002. Crisis management: A leadership imperative. *Leader
to Leader* 26 (Fall): 4–5.

Holling, C.S. 2001. Understanding the complexity of economic, ecological, and
social systems. *Ecosystems* 4: 390–405.

Holling, C.S., and L. Gunderson. 2002. *Panarchy: Understanding transformations
in human and natural systems*. Washington, DC: Island Press.

Hostetter, Edwin C., and Dorothea T. Jinnah. 1993. *Families of adult prisoners*.
Family and Corrections Network. Prison Fellowship Ministries. http://
www.fcnetwork.org/reading/researc.html (accessed 29 November 2006).

Houde, R. 2002. Erik Erikson, 1902–1994, le psychologue de la générativité.
Revue québécoise de psychologie 23, no. 2: 255–68.

Hughes, Della, and Susan P. Curnan. 2000. Community youth development: A
framework for action. *Community Youth Development Journal* 1, no. 1
(Winter): 7–13. http://www.cydjournal.org/2000Winter/hughes.html
(accessed 19 February 2007).

Hunter, S.M. 1985. The relationship between women offenders and their children. PhD dissertation, Michigan State University.

Ignatieff, Michael. 2000. The history that matters most. In *Great Questions of Canada*, ed. R. Griffiths, 7–12. Toronto: Stoddart Publishing.

IGTN. 2005. *International Gender and Trade Network.* http://www.igtn.org/page/507 (accessed 15 October 2006).

Ilchman, Warren F., Stanley L. Katz, and Edward L. Queen, eds. 1998. *Philanthropy in the world's traditions.* Bloomington, IN: Indiana University Press.

Imagine Canada. 2005. The nonprofit and voluntary sector in British Columbia. http://www.nonprofitscan.ca/files/nsnvo/factsheet_voluntary_sector_bc.pdf (accessed 16 January 2006).

International Association of Business Communicators (IABC). 2006. Code of Ethics for Professional Communicators. http://www.iabc.com/about/code.htm (accessed 26 January 2010).

Ipsos-Reid. 2001. Dominion Institute/Ipsos Reid Poll: 5th Annual Canada history quiz. http://www.ipsos-na.com/news/pressrelease.cfm?id=1255 (accessed 26 January 2006).

– 2002. Searching for online health information the number one online activity in Canada. December 17. http://www.ipsos-na.com/news/pressrelease.cfm?id=1696 (accessed 26 January 2006).

Isaacs, W. 1999. *Dialogue and the art of thinking together.* New York: Doubleday.

Ismi, Asad. 2000. Profiting from repression: Canadian firms in Colombia protected by military death squads. *CCPA Monitor* (December 2000–January 2001): n.p.

Jacobs, Jane. 1993. *Systems of survival: A dialogue on the moral foundations of commerce and politics.* New York: Random House.

Johnson, Erica. 2000. Promoting drugs through patient advocacy groups. CBC-TV Marketplace, 14 November. http://www.cbc.ca/consumers/market/files/health/drugmarketing (accessed 1 January 2006).

Johnston, Denise. 1995. Effects of parental incarceration. In *Children of incarcerated parents*, ed. K. Gabel and D. Johnston. New York: Lexington Books.

Jung, Carl. 1981. Archetypes of the collective unconscious. In *Collected Works of C. G. Jung*, vol. 9: *Archetypes and the collective unconscious*, ed. and trans. Gerhard Adler and R. F. C. Hull, 3–41. Princeton, NJ: Princeton University Press.

Kahane, Adam. 2001. How to change the world: Lessons for entrepreneurs from activists. *Reflections. The Society for Organizational Learning Journal* 2 (3) Spring.http://www.solonline.org/reflections/journal/?volume=&issue=&year_id=490567 (accessed 5 November 2006).

Kanter, Rosabeth Moss. 1985. World class leaders: The power of partnering. In *The leader of the future: New visions, strategies and practices for the next era*, ed.

Frances Hesselbein, Marshall Goldsmith, and Richard Beckhard, 89–98. San Francisco: Jossey-Bass.

– 1989. Becoming PALs: Pooling, allying and linking across companies. *The Academy of Management Executive* 3, no. 3: 183–93.

Kanter, Rosabeth Moss, and David V. Summers. 1987. Doing well while doing good: Dilemmas of performance measurement in nonprofit organizations and the need for a multiple-constituency approach. In *The nonprofit sector: A research handbook*, ed. Walter W. Powell, 154–66. New Haven, CT: Yale University Press.

Karoff, H. Peter. 1997. A radical look at gift-giving. Speech given at the Philanthropic Initiative Annual Spring Conference, Cambridge, MA, 4 June.

– 2000. The public and private persona of philanthropy: The donor challenge. Speech given at the 13th Annual Symposium, Indiana University Center on Philanthropy, Bloomington, IN, 25–6 August.

Kazdin, A.E. 1998. Faltering fate. Review of *A faltering fate: Why the past does not predict the future* by M. Lewis. *Contemporary Psychology* 43, no. 8: 533–4.

Kerr, Steven. 1995. On the folly of rewarding A, while hoping for B. *The Academy of Management Executive* 9, no. 1 (February): 7–14.

Klein, Naomi. 2001. A fete for the end of the end of history. *The Nation.* 19 March. http://www.thenation.com/article/fete-end-end-history (accessed 26 January 2010).

Korten, David C. 1991. *Getting to the 21st Century.* Bloomfield, CT: Kumarian Press.

– 1995. *When corporations rule the world.* San Francisco: Berrett-Koehler Publications.

Krauthammer, Charles. 1999. Return of the Luddites. *Time*, 13 December. http://www.time.com/time/magazine/article/0,9171,992853,00.html (accessed 26 January 2010).

Kretzman, John P., and John L. McKnight. 1993. *Building community from inside out: A path toward finding and mobilizing community assets.* Chicago: ACTA Publications.

LaChapelle, David. 2001. Leadership and presence and Helen's hand. http://www.fromthefourdirections.org/Leadership.html (accessed 5 November 2006).

LaFromboise, Teresa, Hardin L. Coleman, and Jennifer Gerton. 1993. Psychological impact of biculturalism: Evidence and theory. *Psychological Bulletin* 114, no. 3 (November): 395–412.

Lai, Chi-tim. 2003. Hong Kong Daoism: A Study of Daoist Altars and Lü Dongbin Cults. *Social Compass* 50, no. 4 (December): 459–70.

Lane, D., and R. Maxfield. 1996. Strategy under complexity: Fostering generative relationships. *Long Range Planning* 29, no.2 (April): 215–31.

Larose, Marni D. 2002. Assets of donor-advised funds totaled $12.3 billion last year, survey finds. *Chronicle of Philanthropy*, 30 May. http://www .philanthropy.com (accessed 10 February 2010).

Lavers, Becky. 2004. Youth development initiative. Report for the Department of Community Services. Halifax, NS: HeartWood Centre for Community Youth Development.

Lawrence, Thomas B., and Cynthia Hardy. 1999. Building bridges for refugees: Towards a typology of bridging organizations. *The Journal of Applied Behavioural Science* 35, no. 1 (March): 48–70.

Lee, Kuan Yew. 2002. Passing the baton. http://straitstimes.asia1.com.sg/ mnt/html/webspecial/lee/lee_about.html (accessed 11 November 2002).

Lines, Rick. 2002. Action on HIV/AIDS in prisons: Too little, too late. Canadian HIV/AIDS Legal Network. http://www.aidslaw.ca/publications/ interfaces/downloadFile.php?ref=179 (accessed 29 November 2006).

Lipman, Harvey. 2001. Survey finds rapid rise in assets and grants of donor-advised funds. *Chronicle of Philanthropy*, 31 May. http://www.philanthropy .com (accessed 10 February 2010).

Livingston, John A. 1994. *Rogue primate: An exploration of human domestication.* Toronto: Key Porter.

Loeber, R., and T. Dishion. 1983. Early predictors of male delinquency: A review. *Psychology Bulletin*, 94, no. 1 (July): 68–99.

Lotz, J., and M.R. Welton. 1997. *Father Jimmy: The life and times of Jimmy Hopkins.* Cape Breton Island, NS: Breton Books.

Lundy, David. 2003. Multiculturalism and pluralization. In *One world or many? The impact of globalisation on mission*, ed. Richard Tiplady, 71–84. Pasadena, CA: William Carey Library.

MacGwire, Scarlett. 1999. Getting the message across: Communication and presentations. McGill-McConnell Program: Master of Management for National Voluntary Sector Leaders, Module 1. McGill University, Montreal, 24 August.

MacMillan, Ian. 1983. Competitive strategies for not-for-profit agencies. In *Advances in Strategic Management*, ed. P. Shrivistava, A. Huff, and J. Dutton, vol. 1., 61–82. Greenwich, CT: JAI Press.

Maehara, Paulette. 2002. Raising funds, raising communities: Trust and the charitable sector. Speech given at the 8th Annual Symposium on Building Trust in Our Sector and Within Our Society, Canadian Centre for Philanthropy, Montreal, Toronto, and Edmonton, 25–6 March.

Mah-Sen, Lily. 2003. Reviewing our transition: How are we doing in implementing the McMaster Plan? Ottawa: Amnesty International Canada (unpublished).

Mauss, Marcel. 1923–4. *The gift: The form and reason for exchange in archaic societies.* Trans. W. D. Halls. London: Routledge.

McDonald, R., and P. Ladd. 2000. *First Nations child and family services joint national policy review. Final Report.* June. Ottawa: Assembly of First Nations.

McGowan, B.G., and K.L. Blumenthal. 1978. *Why punish the children?* Hackensack, NJ: National Council on Crime and Delinquency.

McGregor, Margaret. 1998. *What parents can do about harassment and abuse in sport.* Ottawa: Canadian Association for the Advancement of Women and Sport and Physical Activity.

Menninger, Roy W. 1981. Foundation work may be hazardous to your mental health. Speech given at the Annual Conference of the Council on Foundations, Philadelphia, PA, May. http://www.grantcraft.org/pdfs/articleone.pdf (accessed 28 January 2010).

Milne, G. 2002. *Collaborating with government.* Presentation to the McGill-McConnell Program: Master of Management for National Voluntary Sector Leaders, McGill University, Montreal, 16 April.

Milne, Lorna, The Hon. 2006. *Debates of the Senate,* 1st Session, 39th Parliament, Volume 143, Issue 10, 4 May. http://www.parl.gc.ca/39/1/parlbus/chambus/senate/deb-e/010db_2006-05-04-E.htm?Language=E&Parl=39&Ses (accessed 20 September 2006).

Minister's Task Force on Federal Sport Policy. 1992. *Sport: The way ahead.* Ottawa: Ministry of Supply and Services Canada.

Minot, Stephen. 1998. *Three Genres: The Writing of Poetry, Fiction and Drama.* 6th ed. Upper Saddle River, NJ: Prentice Hall.

Mintz, Jim, Mark Hudson, and Barbara LeBrun. 1996. *Partnerships: Government's new math.* Ottawa: Health Canada, Marketing and Partnerships Division.

Mintzberg, Henry. 1981. Organizational design: Fashion or fit? *Harvard Business Review* 59, no. 3 (January–February): 103–16.

– 1999. Managing quietly. *Leader to Leader* 12 (Spring): 24–30. http://www.leadertoleader.org/knowledgecenter/L2L/spring99/mintzberg.html (accessed 15 June 2002).

Mintzberg, Henry, Bruce Ahlstrand, and Joseph Lampel. 1998. *Strategy safari: A guided tour through the wilds of strategic management.* New York: The Free Press.

Mintzes, Barbara. 1998. Blurring the boundaries: New trends in drug promotion. Amsterdam: Health Action International (HAI–Europe). http://www.haiweb.org/pubs/blurring/blurring.intro.html (accessed 2 February 2010).

Mitroff, Ian. 2004. *Crisis leadership: Planning for the unthinkable.* Hoboken, NJ: John Wiley and Sons.

Mitroff, Ian, and Christine Pearson. 1993. *Crisis management: A diagnostic guide for improving your organization's crisis-preparedness*. San Francisco: Jossey-Bass.

Moore, K.A., and T.G. Halle. 2000. Preventing problems vs. promoting the positive: What do we want for our children? *Child Trends Research Briefs*. http://www.childtrends.org/Files/posdev.pdf (accessed 4 December 2006).

Morris, Jim. 2006. COC plans for bird flu in Turin. The Canadian Press, 13 January 2006.

Morris, P. 1965. *Prisoners and their families*. London: Allen and Unwin.

Moses, Marilyn C. 1995. *Keeping incarcerated mothers and their daughters together: Girl scouts beyond bars*. Washington, DC: National Institute of Justice.

Moskowitz, Milton. 2002. What has CSR really accomplished? Much of the movement has been a public relations smoke screen. *Business Ethics* 16, no. 2 (May/June): 3–4.

Muir, John. 1911. *My first summer in the Sierra*. Boston and New York: Houghton Mifflin. http://www.yosemite.ca.us/john_muir_writings/my_first_summer_in_the_sierra/index.html (accessed 15 June 1992).

Mumola, C. 2000. *Incarcerated parents and their children*. BJS Special Report. Washington, DC: Bureau of Justice Statistics.

Murphy, Brian. 2002. Beyond the politics of the possible: Corporations and the pursuit of social justice. Paper presented to the Corporations as a Factor in Social Justice Forum, Concordia University Institute in Management and Community Development, Montreal, 12–14 June.

Murray, Joseph, and David P. Farrington. 2005. Parental imprisonment: Effects on boys' antisocial behaviour and delinquency through the life-course. *Journal of Child Psychology and Psychiatry* 46, no. 12 (December): 1269–78.

Mustard, J. Fraser, Margaret McCain, and Jane Bertrand. 2000. Changing beliefs to change policy: The early years study. *ISUMA, The Canadian Journal of Policy Research* 1, no. 2 (Autumn): 76–9.

Muttart Foundation. 2000. *Talking about charities: Canadians' opinions on charities and issues affecting charities*. Toronto: Canadian Centre for Philanthropy.

Myerberg, Neal. 1989. What do donors want? *Fundraising Management* (February). http:// www.highbeam.com/doc/1G1-7468743.html (accessed 22 February 2010).

Nadjiwan, Samantha, and Cindy Blackstock. 2003. *Caring across the boundaries: Promoting access to voluntary sector resources for First Nations children and families*. Ottawa: First Nations Child and Family Caring Society of Canada. http:// www.fncfcs.com/docs/VSIFinalReportv2.pdf, (accessed 1 January 2006).

Naim, Moisés. 2000. Lori's war. Interview with Lori Wallach (Public Citizen). *Foreign Policy* 118 (Spring): 29–55.

Napoli, Philip M. 2001. Consumer use of medical information from electronic and paper media. In *The Internet and health communication: Experiences and expectations*, ed. Ronald E. Rice and James E. Katz, 79–98. Thousand Oaks, CA: SAGE Publications.

National Centre on Addiction and Substance Abuse at Columbia University (NCASA). 1999. *No safe haven: Children of substance abusing parents*. New York: CASA.

National Crime Prevention Strategy. 2001. *Jack's troubled career: The costs to society of a young person in trouble*. Ottawa: National Safety and Emergency Preparedness Canada Archive. http://ww4.psepc-sppcc .gc.ca/en/library/publications/economic/jack/index.html (accessed 29 November 2006).

National Youth in Care Network. 1996. *Into the hands of youth: Youth in and from care identify healing needs*. Ottawa: National Youth in Care Network.

Nethercut, D. 2000. The Citizens Jury process. *IAP2 Participation Quarterly* (2nd Quarter): 1–6.

Newcomer, Kathryn E., Harry P. Hatry, and Joseph S. Wholey. 1994. Meeting the need for practical evaluation approaches: An introduction. In *Handbook of practical program evaluation*, ed. Joseph S. Wholey, Harry P. Hatry, and Kathryn E. Newcomer, 1–14. San Francisco: Jossey-Bass.

Nilsson, W.O. 2003. The southern wall: Organizational engagement at Santropol Roulant. Montreal: Santropol Roulant. http://www.santropolroulant.org/ images/southernwallenglish.pdf (accessed 16 January 2006).

Offord, David, Ellen Lipman, and Erik Duku. 1998. Which children don't participate in sports, the arts and community programs? Paper presented at Investing in Children: A National Research Conference, Ottawa, ON, 28 October.

Osborne, David, and Ted Gaebler. 1992. *Reinventing government: How the entrepreneurial spirit is transforming the public sector from schoolhouse to statehouse, city hall to the Pentagon*. Reading, MA: Addison-Wesley.

Ostrower, Francie. 1997. *Why the wealthy give: The culture of elite philanthropy*. Princeton, NJ: Princeton University Press.

Ottawa Citizen. 2001. Failure to admit mistakes at root of Walkerton tragedy study. 17 April: A5.

Paine, Thomas. [1791] 1987. The rights of man. In *The Thomas Paine Reader*, ed. M. Foot and I. Kramnick, 201–364. New York: Penguin Books.

Palmer, Parker J. 1990. *The active life: A spirituality of work, creativity and caring*. New York: Harper and Row.

Participatory Research in India (PRIA). 2002. *Our Journey … 1982–2002*. New Delhi: PRIA Publications.

Patel, Vibhuti. 2000. Globalisation and women's question in India. McGill-McConnell Program: Master of Management for National Voluntary Sector Leaders, Module 3. McGill University, Montreal, October.

Patton, Michael Quinn. 1997. *Utilization-focused evaluation: The new century text.* 3rd ed. Thousand Oaks, CA: SAGE Publications.

Payton, Robert L. 1992. God and money. In *The responsibilities of wealth (Philanthropic studies)*, ed. Dwight Burlingame, 138–44. Bloomington, IN: Indiana University Press

Pembina Institute for Appropriate Development. 2006. *About Pembina.* http://www.pembina.org/about.asp (accessed 28 October 2006).

Pettifog, Ann. 2000. A new world: Life after Jubilee 2000. *Social Democratic Review* 4, no. 4. http://www.icsw.org/publications/sdr/2000_decla-new-world.htm (accessed 31 January 2010).

Phillips, S., and M. Orsini. 2002. *Mapping the links: Citizen involvement in policy processes.* Ottawa: Canadian Policy Research Networks.

Prahalad, C.K., and Gary Hamel. 1990. The core competence of the corporation. *Harvard Business Review* (May/June): 79–90.

Pryor, Mark, Bill Lockyer, Richard Blumenthal, et al. 1999. What's in a nonprofit's name? Public trust, profit and the potential for deception. A preliminary multistate report on nonprofit product marketing. http://www.atg.state.vt.us/upload/1049920007_report-nonprofit_mkting.pdf (accessed 2 February 2010).

Public Health Agency of Canada. 2002. 'What is the population health approach?' http://www.phac-aspc.gc.ca/ph-sp/phdd/approach/index.html (accessed 2 February 2010).

– 2006. *Preparing for an influenza pandemic: A citizen's dialogue on the use of antivirals for prevention. Workbook.* Ottawa: Public Health Agency of Canada.

Public Safety and Emergency Preparedness Canada. 2004. *Corrections and Conditional Release Statistical Overview.* http://ww2.psepc-sppcc.gc.ca/publications/corrections/pdf/stats04/stats_section_e_2004_e.pdf (accessed 4 December 2006).

Putnam, R.D. 2000. *Bowling alone.* New York: Simon and Schuster.

Quann, Nathalie. 2003. *Drug Use and Offending. Questions & Answers* (February). Ottawa: Research and Statistics Division, Department of Justice. http://www.justice.gc.ca/en/ps/rs/rep/qa/qa2002_2/qa2002-2.pdf (accessed 4 December 2006).

Ratzan, Scott C. 1998. Health communication ethics. *Journal of Health Communication* 3, no. 4 (November): 291–4.

Raychaba, Brian. 1993. *Pain, lots of pain: Violence and abuse in the lives of young people in care.* Ottawa: National Youth in Care Network.

Rebick, J. 2000. *Imagine democracy*. Toronto: Stoddart Publishing.

Reis, Tom. 1999. *Unleashing the new resources and entrepreneurship for the common good: A scan, synthesis and scenario for action*. Battle Creek, MI: W.K. Kellogg Foundation.

Richards, M., and B. McWilliams. 1996. Imprisonment and family ties. Home Office Research Bulletin No. 38. London: Home Office.

Rochon Ford, Anne. 1999. *A different prescription: Considerations for women's health groups contemplating funding from the pharmaceutical industry*. Toronto: National Network on Environments and Women's Health.

Rodrick, Dani. 2001. *The global governance of trade: As if development really mattered*. New York: United Nations Development Programme.

Rosso, Henry. 1996. *Rosso on fundraising: Lessons from a master's lifetime experience*. San Francisco: Jossey-Bass .

Rowe, David C., and David P. Farrington. 1997. The familial transmission of criminal convictions. *Criminology* 35, no. 1 (November): 177–202.

Roy, Arundhati. 2003. Confronting empire. Speech presented at the World Social Forum, Porto Alegre, Brazil, 27 January. http://www.zcommunications.org/confronting-empire-by-arundhati-roy (accessed 26 January 2010).

Royal Commission on Aboriginal Peoples (RCAP). 1996. *Report of the Royal Commission on Aboriginal Peoples*. 5 vols. Ottawa: Indian and Northern Affairs Canada. http://www.ainc-inac.gc.ca/ch/rcap/sg/sgmm_e.html (accessed 26 January 2006).

Ruest, Jeanne, N. 2000. National Associations Active in Criminal Justice Round Table on Youth Justice Renewal (9 February). Summary of discussion. Department of Justice. Ottawa. http://www.justice.gc.ca/en/ps/yj/partnership/naacjs.html (accessed 13 December 2006).

Sacks, J. 1938. The social and economic adjustments of the families of a selected group of imprisoned felons. Master's thesis, American Catholic University.

Sapers, Howard. 2006. Speaking notes. 33rd Annual Report to Parliament, 16 October. Ottawa: Office of the Correctional Investigator. http://www.oci-bec.gc.ca/newsroom/speeches/20061016_e.asp (accessed 2 December 2006).

Scheirer, Mary Ann. 1994. Designing and using process evaluation. In *Handbook of practical program evaluation*, ed. Joseph S. Wholey, Harry P. Hatry, and Kathryn E. Newcomer, 40–68. San Francisco: Jossey-Bass.

Schoonover, Stephen. 1999. Schoonover Associates Inc. Leadership self-assessment test. McGill-McConnell Program: Master of Management for National Voluntary Sector Leaders, Module 1. McGill University, Montreal, 22 August.

Schwartz, Peter. 1996. *The art of the long view: Planning for the future in an uncertain world*. New York: Currency Doubleday.

Sczudlo, Walter. 2002. Advancing philanthropy: Ideas and strategies. *The Association of Fundraising Professionals*, 9, no. 3 (May): 17.

Senevirtane, K. 1996. Democracy, transparency don't exist at WTO. Report of an interview with Walden Bello at WTO Ministerial meeting in Singapore, December. Singapore: IPS Inter Press Service. http://www.twnside.org.sq/title/exist-cn.htm (accessed 31 January 2010).

Senge, Peter. 1990. *The Fifth Discipline*. London: Century Business.

Seymour, C. 1998. Children with parents in prison: Child welfare policy, program and practice issues. *Child Welfare* 77, no. 5 (September/October): 469–94.

Sheridan, J. 1996. Inmates may be parents too. *Corrections Today* (August): 100–3.

Smith, Jacquie, Charles Chatfield, and Ron Pagnucco. 1997. *Transnational social movements and global politics: Solidarity beyond the state*. Syracuse, NY: Syracuse University Press.

Stacey, Ralph D. 1996. *Strategic management and organizational dynamics*. London: Pitman Publishing.

Stanton, A.M. 1978. *Female offenders and their children: The effects of maternal incarceration on children*. Ann Arbor, MI: University Microfilms International.

Stanton, S. 1980. *When mothers go to jail*. Lexington, MA: Heath.

Statistics Canada. 1996–7. *National Population Health Survey*. Ottawa: Statistics Canada.

– 2001. *Age and Sex for Population, for Canada, Provinces, Territories, Census Metropolitan Areas and Census Agglomerations, 1996 and 2001 Censuses*. http://www12.statcan.ca/english/census01/products/standard/themes/ListProducts.cfm?Temporal=2001&APATH=3&THEME=37&FREE=0 (accessed 11 December 2006).

– 2002. *Population Counts, Canada, Provinces and Territories, 2001 and 1996 Censuses--100% Data. 2001. Census of Canada* http://www.stats.gov.nl.ca/Statistics/Census2001/PDF/Can-Provs-Terrs_2001.pdf (accessed 11 December 2006).

– 2003a. Adult Correctional Services in Canada, 2001/02. *Juristat* 23 (11). Catalogue no. 85- 002-XPE. http://dsp-psd.pwgsc.gc.ca/Collection-R/Statcan/85-002-XIE/0110385-002-XIE.pdf (accessed 11 December 2006).

– 2003b. *Public Sector Statistics, Financial Management System 2002/03*. Catalogue no. 68-213-XIE. http://www.statcan.ca/english/freepub/68-213-XIE/0000368-213-XIE.pdf (accessed 11 December 2006).

– 2004. *Analysis of Income in Canada 2002*. Catalogue no. 75-203-XIE. http://www.statcan.ca/english/freepub/75-203-XIE/0000275-203-XIE.pdf (accessed 11 December 2006).

– 2005a. Adult Correctional Services in Canada, 2003/2004. *Juristat* 25(8). http://dsp-psd.pwgsc.gc.ca/Collection-R/Statcan/85-002-XIE/0080585-002-XIE.pdf (accessed 22 November 2006).

– 2005b. Crime statistics in Canada, 2004. *Juristat* 25, no. 5: 1. http://dsp-psd .pwgsc.gc.ca/Collection-R/Statcan/85-002-XIE/0050585-002-XIE.pdf (accessed 1 October 2006).

– 2005c. *Population by year, by province and territory.* http://www40.statcan.ca/ l01/cst01/demo02.htm (accessed 30 November 2006).

– 2005d. *Projections of the Aboriginal populations, Canada, provinces and territories 2001 to 2017.* Catalogue no. 91-547-XIE http://www.statcan.ca/cgi-bin/ downpub/listpub.cgi?catno=91-547-XIE2005001 (accessed 6 December 2006).

– 2006a. Adult Correctional Services in Canada, 2004/2005. *Juristat* 26 (5). http://dsp-psd.pwgsc.gc.ca/Collection-R/Statcan/85-002-XIE/85-002-XIE2006005.pdf (accessed 29 November 2006).

– 2006b. Crime Statistics in Canada, 2005. *Juristat* 26 (4): 1. http://dsp-psd .pwgsc.gc.ca/Collection-R/Statcan/85-002-XIE/85-002-XIE2006004.pdf (accessed 7 October 2006).

– 2006c. *Women in Canada Fifth edition. A gender-based statistical report.* Catalogue no. 89-503-XIE. http://www.statcan.ca/english/freepub/89-503-XIE/0010589-503-XIE.pdf (accessed 15 November 2006).

Stein, Janice Gross. 2001. *The cult of efficiency.* Toronto: House of Anansi.

Strasser, Thomas, and James Gallagher. 1994. The ethics of health communication. *World Health Forum* 15: 175–7.

Strategic Planning for Aboriginal Input. 2002. Voluntary Sector Initiative Reports, 3–4 July 2001. www.vsi-isbc.ca/eng/about/pdf/reports_aboriginal.pdf (accessed 1 January 2006).

Sturtevant, William. 1997. *The artful journey.* Chicago: Bonus Books.

Sucupira, J., and L. Mello. 1999. The participatory budget process in Brazil. Paper presented at the International Budget Conference, Cape Town, SA.

Taskforce on the Churches and Corporate Responsibility. 2002. Placer Dome Shareholders Project. http://www.web.net/~tccr/CorpResp/PlacerDome. htm (accessed 7 October 2002).

Taylor, Charles. 1994. *Multiculturalism and the politics of recognition.* Princeton, NJ: Princeton University Press.

Tillich, Paul. 1952. *The courage to be.* New Haven: Yale University Press.

Tiplady, Richard, ed. 2003. *One world or many? The impact of globalisation on mission.* Pasadena, CA: William Carey Library.

Toronto Star. 1991. Junior hockey rebounds on promotion, less violence. 30 March: C1.

– 1999. Business of sport gets ugly. 5 July: E8.

Townson, M. 2000. *A report card on women and poverty.* Ottawa: The Canadian Centre for Policy Alternatives.

TPI. 2000. What's a donor to do? The state of donor resources in America today. Boston: The Philanthropic Initiative (August; revised 6 November). http://www.tpi.org/promoting/publications/WhatToDo.pdf (accessed 23 October 2006).

Trade and Environment Data Base. 2003. TED case study: Bhopal disaster. School of International Service, American University, Washington, DC. http://guruku/.ucc.american.edu/ted/BHOPAL.htm (accessed 15 February 2003).

Trist, Eric. 1983. Referent organizations and the development of inter-organizational domains. *Human Relations* 36, no. 3: 269–84.

Trocmé, Nico, and R. Brison. 1997. Homicide, assault and abuse and neglect: Patterns and opportunities for action. In Health Canada, *For the safety of Canadian children and youth: From injury data to preventive measures.* Ottawa: Minister of Public Works and Government Services.

Trocmé, Nico, David Knoke, and Cindy Blackstock. 2004. Pathways to the overrepresentation of Aboriginal children in Canada's child welfare system. *Social Service Review* 78, no. 4 (December): 577–601.

UDHR. 1948. *Universal declaration of human rights.* Adopted and proclaimed by General Assembly resolution 217 A (III) of 10 December 1948. Geneva: Office of the High Commissioner for Human Rights. http://www.unhchr .ch/udhr/lang/eng.htm (accessed 1 February 2006).

UNICEF. 2005. *Child Poverty in Rich Countries.* Innocenti Report Card No. 6. Florence: UNICEF Innocenti Research Centre. http://www.unicef.org/ brazil/repcard6e.pdf (accessed 12 December 2006).

United Nations Conference on Trade and Development (UNCTAD). 2002. Are transnationals bigger than countries? News release 12 August. Geneva, Switzerland: United Nations.

United States Court of Appeals for the Ninth Circuit in the case of *Doe v. Unocal,* filed on 18 Sept. 2002. Nos. 00-56603, 00-57197 D.C. No. CV-96-06959-RSWL. Case reference Due l v.unocalcorp 395F.3d932.c.9(col.)2002.

United States Department of Health and Human Services (USDHHS). 1999. *Blending perspectives and building common ground: A report to Congress on substance abuse and child protection.* Washington, DC: U.S. Government Printing Office.

– 2000. *Healthy People 2010: Objectives for improving health.* Washington, DC: U.S. Department of Health and Human Services. http://www.healthy-people.gov/document/HTML/Volume1/11HealthCom.htm (accessed 2 February 2010).

United States Department of Justice. 1992. *Survey of state prison inmates.*
Washington, DC: Bureau of Justice Statistics.

United Way. 2002. *People we help: Member and affiliate agencies.* Burnaby, BC:
United Way of the Lower Mainland.

VanderGrift, Kathy. 2000. Stop throwing babies into the river. Lecture,
CRWRC Team Leaders Conference, Hamilton, ON, 19 October.

Varicella Consensus Conference Organizing Committee and Varicella
Consensus Conference Working Group. 1999. Recommendations from the
National Varicella Consensus Conference, Montreal, Quebec, 5–7 May.
Paediatrics & Child Health 4, no. 8 (November–December): 563–8.

Voluntary Sector Initiative. 2002. Minutes, Meeting of Reference Groups,
Vancouver, BC, January 29–30. http://www.vsi-isbc.ca/eng/about/
aboriginal_group_minutes/minutes_jan_29_30.cfm (accessed 1 January
2006).

Von Hofer, Hanns. 2004. Crime and reactions to crime in Scandinavia. *Journal
of Scandinavian Studies in Criminology and Crime Prevention* 5, no. 2
(February): 148–66.

Waddell, Steve, and L. David Brown. 1997. *Fostering intersectoral partnering: A
guide to promoting cooperation among government, business and civil society
actors.* IDR Reports On-Line Library. http://www.jsi.com/idr/online_lib
.htm (accessed 14 February 2003).

Walmsley, Roy. 2005. *World population list.* 6th edition. London: International
Centre for Prison Studies. http://www.kcl.ac.uk/depsta/rel/icps/
world-prison-population-list-2005.pdf (accessed 29 November 2006).

Weatherburn, D., and B. Lind. 1997. *Social and economic stress, child neglect and
juvenile delinquency.* Sydney, Australia: New South Wales Bureau of Crime
Statistics and Research.

Weber, Max. 1968. *On charisma and institution building: Selected papers.* Edited
by S.N. Eisenstadt. Chicago: University of Chicago Press.

Weick, K.E. 1998. Improvisation as a mindset for organizational analysis.
Organization Science 9, no. 5 (September–October): 543–55.

Welch, Jack. 2005. After the storm: The five stages of crisis management. Will
Katrina make us stronger? *Wall Street Journal,* 14 September. http://www
.opinionjournal.com/editorial/feature.html?id=110007256 (accessed
28 January 2010).

West, D.J., and David P. Farrington. 1977. *Who becomes delinquent?* London:
Heinemann.

Westley, Frances, and Harrie Vredenburg. 1991. Strategic bridging: The collaboration between environmentalists and business in the marketing of green
products. *Journal of Applied Behavioural Science* 27, no. 1 (March): 65–90.

Westley, Frances, and Henry Mintzberg. 1989. Visionary leadership and strategic management. *Strategic Management Journal* 10: 17–32.

Wheatley, Margaret J. 1992. *Leadership and the new science*. New York: Berrett-Koehler.

– 2000. Reclaiming Gaia, reclaiming life. In *The fabric of the future*, ed. M. J. Ryan. San Francisco: Conari Press. http://www.margaretwheatley.com/articles/reclaimingaia.html (accessed 3 November 2006).

– 2001. *Listening as healing. Shambhala Sun* (December). http://www.margaretwheatley.com/articles/listeninghealing.html (accessed 3 November 2006).

– 2002. *Turning to one another: Simple conversations to restore hope to the future.* San Francisco: Berrett-Koehler.

Wholey, Joseph S. 1994. Assessing the feasibility and likely usefulness of evaluation. In *Handbook of practical program evaluation*, ed. Joseph S. Wholey, Harry P. Hatry, and Kathryn E. Newcomer, 15–39. San Francisco: Jossey-Bass.

Wingate, Allison. 1995. An investigation into the state of crisis management plans at National Collegiate Athletic Association Division 1-A athletic departments. Master's thesis, University of North Carolina at Chapel Hill.

Wood, Karina, and Jason Clemens. 2002. *Non-profit performance report: An analysis of management, staff, volunteers, and board effectiveness in the non-profit sector. Report based on the analysis undertaken as part of the Donner Canadian Foundation Awards for Excellence in the Delivery of Social Services.* Vancouver: Fraser Institute.

World Health Organization (WHO). 1988. *Ethical Criteria for Medicinal Drug Promotion.* Geneva: World Health Organization.

World Scout Bureau. 1998. Essential characteristics of Scouting. www.scout.org/library/EssChar_E.pdf (accessed 18 March 2003).

Worster, Donald. 1985. *Nature's economy: A history of ecological ideas.* Cambridge: Cambridge University Press.

Wuthnow, Robert. 1995. *Learning to Care: Elementary Kindness in an Age of Indifference.* NewYork: Oxford University Press.

World Social Forum (WSF). 2006. Charter of Principles. http://www.fsmmali.org/rubrique54.html?lang=en (accessed 15 October 2006).

Yankelovich, D. 1999. *The magic of dialogue.* New York: Simon and Schuster.

Zeldin, S., A.K. McDaniel, D. Topitzes, and M. Calvert. 2000. *Youth in decision making: A study on the impacts of youth on adults and organizations.* Madison, WI: Innovation Center/Tides Center, University of Wisconsin Extension.

Zimmerman, Brenda, and Raymond Dart. 1998. Charities doing commercial ventures: Societal and organizational implications. Ottawa: Canadian Policy

Research Network and Trillium Foundation. http://www.cprn.org/en/doc.cfm?doc=556 (accessed 17 January 2007).

Zimmerman, Brenda, Curt Lindberg, and Paul Plsek. 1998. *Edgeware: Insights from complexity science for health care leaders*. Irving, TX: VHA.

Additional McGill-McConnell Papers

Located at the Centre for Voluntary Sector Research and Development
http://www.cvsrd.org/eng/publications.html

The Will to Rise, Dianne Swinemar, 2003 (PDF, 124 Kb)

Storytelling and the Voluntary Sector in Canada - Capturing the Individual and Collective Stories, Liz Weaver, 2005 (PDF, 320 Kb)

Do We Need Another Hero? Understanding Celebrities' Roles in Advancing Social Causes, Stephen Huddart, 2005 (PDF, 312 Kb)

Growth, Change and Organizational Structure - The Evolving Relationship between Form and Function, Geoff Cape, 2002 (PDF, 395 Kb)

Developing Province-Wide Standardization in Volunteer Organizations, Janet H. Napper, 2003 (PDF, 321 Kb)

To Board or Not To Board . . . Why Isn't That a Question?, Kathryn Ann Hill, 2005 (PDF, 156 Kb)

Exploring Organizational Structure – Ideas and Options for the Pembina Institute, Marlo Raynolds, 2003 (PDF, 431 Kb)

The Environmental Youth Alliance – An Exploration of Complexity Science, Doug Ragan, 2005 (PDF, 165 Kb)

Board-Staff Collaboration – Factors for Success, Eric Burton, 2002 (PDF, 444 Kb)

The Learning Organization – Lessons for the Canadian Administrators of Volunteer Resources – A Constructionist and Exploratory Approach, Marjolaine Lalonde, 2005 (PDF, 272 Kb)

New Money, New Demands – The Impact of the Venture Philanthropist, Michael Wolfe, 2002 (PDF, 187 Kb)

Not Just Another Listserv – The Contribution of ACCC Affinity Groups to Knowledge Exchange, Sectoral Initiatives and Innovation, Paul Brennan, 2005 (PDF, 285 Kb)

Inflecting Change in the New City of Montreal – A Contemplation Before Action, Cameron Charlebois, 2003 (PDF, 329 Kb)

Formulating and Implementing a Merger Strategy in the Not-for-Profit Sector, Claude Perras, 2005 (PDF, 177 Kb)

Turnarounds – What Can Nonprofits Learn from the Private Sector?, Karen Takacs, 2001 (PDF, 148 Kb)

Assimilation Versus a Unique Community – An Examination of the Effects of Globalization and Artistic Expression on New Canadians, Linda Balduzzi, 2005 (PDF, 217 Kb)

Information and Communication Technology – Transforming Human Service Organizations, Christine Simmons-Physick, 2003 (PDF, 186 Kb)

Collaboration, Trust and Social Capital – The Dynamics and Effects of Collaboration in the New Health Charities Council of Canada, Yves M. Savoie, 2001 (PDF, 213 Kb)

Promoting Collaborative, Values-Based Decision Making Ways of Better Managing Risk in a Complex World, Sandra Schwartz, 2003 (PDF, 332 Kb)

How Does Oxfam Canada Learn? Organizational Learning in a Real-life Voluntary Sector Organization, Rex Fyles, 2003 (PDF, 628 Kb)

Information and Communication Technology – A Conversation Among Equals?, John Cawley, 2005 (PDF, 472 Kb)

Thought and Action – Perspectives on Leadership and Organizational Change in the Indian Voluntary Sector, Jamie Gamble, 2005 (PDF, 244 Kb)

Hope for a Cure, or Fear of a Curse? National Health Charity Leaders and the Ethical Dilemmas of Emergent Genomic Technologies, Karen L. Ormerod, 2003 (PDF, 258 Kb)

Unleashing Youth Potential – Understanding and Growing Youth Participation in Philanthropy and Volunteerism, Barbara Oates, 2004 (PDF, 147 Kb)

Building an Advocacy Program in a National Federation, Bruce MacDonald, 2003 (PDF, 231 Kb)

Contributors

Shawn Bayes is the executive director of the Elizabeth Fry Society of Vancouver.

Dr Frederick Bird is a research professor in Political Science at the University of Waterloo. Previously, he was a professor in Religious Studies at Concordia University and held the position of Concordia University Research Chair in Comparative Ethics. He is the author or co-author of *The Muted Conscience: Moral Silence and the Practice of Ethics in Business* (1996), *International Businesses and the Challenges of Poverty in the Developing World* (with Stewart Herman, 2004), *International Business and the Dilemmas of Development* (with Emmanuel Raufflet and Joseph Smucker, 2005), and *Just Business Practices in a Diverse and Developing World* (with Manuel Velasquez, 2006).

Cindy Blackstock, PhD, is a member of the Gitksan Nation and is the executive director of the First Nations Child and Family Caring Society of Canada. She is an Atkinson Social Economic Justice Fellow and a J.W. McConnell Family Foundation Social Innovation Generation Fellow.

Charlotte Cloutier, PhD, is currently a SSHRC post-doctoral research fellow at the Saïd Business School, Oxford University. Previously, Charlotte was the executive director of the Newton Foundation, a private foundation making grants in the area of academic nursing; before that she was executive director of the University of Sherbrooke Foundation, in Sherbrooke, Quebec.

Jacquie Dale is the president and CEO of One World Inc., a consulting firm affiliated with the Canadian Council for International Cooperation.

The recipient of two national awards for her work in public engagement, Jacquie is a board member of the Canadian Community for Dialogue and Deliberation.

Jerry V. DeMarco is an adjudicator. He was the first recipient of the City of Toronto's Green Toronto Award for environmental leadership. He is the former managing lawyer for the Sierra Legal Defense Fund.

Jennifer Flanagan is the president and CEO of Actua.

Marc Langlois was the co-founder and former executive director of the HeartWood Centre for Community Youth Development. Marc has a Special Individualized PhD (ABD) from Concordia University. He is currently developing a new organization called Twelve to provide social infrastructure to youth-led community development.

Lily Mah-Sen is a grassroots coordinator for community activism as part of Amnesty International in Canada.

Lynda Manser was the former executive director of the National Youth in Care Network and is currently with the Director Military Family Services as a policy development and research manager.

Margaret McGregor is the CEO of Canadian Interuniversity Sport. Marg has served in senior leadership positions for Team Canada at the Commonwealth Games, Paralympic Games, and Olympic Games.

Elizabeth Moreau is the director of communications and public education for the Canadian Paediatric Society.

Ida Mutoigo is the Canadian director for the Christian Reformed World Relief Committee (CRWRC). She was previously CRWRC's team leader for East and Southern Africa. Prior to that, she was the national coordinator for the ServiceLink volunteer program in Canada.

Alain Roy is the program director for Amnesty International in Canada.

Robert Ryan is the executive director of development for the Canadian Museum of Civilization. Previously, he was associate vice-president for Development and Major Giving for Villanova University, and formerly a vice-president and managing director with the philanthropic consulting firm Grenzebach Glier and Associates in Canada. He has also worked in fundraising for Public Broadcasting in Washington, DC, the University of Ottawa, and CARE Canada.

Bernard Voyer is a director of the Taoist Tai Chi Society of Canada and of the Fung Loy Kok Institute of Taoism. He instructs weekly classes in the Taoist Tai Chi™ internal arts of health at his local branch in Longueuil, Quebec.

Dr Frances Westley is the McConnell Chair in Social Innovation at the University of Waterloo. Previously she was the director of the Gaylord Nelson Institute for Environmental Studies at the University of Wisconsin (at Madison), a professor of management at McGill University, and the director of the McGill-McConnell Program. She is the co-author of *Experiments in Consilience* (with Phil Miller, 2004) and *Getting to Maybe: How the World is Changed* (with Brenda Zimmerman and Michael Patton, 2006).